PREFACE.

HISTORY has been ſtiled, " The evidence of time—The light of truth—The ſchool of virtue—The depoſitory of events." It is calculated for the purpoſes of ſhowing the principles on which ſtates and empires have riſen to power, and the errors by which they have fallen into decay, or been totally diſſolved: and of pointing out the fatal effects of inteſtine diviſions and civil wars, whether ariſing from the ambition, weakneſs, or inattention of princes; or from the mercenary diſpoſition, pride, and falſe policy of miniſters and ſtateſmen; or from miſtaken ideas, and the abuſe, of government and liberty. It ſhould oblige all, who have performed any diſtinguiſhed part on the theatre of the world, to appear before us in their proper character; and to render an account of their actions at the tribunal of poſterity, as models which ought to be followed, or as examples to be cenſured and avoided.

The inſtructions that events afford, are the ſoul of hiſtory; which doubtleſs ought to be a true relation of real facts during the period it reſpects. An eſſential requiſite in an hiſtorian is the knowledge of the truth; and as in

order

PREFACE.

order to perfection he ought to be superior to every temptation to disguise it, some have said, that " he should have neither country, nor particular religion." The compiler of the present history can assure the public, that he has paid a sacred regard to truth, conscious of his being answerable to a more awful tribunal than that of the public; and has labored to divest himself of all undue attachment to every person, country, religious name or profession: whenever the reader is inclined to pronounce him partial, let him recollect, that he also is subject to the like human frailty. A regard to truth has often restrained him from the use of strong and florid expressions, that he might not impose upon the reader a pleasing delusion, and lead him into false conceptions of the events undertaken to be related.

The following work is not confined to the contest between Great Britain and the United States of America, but includes all the other parts of the war which originated from that contest.

In the beginning of the first letter, the reader is acquainted with the reasons that produced an historical account of the first settlers in the Thirteen Colonies, and of their successors, down to the close of 1771. The insertion of what followed to the commencement of hostilities, was necessary for the connecting of the two periods.

The

PREFACE.

The form of letters, inftead of chapters, is not altogether im.ginary, as the author, from his arrival in America in 1770, maintained a correfpondence with gentlemen in London, Rotterdam and Paris, anfwering in general to the prefixed dates.

He apprehended, that by keeping to fuch form, and making the narrative agree with the moment to which it related, and by introducing the various infertions neceffary for the authenticating of facts, a prefent ideal exiftence of paft events might be produced in the mind, fimilar to what is felt when a well-executed hiftorical painting is. examined. The better to fecure this point, feveral parts are written in the prefent tenfe. If the author has failed in the execution, it is hoped that the candid reader will ad.nit of the good intention as an apology.

He has kept, as far as he could, to a chronological order. This has neceffarily interrupted the narrative of particular parts; which, though a difappointment to fome, may prevent the tedioufnefs that might otherwife have been felt by perfons of a different tafte. It may at leaft ferve to prevent or correct the too frequent miftakes of afcribing prior events, partly or wholly to fubfequent facts. The author regrets his not having placed the year at the top of the page, together with the month and day at
the

PREFACE.

the fide, earlier than now appears; and alſo his not having given every European letter the immediate reſemblance of being written to him by a correſpondent. He flatters himſelf, that he has in ſome meaſure compenſated for theſe and other defects, by the general contents of every letter in each volume prefixed to the ſame; by a copious index to the whole at the end of the laſt; and by a collection of maps and plans, about which neither care, nor expence, has been ſpared to render them valuable.

Struck with the importance of the ſcenes that were opening upon the world, in the beginning of 1776, he formed an early deſign of compiling their hiſtory, which he made known to the late commander in chief of the American army; and meeting with the deſired encouragement from him, he applied himſelf to the procuring of the beſt materials, whether oral, written, or printed. Oral communications were minuted down while freſh in the memory; the written were directed immediately to himſelf in many inſtances, in others only imparted: the productions of the European preſs could not be received with any regularity or certainty during the war, but were improved as they could be obtained.

The United States, in congreſs aſſembled, favored him with an inſpection of ſuch of their records as could with propriety be ſubmitted to the

9

peruſal

PREFACE.

perufal of a private perfon; and he was indulged by the late generals Wafhington, Gates, Greene, Lincoln, and Otho Williams, with a liberal examination of their papers, both of a public and more private nature.

He had the opportunity of acquainting himfelf with the records of the firft fettlers in New England; and examined thofe of the Maffachufett's-bay, from their formation as a company to the clofe of the war, contained in near thirty folio manufcript volumes.

Doctor Ramfay's hiftory of the war in Carolina, was communicated to him while in manufcript; and liberty was granted to make full ufe of it: the prefent opportunity is embraced for acknowledging the benefit received from it, and for returning grateful thanks to the Doctor. The Americans remarked, that Dodfley's Annual Regifter contained the beft foreign printed fummary account of their affairs: but it was not poffible for writers on this fide the Atlantic to avoid miftakes. That Regifter and other publications have been of fervice to the compiler of the prefent work, who has frequently quoted from them, without varying the language, except for method and concifenefs. He gathered from every fource of intelligence in his power, while at the place of his refidence near Bofton; and fince his return to his native country in
1786,

PREFACE.

1786, has improved the advantage arising from it.

The accounts here given of American affairs, are so different in several respects from what have been the conceptions of many on each side the Atlantic, that it was necessary to insert a variety of letters, papers and anecdotes, to authenticate the narrative. The publication of these, it is presumed, will obtain credit for such parts as could not with propriety be supported by the introduction of similar proofs.

To write a history worthy the approbation of his friends, and (as far as his powers extended) of the present age, and of posterity; and to convince mankind, that TRUTH *was his care, his search, and what his soul was engaged in,* have been the great objects of

London, Oct. 28, 1788.

* THE AUTHOR.

A
L I S T
O F
S U B S C R I B E R S.

M. P. for Member of Parliament.

A.

HIS Excellency John Adams efq; the late American Plenipo-
tentiary.
Mr. Stephen Abbott, Ipfwich, Suffolk.
Mr. Sergeant Adair, Recorder of London.
Mifs Adair.
Mr. Jofeph Adams.
Mr. Jofeph Ainfley.
Mr. Alderfon, Norwich.
Mr. Thomas Allen, Blackmore, Effex.
Mr. Henry Allnutt, High Wycomb, Bucks.
The Rev. John Andrews, Marden, Kent.
The Rev. Mordecai Andrews, Coggefhall, Effex.
The Antiquaries of Scotland.
The Rev. E. Armftrong, Bath.
Arthur Atherley efq; Southampton.
Mr. Thomas Atkinfon, Huddersfield, Yorkfhire.
Mr. John Audley, Cambridge.

B.

Earl of Briftol.
Gill Badeley, efq; Bath.
Samuel Badeley efq; Walpole, Suffolk, two copies.
The Rev. Ifaac Backus, Middleburgh, Maffachufetts Bay.
The Rev. John Bailey, Clavering, Effex.
Mr. John Banifter, Briftol.
The Rev. Jofeph Barber.
Mr. James Barley, Briftol.
Robert Barlow efq;

LIST OF SUBSCRIBERS.

Mr. John Barnard, Norwich.
Mr. John Barnard.
Mr. Francis Barnet, Fyfield, Effex.
Mr. Edward Barron.
Mr. Edward Barrow, Norwich.
Mrs. Bayne, Hampſtead.
John Beard eſq;
Mr. Joſeph Beldam, Royſton.
Mr. Joſeph Beldam, jun. ditto.
Okey Belfour eſq;
The Rev. Thomas Belſham, Daventry.
William Belſham eſq; Bedford.
Mr. Thomas Bennett.
The Rev. William Bennet, Iſlington:
Mrs. Bernard.
Mr. Peter Bernard, Southampton.
Meſſrs. John and Chriſtopher Berry, Norwich.
The Rev. Mr. Beynon, Great Yarmouth.
The Rev. Thomas Bingham, Ongar, Effex.
William Blake eſq;
Mr. Bezaliel Blomfield, Nayland, Suffolk.
Mr. William Boaden.
Bocking Book Society.
Mr. John Boddy.
Mr. William Booſey, Bocking.
Mr. John Bowman.
Mr. Thomas Bradley.
Daniel Braithwaite eſq;
The Rev. William Brice, Leeds.
Edward Bridgen eſq;
Richard Bright eſq; Briſtol.
Briſtol Education Society.
The Rev. Joſeph Brookſbank, Iſlington.
Mr. Giles Brown, Stobrough, near Wareham.
Mr. Richard Browne.
Robert Brown eſq;
Mr. Nathaniel Bucke, Ipſwich.
Mr. George Buckton.
Bungay Book Society.
Mr. Joſeph Burch.
Bury Book Society.
Mr. John Buſwell.
Mr. William Butler.
Mr. Thomas Button, Nayland.
Mr. Jeremiah Byles, Ipſwich.
Mr. William Byles.

Sir

C.

Sir John Carter, Portſmouth.
Mr. John Calver, Woodbridge, Suffolk.
Mr. Low Carmichael, Ipſwich.
Mr. Jarvis Chambers.
John Channing eſq;
Mr. William Chapman.
Mr. Nathaniel Child.
Mr. John Chaſe, Luton.
Mr. John Clarke.
The Rev. John Clayton, Iſlington.
The Rev. Joſeph Cockin, Rippin, Yorkſhire.
Doctor Cogan, Leyden.
The Rev. Baxter Cole.
Mr. William Cole, Colcheſter.
Mr. James Collins.
Mr. James Conder, Southampton.
Mr. John Conder, Ipſwich.
Mr. Joſeph Conder, Southampton.
Mr. Samuel Conder, Iſlington.
Mr. R. Cooke, Long Melford.
Mr. John Cooper.
Mr. Joſeph Cooper.
The Rev. Samuel Cooper, D. D. Great Yarmouth.
Thomas Cooper eſq; Altringham, Cheſhire.
The Rev. William Cooper for a Book Society at Chelmsford.
Mrs. Eyre Coote, Bath.
Mr. Joſeph Corſbie.
Mr. Bayes Cotton.
James Coulter eſq; Glaſgow.
Dr. Cox, Briſtol.
Mr. Denny Crabb, Keſgrave, Suffolk.
Mr. Benjamin Crackenthorp, Bocking.
John Craig eſq; Glaſgow.
The Rev. William Crathern, Dedham.
Mr. George Crawford, Glaſgow.
Renald Crawford eſq; ditto.
Mr. James Creaſy.
John Crickitt eſq;
Mrs. Cromwell, Hampſtead.
Oliver Cromwell eſq;
Mr. John Cumberland, Bury.
Mr. John Cumming, Riga.
Mr. Timothy Curtis, Hackney.

D.

Mr. Nathaniel Daldy, Ipſwich.
The Rev. Mr. Davidſon, Bocking.
Mr. James Davidſon.
Mr. James Davidſon, Walthamſtow.
The Rev. Benjamin Davies, D. D. Iſlington.

The

The Rev. James Davies, Briſtol.
Philip Davies eſq;
Mr. Thomas Deeble.
Mr. Joſeph Delafield.
Mr. J. L. Deſormeaux.
Lieutenant James Dickinſon, Leeds.
Mr. John Dickinſon.
Mr. William Dickinſon, Portſmouth.
Mr. James Dickſon, Edinburgh.
William Dillwyn eſq;
John Dilly eſq; Southill, Bedfordſhire.
William Dinwoody eſq;
Dr. Diſney.
Mr. J. Dobſon, Ipſwich.
Mr. B. W. Dowſon. Great Yarmouth.
The Rev. William Dunn, Portſmouth.
Mr. William Dymmock, Ipſwich.
Mr. George Dyſon.

E.

Jonathan Eade eſq; Stoke Newington.
Mrs. Earnſhaw, Wakefield, Yorkſhire.
Mr. Thomas Eckley, Hanover, New Jerſey.
Meſſrs. J. and W. Eddowes, Shrewſbury.
Mr. John Edwards, jun. Saffron Walden.
Mr. William Edwards, Briſtol.
The Rev. John Erſkine, D. D. Edinburgh, two copies.
The Rev. J. P. Eſtlin, Briſtol.
The Rev. Caleb Evans, ditto.
Mr. H. F. Evans, ditto.
Mr. John Everett.
Mr. Iſaac Everett, Capell, Suffolk.
Samuel Ewer eſq;

F.

The Marquis de la Fayette, France, twelve copies.
Mr. William Fairclough, Nayland.
Mr. Nathaniel Fenn.
Mr. John Fenwick.
The Rev. Henry Field, Blandford, Dorſet.
Mr. Henry Field.
Mr. John Field, Stoke Newington.
Mr. Oliver Field, Worceſter.
Mr. Thomas Field, Iſlington.
Mr. Charles Finch, Cambridge.
The Rev. Daniel Fiſher, D. D. Hackney.
Mr. Patrick Fitz-Henry, Briſtol.
Joſeph Flight eſq; Hackney.
Thomas Flight eſq; ditto.
Mr. Thomas Flight, jun.

Mr.

Mr. William Flindell, Ipfwich.
Mr. Benjamin Nathaniel Folkard, ditto.
Mr. William Folkard.
The Rev. John Ford, M. D.
Mr. E. K. Fordham, Royfton.
Mr. John Fofter, Bigglefwade, Bedfordfhire.
Mr. Richard Fofter, fen. Cambridge.
Mr. Richard Fofter, jun. ditto.
Mr. George Fownes, Briftol.
Mr. William Fox.
Mr. William Francis, Colchefter.
Mr. William Froft, Bury.
The Rev. Richard Fry, Billericay, Effex.
The Rev. John Fuller, Chefham, Bucks.
Mr. Caleb Furnell.

G.

Mr. Thomas Gibbons.
Gaisford Gibbs efq; Weftbury, Wilts.
Mr. Thomas Gittins, Bowman Hill, Salop.
Mr. William Glafs.
Mr. Samuel Goddard, Ipfwich.
Mr. James Graham, Glafgow.
Mrs. Macaulay Graham, Knightfbridge.
Mr. John Gray, feven copies.
Mr. John Green, Bury.
Mr. Samuel Green.
Mr. Thomas Greenwood.
The Rev. Edward Gregory, Rector of Langar, Nottinghamfhire.
The Rev. John Griffiths, Hitchin, Herts.
Mr. John Griffiths, Penywenallt, Cardiganfhire.
Samuel Gundry, jun. efq; Bridport, Dorfet.

H.

Mr. Henry Owen Hall.
Mr. James Hall.
Mr. John Hall, Ipfwich.
Mr. Luke Hall.
The Rev. Robert Hall, Briftol.
Thomas Hall efq; Harding, Oxon.
Mr. Thomas Hall.
Nathaniel Hardcaftle efq;
Mr. T. D. Harriott.
The Rev. Abraham Harris, Maidftone, Kent.
John Harris efq; Briftol.
Mr. Wintour Harris, ditto, fix copies.
The Rev. —— Harwood, D. D.
Mr. John Hawes, Colchefter.
Mr. Robert Hayward, Bury.
Mr. James Henderfon of Enoch Bank.

Mr.

Mr. John Hepburn, Southwark.
The Rev. Mr. Heptenstall, Beccles, Suffolk.
Mr. John Herring, Norwich.
Mr. Richard Herron.
Mr. John Hewetson.
Mr. Robert Hewetson.
The Rev. T. Hickman, Bildeston, Suffolk.
The Rev. Noah Hill.
The Rev. G. Hobbs, Colchester.
George Hodgson esq; Bromley, Middlesex, six copies.
Mr. Mark Hodgson, ditto, four copies.
Mr. Robert Hodgson, Islington.
Mr. Peregrine Hogg, Hackney.
Ebenezer Hollick, sen. esq; Wittelsford, Cambridgeshire.
T. Brand Hollis esq; F. R. S. S. A. Acad. A, S. New England.
George Sowley Holroyd esq;
Thomas Holroyd esq; Huddersfield.
The Rev. John Horsey, Northampton, for a Reading Society.
Mr. William Horwood.
The Rev. Joseph Houlton, Saffron Walden.
Mr. Thomas Houston.
Mr. Thomas Hovell, Cambridge.
Mr. John Howell, Islington.
Henry Hulton esq; Andover, Hants.
Mr. William Hunt, Birmingham.
The Rev. Henry Hunter, D. D. Charles Square, Hoxton.
Mr. Samuel Hurry, Great Yarmouth.
Mr. Thomas Hurry, jun. ditto.

I.

His Excellency Thomas Jefferson esq; American Ambassador, Paris, six copies.
Mr. John Jackson, Islington.
Mr. John Jacob.
Mr. William Jarrold, Maningtree, Essex.
Mr. Thomas Jefferys.
Edward Jeffries esq; Southwark.
Adam Jellicoe esq;
Mr. Edward Jenden.
Edmund Jenings esq;
Mr. David Jennings.
Mr. David Jennings.
Mr. John Jennings.
Mr. Charles Jerdein.
The Rev. William Jervis, Ipswich.
Mr. James Johns, Littlebury, Essex.
Mr. Thomas Isaac, Witham.

K.

Mr. Ralph Keddey, two copies.

2

Mr.

Mr. Edward Keer, Cretingham, Suffolk.
Mr. William Keer, Badingham, Suffolk.
The Rev. James Kello.
Mr. George Kerfey, Aldham Hall, Suffolk, two copies.
Benjamin King efq; Bedford.
Mr. Benjamin King, Ipfwich.
The Rev. William Kingfbury, Southampton.
The Rev. Andrew Kippis, D. D. F. R. S.
Mr. Thomas Kitchener, Bury.
Mr. John Knill.

L.

Sir Watkin Lewes, M. P. Knight and Alderman.
Mifs Lambe's, Upper Homerton.
Mr. John Lambert, Panfield, Effex.
Mr. W. Langfton.
David Langton efq; Hawkhurft, Kent, two copies.
The Rev. Samuel Lavington, Bideford, Devon.
Mr. Thomas Lawrance.
Mr. B. Leach, Bedford.
Mr. John Leathly.
J. C. Lettfom, M. D.
Mr. Leyfon Lewes, Norwich.
Mr. Samuel Lewin, Hackney.
Mr. William Llewelin, Briftol.
Mr. Chriftopher Load, Briftol.
Capel Lofft efq; Trofton Hall, near Bury.
Walter Logan efq; Glafgow.
Mr. Jofeph Lomas, Iflington.
Mr. John Lowther, Weftbury, Wilts.
Mr. William Lucas, Hitchin.
Mr. J. Luck.
William Peter Lunell efq; Briftol.

M.

The Rev. William Madgwick, Foulmere, Cambridgefhire.
Ebenezer Maitland efq;
Mr. Peter Mallard.
Mr. Philip Mallet
John Manning, M. D. Norwich.
Mrs. Marriott, fix copies.
William Marfhall efq;
Mr. Marfhall.
Mr. Edward Marfh, Norwich.
Mr. Marteneau, ditto.
The Rev. Michael Maurice, Great Yarmouth.
Mr. William Mayhew, Woodbridge.
The Rev. Henry Mayo, L.L. D.
The Rev. Herbert Mends, Plymouth.
Meffrs. T. and J. Merrill, Cambridge.

Jeremiah

LIST OF SUBSCRIBERS.

Jeremiah Meyler efq; of Briftol,
William Middleton efq; M. P. Crowfield Hall, Suffolk.
James Miller efq; Glafgow.
H. B. Millikin efq;
Thomas Milner, M. D. Maidftone.
The Rev. Jofeph Milward, Reeth, Yorkfhire.
Mr. James Mollyner.
Samuel Moody efq;
Mr. John Moore.
The Rev. Thomas Morgan.
Mr. George Henry Mortimer.
Mr. James Mofs, Briftol.
Mr. Jofeph Moul, Saffron Walden.
Mr. Jofeph Mounfher, Portfmouth.
Mr. Thomas Mullet, Briftol.
Mr. Peite Mufgrave, Cambridge.

N.

Mr. R. W. Nafh, Cambridge.
Mr. William Nafh, Royfton.
Mr. E. T. Nealfon, Stoke Newington.
Mr. J. E. L. Nealfon, two copies.
The Rev. Samuel Neely, Great Yarmouth.
Mr. John Newfom.
Mr. William Newfom, Norwich.
The Rev. Samuel Newton, ditto.
The Rev. Samuel Newton, Witham.
Mr. S. Nicklin.
H. H. Norris efq;
Mr. John North.
Mr. J. North, Portfmouth Common.
Mifs Norton, Wakefield.
Mr. George Notcutt, Ifpwich.
Mr. John Notcutt, ditto.
Mr. William Notcutt, ditto.
Mr. Thomas Nunn, Royfton.

O.

Mr. Thomas Ody.
Mr. Benjamin Olding.
Mr. John Olding.
Mr. Samuel Olding.

P.

The Rev. Samuel Palmer, Hackney.
Mr. William Palmer, jun. Great Yarmouth.
William Parker efq; Walthamftow.
The Rev. Edward Parfons, Leeds, Yorkfhire.

Mr.

Mr. George Paterfon.
Mr. James Payton.
Mr. James Pearfon.
Mr. Michael Pearfon.
Charles Peers efq; Portfmouth Common.
The Rev. Samuel Perry, Weathersfield, Effex.
The Rev. N. Phene, Bradford, Wilts.
Mr. Nicholas Phene.
The Rev. Daniel Philipps, Palgrave, Suffolk.
George Phillips efq; Manchefter.
William Pickett efq;
Mr. Thomas Pickles.
Mr. Cruttall Pierce.
Mr. Edward Pierce, Maidftone.
Charles Piefchell efq;
Mr. Thomas Jordan Pine, Maidftone.
Mr. Thomas Pitter.
Mr. Stephen Ponder.
Richard Poore efq; Andover.
Mr. George Prentis, Maidftone.
Mr. William Pretyman.
The Rev. Richard Price, D. D. F. R. S. &c. &c. Hackney.
Robert Price efq;
Mr. John Prince, Linton.
Mr. John Protheroe, Briftol.

R.

Jofeph Read efq;
The Rev. Abraham Rees, D. D. F. R. S.
Mr. Thomas Reeves.
The Rev. John Reynolds.
The Rev. John Rippon, A. M. three copies.
Mr. Alexander Ritchei, Glafgow.
Mr. James Robbins, Long Afhton, Somerfetfhire.
Mr. Thomas Robinfon.
Mr. Thomas Robinfon, Bury.
The Rev. Mr. Robotham, Congleton, Chefhire.
Mr. John Rodbard, Ipfwich.
Mifs Rodbard, Hackney.
Thomas Rogers efq; Newington Green.
Jeffe Rozea efq;
Mr. J. T. Rutt.

S.

Mr. John Salmon, Nayland.
Mr. Edward Sargeant.
Mr. Thomas Nicol Scott, Ipfwich.
The Rev. Ruffel Scott, Portfmouth.
Mr. William Hendley Scott.
Mr. Richard Scrivener, Framlingham, Suffolk.

I

Mr. James

Mr. James G. Searle, Saffron Walden.
Mr. James Searle, ditto.
Mr. John Searle, ditto.
John Semple esq; Earnock.
Mr. Nathaniel Sergeant.
Mr. Benjamin Sermon.
Mr. B. Sewell, Norwich.
Mr. Robert Sewell, jun. ditto.
Mr. Clement Sharp, Rumsey, Hants.
Mr. Richard Sharp.
The Rev. John Sheldon, Canterbury.
Mr. Robert Sheldrak, Hadleigh, Suffolk.
Mr. John Shelly, Great Yarmouth.
Mr. Thomas Shewell, Ickleford, Herts.
Samuel Shore, jun. esq.
Thomas Shrimpton esq; High Wycomb.
Mr. Richard Simpson, Cambridge.
Mr. T. Simpson.
Philip Slater esq; Stoke Newington.
Joseph Smith esq; Bristol.
The Rev. Mr. Smith, Bedford.
Colonel William Smith, New York.
Mr. Joseph Smitheman, Braintree.
The Rev. Joseph Sowden, Booth, Yorkshire.
Archibald Speirs esq; Eldersley.
Mrs. Speirs, Dowager, ditto.
Peter Speirs esq; Culcruch.
Mr. Isaac Spelman, Great Yarmouth.
The Rev. John Stafford, D. D.
Mr. Jonathan Stammers, Nayland.
Mr. Thomas Stammers, Melton, Suffolk.
The Rev. Samuel Stevens, Honiton, Devon.
Mr. William Steward, Great Yarmouth.
Mr. C. Stibbs.
Thomas Stiff esq.
Walter Stirling esq; Glasgow.
Mr. Thomas Stock.
Joseph Stonard esq.
Mr. Nathaniel Stonard, Bow.
John Hurford Stone esq; Hackney.
Samuel Stratton, sen. esq; ditto.
Miss Stratton, ditto.
Thomas Stratton esq; ditto.
Samuel Stratton, jun. esq.
Mr. John Strutt, Rickmansworth, Herts.
Mr. Richard Suatt.

Mr. John

LIST OF SUBSCRIBERS.

T.

Mr. John Tabor, Bocking.
Mr. Robert Tabor, Colcheſter.
Mr. Robert Tabor, jun. ditto.
Mr. Samuel Tabor, Rotterdam.
Mr. John Bayly Tailer, Woodbridge.
Clement Taylor eſq; Maidſtone, M. P.
Mr. David Taylor, Harlow.
Mr. John Taylor, Ipſwich.
Mr. Richard Taylor, Norwich.
Mr. Samuel Taylor, Southampton.
Mr. William Taylor, jun. of Norwich.
Mr. William Taylor.
John Thompſon eſq; Craydon, ſix copies.
Mr. John Thompſon, jun. two copies.
Andrew Thomſon eſq; Glaſgow.
The Rev. Thomas Toller, Iſlington.
Mr. Benjamin Tomkins.
Joſeph Tomkins eſq; Abingdon, Berks.
William Tomkins eſq; ditto.
The Rev. Iſaac Toms, Hadleigh.
Mr. William Tomſon.
Mr. Abraham Toulmin.
Samuel Toulmin eſq.
Mr. William Toulmin, Hackney.
The Rev. Joſeph Towers, D. D.
John Towgood eſq.
Matthew Towgood eſq.
The Rev. Meredith Townſend, Stoke Newington.
Mr. Arthur Tozer, Briſtol.
Mr. John Travis, Kingſton upon Hull.
Mr. William Travis, ditto.
Mr. John Trigg, Melbourn, Cambridgeſhire.
The Rev. Nathaniel Trotman, Clapton.
Mr. John Trumbull.
The Rev. Daniel Turner, Abingdon.
Mr. Daniel Turner, Hackney.
Mr. James Turner, Great Yarmouth.

V.

Mr. Elias Vanderhorſt, Briſtol.
Benjamin Vaughan eſq.
Mr. Francis Virgo.
Mr. William Unwin, Bow.
Mr. John Vowell, jun.

W.

Mrs. Wade, Colchester.
Mr. James Walker, Great Yarmouth.
The Rev. Matthew Walker, Saffron Walden,
Mr. Thomas Walters.
Mr. Henry Wardall.
Mr. Daniel Watkinson, Felsted, Essex.
Mr. Robert Watkinson.
Mr. George Watson, Saxlingham, Norfolk,
Mr. John Watson.
Mr. Job Watts, Bristol.
Mr. Nathaniel Watts, ditto.
Mr. Francis Weaver, ditto.
Mr. James Webb.
The Rev. Joshua Webb.
Mr. Nathaniel Wedd, Newton, Cambridgeshire.
Mr. William Wedd, Foulmere.
Mr. William Weightman.
George Welch esq.
Messrs. Welles, Grosvenor and Co. twelve copies.
Mr. John Wenham, Harlow.
James West esq.
James Welton esq.
Mr. J. T. Wheeler, Bristol.
The Rev. Thomas Whitehurst, A. M. Rector of Colmworth,
  Bedfordshire.
Mr. William Whitley.
James Whittle esq.
Mr. Thomas Whitty, Bristol.
The Rev. John Wiche, Maidstone.
The Rev. Aaron Wickens, Dunmow, Essex,
Mr. John Wilkinson, Saffron Walden.
Mr. William Wilshere, Hitchin.
Mr. William Wilshere, jun. ditto.
Mr. Wilson.
Mr. Thomas Wilson.
The Rev. John Winter, Newbury, Berks.
The Rev. Robert Winter, Hammersmith.
Thomas Wittenoom esq.
The Rev. Mr. Wood, Leeds.
Michael Woodhull esq.
The Rev. Hugh Worthington, Islington.
The Rev. Thomas Wren, D. D. Portsmouth.
John Wright, M. D. Bristol.
Mr. John Wright.
The Rev. Mr. Wright, Ipswich.

AMERICAN

AMERICAN SUBSCRIBERS,

Whofe Names have been tranfmitted from VIRGINIA.

His Excellency George Wafhington efq; two copies.

The Titles belonging to the following Gentlemen not being known, their Names only are given.

James Adam.
Samuel Arell.
W. Brown.
John Carter.
Richard Conway.
John Dundas.
Philip Dalby.
William Deakins.
John Fitzgerald.
Richard Gray, Winchefter.
S. and T. Hanfon.
Edward Harper.
William Hartfhorne.
James Hendricks.
George Hollingfworth.

Hove and Harrifon.
Charles Lee.
Samuel Love.
William Lyles.
Daniel M'Pherfon.
John Muir.
William Murphy.
William Paton.
Thomas Porter.
Dennis Ramfay.
Robert Sanderfon.
Jeffe Taylor.
Edward K. Thompfen.
George Torien.
Jofiah Watfon and Co.

SUBSCRIBERS IN THE MASSACHUSETTS.

M. C. for fuch as have been Members of Congrefs.

His Excellency James Bowdoin efq; late Gov. three copies.
His honor Thomas Cufhing efq; late lieut. governor.
His honor Benjamin Lincoln efq; lieut. gov. two copies.
Samuel Adams efq; M. C. Bofton.
Mr. John Andrews.
Nathaniel Appleton efq.
Mr. Luke Baker.
The Rev. Thomas Barnard, A. M. Salem.
Jofeph Barrell efq; Bofton.
Mr. T. Brattle, Cambridge.
Samuel Breck efq; Bofton, two copies.
Mr. M. Brimmer, Roxbury.

Captain John Callahan, Bofton.
Mr. Jofeph Callender.
Richard Cary efq; Charleftown.
Benjamin Clarke efq; Roxbury.
The Rev. John Clarke, A. M. Bofton.
Caleb Davis efq;
Thomas Dawes, fen. efq.
Captain John Derby, Salem, three copies.
Samuel Dexter efq;
Mr. Elifha Doane, Bofton.
Mr. Ebenezer Dorr.
The Rev. Jofeph Eckley, A. M.
The Rev. John Eliot, A. M.
Mr. Samuel Eliot.
William Erving efq.
Royal Flint efq.

The

AMERICAN SUBSCRIBERS.

The Rev. Jonathan French, A. M. Andover.
Elbridge Gerry efq; M. C. Marblehead.
Mofes Gill efq; Bofton, two copies.
D. S. Greenough efq; Roxbury.
Dr. Lemuel Hayward, Bofton.
J. Henfhaw efq;
Jofhua Henfhaw efq;
Stephen Higginfon efq; M. C. two copies.
The Rev. Simeon Howard, D.D.
William Hyflop efq; Brookline.
Henry Jackfon efq; Bofton.
Mr. James Jackfon, Roxbury.
Jonathan Jackfon efq; M. C. Bofton.
John Coffin Jones efq; two copies.
The Rev. John Lathrop, D. D.
Thomas Lee efq; Cambridge.
James Lovell efq; M. C. Bofton.
John Lowell efq; M. C. two copies.
Mr. Ifaac Lucas.
Mr. John Lucas.
Mr. William Martin.
Jonathan Mafon, fen. efq;
Jonathan Mafon, jun. efq;
Mr. Timothy Newell.
The Rev. Daniel Oliver, A. M.
Mr. Jofeph Peirce.

T. Penny efq; [now of Jamaica.]
Wm. Phillips, fen. efq; Bofton.
Mr. William Phillips, jun.
The Rev. Eliphalet Porter, A. M. Roxbury.
Mr. Simeon Pratt.
John Read efq;
Mr. Samfon Reed, Bofton.
Thomas Ruffell efq; fix copies.
Mr. Nathaniel Seaver.
Mr. William Shattuck.
The Rev. Ifaac Skillman, A. M.
Dr. John Sprague, Dedham.
The Rev. Sam. Stillman, A.M. Bofton.
Mr. Ebenezer Storer.
Increafe Sumner efq; Roxbury.
Mr. John Sweetfer, jun. Bofton.
The Rev. Peter Thacher, A. M.
Mr. William Thompfon.
Mr. Elifha Ticknor.
Mr. Edward Tuckerman.
Jofeph Ward efq;
Benjamin Waterhoufe, M. D.
Mr. Jofiah Waters.
Mr. Arnold Welles.
Mr. Samuel Whitwell.
The Rev. Ebenezer Wight, A.M.
The Rev. Jofeph Willard, D.D. Prefident of the Univerfity at Cambridge.
Mr. Jofeph Williams, Roxbury.
John Winflow efq; Bofton.

RHODE ISLAND.

Jabez Bowen efq; Providence.
Meffrs. John Brown and Francis.
Mr. Nicholas Brown.

Mr. Caleb Greene, Warwick.
Mr. John Jenckes, Providence.
Mr. Jofeph Varnum, Dracutt.

Daniel Buck efq; Norwich, VERMONT.

Sir John Temple, Britifh Conful, NEW YORK.

John Bavard efq; M. C. PHILADELPHIA.

Rufus Fairbanks efq; Halifax, NOVA SCOTIA.

CONTENTS.

CONTENTS.

CONTENTS.

ERRATA befide thofe at the End of the Volume.

Page 4, line 20, *read* Brown, a fiery zealot—l. 22, *dele* a fiery zealot. P. 12. l. 21, *read* tyrant, Philip II. of Spain. P. 20, l. 7, *read* elected by the planters. P. 23, l. 18, *read* declared fo late as. P. 27, l. 5, *read* ceafed in 1640. P. 32, l. 20, *read* the jurifdiction. P. 35, l. 21, *read* the three laft colonies, Maffachufetts, Connecticut, and New Haven. P. 39, l. 10, *read* colonies of the Maffachufetts and New Hampfhire. P. 44, l. 3, *read* mentioned hereafter. P. 77, laft line, *read* James II. P. 118, l. 11 *read* the London diffenting deputation. P. 166, l. 10, *read* the Minifters of Charles II. down to thofe of the. P. 290, l. 13, *dele* generality of the. P. 308, l. 19, *read* not folely to any. P. 427, l. 3, *for* other *read* diftrict.

I

THE

RISE, PROGRESS, AND CONCLUSION

OF THE

NORTH AMERICAN REVOLUTION.

———————

L E T T E R I.

Roxbury, December 26, 1771.

MY GOOD SIR,

TO your properly underſtanding the nature and origin of the uneaſineſs, that has ſo ſtrongly agitated
the colonies of late years, and ſtill exiſts though now ſome-
what abated; and which has been occaſioned by parliamentary taxation and the modern meaſures of government; you muſt be acquainted with the ſentiments
and hiſtory of the firſt ſettlers, no leſs than of their
deſcendants and ſucceſſors.

Several of the moſt zealous and eminent proteſtants,
in the reign of *Edward* the VIth, oppoſed the popiſh
ceremonies and habits, though otherwiſe united to their
brethren in religious tenets. The oppoſition became
more general and determined, after hundreds of them
fled to, and reſided in foreign parts, in order to eſcape
the *Marian* perſecutions. There the ſentiments of
numbers, through their intercourſe with proteſtants of

 other

other nations, were much changed and improved; and they were more than ever defirous of proceeding further in the reformation, than was directed by the service-book of king *Edward*.

1558. Upon the acceffion of *Elizabeth*, the refugees returned to *England*, loaded with experience and learning, but in the utmoft diftrefs and poverty. Thofe of the clergy, who could comply with the queen's eftablishment, were quickly preferred. The reft, after being admitted to preach awhile, were fufpended, and reduced to former indigence. Several were offered bifhoprics, but declined the tender, on account of the garments, ceremonies, &c. while the neceffity of the times, and the flattering hope of obtaining hereafter an amendment in the conftitution of the church, induced others to accept preferments, though with trembling.

The queen affected much pomp in religion; was fond of the old popifh ceremonies, in which fhe had been educated; and thought her brother king *Edward* had gone too far in demolishing ornaments.

The clergy and laity, who fought after greater eccle-fiaftic purity, in vain ftruggled hard for the abolifh-ment of popifh ceremonies and habits; or, at leaft, leaving the ufe of them, in divine fervice, indifferent. They obtained nothing but the honorable nick-name of PURITANS. The queen proved an inflexible bigot, and would be obeyed, or punifh. The parliament, in their firft feffion, had very injudicioufly paffed the two acts of Supremacy and Uniformity, without guarding them properly; and, by a claufe in the latter, delivered up to the crown all ecclefiaftic jurifdiction. Men of folid

folid learning and piety, of fober lives, popular preachers, profeffed enemies to popery and fuperftition, and of the fame faith, in point of doctrine, with the conformifts, were fufpended, deprived, imprifoned and ruined, for not complying with the ufe of thofe garments and cere- monies, which their opponents acknowledged to be in- different in themfelves ; while the fufferers adjudged fuch compliance finful, from their having been abufed to idolatry, and ferving as marks and badges of that reli- gion they had renounced.

All the puritans of thefe times were defirous of re- maining in the church, might they be indulged as to the habits and a few ceremonies, though they were far from being fatisfied with the hierarchy, and had other ob- jections befide thofe for which they had been deprived. Inftead of indulgence, their grievances were multiplied ; and the penal laws were rigoroufly executed. However, the body of the conforming clergy being extremely illiterate and ignorant, the deprived minifters were em- ployed as curates or lecturers ; and received, for their fervices, a fmall confideration from the incumbent, to- gether with the voluntary contribution of the parifh. By their warm and affectionate preaching and eminent faithfulnefs, they gained the hearts of the common people, who were the more attached to them, the more cruelty was exercifed upon them ; and who had the utmoft averfion to the popifh garments, as their hatred to popery increafed. The preachers appealed to the fcriptures. Their hearers fearched them carefully ; ob- tained more and clearer difcoveries of the popifh fuper- ftitions ; grew in their abhorrence of them ; venerated the divine inftitutions ; and longed to have the worfhip

of

of the church rendered more pure and primitive. The popularity of the deprived minifters drew numbers from neighbouring parifhes. *Puritanifm* fpread and gained ground by being perfecuted. Its growth was the greateft grief to the queen and archbifhop Whitgift. But neither the fupreme head of the church, nor the primate of all *England*, had policy or chriftianity enough to apply the proper remedy, in granting *liberty of confcience*. Inftead of that, new acts were paffed, and greater feverities practifed. Such inhuman proceedings, againft proteftants of good moral characters, did not pafs unnoticed. They were the fubjects of converfation. The right of acting thus toward fellow-creatures, and its non-agreement with the mild and benevolent principles of Chriftianity, were freely canvaffed. The fupreme head and chief dignitaries of the *Englifh* church being fuch intolerable perfecutors, it became a queftion, " Is fhe any longer a *true church* of Chrift, and are her minifters *true* minifters ?"

At length one *Robert Brown*, defcended from an ancient and honorable family, and nearly related to Lord Treafurer *Cecil*, a fiery zealot, travelled through the country, 1586. a fecond time, holding forth, wherever he went, againft *bifhops, ecclefiaftic courts, ordaining of minifters,* &c. and gathered a *feparate* congregation. The parties held, that the *church of* ENGLAND was not a *true* church; that her minifters were not *rightly* ordained; that her difcipline was *popifh* and *anti-chriftian*; and that all her ordinances and facraments were *invalid*. Therefore they would not join with her members, in *any part* of public worfhip. They not only renounced communion with the *church*

of

of ENGLAND, but with *all* other reformed churches, except they were of their own model.

Thefe *feparatifts* were called *Brownifts*, which was long afterward the common name for all that feparated *totally* from the church of *England*, even when they difowned the rigid principles of *Brown* and his congregation. We muft carefully diftinguifh the *Brownifts* from the *Puritans*. Moft of the latter were for keeping within the pale of the church, apprehending it to be a *true* church in its *doctrines* and *facraments*, though defective in *difcipline* and corrupt in *ceremonies*. They thought it *unlawful* to feparate; fubmitted to fufpenfions and deprivations: when driven out of one diocefe, took fanctuary in another, being afraid of incurring the guilt of *fchifm*; and were the chief writers againft the *Brownifts*.

A frefh effort was made to crufh the *non-conformifts*. 1593. A moft obnoxious act was paffed, for punifhing all who refufed to come to church, and every one, who perfuaded others to oppofe the queen's authority in ecclefiaftic caufes, or was prefent at any conventicle or meeting. The punifhment was imprifonment without bail, till the convicted agreed to conform and make a declaration of his conformity. In cafe the offender did not fign the declaration within three months, he was *to abjure the realm, and go into perpetual banifhment*. If he departed not within the time limited, or returned afterward without the queen's licenfe, he was *to fuffer death without benefit of clergy*. By this act, the cafe of nonconformifts was worfe than that of felons at common law. The ftatute was levelled againft the laity, no lefs than the clergy. The moderate puritans evaded it, by going to church when prayers were nearly ended,

and

and by receiving the facrament when adminiftered with fome latitude. The weight of it fell upon the *Brownifts*, whofe fentiments had gained ground, fo that they were increafed to near twenty thoufand, befide wives and children, according to the opinion of *Sir Walter Raleigh*, given in the houfe of commons, when the bill was read the fecond time and debated *.

Several were *put to death*, about this period; which excited an odium againft the bifhops and high com-miffioners, who were univerfally known to have been at the bottom of the proceedings againft them. It was refolved therefore, to fend the remainder of the im-prifoned into banifhment, inftead of continuing to execute them. Others preferred a voluntary exile, rather than be expofed to the mercilefs perfecutions that awaited them in their native country. Is it ftrange, that thefe perfons, thus forced or frightened out of it, for claiming and exercifing the common right of human nature, that of judging for themfelves in matters of religion, fhould at length think, that their allegiance terminated with their departure; or, that thofe who commiferated them inclined to the fame fentiment?

The parliament, efpecially the lower houfe, perceiving how the queen, and many of the bifhops and ecclefiaftics, abufed their fpiritual power; what mifchiefs they brought upon the church; and the miferies to which honeft men were reduced for mere difference in religious fentiments; attempted repeatedly to regulate matters, and to redrefs the hardfhips of the non-conformifts, but was ftopt by her majefty, in the moft dictatorial manner. Some of the members, roufed by fuch unwarrantable

* Townfhend's Hiftorical Collections, p. 76.

acts

acts of fovereignty, fpake boldly and freely upon the occafion, and cenfured the arbitrary proceedings of the bifhops. The queen added to her other faults, that of fending them to the Tower. But, though fhe could awe the parliament, imprifon its members, and protect her favorite bifhops; fhe could not overpower the confciences of the non-conformifts.

A number of religious people, upon the borders of *Nottinghamfhire, Lincolnfhire* and *Yorkfhire,* having fuf-fered perfecution patiently for years, and fearched the fcriptures diligently, were at length fully of opinion, that the *ceremonies* of the *Englifh* church were *unlawful*; that the lordly power of her prelates was contrary to the *freedom* of the gofpel; and that her offices, courts and canons had no warrant in the word of God; but were *popifh.* They determined therefore to fhake off that yoke of bondage, viz. human impofitions, brought into the church by popifh policy and power, againft the fuperior law of Chrift, the genius of his plain religion, and chriftian liberty. They refolved, as the Lord's free 1602. people, " *to join themfelves by covenant into a churchftate; and, agreeable to prefent or future knowledge, to walk in all the ways of God, according to their beft abilities, whatever it cofts them* *."

The affembly, owing to the diftance of habitations, 1606. was obliged to form itfelf into two diftinct religious focieties; the one, with which is our concern, foon had for its paftor the famous Mr. *John Robinfon.* The church kept together about a year; but being extremely haraffed by perfecutors, concluded upon removing to *Holland.* The pious refugees repaired to and fettled at Amfterdam;

* Prince's New England Chronology, Part I. p. 4.

B 4   but

but after a while removed to *Leyden*; where they were highly refpected, and would have been allowed fome public favor, had it not been for fear of offending England. By hard and continued labor they obtained a living. The *Dutch* employed them before others, for their honeft and exemplary behaviour; and readily trufted them when in want of money. Matters, however, were not altogether to their mind; and fome of the moft 1617. fenfible began to think of another removal. It was imagined, that, if a better and eafier place of living could be had, numbers would join them. The morals of the Dutch were too diffolute; and they were afraid, that their offspring would become irreligious. Befide, they had an ardent, noble, and godly defire, of laying a foundation for fpreading the religion of *Jefus* over the remote regions of the earth; and of handing down to future ages, what they thought to be, the pure and unadulterated worfhip of the great JEHOVAH. They therefore directed their views to *America*. To thofe who objected—the length and danger of the voyage, the difficulties and calamities to which they fhould be expofed, the barbarities and treacheries of the *Indians*, and their inability to fupport the expenfe—it was anfwered, " The difficulties are not invincible, and may be overcome by fortitude and patience; the ends propofed are good and honorable; the calling lawful and urgent; the bleffing of God may therefore be expected. We live but as exiles now, and are in a poor condition. The truce with the *Spaniards* is haftening to a clofe. Nothing but preparations for war are going forward. The *Spaniards* may be as cruel as the *Savages*; and famine and peftilence may be as fore in *Holland* as in *America*."

After

After ferious and folemn application to God for direction, they concluded on carrying the propofal of
croffing the *Atlantic* into execution; endeavouring
to live in a diftinct body by themfelves, under the
general government of the *Virginia* Company; and
fuing to his majefty, king *James*, for *full liberty and
freedom of confcience.*

The Virginia Company were ready to give them a
patent, with as ample privileges as they could grant;
but, notwithftanding the great intereft made by gentlemen of the firft character, and by the chief fecretary
of ftate, the king and bifhops refufed to allow the refugees (though at the diftance of 3000 miles) liberty
of confcience under the royal feal. All they could obtain from his majefty, was a promife that he would
connive at, and not moleft them, provided they carried
themfelves peaceably; but he would not tolerate them
by his public authority. Upon this occafion it was
wifely obferved, " If his majefty's promife is no fecurity, a further confirmation will be of little value; though
it has a feal as broad as the houfe-floor, it will not
ferve the turn, for there will be means enow found,
when wanted, to recall or reverfe it; and we muft reft
herein on God's Providence." This reafoning, and the
hope of being placed beyond the reach of ecclefiaftic
courts, prevailed. They refolved to venture; and,
after long attendance, much coft and labor, obtained a
patent.   1619.

They agreed, that the minor part of younger and
ftronger men, with Mr. *Brewfter*, an elder of the church,
fhould go firft, and that the paftor, Mr. *Robinfon*, fhould
remain behind with the majority, for a future favorable
opportunity.

opportunity. Their enemies whifpered, that the States of *Holland* were weary of their company; but the reverfe was evident from the following occurrence, viz. the magiftrates of the city, when reproving the *Walloons* in open court, faid, " *Thefe* Englifh *have lived now ten years among us, and yet we never had any accufation againft any of them, whereas your quarrels are continual.*"

1620.
July
22.
The colony, deftined for America, failed from *Delft-Haven* for *Southampton*; and there met a fhip, having fome Englifh friends on board, who propofed removing with them. Both veffels proceeded to fea; but returned twice into port, on account of defects in the one from Delft, which was difmiffed. Part of the company returned to *London*, the remainder betook themfelves to the fhip, and failed from *Plymouth* the 6th of September. After many delays, difficulties and dangers, they made *Cape Cod* at break of day on the 9th of November, and entered the harbour on the 10th. They offered up their devout and ardent acknowledgments to God for his protection, and had thoughts of landing; but remarking, that they were out of the limits of their patent, and in a fort reduced to a ftate of nature; and hearing fome, who came from London, hint, *there is now no authority over us*; they, while on board, formed themfelves into a Civil Body Politic under the crown of *England*, for the purpofe of framing " juft and equal laws, ordinances, acts, conftitutions and offices," to which they promifed " all due fubmiffion and obedi-ence." This *contract* was fubfcribed by forty-one per-
Nov.
11.
fons, on Saturday the 11th of November. The whole company of fettlers, men, women, children and fervants, amounted to no more than one hundred and one,
the

the exact number that left England—for one had died, but another was born, upon the paffage.

Enfeebled and fickly, we now behold them at the diftance of 3000 miles, not only from their native country, but the hofpitable land where they lately refided for years, when unfeeling perfecution drove them into a voluntary banifhment. They have a long and dreary winter before them, and are upon the ftrange coaft of an uncultivated wildernefs, without a relation or friend to welcome their arrival, or an houfe to fhelter them; without even a kind inhabitant to comfort them by tender acts of humanity, much lefs a civilized town or city, from which fuccour may be obtained on an emergency. Thus circumftanced, they are employed in making difcoveries, till the 20th of December, when they conclude upon a place for immediate fettlement, which they afterward name *New-Plymouth*, in grateful remembrance of the laft town they left in their native country.

The winter proved remarkably mild * for the American climate, though exceffively fevere to an Englifh conftitution; and, what with diforders brought upon them through uncommon labors and fatigues, and their being expofed to the rigours of the feafon; and what with the fcurvy and other difeafes occafioned by a tedious voyage, and the want of proper accommodations while making it, they buried by the end of March 1621, forty-four of their little fociety, of whom one and twenty were fubfcribers to the *contract*. The number of their dead increafed to fifty by the beginning of November, when, to their great joy, a veffel arrived

1621.

---

* *Wood*'s New England's Profpect. Ed. 1764. p. 5.

with

with thirty five settlers from London. It was years before their plantation amounted to three hundred people: when nearly so, the Council established at *Plymouth*, in the county of *Devon*, for the planting, ruling, ordering 1630. and governing of *New England* in *America*, granted Jan. them a *Patent*, by which their lands were secured against 13. all English claims.—Be it noted, that they early agreed with, and satisfied the *Indian* proprietors.

It would have been astonishing, had not these planters brought with them opinions favorable to liberty. The arbitrary proceedings of *Elizabeth* and *James* produced a spirit of inquiry; and induced the sufferers and others to canvass the equity of those powers, which were so improperly exercised. When the film of prejudice was removed, it was easy to discern that tyranny, whether in church or state, could not be vindicated by reason or revelation; and that Heaven's permitting it, was no more a countenance to that, than any other wickedness. Beside, the *Plymouthians* had lived for years among a people, who had been engaged in a bloody war, with a cruel unrelenting tyrant, whose sovereignty they had renounced. The frequent conversation that must have passed between the Dutch and English refugees, must have improved the attachment of the last to the cause of freedom. It might also have been hinted to them, that it began to be the sentiment of some English nobles and principal commoners, that in case of a removal to America, persons, without any charter from the crown, were at liberty to establish what form of government they pleased; and to set up a new state, as fully to all intents and purposes, as though they were making their first entrance into civil society.

No

No wonder then, efpecially confidering the general
equality prevailing among them, that the *Plymouthians*,
by their contract before landing, formed themfelves
into a *proper Democracy*; and that it was entered in the
Plymouth records of 1636, " *Finding, that as free born* 1636.
fubjects of the ftate of ENGLAND, *we hither came with* 15.
all and fingular the privileges belonging to fuch; *in the firft*
place we think good, that it be eftablifhed for an act, that,
according to the [*rights* fuppofed to be wanting] *and due*
privileges of the fubjects aforefaid, no impofition, law or
ordinance be made or impofed upon them at prefent or to
come; but fuch as fhall be made and impofed by confent, ac-
cording to the free liberties of free born fubjects of the ftate
and kingdom of ENGLAND, *and no otherwife.*"   They
meant to continue their allegiance to the crown; to retain their connection with the mother country; to adopt
the general laws of England for the rule of government,
wherein they fuited; and to be governed by their own
particular acts in other inftances.

Perfons, devoted to church authority and particular
national eftablifhments, may exclaim againft the *Ply-*
mouthians for their religious fentiments : but a fair and
brief ftatement of them, it is apprehended, will be thought
the beft defence that can be offered, by thofe who candidly examine the *New Teftament*, and are properly impreffed with the words of our Saviour—*My kingdom is*
not of this world.

When Mr. *Robinfon* and his affociates feparated from
the church of England, they were rigid *Brownifts*.   After
his removal to Holland, and there converfing with
learned divines, he, being a gentleman of a liberal
mind and good difpofition, became moderate, as did
his

his people; so that they who continued rigid *Brownists* would hardly hold communion with them. Mr. *Robinson* and his society did not require of those who joined them, a renunciation of the church of England. They also acknowledged the other reformed churches for true and genuine; allowed their own members occasional communion with them, in the word preached, and in the prayers conceived by the preacher before and after sermon, but not in the sacraments and discipline; and admitted their members, known to them to be pious, to occasional communion with themselves in the sacraments. Still it is to be remarked, that they were not admitted, because of their being members of such churches, but on account of their known piety: their belonging to and continuing in such churches, was not an argument for rejecting them; nor was it the argument for their reception. Mr. *Robinson*, however, by his conversation and writings, proved a principal in ruining *Brownism*; and, in the opinion of some was the father, of others the restorer, of the *independent* or *congregational* churches. Congregational is the term used in *New England*, the other is discarded, as seeming to imply too great a separation from sister churches.

The *Plymouthians* held, that the Bible was the sole religious code of protestants; and that every man had a right to judge for himself, and to try all doctrines by it, and to worship according to what he apprehended that directed. In doctrinal tenets they agreed with the articles of the church of England. The main difference between them and other reformed churches, was about hierarchy. They maintained, that no particular church ought to consist of more persons than

could

could worſhip in one congregation; that every man ought, in appearance, to be a true believer in Chriſt and ſubject to his authority; that when there was a ſuitable number of ſuch believers, who thought themſelves bound in conſcience to do it, they had a right to imbody into a church, by ſome certain contract or covenant, expreſſed or implied; and that, being imbodied, they were to chooſe all their officers, who were paſtors or teaching elders, mere ruling elders meant to aſſiſt the former, and qualified to teach occaſionally, and deacons who were to manage the temporalities of the church, to take care of the poor, and to officiate at the Lord's table by providing the bread and wine, laying the cloth, carrying the elements, &c. [The cuſtom of having ruling elders has now ceaſed.] The elders of both kinds were to form the preſbytery of overſeers and rulers. They alſo held, that no churches or church officers had any power over other churches or officers, to control or impoſe upon them, all having equal rights and privileges. Their own officers were removable by them upon juſtifiable reaſons; in caſe of capital errors, groſs miſconduct and the like. When they baptized, they rejected the ſign of the croſs, and other ceremonies not enjoined by ſcripture. They received the elements of the Lord's ſupper, in the table poſture of the day and place in which they lived. Excommunication they deemed to be wholly ſpiritual; and denied, that the church or its officers had any authority to inflict temporal pains and penalties. They conſidered no days as holy, but the Lord's day, which they obſerved with great ſtrictneſs. Solemn faſtings and thankſgivings, as the aſpects of Providence required, they had a pious

7

regard

regard to, as agreeable to both natural and revealed religion.

A better set of emigrants never crossed the *Atlantic*. " They were a plain, frugal, industrious, conscientious and loving people; and, for the day in which they lived, and considering their education, possessed a good share of politeness. The important light in which they viewed morality, led them, in many instances, to such critical exactness, as would be deemed by the moderns ridiculous; from thence however the community derived substantial benefits. They have been stigmatized as enthusiasts; but nothing like enthusiasm is to be met with in the records of any of their transactions, either civil or ecclesiastic. Their piety indeed was eminent and fervent, but it was also rational; and their religion was that of the Bible, and had a proper influence upon their conduct."

The *Plymouthians* having cleared the way for other sufferers to settle in *America*, with less difficulty and danger than what they had experienced; the fame of their plantation spreading through the western parts of *England*; and the government in church and state growing more and more oppressive; the territory of the 1628. *Massachusett's-Bay* was purchased of the *Plymouth-Council*, and a company soon formed, who consulted on settling a plantation, to which non-conforming *puritans* might emigrate in order to enjoy their own principles in full security. Their sufferings had been moderated for a few years before *Elizabeth*'s death. The queen was far advanced in life; the next heir to the crown was a *presbyterian,* who had subscribed to the *Scotch* national covenant, and, with hands uplifted to heaven, had pronounced, " The
Scotch

Scotch kirk is the pureft in the world, and the fervice of the kirk of *England* an evil faid mafs in *Englifh;* that wants nothing of the mafs but the liftings :" he had interceded for fome of the perfecuted minifters; and the bifhops were cautious of acting againft a party, for whom king *James* had declared : but upon his afcending the throne, the fears of the high church-men and the hopes of the non-conformifts were foon ended. It was not long before the king became in the church a furious perfecutor of the non-conformifts, and in the ftate as errant a defpot as his cowardice would allow. In ftigmatizing for *Puritans,* all who ftood by the laws of the land and oppofed his arbitrary government, though ftrenuous churchmen, he ftrengthened the caufe of the *church-puritans :* the former, called by way of diftinction *ftate-puritans,* joining the latter, both together became at length the majority of the nation.

Still the times were not mended; and the death of *James* made way for their becoming much worfe. King *Charles* unfortunately took for his bofom counfellor, in religious affairs, bifhop *Laud,* the moft unqualified perfon for the purpofe of any to be found in his three kingdoms : he alfo refigned himfelf up to arbitrary councils.

The lowering profpect thickened apace; the *Maffachufetts* Company therefore provided a fafe retreat, in feafon. They applied immediately to the improvement of their purchafed territory; and fent out Capt. *John Endicott* and others, with fervants, to begin a plantation; who arrived at (what is now named) *Salem.* They foon after petitioned for a *royal charter,* hoping that their exiftence and powers would be thereby fecured and promoted.

1629. moted. They fucceeded, and a charter of incorporation
Mar.
4.
was granted, making them a body politic, by the name
of " The Governor and Company of the *Maffachufetts-
Bay* in *New England*," with as full powers as any other
corporation in the realm of *England*. The grant and
fale of the *Plymouth-Council* was confirmed. Till the
annual election by the company could commence,
the governor, deputy-governor, and eighteen affiftants
were fpecified. The mode of governing, and of admitting freemen was prefcribed. They were empowered
to elect and conftitute fuch other officers, as might be
thought requifite for the managing of their affairs; and
to make laws and ordinances, not contrary to the laws
and ftatutes of the realm, for the good of the faid company, and the government of their lands and plantation,
and the inhabitants thereof. They were allowed to
tranfport perfons, whether fubjects or ftrangers, weapons,
merchandife, &c. *any law to the contrary notwithftanding*
—fuch was the difpenfing power the king affumed. He
alfo exempted them from paying cuftom or fubfidy for
feven years: the governor and company, their factors
and affigns, were to pay neither that nor any taxes IN
New England for the *fame fpace*. All were freed from
duties upon goods imported or exported for 21 years,
except the old 5 per cent. cuftom upon imports after
the expiration of the feven years. All his majefty's
fubjects going to and inhabiting the company's lands,
together with their children, were to enjoy all the liberties of free and natural fubjects, within any of his dominions, the fame as though born in England. The
king could mean only, that, by removing to and refiding
in the Maffachufetts, they fhould not forfeit for themselves,

felves or children, the privileges of *Englishmen*, and be
treated as foreigners; and not, that they fhould be governed by laws and officers of their own making or
choofing, perfonally or by reprefentation; for they were
evidently diftinguifhed from the governor and company
(of whom it appears to be fuppofed, that they were to
remain in England) as thefe were authorized to adminifter the oaths of fupremacy and allegiance to all
and every perfon or perfons, who fhould hereafter go to
inhabit the lands and premifes of the company. Befide,
the governor and company were entrufted with the
power of making laws, ordinances, &c. not contrary
to the laws of England; of fettling the government,
and magiftracy of the plantation, and its inhabitants;
of naming all the officers; and of fetting forth their
feveral duties, powers and limits; and the king commanded that all fuch laws, ordinances, &c. fhould be
publifhed, in writing, under the common feal of the
company, and thereupon be carefully obferved and put
into execution, according to their true meaning. The
charter * does not once mention *liberty of confcience* or
toleration; though one † hiftorian has inadvertently advanced, that " free liberty of confcience was likewife
granted to all who fhould fettle in the *Maffachufetts-Bay*,
to worfhip God in their own way;" and another ‡,
" the charter granted toleration to all chriftians, except
papifts." The affertions apply only to the charter
granted by king *William* and queen *Mary*.

* See the Charter in *Hutchinfon*'s Collection of Papers, p. 1—23.
† *Neale*'s Hiftory of the Puritans, 4to. Vol. I. p. 543.
‡ *Hutchinfon*'s Hiftory of the *Maffachufetts-Bay*. Vol. II. p. 3.

C 2   The

1629.   The company, in the exercife of their chartered powers,
April
30. determined that a governor and council of twelve, refiding on the plantation, fhould have the fole ordering of
its affairs and government. They appointed Capt. *Endicott* governor, and feven gentlemen going from England
to be counfellors, and directed how the other five fhould
be elected, together with a deputy-governor and fecretary.

Meffrs. *Higginfon, Skelton, Bright, John* and *Samuel
Browne* were of the feven counfellors nominated by the
company. The three firft, being minifters, had declared themfelves to be of one judgment, and to be
fully agreed in the manner how to exercife their miniftry. The company's committee in their letter to
governor *Endicott*, expreffed good hopes on account of
it; and at the fame time recommended Meffrs. *John* and
Samuel Browne as men whom they much refpected, being
fully perfuaded of their fincere affections to the good of
the plantation *. The minifters and paffengers coming
to fettle in it, were epifcopally inclined when they left
England; though they could not conform to many ceremonies and cuftoms, nor fubmit to, what they judged,
different corruptions, impofed upon their confciences by
the king and prelates. They were alfo ftrongly prejudiced againft the *feparatifts*, in which clafs the *Plymouthians* were numbered. But long before they arrived, or even failed, a Dr. *Fuller*, a deacon of the
church at Plymouth, and well verfed in its difcipline,
having been fent for, on account of a fatal ficknefs
which broke out among the emigrants after their arrival
at *Salem*, had, by his converfation with Capt. *Endicott*,
taken off the ill effect of common report, and brought

Suffolk Records.

                                                    him

him to think favorably of the outward form of worship espoused by the *Plymouthians*. The influence of the doctor's intercourse with the *Salem* settlers cannot be thought to have been confined to the captain. When the business of organizing a church was brought forward after the arrival of the counsellors, the matter was frequently canvassed, and at length it was determined to form it, nearly upon the plan of the one at Plymouth; and to invite the latter to be present, by their messengers, at the solemn ordination of the ministers Messrs. *Skelton* and *Higginson*. Notwithstanding cross winds the Plymouth messengers were time enough to give the right hand of fellowship, by which ceremony the two churches professed mutual affection and communion.

Aug. 6.

Probably, none of the newly arrived settlers had the least idea of such ecclesiastic proceedings, when they left England; but thought very differently. Some continued to do so; for Mr. *Bright*, disagreeing in judgment from the other ministers, removed to a distance before their ordination; and Messrs. *John* and *Samuel Browne*, dissatisfied with the proceedings of the society, separated with several who were like minded, and sat up another. Governor *Endicott*, being of a hot temper and not possessed of the greatest prudence, summoned the brothers before him, as ringleaders of a faction; and apprehending that their conversation and conduct would occasion divisions, sent them back to *England*, against their own inclination, notwithstanding their being counsellors, thinking himself justified by his public orders.

Let us return to the Company in *England*.

C 3

Mr.

Mr. *Matthew Craddock*, the governor, propofed at the general court, that, for the advancement of the plantation, the encouragement of perfons of worth and quality to tranfplant themfelves and families, and other weighty reafons, the government of the plantation fhould be transferred to its inhabitants, and not be continued in fubordination to the company at *London*. The matter was debated; and it was agreed, that the perfons prefent fhould ferioufly confider the bufinefs againft the next general court; it was alfo requefted, that they would, in the mean while, conduct with that privacy, that the affair might not be divulged. At a month's end they met, and confented that the government and patent fhould be fettled in *New England*, if it could be done legally. They foon after received letters refpecting the difference between governor *Endicott* and Meffrs. *John* and *Samuel Browne*; and fearing that thefe two had in their private letters defamed the plantation, they opened and read a number of them, and ordered that none from Mr. *Samuel Browne* fhould be delivered; however, upon application from the brothers, they directed that they fhould have a copy of the accufation fent againft them from *New England*. The company's letters upon this bufinefs, one to Meffrs. *Skelton* and *Higginfon*, and another to governor *Endicott*, intimated, that there had been in the parties addreffed a degree of intemperance; that direct or oblique afperfions had been thrown out againft the ftate; and that undigefted counfels had been too fuddenly put into execution. They befides expreffed an apprehenfion, left, through an ill conftruction, the fame might make the company obnoxious to any adverfary *.

* Suffolk Records.

The

The difference that happened in the plantation, the treatment of the *Brownes*, and the reports circulated by them, undoubtedly occasioned much talk Many would think it ſtrange, that, while the charter was totally ſilent upon the head of religion, and ſeveral of the grantees and company, though ſtrongly oppoſed to the tyrannies of the high churchmen, were real epiſcopalians, perſons of this profeſſion ſhould be debarred the right of worſhipping according to their own judgment and conſcience, and be even expelled the plantation. Theſe occurrences moſt probably forwarded the plan of Mr. *Craddock*. The advice of learned council was ordered to be taken, and it was conſidered how to execute the projected removal without offending government.

Among the other weighty reaſons which induced them to remove, we muſt include the hope of getting beyond the reach of *Laud* and the high commiſſion court: for the Maſſachuſetts general court declared in 1651, " That ſeeing juſt cauſe to fear the perſecution of the then biſhop and high commiſſion, for not conforming to the ceremonies, they thought it their ſafeſt courſe to get to this outſide of the world (America) out of their view, and *beyond their reach*."

The company, at a general court, proceeded to a Oct. new election of officers, who were to repair to and ſettle 20. in *New England*. They choſe for governor *John Winthrop*, eſq; of *Groton* in *Suffolk*, a gentleman well known for his piety, liberality, wiſdom and gravity. The buſineſs of transferring the patent and corporation, and of taking over new ſettlers, was proſecuted with vigor. The enterpriſe produced a general rumor, as its extent and magnitude, the number and principles of the

perſons engaging in it, opened upon the public. The
intentions of the parties being ſuſpected, and jealouſies
ariſing concerning them, governor *Winthrop* and other
gentlemen, to remove prejudices, conciliate the minds
of the diſaffected, and recommend themſelves and their
expedition to the favorable regards of all ſerious chriſ-
1630. tians of the epiſcopal perſuaſion, addreſſed their brethren
Ap. 7. in and of the church of *England*, and afterward ſailed
from *Yarmouth* in the iſle of *Wight*, for *America*. The
ſigners of the addreſs, pray in the moſt ſolemn manner to
be conſidered as their brethren, and deſire it to be noted,
that the principals and body of their company eſteem it
their honor to call the *church of* ENGLAND their dear
mother. They acknowledge, that ſuch hope and part
as they have obtained in the common ſalvation, they
have received in her boſom, and ſuck'd from her breaſts.
They declare themſelves members of her body; and
that, while they have breath, they ſhall ſincerely endeavour her welfare. They pronounce themſelves a church
ſpringing out of her own bowels. Their profeſſions are
made in the ſtrongeſt language *.

June   The company arrived at *Salem*; and ſoon were in
12.   number more than fifteen hundred perſons, from different counties in England. They applied themſelves
early to the forming of churches; but, the Rev. Mr.
Cotton (who came from *Boſton* in *Lincolnſhire* to take
leave of his departing friends at *Southampton*) having
told them to adviſe with the *Plymouthians*, and to do nothing to offend them, and a precedent exiſting in the
church at *Salem*, they diſmiſſed all the peculiarities of
epiſcopacy, and preferred the congregational mode in

* *Hutchinſon's* Hiſtory, Vol. I. p. 487.

general.

general. However, they had no settled plan of church discipline, till after the arrival of Mr. *Cotton,* who was 1633. considered as a kind of oracle in both civil and sacred matters, and gradually moulded all their church administrations, and thus determined the ecclesiastic constitution of the colony; therein verifying what Mr. *Robinson* had judiciously predicted, when he said, " Many of those who have both wrote and preached against me and my people, were they in a place where they could have liberty and live comfortably, would do as we do *."

Governor *Winthrop* inserted, in his manuscript history, a couple of anecdotes, of an earlier date than Mr. Cotton's arrival, which may amuse you. " July 30, 1631, Mr. *Ludlow* in digging the foundation of his house at *Dorchester,* found two pieces of *French* money, one was coined 1596. They were in several places, above a foot within the firm ground." " June 13, 1632, At *Watertown* there was, in the view of divers witnesses, a great combat between a mouse and a snake; and after a long fight, the mouse prevailed and killed the snake. The minister of Boston, Mr. Wilson, a very sincere holy man, gives this interpretation—" The snake is the devil, the mouse is a poor contemptible people whom God has brought hither, and who shall overcome satan here, and dispossess him of his kingdom." " At the same time he told the governor, that before he resolved to come into the country, he dreamed that he was here, and saw a church arise out of the earth, which grew up and became a marvellous goodly church." He might think his dream divine; but it is easily accounted for as a common event, arising with the church-build-

* Prince's Chronology, p. 238.

ing

ing out of a lively imagination, warmed and directed
by a preponderating inclination. If, instead of interpret-
ing the combat, he had only mentioned, that the event
suggested to him such thoughts, and such an improvement, he would have evidenced more judgment and an
equal degree of wisdom in seizing the happy circumstance.

The colony increased apace, by frequent and numerous
accessions. But " it appears by private letters, that
the departure of so many of the best, both ministers
and private christians, did breed sad thoughts in those
behind of the Lord's intention in the work, and an apprehension of some evil days to come upon England;
yea, it began to be viewed by the council as a matter
of state, so that warrants were sent to stay the ships,
and to call in the patent; but, upon the petition of the
ship-masters, alleging how beneficial the plantation
was, they were released: Mr. Craddock, however, had
strict charge to deliver in the patent, and wrote to the
company to send it home upon receipt of his letter.
1634. The governor and assistants consulted about it, and re-
July. solved to answer Mr. Craddock, but not to return any
answer or excuse to the council, for the present *."

On the death of the duke of *Buckingham*, *Laud* became the king's prime minister in all affairs of both
church and state; and, on the death of archbishop
Abbot, he was exalted to the see of *Canterbury*. Possessed of such powers, he, by his pliant tools, *made
havock of the church, haling and committing to prison* conscientious ministers and laymen, who would not bend to
his antiscriptural impositions, so that the people were
scattered abroad, and passed over the *Atlantic* into the

* Governor Winthrop's MS, History.

wilds

wilds of *America*. The daily inroads of the court, on the civil rights of the fubject, helped forward the emigration.

From the beginning of the colony, until the emigration ceafed, through a change of affairs in England, 1640, there arrived in 298 veffels about 21200 fettlers (men, women and children) or 4000 families, but they did not all confine themfelves to the *Maffachufetts*. Notwithftanding the numbers that repaired thither, when Joffelyn vifited Bofton, in 1638, " he found it rather a village than a town, there being not above 20 or 30 houfes." Thefe fettlers were no lefs ftrenuous for their own particular rights and privileges than the Plymouthians. When the governor and company removed from *London* to the *Maffachufetts*, they renounced the appearance of a corporation, and affumed the form of a commonwealth, varying, as it fuited them, from the directions of the charter. The change of place and circumftances prevented their keeping to it in certain inftances, though not in others; but they could eafily fatisfy themfelves as to any violations; for " they apprehended themfelves fubject to no other laws or rules of government, than what arofe from natural reafon and the principles of equity, except any pofitive rules from the word of God *." Perfons of influence among them held, that birth was no neceffary caufe of fubjection; for that the fubject of any prince or ftate, had a natural right to remove to any other ftate or quarter of the world, when deprived of liberty of confcience; and that upon fuch removal his fubjection ceafed. They called their own a voluntary civil fubjection, arifing

* Hutchinfon's Letter of December 7, 1762.

merely

merely from a mutual compact between them and the king, founded upon the charter. By this compact they acknowledged themfelves bound; fo that they could not be fubject to or feek protection from any other prince, neither could make laws repugnant to thofe of *England*, &c. but, on the other hand, they maintained, that they were to be governed by laws made by themfelves, and by officers of their own electing *. They meant to be independent of Englifh parliaments; and therefore, when their intimate friends were become leading members in the houfe of commons, and they were advifed, on account of the great liberty to which king Charles left the parliament, to fend over fome to folicit for them, and had hopes given that they might obtain much, the governor and affiftants, after meeting in council upon the occafion, " declined the motion, for this confideration, that, if they fhould put themfelves under the protection of the parliament, they muft then be fubject to all fuch laws as they fhould make, or at leaft fuch as they might impofe upon them, in which courfe (though they fhould intend their good, yet) it might prove very prejudicial to them †."

Whatever approbation fuch fentiments may meet with from the friends of liberty, thefe muft regret the inconfiftencies to which human nature is fubject, in thofe very perfons whofe experience fhould have taught them, to do unto others, as they would that others fhould have done unto them, when they themfelves were fuffering under the relentlefs hand of arbitrary government. But,

* Hutchinfon's Hiftory, Vol. I. p. 251, and 252.

† Extract from Governor *Winthrop*'s MS. Hiftory, fent me by Governor *Trumbull* from *Connecticut*.

what

what is man! So early as the second general court after 1631.
the arrival of the governor and company, instead of May 18.
resolving to admit all the suitable and deserving, to a
generous participation of their freedom, they passed the
pernicious and disingenuous order, " For time to come
no man shall be admitted to the freedom of this body
politic, but such as are members of some of the churches,
within the limits of the same *." They soon after concluded, that none but such should share in the administration of civil government, or have a voice in any
election. Thus a powerful and mischievous alliance was
formed between the churches and the state. The
ascendency of the clergy was secured and much increased;
for no one could be proposed to the church for a member, unless the minister allowed it. The ministers were
consulted by the general court, in all matters of great
moment; and nothing was determined in such cases,
without a formal reference to them; who, of course,
used their influence with the people, to procure an approbation of the measures which they themselves had
advised †.

Instead of the freemen's appearing personally in the 1634.
general court, they for the first time sent deputies, to the May.
number of twenty-four. This was a variation from the
charter, which gave no power to admit representatives.
These with the governor, deputy governor, and assistants, formed the legislature of the colony, met and voted
together in one apartment till March 1644, when it was
ordained, that the governor and assistants should sit

---

* Massachusetts Records, Vol. I.   † Hutchinson's History,
Vol. I. p. 424.

apart:

apart: and thus commenced the houfe of reprefentatives, as a diftinct body.

The general court affumed fpiritual jurifdiction. Being church members, they might fuppofe they reprefented the churches, no lefs than the colony. They would 1636. approve of no churches, after a certain period, unlefs Mar. they had the approbation of the magiftrates and elders 8. of moft of the churches within the colony; nor would admit to freedom any of their members. They preffed colonial uniformity in religion, till they became perfe- cutors *. Whatever apology may be made for the treat- ment given to epifcopalians, baptifts and quakers, the colony cannot be cleared from the charge of perfe- cuting: that, however, will not juftify thofe who per- fecute with reproaches and ill-will the prefent genera- tion, now reprobating the intolerance of their forefathers, which at that period was, more or lefs, the ftain of moft religious parties. "It was not peculiar to the Maffa- chufetts people to think themfelves bound in confcience, to ufe the fword of the civil magiftrate to convince, or cut off heretics, that fo they might not infect the church, or injure the public peace †." The true grounds of liberty of confcience, were not then known or embraced by many fects of chriftians. But remember that the *Maffachufetts-Bay* now furpaffes the mother country, in its regard for the facred and civil rights of mankind. It not only exempts thofe of other denominations from paying to the fupport of its own colonial eftablifhments; the congregational churches; and has been a great num- ber of years in this laudable practice: but it protects all

* Maffachufetts Records, in many places.   † Mr. John Calender's Century Sermon.

I

proteftants

proteftants without requiring any qualifying fubfcriptions or tefts, and excludes none by partial laws from the exercife of civil power.

The government was in divers refpects abfolute. Both magiftrates and general court often judged and punifh-ed, in a fummary way, without a jury, according to difcretion, as occafions occurred. It was four years before it was enacted or ordered, that no trial fhould pafs upon any for life or banifhment, but by a jury of freemen: and within three years after, that law was 1637. violated even by the general court. They exercifed, while fitting, legiflative, judicial, and executive powers —a practice which muft ever be dangerous to the rights of a people, even when allowed to their own annual reprefentatives.

The country at length grew uneafy at thefe proceed-ings; were fufpicious that the general court affected arbitrary government; and earneftly expected a body of laws to direct and protect them in all their juft rights and privileges *. It was the more neceffary to comply with the prevailing expectation, for the bufinefs had been long in agitation: not only fo, but a great majority of the inhabitants were not freemen, not being members of the congregational churches, or declining to take up their freedom, in order to fecure an exemption from ferving in civil offices. It was not, till 1648 that the 1648. body of laws was digefted and printed.

The conduct of the colony on the one hand, and the inveteracy of the Englifh adminiftration on the other, would certainly have produced a revocation of the charter, and probably the ruin of the plantation, had

* Maffachufetts Records for the 4th of November, 1646, Vol. I.

not

not the difturbances in England prevented. It became a favorite, upon the change that followed them ; and, while *Oliver Cromwell* ruled, met with the utmoft indulgence. From 1640 to 1660, it approached very near to an independent commonwealth *. The houfe of commons, in a memorable refolve of the 10th of March, 1642, paffed in favor of it, gives *New England* the title of *kingdom* †. The commiffioners for *New England*, fent over by king *Charles* II. affert in their narrative ‡, that the colony folicited *Cromwell* to be declared a free ftate, which is not unlikely.

It has been already mentioned, that all the perfons paffing over to the *Maffachufetts* did not confine themfelves to that colony.

1635. Several families removed to *Connecticut* river, by mutual agreement with their fellow emigrants that remained behind. Plantations were formed at *Hartford, Windfor,* and *Weathersfield.* The inhabitants being foon after fully fatisfied, that they were out of the Maffachufetts limits, and of courfe jurifdiction, entered into 1639. a combination among themfelves ; became a body politic, without reftraining the freedom of their civil government to the memberfhip of their churches ; and proceeded to the choice of magiftrates and reprefentatives. By the articles of government, it was determined that there fhould be annually two general courts ; and that no perfon fhould be chofen governor more than once in two years. But it muft be obferved, that the fame year, in which the families removed from the Maffachufetts, Lords *Say* and *Brooke,* with other

* Hutchinfon's Hiftory, Vol. II. p. 2 and 3.   † Ibid. Vol. I. p. 115.   ‡ Hutchinfon's Collection, p. 420.

gentlemen,

gentlemen, having obtained a grant, John Winthrop, efq; was appointed governor, took poffeffion of Connecticut river, and began to erect a fort (which he called Say-Brooke) to fecure the mouth of it. He was fupplied with men, provifions and all things neceffary, by a veffel from England, fent by the grantees, which arrived the latter end of November. Some of the grantees had in contemplation tranfporting themfelves, families and effects, to the territory they had obtained; but the defign of emigrating was laid afide, when matters began to take a new turn in their native country; and at length the agent, Mr. *Fenwick*, was authorized to difpofe of their lands, which were purchafed, in 1644, by the people who had removed from the Maffachuffetts.

Two large fhips arrived at the *Maffachufetts-Bay* 1637. with paffengers from *London*. Great pains were taken to prevail upon them to remain in the colony; but they hoped by removing to a confiderable diftance, to be out of the reach of a general governor, with whom the country was then threatened. They fent to their friends in *Connecticut* to purchafe of the natives the lands lying between them and *Hudfon*'s river. They laid the foundation of a flourifhing colony, of which *New Haven* was the capital. They, as Connecticut, formed a government, much like the Maffachufetts, by a voluntary agreement, without any charter, or commiffion, or authority whatfoever, from the crown or other powers in England. They admitted no one to any office civil or military, or to have a voice in any election, except he was a member of one of the churches in New England. They had no jury, either in civil or criminal cafes.

Vol. I.   D   *Connecticut*

Connecticut and New Haven continued two distinct colonies for many years. At length the general court of Connecticut determined to prefer an address and petition to Charles II. professing their subjection and loyalty to his majesty, and soliciting a royal charter; and John Winthrop, esq; who had been chosen governor, was appointed to negotiate the affair with the king. He suc-

1662. ceeded and a royal charter was obtained, constituting the
Apr.
23. two colonies for ever one body corporate and politic. New Haven took the affair ill; and for some time declined the union. But difficulties were amicably settled

1665. at last, and the colonies united by agreement.

The royal charter established a pure democracy. Every power, as well deliberative as active, was invested in the freemen of the corporation or their delegates, and the colony was under no obligation to communicate the acts of their local legislature to the king. It was the same as to the *royal* charter, granted the next year to *Rhode Island and Providence Plantations* *.

1685. In July various articles of high misdemeanor were exhibited against the governor and company of Connecticut; and orders were given to issue a writ of *quo warranto* forthwith against the colony. The next year two writs were served by Mr. *Randolph*; and after them a third in December. This is taken notice of by the governor and company in their letter of Jan. 26, 1686-7, wherein they mention their readiness to submit to his majesty's royal commands; and that, " if it be to conjoin them with the other colonies and provinces under Sir *Edmund Andros*, it would be more pleasing than to

* Chalmers's Political Annals, under Connecticut and Rhode-Island.

be

be joined with any other province." Such profeſſed
ſubmiſſion probably prevented the *quo warranto*'s being
proſecuted with effect; and produced an order to Andros
to accept the ſurrender of the charter and the ſubmiſſion
of the colony.   Sir Edmund went to *Hartford* in October; but when at night he expected the charter would
have been ſurrendered into his hands, the candle was
blown out, and the charter withdrawn from the table,
carried off and ſecreted by one of the company : whoſe
extraordinary ſervice was afterward rewarded, by the
general aſſembly with five ſhillings, agreeable to the
plain ſimple manners of the people.   He however publiſhed in the general court his orders and commiſſion,
which every one tacitly obeyed.   He diſſolved the former government, and aſſumed the adminiſtration, receiving into his legiſlative council the late governor and
ſecretary, for the better carrying on the buſineſs of the
colony.   The ſubſequent revolution in England brought
matters back, after a while, to their former courſe ; as
the legal validity of the charter was admitted.

The peopling of theſe three laſt colonies was owing
chiefly to the *Puritan Miniſters*, who, being ſilenced at
home, repaired to *New England*, that they might enjoy
liberty of conſcience ; and drew after them vaſt numbers of their friends and favorers.   They amounted
to ſeventy-ſeven before 1641 ; and though all were not
perſons of the greateſt learning and abilities, they had a
better ſhare of each than moſt of their neighbouring clergy
at that period ; and were men of eminent ſobriety and virtue, plain, ſerious, affectionate preachers, exactly conformable to the doctrines of the church of *England*, and labored much to promote a reformation of manners in

their feveral parifhes. Many planters, who accompanied or followed them, were gentlemen of confiderable fortunes and of no mean education, who fpent their eftates in New England, and were at the charge of bringing over many poor families, that were not able of themfelves to bear the expenfe *. The body of laity and clergy, collectively confidered, furnifhes fuch a glorious conftellation of characters, as would employ the pen of a firft-rate writer to do them juftice; notwithftanding what has been above remarked of their governmental miftakes.

The dangers to which the *New England* colonies were early expofed, induced them to think of confederating for their mutual fafety. Articles were drawn up in 1638; but they were not finifhed and ratified till the feventh of September 1643; from which time we are to look upon *Plymouth, Maffachufetts, Connecticut* and *New Haven* as one body, in regard to all public tranfactions with their neighbours, though the private affairs of each colony were ftill managed by their own courts and magiftrates.

1643. Sept. 7.

Pafs we on to the fettlement of the other *New England* colonies.

Mr. *Roger Williams,* who fucceeded Mr. *Skelton,* upon his deceafe, as paftor of the church at Salem, being banifhed from the Maffachufetts, repaired with twelve companions to the *Narraganfet* country, and had land given him by the *Indian Sachem Canonicus;* of whom he afterward purchafed the large tract, lying between *Pawtucket* and *Pawtuxet* rivers (the great falls and the little falls; as the Indian names fignify,) and ftiled it

1635.

Neale's Hiftory of *New England,* Vol. I. 214—217.

Providence

Providence " from a fenfe of God's merciful Providence to him in his diftrefs." The authority and power of *Miantonomy*, another Sachem, and his uncle *Canonicus*, awed all the Indians round to affift him and his few af-fociates. · When the determinations of the Maffachufetts general court (occafioned, by what they called antino-mian difputes) banifhed many and induced others to leave the colony, the heads of the party were entertained in a friendly manner by Mr. *Williams*; who advifed 1638. them to feek a fettlement on *Rhode Ifland*, and was very inftrumental in procuring it of the Indian Sachems.

They, to the number of eighteen, incorporated them-felves, and began fettling the ifland. The plantations there and at Providence increafed apace, owing to the liberal fentiments of the firft fettlers: and in 1643 Mr. *Williams* went to England as agent, and obtained " a 1644. free and abfolute charter of incorporation of *Providence* Mar. and *Rhode Ifland* Plantations, empowering them to rule 16. themfelves, by that form they might voluntarily agree upon." They agreed upon a democratic. Mr. *Williams* juftly claims the honor of having been the firft le-giflator in the world, in its latter ages, who effec-tually provided for, and eftablifhed, a free, full, and abfolute liberty of confcience. This was the chief caufe that united the inhabitants of *Rhode Ifland* and thofe of *Providence*, and made them one people, and one colony. The foundation principle on which this colony was firft fettled, was, that " *every man who fubmits peaceably to the civil authority, may peaceably worfhip God according to the dictates of his own confcience without moleftation.*" When the colony was applied to in 1656 by the four *United Colonies* " to join them in taking effectual methods to

fuppref

suppress the quakers, and prevent their pernicious doctrines being propagated in the country;" the assembly returned for answer " We shall strictly adhere to the foundation principle on which this colony was first settled."

1663.
July
8.

King *Charles* II. granted an ample charter, whereby the colony was made a body corporate and politic, by the name of the *Governor and Company of the English Colony of Rhode Island and Providence Plantations in New England in America.* The charter reserved only allegiance to the king, without the smallest share of the legislative or executive powers.

1685.

A writ of *quo warranto* was issued out against the colony, which was brought June 26, 1686. The assembly determined not to stand suit. After the revolution, they were allowed by government to resume their charter, no judgment having been given against it.

New Hampshire and the *Main* were settled about the same time with the *Massachusetts,* by different proprietors who had obtained patents; and whose views were to enrich themselves, by the fishing trade at sea, and the beaver trade ashore. Religion had little concern in the settlements: but it had some in the plantation of *Exeter,* on the river *Pascataqua;* which was began by Mr. *Wheelwright* (a minister banished from the Massachusetts, on account of the antinomian dissensions with which the colony was convulsed,) and by a number of his adherents. They formed themselves into a body politic. Three other distinct governments were also established on the branches of the said river. These governments, being altogether voluntary, had no security as to their continuance; and the several settlers were

3   too

too divided in opinion to form any good general plan of permanent adminiſtration. Therefore the more conſiderate among them treated with the Maſſachuſetts, about taking them under its protection; which fully ſuited the wiſhes of that colony, as it afforded the heads of it the opportunity of realizing the conſtruction they had put upon a clauſe of their charter, by which they extended their line, ſo as to comprehend both *New Hampſhire* and the *Main.* The buſineſs terminated in the incorportion of the two colonies, on condition that the inhabitants of each ſhould enjoy equal privileges. They continued long united, and were of one heart and mind in civil and religious affairs *. When ſeparated by the king's commiſſion for the government of *New Hampſhire*, the new aſſembly at their firſt meeting, in a letter of March 25, 1680, to the governor of the Maſ- 1680. ſachuſetts, to be communicated to the general court, expreſſed their full ſatisfaction in the paſt connection; a grateful ſenſe of the care that had been exerciſed over them; and of their having been well governed; and an unfeigned deſire, that a mutual correſpondence between them might be ſettled †.

The towns in the province of *Main*, after a time, fell into a ſtate of confuſion. The Maſſachuſetts took that opportunity, for encouraging the diſpoſition which prevailed in many of the inhabitants to ſubmit to their juriſdiction; and, to forward their compliance, granted 1652. the people larger privileges than were enjoyed by their own; for they were all freemen upon taking the oath, whereas every where elſe no one could be made free, unleſs he was a church member. The province was

Hutchinſon's Hiſtory, Vol. I. p. 268.　　† Ibid. p. 328.

　　　　　　made

made a county, by the name of *Yorkſhire:* and the towns
ſent repreſentatives to the general court at *Boſton.* Though
the major part of the inhabitants were brought to conſent to this regulation, great oppoſition was made by
ſome principal perſons, who ſeverely reproached the
Maſſachuſetts, for uſing force in order to reduce the
province: but the people experienced the benefit of
it, and were contented. They continued in union
with the Maſſachuſetts until 1665, when a ſhort ſeparation commenced.

You have now a ſketch of the ſettlement of all *New
England.* It would have been far more conciſe, had it
not been neceſſary, to correct the miſtakes frequently
committed, by thoſe who publiſh on the ſubject; and
to remove the reproaches caſt upon the bulk of the inhabitants, on account of their religious profeſſion.
Whether there was any material difference between
them and the other colonies, in regard to the opinion
they entertained of their civil rights, you will be able
to obſerve in the courſe of your reading. Their judgment in reſpect to the exerciſe of parliamentary powers
over them, may be further known by what *Randolph*
wrote concerning the Maſſachuſetts, in his narrative and
letters, after the reſtoration; from whence " *it ſeems to
have been a general opinion that acts of parliament had no
other force, than what they derived from acts paſſed by the
general court to eſtabliſh or confirm them.*"

1676.   *Randolph* declared, " No law is in force or eſteem there,
but ſuch as are made by the general court; and therefore it is accounted a breach of their privileges, and a
betraying the liberties of the commonwealth to urge the
obſervation of the laws of *England.*"—" No oath ſhall
be

be urged, or required to be taken by any perfon, but such oath as the general court hath confidered, allowed, and required."—" There is no notice taken of the act of navigation, plantation, or any other laws made in *England* for the regulation of trade."—" All nations have free liberty to come into their ports, and vend their commodities without any reftraint; in this as well as in other things, that government would make the world believe they are a free ftate, and do act in all matters accordingly."—" The magiftrates have continually difobeyed his majefty's command in his royal letters of 1662, 64, 65, 66, and thofe of March laft; ever referving to themfelves a power to alter, evade and difannul any law or command not agreeing with their humor, or the abfolute authority of their government, acknowledging no fuperior."—" He (the governor) freely declared to me, that the laws made by your majefty and your parliament obligeth them in nothing, but what confifts with the intereft of the colony; that the legiflative power is and abides in them *folely* *."

The *Maffachufetts* general court, in a letter to their agents, mentioned, that not being reprefented in parliament, they looked not upon themfelves to be impeded in their trade by the acts of trade and navigation, and that thefe could not be obferved by his majefty's fubjects in Maffachufetts without invading their liberties and properties, until the general court made provifion therein by a law, which they did in October. Notwithftanding

1679.

---

* See Hutchinfon's Collection of papers, p. 477—506. The Maffachufetts affembly in their anfwer to governor Hutchinfon in 1773 quote the above paffages in fuch a manner and to fuch a purpofe, as expreffes their opinion of the truth of what Randolph declared.

such law, and a subsequent order Feb. 15, 1681, " that the act of navigation and the act for encouragement of trade, be published in Boston by beat of drum, and all-clauses in said acts relating to the plantation be strictly observed," *Randolph* complained to the commissioners of the customs in England, because of their not being duly observed. When the people found themselves in danger of a *quo warranto*, they agreed upon such emendations of their acts of trade, as to make them accord in all things with the laws of England. But it was too late. A *quo warranto* was sent them, and brought by

1683. *Randolph*, Nov. 3, 1683; and the next year a writ of
Nov.
3.   *scire facias* was prosecuted in the court of chancery against the governor and company, and judgment given, that the charter should be annihilated. Considering the temper of *Charles* II. it is rather matter of astonishment, that the sentiments and conduct of the Massachusetts government did not provoke him to vacate the charter much sooner. However mortifying, yet it would have been more prudent, to have declined contending with the king, when they knew that they must be vanquished, than virtually to bid him defiance. Such submission might not have saved them from the arbitrary government that followed, but could have been of no disservice, had there not been a subsequent revolution: that event taking place, it would have been extremely beneficial. They might have been allowed to resume their charter, nearly, if not wholly.

Before we proceed to the southward, let it be noted,
1672. that in 1672 the English parliament enacted by law, " That if any vessel, which by law may trade in the plantations, shall take on board any enumerated commodities,

modities, and a bond fhall not have been given with
fufficient fecurity to unlade them in England, there
fhall be rendered to his majefty, for fugars, tobacco,
ginger, cocoa nut, indigo, logwood, fuftic, cotton wool,
the feveral duties mentioned in the law, to be paid in
fuch places in the plantations, and to fuch officers as
fhall be appointed to collect the fame: and for their
better collection, it is enacted, that the whole bufinefs
fhall be managed, and the impofts be levied by officers
appointed by the commiffioners of the cuftoms in England." This is the firft act that impofed cuftoms on the
colonies alone, to be regularly collected by colonial
revenue officers. But the beft affected colonies,
Barbadoes, Virginia and Maryland, confidering the
laws of trade either as inconfiftent with their privileges,
or deftructive of their infant commerce, hefitated to
obey, or eluded the provifions of the laws; and trafficked
without reftraint, wherever hope of gain directed their
navigators. Charles II. reprimanded them, and his
fucceffors gave ftanding inftructions upon the head, but
without effect *.

Governor *Nicholfon* of Maryland wrote to the board
of trade, Auguft 1698, " I have obferved that a great
many people in all thefe provinces and colonies, efpecially in thofe under proprietaries, and the two others
under Connecticut and Rhode Ifland, think that no law
of England ought to be in force and binding to them
without their own confent; for they foolifhly fay, they
have no reprefentatives fent from themfelves to the parliament of England: and they look upon all laws made
in England, that put any reftraint upon them, to be

* Chalmers's Political Annals, p. 313.

great

great hardfhips." Thefe were tne colonial fentiments two years after paffing the famous declaratory act of William and Mary, which you will find mentioned below. Molyneux's Cafe of Ireland, afferting openly the fame doctrines, was firft puoiifhed in Feb. 1697-8.

The colony of *New-York* demands our next attention. The Dutch had fettled, and named it the *New Netherlands*. 1664. Charles II. refolved upon its conqueft in 1664, and in March granted to his brother the duke of York, the region extending from the weftern banks of Connecticut to the eaftern fhore of the *Delaware*, together with *Long Ifland*, conferring on him the civil and military powers of government. Colonel *Nichols* was fent with four frigates and three hundred foldiers to effect the bufinefs. The Dutch governor being unable to make refiftance, the New Netherlands fubmitted to the Englifh crown, in September, without any other change than of rulers. Few of the Dutch removed: and Nichols inftantly entered upon the exercife of his power, as deputy governor of the duke of York, the proprietary.

1673. In July 1673, the Dutch repoffeffed themfelves of the province, by attacking it fuddenly when in a defencelefs ftate. By the peace in February following it was reftored. The validity of the grant, while the Dutch were in quiet poffeffion having been queftioned, the duke of York thought it prudent to obtain a new one the following June: and *Edmund Andros* having been appointed governor, the Dutch refigned their authority to him in October. Thus was New-York regained: but the inhabitants were again enflaved to the will of the conqueror; for, being admitted to no fhare in the legiflature, legiſlature, they were ſubject to laws, to which they had never aſſented.

To be relieved from a ſervitude that had degraded 1681. the colony, and now gave diſſatisfaction to every one, the council, the court of aſſizes and the corporation of New-York, concurred in ſoliciting the duke, " to permit the people to participate in the legiſlative power." The duke, though ſtrongly prejudiced againſt democratic aſſemblies, yet in expectation that the inhabitants would agree to raiſe money to diſcharge the public debts, and to ſettle ſuch a fund for the future as might be ſufficient for the maintenance of the government and garriſon, informed the lieutenant-governor, in 1682, 1682. that " he intended to eſtabliſh the ſame frame of government as the other plantations enjoyed, particularly in the chooſing of an aſſembly."

Mr. Dongan was appointed governor in September, and inſtructed to call an aſſembly, to conſiſt of a council of ten, and of a houſe of repreſentatives, choſen by the freeholders, of the number of eighteen members. The aſſembly was empowered to make laws for the people, agreeable to the general juriſprudence of the ſtate of England, which ſhould be of no force, however, without the ratification of the proprietary. " Thus the inhabitants of New-York, after being ruled almoſt twenty years at the will of the duke's deputies, were firſt admitted to participate in the legiſlative power."

An aſſembly was called on governor Dongan's arrival, 1683. which paſſed an act of general naturalization, in order to give equal privileges to the various kinds of people then inhabiting the province: together with an act " declaring the liberties of the people;" as alſo one
" for

" for defraying the requisite charges of government for
a limited time." The legislature was convened once
1684. more in August 1684, when it explained the last act.
These seem to have been the only assemblies called prior
to the revolution.

When the duke became king of England, he refused
to confirm that grant of privileges to which as duke he
had agreed. He established a real tyranny, and reduced
New-York once more to the deplorable condition of a
conquered province.

New Jersey, which was also taken from the *Dutch* (who
were considered as having no right to any of their settlements in these parts of America) was included in the
grant to the duke of York. The duke disposed of it
to Lord *Berkely* and Sir *George Carteret* ; who, being sole
1664. proprietors, for the better settlement of it, agreed upon
certain constitutions of government, so well relished,
that the eastern parts were soon considerably peopled.
One of the stipulations was, " no qualified person,
at any time, shall be any ways molested, punished, dif-
quieted or called into question, for any difference in
opinion or practice in matters of religious concernments,
who does not actually disturb the civil peace of the
province; but all and every such person and persons,
may, from time to time, and at all times, freely and
fully have and enjoy his and their judgments and consciences, in matters of religion, they behaving themselves peaceably and quietly, and not using this liberty
to licentiousness, nor to the civil injury or outward difturbance of others; *any law, statute, or clause contained,
or to be contained, usage or custom of the realm of England,
to the contrary thereof in any wise notwithstanding* *."

* Smith's History of New-Jersey, p. 513.

The

The lords proprietors further agreed, " for the better security of all the inhabitants in the province—That *they are not to impose*, NOR SUFFER TO BE IMPOSED, *any tax, custom, subsidy, tallage, assessment, or any other duty whatsoever, upon any colour or pretence, upon the said province and inhabitants thereof, other than what shall be imposed by the authority and consent of the general assembly* *." What can more strongly express the then opinion of Lord *Berkely* and Sir *George Carteret*, as to the parliament's having no right to tax the inhabitants of the province, possessed by them as lords proprietors !

Lord *Berkely* sold his moiety of the province to *John* 1674. *Fenwick*, in trust for *Edward Byllinge* and his assigns. After which the proprietors, *E. Byllinge, William Penn, Gawen Lawrie, Nicholas Lucas*, and *Edmond Warner*, of the quaker persuasion, agreed with Sir *George Carteret* 1676. upon a division ; and that his moiety should be called *New East-Jersey* and theirs *New West-Jersey*. The agreement respecting the *not imposing or suffering to be imposed any tax, &c.* was adopted : the other stipulation is worded somewhat differently—" No men, nor number of men upon earth, hath power or authority to rule over men's consciences in religious matters ; therefore it is consented, agreed and ordained, that no person or persons whatsoever, within the province, at any time or times hereafter, shall be any ways, upon any pretence whatsoever, called in question, or in the least punished or hurt, either in person, estate or privilege, for the sake of his opinion, judgment, faith or worship towards God in matters of religion ; but that all and every such person and persons, may from time to time, and at all times, freely and fully have and enjoy his and their

* Ibid. p. 517.

judgments

judgments, and the exercise of their consciences, in matters of religious worship, throughout all the province *." It was also agreed, " that all elections be not determined by the common and confused way of cries and voices; but by putting balls into balloting boxes, to be provided for that purpose, for the prevention of all partiality, and whereby every man may freely choose according to his own judgment and honest intention †."

Soon after, many quakers resorted to *West-Jersey* from England, and the country filled apace. But the people early experienced the dreadful effects of arbitrary power. Major *Andros*, the governor of *New-York*, imposed 10 per cent. on all goods imported at the *Hoar-kill* ‡, and demanded 5 per cent. of the settlers at arrival or afterward, though neither *West-Jersey*, nor the *Hoar-kill*, was legally under his jurisdiction. They complained of the hardship from the first, but bore it patiently, till about 1680, when application was made to the duke of York, who referred the matter to the council, where it rested for a considerable time, and then was reported in their favor, and the duty ordered to be discontinued. Among the arguments used by Messrs. *William Penn*, *George Hutchinson* and others, chiefly if not all quakers, in the paper presented to the duke's commissioners, were these, " Powers of government are expressly granted, in the conveyance Lord Berkely made us; for that only could have induced us to buy it; and the reason is plain, because to all prudent men, the government of any place

* Smith, p. 528, 529.   † Ibid. 536.
‡ Corrupted by time into *Whore-kill*. The names of many rivers, in New-York government particularly, terminate with *kill*, which means both river and rivulet.

is

is more inviting than the foil; for what is good land
without good laws; the better, the worfe. And if we
could not affure people of an eafy and free, and fafe
government, both with refpect to their fpiritual and
worldly property, that is, an uninterrupted liberty of
confcience, and an inviolable poffeffion of their civil
rights and freedoms, by a juft and wife government, a
mere wildernefs would be no encouragement; for it were
a madnefs to leave a free, good, and improved country,
to plant in a wildernefs; and there adventure many
thoufands of pounds, to give an abfolute title to another
perfon to tax us at will and pleafure. Natural right and
human prudence oppofe fuch doctrine all the world
over, as fays, " that people, free by law under their prince
at home, are at his mercy in the plantations abroad."
The king's grant to the duke of York, is plainly re-
ftrictive to the laws and government of England. Now,
we humbly conceive, it is made a fundamental in our
conftitution and government, that the king of England
cannot juftly take his fubjects goods without their confent: this needs no more to be proved than a principle;
'tis *jus indigene*, an home-born right, declared to be
law by divers ftatutes; as in the great charter, ch. 29,
and 34. Ed. III. ch. 2; again 25 Ed. ch. 7 *. To give
up the power of making laws is to change the government, to fell or rather refign ourfelves to the will of
another; and that for nothing: for we buy nothing of
the duke, if not the right of an undifturbed colonizing,
with no diminution, but expectation of fome increafe

* The manufcript copy contains a number of authorities from
Bracton, Fortefque, the Petition of Right, &c. See Smith, p. 120,
the note.

of thofe freedoms and privileges enjoyed in our own country. We humbly fay, that we have not loft any part of our liberty, by leaving our country; but we tranfplant to a place, with exprefs limitation to erect no polity contrary to the eftablifhed government (of England), but as near as may be to it; and this variation is allowed, but for the fake of emergencies; and that latitude bounded with thefe words, *for the good of the adventurer and planter.* This tax is not to be found in the duke's conveyances, but is an after bufinefs. Had the planters forefeen it, they would fooner have taken up in any other plantation in America—[a plain intimation that no fuch tax was impofed in any other American plantation.] Befide, there is no end of this power; for fince we are by this precedent affeffed without any law, and thereby excluded our Englifh right of common affent to taxes; what fecurity have we of any thing we poffefs? We can call nothing our own, but are tenants at will, not only for the foil, but for all our perfonal eftates; we endure penury, and the fweat of our brows, to improve them at our own hazard only. This is to tranfplant from good to bad. *This fort of conduct has deftroyed government, but never raifed one to any true greatnefs* [*]."

The paper prefented to the duke's commiffioners, evidently proves, that it was the opinion of thefe gentlemen, who were quakers, that no tax could be juftly impofed upon the inhabitants, without their own confent firft had, and by the authority of their own general affembly. The report of the council in favor of the aggrieved, and the relief that followed, were virtual

[*] Smith, p. 117—123.

conceffions

conceffions to the fame purport. This will not be judged wholly unprecedented by thofe who are acquainted with what happened relative to the county-palatine and city of *Chefter* in the 35th year of the reign of *Henry* VIII. 1543. The inhabitants complained in a petition to the king, that for want of knights and burgeffes in the court of parliament, they fuftained manifold damages, not only in their lands, goods and bodies, but in the civil and politic governance and maintenance of the common-wealth of their faid county: and that while they had been always bound by the acts and ftatutes of the faid court of parliament, the fame as other counties, cities and boroughs, that had knights and burgeffes in faid court, they had often been touched and grieved with acts and ftatutes made within the faid court, as well de-rogatory unto the moft ancient jurifdictions, liberties and privileges of the faid county-palatine, as prejudicial unto the commonwealth, quietnefs and peace of his majefty's fubjects. They propofed to the king, as a remedy, that it would pleafe his highnefs, that it be enacted, with the affent of the lords fpiritual and temporal, and by the commons in parliament affembled, that from the end of the feffion the county-palatine fhall have two knights for the faid county, and likewife two citizens to be bur-geffes for the city of Chefter. The complaint and remedy were thought to be fo juft and reafonable, that the relief for which they prayed was granted, and they were admitted to fend reprefentatives to parliament, to guard their interefts and to fecure their liberties and privileges.

The reafons for my paffing from the Jerfeys to Vir-ginia will foon be obvious.

E 2

Virginia

Virginia was the original name for all the Englifh North American continental claims, given in honor to the virgin queen, Elizabeth. King James, being applied to, granted letters patent to a body of gentlemen 1606. on the 6th of April, 1606, with powers to divide themfelves into two diftinct companies, the one confifting of London adventurers, called the firft or fouthern colony of Virginia; the fecond or northern colony, compofed of merchants belonging to Briftol, Plymouth, and Exeter. The territory granted to the firft or fouthern colony was generally called *Virginia*, without any diftinguifhing epithet; and retained that name after the fecond or northern colony obtained the name of New-England in 1614.

The London company applied their attention immediately to the forming of a fettlement, and fent off a hundred and ten emigrants, who arrived on the coaft of 1607. Virginia April 29th, 1607 : a party landed on the promontory, called, in honor of the prince of Wales, *Cape Henry*; afterward proceeded to and took poffeffion of a peninfula in James-river, and began a fettlement at *James-town*. The inftructions given by the company of proprietors, when they fent out their fecond fupply the following year, fhow that the moft active projectors in England had for their chief objects difcovery and gain, rather than colonization.

1609. A new charter was obtained : many of the firft nobility and gentry were added to the former proprietors, and were incorporated by the name of " The Treafurer and Company of adventurers, of the city of London, for the firft colony of Virginia." To them was granted in abfolute property the lands extending from Cape Comfort

fort along the fea-coaft fouthward 200 miles, from the
fame promontory 200 miles northward, and from the
Atlantic weftward to the South-fea. The company was
empowered to make ordinances for the colony, and for
thofe on the feas going thither. There was granted to
the treafurer and company and their affigns, a freedom
from all fubfidies in Virginia for 21 years, and from all
impofitions on importations and exportations to and
from England, or any other of the king's dominions,
" except only the five pounds in the hundred due for
cuftoms." Little was conceded to the emigrants by
the charter; and much conferred on the corporation.
The colonifts were to be governed by the ordinances of
a corporation refiding in England, in which they were
not reprefented, and over the deliberations of which
they had no control. The powers of the corporation
were indeed controlable, as it was fubject to the fuper-
intendence of the courts of juftice within the realm,
which could compel it to act agreeable as well to the
grant, as to the laws of the ftate.

The adventurers, warmed with golden dreams of
great riches, foon fitted out nine fhips, with 500 emigrants, and every neceffary for the eftablifhment of a
permanent colony, excepting fuitable encouragement to
the fettlers. Lord Delaware was appointed captain-
general for life. Only feven veffels arrived fafe.

When Mr. Smith, who had governed the colony,
departed for England, he left behind him 500 perfons,
of whom, what with bad management, diffenfions,
attacks from the Indians, wafte of provifions, which occafioned a famine, &c. there remained only fixty of all ages
and fexes, at the expiration of fix months. When Sir

E 3 *Thomas*

1610. *Thomas Gates* the lieutenant-governor arrived in May, and faw the calamitous fituation of affairs, he concluded on embarking the colonifts and failing for England: but before he could proceed to fea, Lord *Delaware* arrived with three fhips, bringing abundant fupplies, and carried back with him to James-town the feeble remains of the colony. He foon re-eftablifhed matters; but his health obliging him, he failed for England the beginning 1611. of the fubfequent year, leaving about 200 colonifts, poffeffed of health, plenty, and peace with their neighbours. After his departure they relapfed; but his fucceffor, Sir *Thomas Dale*, arriving in May with more emigrants, cattle, and provifion for a year, things were again reftored. This fame year the adventurers obtained a new charter, by which the two former were confirmed, and they had alfo granted to them all the iflands fituated in the ocean, within 300 leagues of any part of the Virginia coaft. The corporation was now confiderably new modelled, and, in order to promote the effectual fettlement of the plantation, licenfe was given to open *lotteries* in any part of England. The lotteries, alone, which were the firft ever granted in England, brought 29,000 l. into the company's treafury. At length, being confidered as a national evil, they attracted the notice of parliament, were prefented by the commons as a grievance, and in March, 1620, fufpended by an order of council.

Sir *Thomas Gates* was difpatched with fix large fhips, carrying 300 colonifts, 100 cattle, and ufeful fupplies. He arrived in Auguft: and parties were fent out from James-town to form diftant fettlements. He returned 1614. the beginning of 1614, and the adminiftration devolved

once

once more on Sir *Thomas Dale*, to whom the Virginians owe the introduction of landed property. In 1615, fifty 1615. acres of land were granted to every emigrant and his heirs, and the same quantity to every person imported by others. Dale sailed for England in the beginning of 1616, giving up the trust to Sir *George Yeardley*, as 1616. deputy governor, and in this year the cultivation of tobacco was introduced. It was originally carried from Tobago to England. Mr. *Argal*, a new deputy, arrived in May, 1617. He published a variety of edicts, and 1617. was guilty of those wrongs and oppressions, that the treasurer and council appointed *Yeardley* captain-general, and empowered him to examine into and redress grievances. Sir George arrived April, 1619, bringing with 1619. him several instructions favorable to freedom, and soon declared his intention of calling a general assembly, which gave the greatest joy to men, who had been hitherto subjected to the arbitrary orders of their prince, to the interested ordinances of an English corporation, or to the edicts of a haughty governor; and who enjoyed none of those liberties which Englishmen claim as their birth-right.

In June, Yeardley, pursuant to his instructions from the company, issued writs for the election of delegates, called burgesses. The colony had been divided into seven hundreds or distinct settlements, which seemed to enjoy some of the privileges of boroughs; and from this circumstance the democratic branch of the assembly has been called to this day the house of burgesses, though composed almost entirely of the representatives of counties. The assembly, formed of the governor and council of state, who were appointed by the treasurer and com-

pany, and of the burgeffes chofen by the people, met
together in one apartment, and tranfacted affairs like the
parliament of Scotland of old, which mode continued till
after the reftoration of Charles II. Thus convened, and
thus compofed, the legiflature " debated all matters
thought expedient for the good of the whole." The
laws were tranfmitted to England, for the approbation
of the treafurer and company, without whofe confirmation they were of no validity. The introduction of an
affembly was attended with the happieft effects. The
emigrants, for the firft time, refolved to fettle themfelves, and to perpetuate the plantation. The affembly
thanked the company for their favor, and begged them
" to reduce into a compendious form, with his majefty's
approbation, the laws of England proper for Virginia,
with fuitable additions ;" giving as a reafon, " that it
was not fit that his fubjects fhould be governed by any
other rules, than fuch as received their influence from
him." This year the treafurer and council received a
letter " commanding them to fend a hundred diffolute
perfons (convicts) to Virginia." They were accordingly
tranfported ; " and were at that period very acceptable
to the colonifts," though the unlimited practice of
emptying the Englifh jails on the American continent has of late years been complained of as a nuifance.
1620. The fubfequent year muft, on account of the introduction of *African flaves* into the colonies, be ftigmatized as a much viler æra. The Hollanders were not
then precluded by any law from trading with the colonies. A Dutch veffel carried to Virginia a cargo of
negroes, and the Virginians, who had themfelves juft
emerged from a ftate of flavery, became chargeable
with

with reducing their fellow-men to the condition of brutes.

In July, the treasurer and company carried into exe- 1621. cution a resolution formerly taken, for establishing a proper constitution for the colony.   The ordinance they passed, declared, that there should be two supreme councils in Virginia, the one to be called the council of state, to be appointed and displaced by the treasurer and company, and which was to advise the governor in governmental affairs; the other was to be denominated the general assembly, and to consist of the governor and council, and of two burgesses, to be chosen, for the present, by the inhabitants of every town, hundred, and settlement in the colony.   The assembly was to determine by the majority of the voices then present, and to enact general laws for the colony, reserving to the governor a negative voice.   They were to imitate the laws and customs, and judicial proceedings used in England. " No acts were to be in force till confirmed by the general court in England: on the other hand, no order of the general court was to bind the colony, till assented to by the assembly."   The company having offered territory to those who should either emigrate themselves, or engage to transport people to the colony, found this policy so successful, that upward of 3500 persons emigrated to Virginia during this and the two preceding years.

This year was remarkable for a massacre of the colo- 1622. nists by the *Indians*, which was executed with the utmost subtilty, and without any regard to age, sex, or dignity. A well concerted attack on all the settlements, destroyed, in one hour, and almost at the same instant, 347 persons, who were defenceless and incapable of making resistance.

refiftance. The emigrants, notwithftanding the orders they had received, had never been folicitous to cultivate the good-will of the natives; and had neither afked permiffion when they occupied their country, nor given a price for their valuable property, which was violently taken away. The miferies of famine were foon fuper-added to the horrors of maffacre. Of eighty plantations, which were filling apace, only eight remained; and of the numbers which had been tranfported thither, no more than about 1800 furvived thofe manifold difafters.

Frequent complaints having been made to king James of the oppreffions of the treafurer and company, and the before-mentioned calamities being attri-buted to their mifconduct or neglect, it was determined that a commiffion fhould iffue to inquire into the affairs of Virginia and the Somer-ifles, from the earlieft fettle-ment of each. Upon the report of the commiffioners, the king concluded on giving a new charter, and re-quired of the company the furrender of former grants, which being refufed, a writ of *quo-warranto* iffued in 1623. November, againft the patents of the corporation : and judgment was given by the court of King's-bench againft 1624. the treafurer and company, in Trinity-term, 1624

Thefe proceedings " were fo conformable to the general ftrain of the arbitrary adminiftration of that reign, that they made little impreffion at the time, though the Vir-ginia company was compofed of perfons of the firft qua-lity, wealth, and confequence in the nation." The com-pany probably would not have exercifed fo tame and fubmiffive a fpirit, had they not been wholly difappoint-ed in their vifionary profpects, and met with confider-able loffes, inftead of acquiring enormous profits. They had

had obtained from individuals, who sported in their lotteries from the hope of sudden riches, £. 29,000: but
the transportation of more than 9000 English subjects
had cost them £. 150,000. They did not however
abandon the colony in its distress, while they continued
a corporation. Timely supplies were sent from England
to the Virginia settlers, which so animated them, that
they carried on an offensive war against the Indians,
pursued them into their fastnesses, and drove them from
the neighbourhood of those rivers, where they had fixed
their own plantations.

As to king *James*, he " assuredly considered the colonies as acquired by conquest; and that they ought to
be holden of his person, independent of his crown or
political capacity; and might be ruled according to his
good will, by prerogative: and he endeavoured, agreeable to the strange œconomy of his reign, to convert
them into a mere private estate, descendable to his personal heirs *."

The Virginia company being dissolved, James took
the colony under his immediate dependence, which occasioned much confusion. Upon his death king *Charles*, 1625.
being of the same judgment with his father as to the
government of Virginia, determined to tread in the
same steps. In May he named a new governor and
council for Virginia, and invested them with an authority fully legislative and arbitrary. They were empowered to make and execute laws, to impose taxes,
and enforce payment. Neither the commission nor
instructions mentioned expressly, or even alluded to an

---

* See Chalmers's Political Annals under the head of Virginia, for
many of the preceding and subsequent articles respecting that colony.

assembly,

affembly, to the laws of England, or to the acts of
the provincial legiflature, as a rule of government.
They were required to tranfport colonifts into England,
to be punifhed there for crimes committed in Virginia.
This fyftem increafed the colonial diffatisfaction, which
continued for years, till the Virginians received a letter
containing the royal affurance, that " all their eftates, trade,
freedom, and privileges, fhould be enjoyed by them in
as extenfive a manner, as they enjoyed them before the
recalling of the company's patent." On this they were
reconciled, and began again to exert themfelves in
making improvements *.

Being left for fome years in a manner to themfelves,
they increafed beyond expectation. They remained
under the adminiftration of their late governors, and
other officers, who refpected their privileges becaufe
they loved the colony. The governor, whom Charles
had been anxious to appoint, had no opportunity of
exercifing thofe illegal and extraordinary powers with
1627. which he had been invefted. His death in 1627 put
an end to his authority, and prevented the colony's
feeling its full extent. His fucceffor *John Harvey*, efq;
1629. was nominated in March 1629; and his commiffion
and inftructions were precifely the fame with thofe of
the former. He departed foon after for Virginia. The
fpirit of his adminiftration was an exact counterpart of
what had too long prevailed in England. He was fevere in his extortions, proud in his councils, unjuft and
arbitrary in every department of his government. The
Virginians, roufed almoft to madnefs by oppreffion, feized
and fent him prifoner to England, accompanied with

* Bland's Inquiry into the rights of the Britifh colonies.

two

two deputies, to reprefent their grievances and his mifconduct.   His behaviour was fo thought of, that he
was honored with a new commiffion which confirmed
former powers, and he was fent back to Virginia in
April 1637.   After that, his government was fo excef- 1637.
fively oppreffive and cruel, that the complaints of the
colonifts became at length too loud to be longer neglected, and his commiffion was revoked in Jan. 1638-9. 1639.
During his ten years adminiftration, the Virginians were
ruled rather as the vaffals of an eaftern defpot, than as
fubjects entitled to Englifh liberties; but it is to their
credit, that, having tafted the fweets of a fimple government, they oppofed with a firm fpirit, during the reign
of Charles, the attempts of thofe who endeavoured to
revive the patents, and to reftore the corporation.

Sir *William Berkely* was appointed governor the be- 1639.
ginning of 1639.   His inftructions evidenced a prodigious change in colonial policy, which muft be partly
afcribed to the then ftate of affairs in England.   He was
directed to fummon all the burgeffes of the plantations,
who with the governor and council were to conftitute
the grand affembly, with power to make acts for the
government of the colony, as near as might be to the
laws of England—to caufe fpeedy juftice to be admi-
niftred to all, according to Englifh forms —and to forbid
all trade with foreign veffels except upon neceffity.
Thus were the Virginians reftored to that fyftem of
freedom, which they had derived from the Virginia
company, and which the writ of *quo warranto* had involved in the fame ruin with the corporation itfelf.

Civil diffenfions however took place, which were imbittered by religious differences, and inflamed by acts
                                        made

made to prohibit the preaching of the doctrines of the puritans. The discontented party presented a petition to the house of commons, in the name of the assembly, " praying for the restoration of the ancient patents and corporation government." But the governor, council, and burgesses, no sooner heard of the transaction, than they transmitted an explicit disavowal of it. They sent also an address to king *Charles*, acknowledging his bounty and favor toward them, and earnestly desiring

1642. to continue under his immediate protection. In 1642 they declared in the form of an act, " that they were born under monarchy, and would never degenerate from the condition of their births, by being subject to any other government." Nothing could be more acceptable than this act, which being presented to the king at *York*, drew from him an answer, in which he gave them the fullest assurances, that they should be always immediately dependent upon the crown, and that the form of government should never be changed.

They remained unalterably attached to the cause of their sovereign. But when the Commons of England had triumphed over their European opponents, their attention was turned to the plantations; and an ordinance was passed

1650. in October 1650, " for prohibiting trade with *Barbadoes*, *Virginia*, *Bermuda*, and *Antego*." It recited, that " in Virginia, and other places in America, there are colonies, which were planted at the cost, and settled by the people, and by the authority of this nation, which ought to be subordinate to, and dependent upon England—that they ever have been, and ought to be, subject to such laws and regulations as are, or shall be made by the parliament—that divers acts of rebellion have been committed

committed by many perfons inhabiting Virginia, whereby
they have fet up themfelves in oppofition to this commonwealth." It therefore declared them " notorious rob-
bers and traitors." Perfons in power generally reafon
alike againft thofe who oppofe their authority, and difpute the legality or equity of their meafures, whatever
might be their own fentiments when in a lower ftatio,
and while aggrieved by fuperiors. The ordinance authorized the council of ftate to fend a fleet thither, and
to grant commiffions to proper perfons to enforce to
obedience all fuch as ftood oppofed to the authority of
parliament. In confequence hereof commiffioners were
appointed, and a powerful fleet and army detached, to
reduce all their enemies to fubmiffion. They were to
ufe their endeavours, by granting pardons and by other
peaceful arts, to induce the colonifts to obey the ftate of
England: but, if thefe means fhould prove ineffectual,
then they were to employ every act of hoftility; to free
thofe fervants and flaves of mafters oppofing the government, that would ferve as foldiers to fubdue them;
and to caufe the acts of parliament to be executed, and
juftice to be adminiftered, in the name of the commonwealth. After the arrival of the commiffioners with
the naval and military force, the Virginians refufed to
fubmit, till articles of furrender had been agreed upon,
by which it was ftipulated, " The plantation of Virginia, and all the inhabitants thereof, fhall enjoy fuch
freedoms and privileges as belong to the free people of
England. The general affembly, as formerly, fhall
convene, and tranfact the affairs of the colony. The
people of Virginia fhall have a free trade, as the people
of England, to all places, and with all nations. Virginia

ginia fhall be free from all taxes, cuftoms, and impofitions whatfoever; and none fhall be impofed on them
without confent of the general affembly; and neither
forts nor caftles fhall be erected, nor garrifons maintained without their confent *."

The hardfhips the *Virginians* experienced from reftrictions on their trade under *Oliver Cromwell*, together
with their attachment to the royal family, induced
them to feize the occafion of the death of the protec-
tor's governor, for applying to Sir *William Berkely*, who
had lived privately during the revolutions of the day,
to refume the government of the colony, to which he
confented, on their folemnly promifing to venture their
lives and fortunes with him for Charles II. Before
they had heard of the death of Cromwell, *Charles* was
proclaimed by them king of England, Scotland, Ireland,
and Virginia. During the diftreffes to which the royalifts
were expofed in England prior to this event, they reforted
to that colony, fo that Virginia contained about 30,000
perfons at the reftoration. Sir William Berkely, in his
anfwer to the inquiries of the lords of the committee
1671. of the colonies writes, June 20, 1671, " there are
40,000 perfons, men, women, and children, 2000 black
flaves, and 6000 chriftian fervants for a fhort time."
You will not have your good opinion of him heightened
for his adding—" I thank God there are no free fchools,
nor printing, and I hope we fhall not have them thefe
hundred years. For learning has brought difobedience,
and herefy, and fects into the world, and printing has

* Bland's Inquiry into the rights of the Britifh colonies.

divulged

divulged them and libels againſt the beſt government.
God keep us from both * !"

You will remark, that, however zealous the Virginians were to honor the Charles's with their loyalty, they
boldly declined complimenting king, commonwealth,
and proteƈtor, with their liberties.

Maryland comes now to be confidered.

Sir *George Calvert* was one of the original aſſociates
in the great Virginia company, and continued a member of that corporation during its exiſtence: and, as
fecretary of ſtate, he aƈted as one of the committee of
council for the affairs of the plantations while James I.
lived. Sir George, in his reign, having thought proper
to alter his religious ſentiments and embrace popery,
ingenuouſly avowed the change. The king pleaſed
with his ſincerity, granted him a part of *Newfoundland,*
which the French at length obliged him to abandon.
His majeſty further teſtified his regard, by creating
him lord Baltimore of Ireland. King *Charles,* to com-
penſate for his loſs of the Newfoundland territory, gave
him a grant of the country on the north ſide of the
Cheſapeak-bay.

His lordſhip died April 15, 1632, before the patent 1632.
was made out; on which his ſon Cecil took it out in
his own name the June following. Charles, in honor
to his royal conſort Henrietta Maria, named the colony
Maryland; and, being deſirous of gratifying the proprietary all in his power, inveſted him with as much
fovereignty as could well conſiſt with an immediate ſub-
jeƈtion to the crown of England. His lordſhip, with
the aſſent of the freemen or their delegates, whom he

* Chalmers's Political Annals, under Virginia.

was required to affemble for that purpofe, might make laws of what kind foever for the province, fo that they were not repugnant, but agreeable to the jurifprudence and rights of the realm of England; and he was authorized to execute the acts of the affembly. There vas no claufe in the charter obliging him to tranfmit their acts to the king for approbation or diffent: nor any faving of the royal interference in the government of the colony. Charles referved to himfelf, and his heirs for ever, impofts, duties, and cuftoms, which the colonifts were bound to pay; but declared in the fame charter, " We, our heirs and fucceffors, fhall at no time fet and make, or caufe to be fet, any impofition, cuftom, or taxation, on the inhabitants of the province, for their lands, goods, tenements, or chattels, within the faid province." By this claufe the king covenanted for himfelf, heirs, and fucceffors, that, having referved for ever the impofts, duties, and cuftoms, he would not contribute toward fetting upon the inhabitants any impofition, cuftom, or taxation, for their lands, goods, tenements, or chattels, within the faid province; and therein bound both himfelf and them, not to affent to any bill fubjecting the inhabitants to an internal taxation by an external legiflation.

The firft emigration confifted of two hundred gentlemen of confiderable fortune and rank, with their adherents, chiefly Roman Catholicks, who hoped to enjoy liberty of confcience, under a proprietary of their own profeffion. They failed from England in November, 1633. and landed in Maryland the beginning of 1633. Governor *Calvert*, brother to lord Baltimore, very wifely and juftly purchafed by prefents of various goods, the rights of the Indians, and with their free confent took poffeffion

poffeffion of their town, which he called St. Mary's.
The country was fettled with fo much eafe, and furnifhed with fo many conveniences, that emigrants repaired thither in fuch numbers, that the colony foon
became populous and flourifhing. A third affembly of
freemen was held at St. John's in February 1638-9, 1639.
when an act was paffed, " for eftablifhing the houfe of
affembly." It enacted, that thofe who fhall be elected
purfuant to writs iffued, fhall be called burgeffes, and
fhall fupply the place of the freemen who chofe them—
that the gentlemen fummoned by the fpecial writ of the
proprietary, and thofe freemen who fhall not have voted
at any of the elections, together with the governor and
fecretary, fhall be called " the houfe of affembly"—
that all acts affented to by that body, fhall be deemed
of the fame force, as if the proprietary and freemen
had been perfonally prefent. Slavery feems to have
gained an early eftablifhment in Maryland, for an act
of this affembly defcribes " the people" to confift of all
chriftian inhabitants, " flaves only excepted." The
perfecuting laws which were paffed by the Virginians,
foon after this period, againft the puritans, made the
latter emigrate in confiderable numbers to Maryland,
that they might enjoy, under a popifh proprietary, that
liberty of confcience of which they were deprived by
fellow proteftants

In 1642 the burgeffes " defired that they might be 1642.
feparated, and fit by themfelves, and have a negative"—
fuch was their progrefs in entertaining juft conceptions
of their own democratic rights. The governor did not
grant their requeft; but they were afterward more fuccefsful. The affembly of 1649 was affuredly divided 1649.

into

into two parts, and tranſacted buſineſs in the form of an upper and lower houſe. That aſſembly which convened in April enacted, that no perſons profeſſing to believe in Jeſus Chriſt ſhall be moleſted in reſpect of their religion, or in the exerciſe thereof, or be compelled to the belief or exerciſe of any other religion againſt their ,conſent, ſo that they be not unfaithful to the proprietary, or conſpire againſt the civil government—that thoſe reproaching any with opprobrious names of religious diſtinction, ſhall forfeit ten ſhillings to the perſons injured—that any one ſpeaking reproachfully againſt the bleſſed Virgin, or the apoſtles, ſhall forfeit five pounds—but blaſphemy againſt God ſhall be puniſhed with death.

1650.   In 1650 a law was paſſed " for ſettling this preſent aſſembly." It enacted, that thoſe who were called by ſpecial writ ſhall form the upper houſe—that thoſe who were choſen by the hundreds ſhall compoſe the lower houſe—and that all bills which ſhall be aſſented to by the two branches of the legiſlature thus eſtabliſhed, and aſſented to by the governor, ſhall be deemed the laws of the province, and have the ſame effect as if the freemen were perſonally preſent. There was alſo paſſed " an act againſt raiſing money without the conſent of the aſſembly." It mentioned, " That no taxes ſhall be aſſeſſed or levied on the freemen of the province without their own conſent, or that of their deputies, firſt declared in a general aſſembly." The printed words and early date of this Maryland act demand particular notice. The acts of the general aſſembly and governor were of the ſame force in their own province, as acts of parliament in England; and could not be repealed with-

out

out the concurring affent of the proprietary, or his deputy, with the other two eftates.

Carolina follows Maryland in the order of exiftence.

A few adventurers emigrated from the Maffachufetts, and fettled round *Cape Fear*, about the time of the reftoration. They confidered mere occupancy, with a transfer from the natives, without any grant from the king, as a good title to the lands which they poffeffed. They deemed themfelves entitled to the fame " civil privileges" as thofe of the country whence they had emigrated. For years they experienced the complicated miferies of want. They folicited the aid of their countrymen : and the general court, with an attention and humanity which did it the greateft honor, ordered an extenfive contribution for their relief. But the final fettlement of the province was effected equally through the rapacity of the courtiers of Charles II. and his own facility in rewarding thofe, to whom he was greatly indebted, with a liberality that coft him little. The pretence, which had been ufed on former occafions, of a pious zeal for the propagation of the gofpel among the Indians, was fuccefsfully employed to procure a grant of the immenfe region, lying between the 36° of north latitude, and the river St. Matheo under the 31°. March 24, 1663, this territory was erected into a pro- 1663. vince by the name of *Carolina*; and conferred on Lord *Clarendon*, the Duke of *Albemarle*, Lord *Craven*, Lord *Berkeley*, Lord *Afhley*, Sir *George Carteret*, Sir *John Colleton*, and Sir *William Berkeley*, as abfolute lords proprietaries for ever, faving the fovereign allegiance due to the crown. The charter feems to have been copied from that of Maryland, fo extenfive in its powers, and fo

noble

noble in its privileges. The noblemen held their firſt meeting in May; and, at the deſire of the New England people above-mentioned, publiſhed propoſals to all that would plant in Carolina. They declared, that all perſons ſettling on Charles-river, to the ſouthward of Cape Fear, ſhould have power to fortify its banks, taking the oath of allegiance to the king, and ſubmitting to the government of the proprietaries—that the emigrants might preſent to them thirteen perſons, in order that they might appoint a governor and a council of ſix for three years—that an aſſembly, compoſed of the governor, the council, and delegates of the freemen, ſhould be called as ſoon as circumſtances would allow, with power to make laws, not contrary to thoſe of England, nor of any validity after the publication of the diſſent of the proprietaries—that every one ſhould enjoy the moſt perfect freedom in religion—that during five years, every freeman ſhould be allowed one hundred acres of land, and fifty for every ſervant, paying only an half-penny an acre—and that the ſame freedom from cuſtoms, which had been confirmed by the royal charter, ſhould be allowed to every one.

The proprietaries appointed Sir *William Berkeley*, then governor of Virginia, general ſuperintendent of the affairs of the county of Albemarle, within the boundaries of which, a ſmall plantation, of the New Englanders probably, had been eſtabliſhed for ſome years, on the north eaſtern ſhores of the river Chowan. Sir William Berkeley repaired to the county, confirmed and granted lands on the conditions before-mentioned, appointed Mr. Drummond the firſt governor, and likewiſe other officers, and then returned to Virginia.

The

The affembly of 1666, being diffatisfied with the
tenures by which they held their lands, petitioned the
proprietaries, that the people of Albemarle might hold
their poffeffions on the fame terms on which the Virginians enjoyed theirs, and were gratified.

The proprietaries appointed *John Yeamans*, a refpecta- 1665.
ble planter of Barbadoes, commander in chief of Clarendon county, ftretching from Cape Fear to the river
St. Matheo; and he was at the fame time created a
baronet. To fecure its profperity, the fame powers
were conferred, and the fame conftitution eftablifhed,
as thofe which had made Albemarle happy.

A fettlement was alfo now projected to the fouthward
of Cape Romain, which acquired the name of Carteret.
Thus a variety of feparate and independent colonies,
each of which had its own government, its own affembly,
its own cuftoms and laws, were eftablifhed in Carolina.

In June the proprietaries obtained a fecond charter, 1665.
which recited and confirmed the former. They were
enabled to make laws for the province, with the confent
of the freemen or their delegates: and likewife to grant
titles of honor by the creation of a nobility. No one
prerogative of the crown was referved, except the fovereign dominion.

Samuel Stevens efq; was appointed governor of 1667.
Albemarle in October, and was commanded to act
agreeable to the advice of a council of twelve, the one
half of which he was to appoint, the other was to be
chofen by the affembly. The affembly was to be compofed of the governor, the council, and twelve delegates
chofen annually by the freeholders. Various regulations
provided for the fecurity of property; and no taxes

were

were to be impofed without the confent of the affembly. The proprietaries might mean no more, than that neither they, nor the governor and council, fhould impofe taxes without the confent of the affembly: but the mode of expreffion tended to confirm the people at large in the opinion of their being exempted from all taxes which had not the confent of their own affembly. The fettlers had their lands confirmed, and granted to be now held by the free tenure of foccage, expreffing a certain rent and independence. All men were declared entitled to equal privileges, on taking the oath of allegiance to the king, and of fidelity to the proprietaries.

1669. It was not till 1669 that an affembly conftituted as above-mentioned was convened: when it was enacted—" none fhall be fued, during five years, for any caufe of action arifing out of the country—and none fhall accept a power of attorney, to receive debts contracted abroad." Hence this colony was long confidered as the refuge of the criminal, and the afylum of the fugitive debtor.

The proprietaries, at length diffatisfied with every fyftem which they had hitherto devifed for the government of their province, figned, in July, a body of *fundamental conftitutions* compiled by the celebrated *Locke*, giving as a reafon, " That we may eftablifh a government agreeable to the monarchy of which Carolina is a part, and may avoid making too numerous a democracy."

By this edict a palatine was to be chofen from among the proprietaries for life; who was to act as prefident of the palatine court, compofed of the whole; which was intrufted with the execution of the powers of the charter. A body of hereditary nobility was created, and

denominated

denominated landgraves and caciques; the former were to be invested with four baronies, each consisting of 12,000 acres; the latter to have two, containing one half of that quantity: and these estates were to descend with the dignities inseparably. There were to be as many landgraves as counties; and twice as many caciques, but no more. Two fifths of the counties, styled signiories and baronies, were to be possessed by the nobility; the other three fifths, called the colonies, were to be left among the people.

The provincial legislature, dignified with the name of parliament, was to be biennial, and to consist of the proprietaries, alias landgraves, or the deputy of each, of the cacique nobility, of the representatives of the freeholders of every district, who were to meet in one apartment, and every member to enjoy an equal vote: but no business was to be proposed till it had been debated in the grand council, whose duty it was to prepare bills for the parliamentary consideration. The grand council was to be composed of the governor, the nobility, and the deputies of the proprietaries, these being absent; and was invested with the executive of the province. The church of England alone was to be allowed a public maintenance by parliament; but every congregation might tax its own members for the support of its own ministers; and to every one was allowed perfect freedom in religion. However the most degrading slavery was introduced, by investing in every man the property of his negro *.

These constitutions, consisting of 120 articles, and containing a great variety of perplexing regulations,

* Locke's Works, Vol. IV. p. 519, &c. 1779.

were

were declared to be the sacred and unalterable rule of
government in Carolina for ever: and yet they were
never altogether adopted. The parties engaged in this
act of legiflation fhould have reflected, that the inhabitants had fettled on conditions, which it was no longer
in their power to abrogate ; and that, in the forms of
government which had been actually eftablifhed, the
people had acquired an intereft which could not be taken
away without their confent.

1670. A number of emigrants were fent in January, under
William Sayle, Efq; appointed governor of that part of the
coaft which lies fouth-weftward of Cape Carteret, to form
a colony at Port-Royal. They arrived fafe: and as it
was found impracticable to conform to the conftitutions,
it was determined to keep as clofe to them as poffible.
Sayle dying, Sir *John Yeamans* had his command ex-
1671. tended to and over this colony, in Auguft, 1671. This
year, planters reforted from Clarendon on the north, and
Port-Royal on the fouth, to the banks of Afhley-river,
for the convenience of pafture and tillage; and laid on
the firft high land the foundation of old Charles-Town.
The proprietaries promulgated temporary laws, till
through a fufficient number of inhabitants, government
could be adminiftered according to the fundamental
conftitutions. The temporary laws were of no long
duration, being derided by a people without whofe confent they had been eftablifhed.

1674. In May, *Joseph Weft* efq; was appointed governor of
the fouthern colony, in the room of Sir John Yeamans,
with whofe conduct the proprietaries were diffatisfied.
But the difficulty of eftablifhing the colony was not
overcome for years not till people repaired to it at
                                                    their

their own expence, and men of estate ventured thither
under the full persuasion of being fairly treated. In
expectation of such treatment, the dissenters, being
harassed by persecutions in England, and dreading a
popish successor, emigrated to Carolina in great numbers, and made a considerable part of the inhabitants.
They acquired the honor of introducing religion into
the province, while they strengthened it also by their
personal accessions. But the promising appearances of
the country inviting over many of a very different stamp,
after a while disturbances followed.

The planters being informed, that the *Oyster-point*, so
delightfully formed by the confluence of the rivers
Ashley and Cooper, was more convenient than what
was fixed upon eight years before, and the proprietaries
encouraging their inclination, they began to remove,
and in the subsequent year laid the foundation of the 1680.
present Charles-town, and built thirty houses. It was
instantly declared the *port* for the purposes of traffic,
and the *capital* for the administration of government.
It was long unhealthy; but the adjacent country being
now cleared and cultivated, it is allowed to enjoy the
most salubrious air of Carolina.

Though the province had been formed into manors
and baronies, it was not till 1682, that it was divided 1682.
into three counties. In the Autumn of this year, governor West held a parliament; and afterward immediately resigned his administration to Mr. Joseph Moreton.
Thence commenced a reiterated change of governors.
Kyrle, West, Quarry, Moreton, were successively appointed. There was a similar change of every public
officer. These changes produced turbulency and faction.
But

But prior to this period, an infurrection broke out in
the colony of Albemarle, in December, 1677. At the
end of two year's fuccefsful revolt, Culpeper, who was
deeply concerned in the bufinefs, was difpatched with
another perfon to England with a promife of fubmiffion to
the proprietaries, on certain conditions. When about
to return, after executing his truft, he was impeached
by the commiffioners of the cuftoms, for acting as collector without their authority, and embezzling the king's
revenue in Carolina. He was feized on board a veffel
in the Downs, brought back, and in Trinity-term, 1680,
tried by virtue of the ftatute of *Henry* VIII. on an in-
dictment of high-treafon committed without the realm.
The famous Lord Shaftefbury, then in the zenith of his
popularity, appeared on his behalf, and reprefented, contrary to the moft undoubted facts, " That there never
had been any regular government in Albemarle, that
its diforders were only feuds between the planters, which
could only amount to a riot." On this *Culpeper* was
acquitted. He is the firft colonift who appears to have
been regularly tried in the court of King's-bench upon
that ftatute * : but he was not tranfported from America in
order to trial. His acquittal induced the proprietaries to
refolve upon governing, in future, according to the portion
of obedience, which the infurgents fhould be difpofed
to yield. They recommended, however, an healing
difpofition. But the perfons bearing the chief fway,
being actuated too much by a vindictive fpirit, proceeded againft their opponents by imprifonment, fine,
and banifhment. The fcenes of anarchy produced by
thefe meafures were not changed, nor the condition of

1677.

1680.

Chalmers's Political Annals, B. I, p. 537, 538.

7

the

the colony mended by the arrival of governor *Seth Sothel,* in 1683, who was fent in hope of quieting the 1683. diforders by his authority, as he had purchafed Lord Clarendon's fhare of the province. He was guilty of that bribery, extortion, injuftice, rapacity, breach of truft, and difobedience of orders, for five years, that the inhabitants, driven almoft to defpair, feized him with a view of fending him to England to anfwer to their complaints : but upon his intreaties, and offering to fubmit their mutual accufations to the next affembly, they accepted his propofal. The affembly gave judgment againft him in all the above-mentioned particulars, and compelled him to abjure the country for twelve months, and the government for ever.

Charles-town having been made the provincial port, the firft collector was eftablifhed there in 1685. The 1685. governor and council were at the fame time ordered, " Not to fail to fhow their forwardnefs in affifting the collection of the duty on tobacco tranfported to other colonies, and in feizing fhips that prefumed to trade contrary to the acts of navigation." Little regard was paid to orders fo contrary to the views of every one. An illicit trade was not only practifed, but juftified under a claufe of the patent, *which the people believed to be of fuperior force to the law.* Though the royal grant of 1665 was paffed fubfequent to the act of navigation, the prefent exemption was infifted upon, with the fame fpirit that it was contended during this reign, that a king of England may difpenfe with the law. The principle of the Carolinians, and the doctrine fo fafhionable at the court of James, were therefore exactly the fame.

James

1686. *James Colleton,* efq; a proprietary, was appointed governor, in Auguft. The next year he called an affembly, in which he and his party took upon them to pafs fuch laws as loft him the affections of the people. During the ferments that followed, Seth Sothel, whom we have feen banifhed from Albemarle, fuddenly arrived at Charles-town. Countenanced by a powerful party, and prefuming on his powers as a proprietary, he feized the 1690. reins of government in 1690, notwithftanding the oppofition of governor and council. A general return of members was procured, who readily fanctified by their votes whatever was dictated by thofe that had thus acquired power. Colleton, whofe conduct had been far from blamelefs, was inftantly impeached of high crimes and mifdemeanors, difabled from holding any office, and banifhed. Others were fined, imprifoned, and expelled the province. The proprietaries appointed 1692. a new governor; and the next year, upon the requifitions of the Carolinians, abrogated Mr. Locke's fyftem of laws, *the fundamental conftitutions,* which far from having anfwered their end, introduced only diffatisfaction, and diforders, that were not cured till the final diffolution of the proprietary government *. The operation and fate of Mr. Locke's fyftem may convince us of this truth, that a perfon " may defend the principles of liberty and the rights of mankind, with great abilities and fuccefs; and yet after all, when called upon to produce a plan of legiflation, he may aftonifh the world with a fignal abfurdity †."

* Moft of what is faid upon Carolina is taken from Chalmers's Political Annals, under the head of that province.

† A Defence of the American Conftitutions of Government, by John Adams, efq; p. 365.

Governor

Governor *Archdale* arrived at Carolina in Auguft. 1695. He managed with great prudence, and fucceeded fo well that the affembly voted him an addrefs of thanks. He was fucceeded by *Jofeph Blake* efq; whofe fentiments were fo liberal, that, though a diffenter, he prevailed with the affembly to fettle 150 l. *per annum* upon the epifcopal minifter of Charles-town for ever, and likewife to fur-nifh him with a good houfe, a glebe, and two fervants. A very different fpirit wrought in the earl of Bath, when he fucceeded to the power of palatine, and became 1701, eldeft proprietary. Being a zealot for the church of England, he was ambitious of eftablifhing its worfhip, and of excluding non-epifcopalians from a fhare in the government of Carolina; a fimilar principle was at that time too prevalent in England. His views were feconded by the pliablenefs of governor *Moor*, who was after a while fucceeded by Sir *Nathaniel Johnfon*. Then the affembly being convened, a bill was brought in for the more effectual prefervation of the government, by re-quiring all perfons chofen members of the affembly, to conform to religious worfhip, and receive the facrament of the Lord's-fupper, according to the ufage of the church of England. By this act, all diffenters were dif-qualified from fitting in the affembly, though legally elected, and the candidate who had the greateft number of voices, after the difqualified diffenter, was to be ad-mitted. The paffing of this act was unconftitutional and oppreffive. Another bill was paffed for eftablifhing religious worfhip in the province, according to the church of England, and alfo for the erecting of churches, the maintenance of minifters, and the building of convenient parfonages. Both thefe acts were afterward

4   figned

signed and settled by John Lord Granville, then palatine, for himself and the other proprietors. In consequence of the last act, many oppressions were committed by the government against the dissenters; who labored under these and other grievances, till the matter at length was brought before the house of lords, who, having fully weighed the same, addressed the queen in favor of the Carolinians; and the laws complained of 1706. were declared null and void.

An Indian war having broken out in Carolina, and the proprietaries finding themselves unable to maintain it against the Indians, while these were supported by the 1728. French and Spaniards, resolved to surrender their charter to the crown. One-eighth of the province belonged to Lord Carteret. The proprietors of the other seven-eighths were to receive for their cession 17,500 l. together with 5000 l. more, due to them from the province on account of outstanding debts. The surrender and payment was confirmed by a British act of parliament, wherein was a clause, reserving alway to John Lord Carteret, his heirs, executors, administrators, and assigns, all such estate, right, and title to one-eighth part of the share of the said provinces or territories, and to one-eighth part of all arrears, as was his due. After passing the act, the British government applied itself in earnest to encourage this colony, and *Robert Johnson*, esq; was appointed governor, and continued such till he died in 1735. 1735; in which year Carolina was divided into two colonies, North and South, and each placed under a separate governor *.

* The Modern Universal History, Vol. XL. 1763.

Pennsylvania

Pennsylvania and the *Delaware Counties* next demand our attention. Mr. *William Penn,* one of the joint purchasers of the western part of the Jerseys, having received the most exact information of the country to the westward of the Delaware, while engaged in the administration of the joint purchase, became desirous of acquiring a separate estate.

He presented a petition to *Charles* II. in June, stating 1680. not only his relationship to the late admiral; but that he was deprived of a debt due from the crown, when the exchequer was shut. He prayed for a grant of lands, lying to the northward of Maryland and westward of the Delaware; and added, that, by his interest, he should be able to settle a province which might, in time, repay his claims. Having the prospect of success, he copied from the charter of Maryland the sketch of a patent which in November was laid before the attorney-general for his opinion. Penn had the same object in view as Lord Baltimore had, the guarding against the exertions of prerogative, which experience had taught both were very inconvenient. The attorney-general declared the clause of exemption from taxation illegal: and chief justice North, being of the same opinion, and observing its tendency, added the saving of the authority of the English parliament, so that it was stipulated by the king, for himself and his successors, " that no custom or other contribution shall be laid on the inhabitants or their estates, unless by the consent of the proprietary, or governor and assembly, or *by act of parliament in England.*"

The next year the patent was granted, in consideration 1681. of " the merits of the father, and the good purposes of the son, in order to extend the English empire, and to

VOL. I.   G   promote

promote ufeful commodities." It was provided by fit
claufes, that the fovereignty of the king fhould be preferved; and that acts of parliament, concerning trade
and navigation and the cuftoms, be duly obferved.
Penn was empowered to affemble the freemen, or their
delegates, in fuch form as he fhould think proper, for
raifing money for the ufes of the colony, and for making
ufeful laws, not contrary to thofe of England, or the
rights of the kingdom. A duplicate of the acts of the
affembly was to be tranfmitted within five years to the
king in council, and the acts might be declared void
within fix months, if not approved.

The novel introduction of the claufe fubjecting the
inhabitants of Pennfylvania to taxation by act of parliament, might afford an argument againft being fo taxed,
to all the colonies whofe charters contained no fuch
claufe. Dr. Franklin being afked, when examined by
the houfe of commons, in the time of the ftamp act,
" Seeing there is in the Pennfylvania charter, an exprefs
refervation of the right of parliament to lay taxes there,
how could the affembly affert, that laying a tax on them
by the ftamp act was an infringement of their rights ?"
anfwered, " They underftand it thus—By the fame
charter and otherwife they are entitled to all the privileges and liberties of Englifhmen. They find in the
great charters and the petition and declaration of rights,
that one of the privileges of Englifh fubjects is, that
they are not to be taxed, but by their own confent:
they have therefore relied upon it, from the firft fettlement, that the parliament never would or could, by
colour of that claufe, tax them till it had qualified itfelf
for the exercife of fuch right, by admitting reprefentatives

tives from the people to be taxed." You will recollect governor Nicholſon's writing in 1698, " a great many people in all the colonies, eſpecially in thoſe under pro- prietaries, think that no law of England ought to be binding to them without their own conſent; for they fooliſhly ſay, they have no repreſentatives ſent from themſelves to the parliament of England." [p. 43.]

The Pennſylvanians, it may be noted, were not de- clared by the patent to be Engliſh ſubjects. There was no expreſs ſtipulation, as had been inſerted in all other colonial patents, " that the Pennſylvanians and their deſcendants ſhould be conſidered as ſubjects born within the realm;" for the lawyers who reviſed it, con- ſidered ſuch declarations as nugatory, ſince they were inferred by law *. If the right of the Engliſh parlia- ment to tax the colonies could alſo have been inferred by law, why was not the expreſs reſervation of that right conſidered likewiſe as nugatory?

In May, Penn detached Mr. Markham, his kinſman, with a ſmall emigration, in order to take poſſeſſion of the country, and prepare it for a more numerous colony. Care was taken to order an humane attention to the rights of the Indians.

The frame of government for Pennſylvania was pub- 1682. liſhed in April. It was forced from the proprietary by friends, who would not have ſettled his country, unleſs gratified in whatever they demanded. It underwent a ſimilar fate with the conſtitutions of Locke; and after a variety of alterations, was at length wholly laid aſide, and a ſimpler form eſtabliſhed. As a ſupplement to the frame, there was publiſhed, in the ſubſequent May, a

* Chalmers's Political Annals, under the head of Pennſylvania.

body

body of laws agreed upon in England by the adventurers, which was intended as a great charter; and does honor to their wifdom as ftatefmen, to their morals as men, and to their fpirit as colonifts.

Mr. *Penn* defirous of carrying his region fouthward to the Chefapeak, was continually foliciting the duke of York, for a grant of the *Delaware colony*. The prince at length wearied out, conveyed in Auguft the town of Newcaftle, with a territory of twelve miles round; as alfo that tract of land extending fouthward from it upon the Delaware to Cape Henlopen. It was known to both parties, that the title of what was now granted was extremely exceptionable, as the duke could transfer no other right than mere occupancy in oppofition to the legal claim of Lord Baltimore. Penn, however, who was intent on his own intereft in thofe parts, immediately affumed the powers of jurifdiction.

When, for the firft time, he arrived on the banks of the Delaware, October the 24th, he found them inhabited by 3,000 perfons, compofed of Swedes, Dutch, Finlanders, and Englifh. Not only his own colonifts, but the reft, received him with joy and refpect. He was accompanied thither by about 2000 emigrants, who being either quakers or other diffenters, wifhed to enjoy their peculiarities and religion, in a country that offered a peaceful afylum to the perfecuted. Mr. Penn immediately entered into a treaty with the Indians, and, agreeable to the bifhop of London's counfel, purchafed from them as much of the foil' as the circumftances of the colony required, for a price that gave them fatisfaction: he alfo fettled with them a very kind correfpondence. In December, he convened the firft affembly

at

at Chefter, confifting of feventy-two delegates from the fix counties, into which they had divided Pennfylvania and the Delaware colony, foon after denominated the *territories*. The inhabitants propofed that the deputies might ferve both for the provincial council and general affembly; three out of every county for the former, and nine for the latter. Their propofals were paffed by the affembly without hefitation into an act of fettlement. The perfons returned were declared to be the legal council and affembly, and every county was empowered to fend the fame number in future, which in the fame manner fhould conftitute the legiflature; and after the addition of a few other explanations, the modified frame of government was folemnly recognifed and accepted. Then an act was paffed, annexing the territories to the province, and communicating to the one the fame privileges, government, and laws, as the other already enjoyed. Every foreigner who promifed allegiance to the king, and obedience to the proprietary, was at the fame time declared to be a freeman, and entitled to his rights. By the legiflative regulations, eftablifhed as fundamentals by this affembly, factors who wronged their employers were to make fatisfaction and one-third over—not only the goods, but the lands of the debtor were fubjected to the payment of debts—every thing which excited the people to rudenefs, cruelty, and irreligion, was to be difcouraged and feverely punifhed—no perfon acknowledging one God, and living peaceably in fociety, was to be molefted for his opinions or practice, or to be compelled to frequent or maintain any miniftry whatfoever. It was a principle of the great charter, " that children fhall be taught fome ufeful

G 3   trade,

trade, to the end that none may be idle, but the poor may work to live, and the rich, if they become poor, may not want."

Penn, diffatisfied with the act of fettlement, without difficulty created a fecond frame, agreeing partly with the firft, modified according to the act of fettlement in certain particulars, and in fome meafure effentially different from both : to which he procured the affent of the next affembly, in 1683; but which in time fhared the fate of the former.

1684. He departed for England. The moft violent diffenfions followed almoft inftantly upon it, the provincial council and the affembly contending eagerly with regard to their mutual privileges and powers. Tranquility was not reftored by the deputy governor Blackwell, who entered upon his government in December 1688.

1685. Toward the clofe of this year Mr. Penn obtained a new grant of the Delaware colony, which he had been foliciting for fome time.

1688. The Penfylvanians and their rulers, when Blackwell entered upon his adminiftration, were fo much engaged in their own contefts and purfuits, and fo actuated by the principles of their fuperior [the proprietary, whofe attachments to James II. during thofe days are well known] that they feem to have difregarded that fignal revolution which transferred their allegiance and Pennfylvania to the prince and princefs of Orange : for the very laws and government of the province were adminiftered in the name of the abdicated monarch, long after William and Mary had been formally proclaimed in other colonies.

It

It is a fingularity in the hiftory of this province, that neither its various fyftems, nor its fundamental laws, were communicated to the king for diffent or approbation, though ftrongly enforced *.

Penn's adherence to James carried him to fuch lengths, that he was confidered as an inveterate enemy to the proteftant eftablifhment, and was for fome time excepted out of the acts of grace publifhed by William and Mary; who appointed colonel *Fletcher*, by the fame commiffion, governor both of New-York and Pennfylvania. In the commiffion no manner of regard feems to have been had to the original charter. But when the affembly met, though fixteen fhort in number to what had been before ufual, through the change made in the writs, they paffed a vote, *nem. con.* " That the laws of this province, which were in force and practice before the arrival of this prefent governor, are ftill in force : and that the affembly have a right humbly to move the governor for a continuation or confirmation of the fame." That and fubfequent affemblies fhowed fuch a fixed determination to fecure their rights, that neither governor nor lieutenant governor could bring them to bend to their wifhes.

In 1696 Penn had fo well managed matters at the 1696. court of England, that he was reftored to his right of naming a governor: and in the beginning of 1700 he 1700. went to Pennfylvania in perfon. After the meeting of feveral affemblies, he convened one in September 1701, 1701. and informed them of the indifpenfable neceffity he was under of going to England, to obviate fome ill offices done by his and their enemies with the government

* Chalmers's Annals.

there;

there; but offered to do every thing that was in his power to fecure to them their privileges and properties. The affembly, in their anfwer, expreffed their diffatisfaction at the ftate of both, and required further fecurity; to which he gave evafive anfwers, but offered to leave the nomination of the deputy governor to themfelves: they declined it, and went upon a new charter of privileges.

This introduced a breach between the members of the province, and thofe of the territories; the latter infifting upon fome particular privileges, which, when refufed by the others, made them withdraw from the meeting, and it required all the authority and addrefs of the proprietary to make up the breach. At laft, after great heart-burnings on both parts, juft when Mr. Penn was about to embark, a charter of privileges was prefented to him, and being ratified by him, became the rule of government in Pennfylvania. By this important charter liberty of confcience is granted; and all chriftians, of whatever denomination, taking the proper oaths of allegiance and fidelity, are enabled to ferve the government, either legiflatively or executively. The exclufion of all perfons from the legiflative and executive branches, however eminently qualified, and well behaved as members of civil fociety, unlefs they are chriftians, does not accord with that general liberty which ought to prevail in national communities, now that the exiftence of all theocracy is ended by the introduction of the kingdom of Chrift. The piety of the theorift, and the fubtilty of the politician, defirous of fecuring the fupport of chriftians, may introduce the exclufion into

                                                            written

written or printed agreements, but cannot eftablifh a
practical exclufion of perfons oppofed to chriftianity.
He muft be both fimple and uninformed, who will not
admit, that many deifts have ferved the Pennfylvania
and other excluding governments, either legiflatively or
executively.

By the fecond article of the charter it is provided,
that an affembly fhall be yearly chofen by the freemen,
to confift of four perfons out of each county, or of a
greater number, if the governor and affembly fhall fo
agree, on the 1ft of October for ever, and fhall fit on
the 14th following, with power to choofe a fpeaker and
other their officers, and be judges of the qualifications
and elections of their own members; fhall fit upon their
own adjournments, prepare bills, impeach criminals, and
redrefs grievances; and fhall poffefs all other powers and
privileges of an affembly, according to the rights of the
free-born fubjects of England, and the cuftoms obferved
in any of the king's plantations in America. If any
county or counties fhall neglect to fend deputies, thofe
who meet, provided they are not fewer in number than
two thirds of the whole, fhall be confidered as the legal
reprefentatives of the province.

By the eighth article, in cafes of fuicide, all property
is to defcend to the next heirs, as if the deceafed had
died a natural death: nor is the governor to be entitled
to any forfeiture, if a perfon fhall be killed by cafualty
or accident. The fame article provides, that no act,
law, or ordinance whatfoever, fhall at any time hereafter
be made, to alter or diminifh the form or effect of this
charter, or of any part of it, without the confent of
the governor for the time being, and fix parts in feven

of

of the affembly met—that the firft article, relating to
liberty of confcience, fhall be kept without any alteration inviolably for ever—and that William Penn, for
himfelf, &c. does folemnly declare, that neither he, &c.
fhall do any thing whereby the liberties, in this charter
contained, nor any part thereof, fhall be infringed; and
that if any thing fhall be done by any perfon contrary
thereto, it fhall be held of no effect.

This new conftitution differed greatly from the original. The governor might nominate his own council,
and he was left fingle in the executive part of the government, and had liberty to reftrain the legiflative, by
refufing his affent to their bills. The affembly, on the
other hand, acquired the important privilege of pro-
pounding laws, as well as of amending or rejecting
them; but though this new conftitution was thankfully
accepted by the province, it was unanimoufly rejected
by the territories; and affairs ftood in this untoward
ftate when the proprietary failed for England. The reprefentatives of the province and thofe of the territories
divided, and acted as two diftinct bodies: and the attempts to unite them proved ineffectual.

The *territories* confifted of the three counties, *Newcaftle*, *Kent*, and *Suffex* on the Delaware, and are commonly known by the name of the three *Lower Counties
on the Delaware*.

Notwithftanding Mr. Penn is celebrated as the wifeft
of legiflators, the affembly, about the year 1704, unanimoufly came to nine refolutions, in which they complain
with great grief of him, " for undermining his own
foundations; and by a fubtle contrivance, laid deeper
than the capacities of fome could fathom, finding a way

to

to lay afide the act of fettlement, and diffolve his fecond charter *." He was likewife charged with having extorted from the province great fums of money. They complained alfo of the abufes of furveyors, the clerks of the courts, and juftices of the peace, who, they faid, were all put in by the proprietary, fo that he became his own judge in his own caufe. Thefe and other matters were the heads of a reprefentation, or rather remonftrance, drawn up and fent to Mr. Penn then in England, in which he is reprefented as an oppreffor, and as falfifying his word in almoft every refpect with the provincials †.

The difputes which fubfifted in Pennfylvania were greatly augmented by the intemperance of the quakers themfelves, who, notwithftanding all their zeal for liberty of confcience, perfecuted, about or foon after 1694, George Keith (who had been one of their moft famous preachers) upon his conforming to the church of England; and went fo far as to throw him into prifon. They apologized for their conduct by pleading, that they did not punifh him for his religious principles, but for having infulted the civil government ‡. If this was a good plea, the New Englanders might gain great advantages from it, in vindicating themfelves as to many of the feverities they practifed upon the quakers, who infulted their civil governments, beyond what will be eafily credited by thofe, who have not had the opportunity of knowing the tranfactions of that period, or are not acquainted with the abufive language of fome of the then leaders of that

* Chalmers's Annals, p. 654.
Hiftory, Vol. XLI. p. 19. 1764.

† The modern Univerfal
‡ Ibid. p. 20.

denomination

denomination—language which the body of modern quakers will not vindicate.

It only remains to give a concise account of the settlement of *Georgia*.

1732.   In 1732 a number of gentlemen, confidering the vaft benefit that might arife from the tract of land lying between the Savannah and the river Alatamaha, petitioned the king for a charter, which was accordingly granted on the ninth of June. They meant, that the country fhould be made a bulwark for the fouthern colonies againft the Spaniards; and fhould give employment to numbers of people, who were burdenfome at home to their friends and parifhes. The charter conftituted them a corporation, by the name of truftees for eftablifhing a colony, by the name of Georgia, including the country from the moft northern ftream of the Savannah, to the moft fouthern ftream of the Alatamaha. The corporation was to fubfift for 21 years; and after the expiration of that term, the governor and all officers were to be appointed by the crown.

Toward the end of Auguft Sir Gilbert Heathcote recommended, in the ftrongeft terms, to the directors of the bank, the interefts of the colony. His fpeech had the defired effect, and the members of the court, after his example, contributed largely toward the undertaking, as did great numbers of the nobility, gentry, clergy, and others; and the parliament granted 10,000*l*. By the beginning of November, about a hundred and fixteen colonifts prefented themfelves, moft of them laboring people; and were furnifhed with working tools of all kinds, ftores, and fmall arms. Mr. *Oglethorpe*, one of the truftees, generoufly attended the firft fet of

emigrants

emigrants to Carolina, where they arrived in good health on the 15th of January following. The Carolinians 1733. made them a present of 100 breeding cattle, besides hogs, and twenty barrels of rice; and furnished them with a party of horse and with scout boats, by the help of which they reached the Savannah, where Mr. Oglethorpe, ten miles up the river, pitched upon a spot for a town; and on February the 9th the building of the first house commenced. The colonists were most generously assisted by the Carolinians and their governor, Colonel Bull, not only with their purses, but their labor, in raising the new town, named Savannah from the river.

Mr. *Oglethorpe* was waited upon by a numerous deputation from the Lower Creek nation, with whom he concluded a treaty; and soon after sat out for Charles-town on his return to England, where he arrived in 1734, bringing with him several Indian chiefs 1734. and a war captain. But before the end of March this year, more emigrants to the amount of six hundred, were either sent over by charity, or went at their own expence.

On the 30th of October the Indians embarked for their own country, having had an allowance while in London of 20 l. a week, of which they spent little, as they commonly eat and drank at the tables of persons of the highest distinction. They moreover received presents to a very considerable amount. They embarked at Gravesend in a ship which carried over a number of Saltzburghers, being German protestants, who, with others of their countrymen that followed, settled on the Savannah a town they called Ebenezer, and which by their habits of industry and sobriety soon became considerable. The Georgians made a surprising

progress

progress in clearing their lands and building their houses; and, as an encouragement, the British parliament granted them a supply of 26,000 *l*. which, with very great private donations, was expended upon strengthening the south part of Georgia. This being a necessary service for the colony, the trustees pitched upon the highlanders of Scotland, 160 of whom went 1735. over in 1735, settled themselves upon Altamaha river, and gave the name of Darien to a fort they built there, to which they afterward added a small town called New Invernefs.

1736.   In February Mr. Oglethorpe, with about 300 paffengers on board two ships, anchored in the road of Savannah. He soon began building another town named Frederica.

1737.   A misunderstanding subsisting between the courts of London and Madrid, and advice being sent from South Carolina to Britain, that the Spaniards at St. Augustine and the Havannah were making preparations for attacking Georgia, the government, at the request of the trustees, sent thither a regiment of 600 men, any of whom at the end of seven years might have a regular discharge, and be entitled to a grant of twenty acres of land. The parliament this year granted the colony another supply of 20,000 *l*. which enabled the trustees to send over a fresh embarkation of persecuted proteftants.

On the breaking out of the war between England and Spain, Mr. Oglethorpe, being invested with a general's command, proceeded with a body of troops to attack St. Augustine in 1740, but the expedition proved unfortunate.

In

In 1742 Georgia was invaded by about 5000 Spaniards 1742. and Indians from St. Auguftine, in about fifty veffels of various kinds, who were repulfed by the general at the. head of the Englifh forces, and a fmall body of Indians. Had the Spanifh defcent proved fuccefsful, the Carolinians muft have been in imminent danger: but the general's good conduct fecured them, and he received congratulatory letters of thanks from feveral of the American governors, for his great and important fervices *.

, On the review of what you have read, you will note, that the colonifts were very early in declaring, that they ought not to be taxed, but by their own general courts, and that they confidered fubjection to the acts of a parliament in which they had no reprefentatives from themfelves, as a hardfhip—that like true born Englifhmen, when grievoufly oppreffed by governors or others, they refifted, depofed, and banifhed; and would not be quieted till grievances complained of were redreffed— and that not a colony, Georgia excepted, was fettled at the expence of government. Toward the fettlement of the laft, parliament granted 56000 l. at three different periods.

* Modern Univerfal Hiftory, Vol. XL. p. 453—463. 1763.

L E T

LETTER II.

Roxbury, July 9, 1772.

THE prefent letter begins with fome fpecial colonial tranfactions fubfequent to the glorious revolution.

Upon information of the acceffion of William and Mary, the fort at New York was feized by the rabble, while the lieutenant governor Nicholfon and the council waited with anxiety for orders to proclaim their new fovereign. On this occafion, Jacob Leifler placed himfelf at the head of the infurgents; and notwithftanding the proteft of the council, poffeffed himfelf by force of a letter tranfmitted by king William to the lieutenant governor, or to fuch as for the time execute the law, and inftantly affumed the name and exerted the authority of governor. He convened two feffions of affembly in 1690, which paffed various laws. But colonel Sloughter, who had been appointed governor in Auguft, 1689, arriving in March, 1691, Leifler was made prifoner, and, with others, condemned for treafon and murder: he and his principal advifer were executed. A legal general affembly was now convened. The precaution taken in the declaration and bill of rights, by the convention and parliament, to ftate the claims of Englifhmen, might naturally induce the Yorkers to propofe fomewhat fimilar for themfelves, had there been no prior propenfity to that bufinefs. But the prevailing
opinion

1691.

opinion of the colonists naturally dictated to them the
seizing of the present favorable opportunity. The New
York general assembly passed " an act, declaring what
are the rights and privileges of their majesties subjects
within the province." The law enacts, " That the supreme legislative power and authority under their majesties, shall for ever be, and reside in a governor and
council appointed by their majesties, their heirs and successors ; and the people by their representatives met and
convened in general assembly." It further enacts, " *That
no aid, tax, tallage,* &c. *whatsoever, shall be laid, assessed,
levied, or required, of or on any their majesties subjects
within the province,* &c. *or their estates, upon any manner of
colour or pretence whatsoever, but by the act and consent of
the governor and council, and representatives of the people,
in general assembly met and convened.*" This memorable
act was a virtual declaration, that the inhabitants of the
colony had a right to be represented in assembly, and
enjoyed it not as a privilege, through the grace of the
crown *. Six years after, in 1697, a negative was put
upon the act, probably by the regency, while the king
was absent, which was from April the 26th, to the middle of November, when he returned after the peace of
Ryswick was settled.

The *Massachusetts* petitioned for a renewal of their
former charter, but it could not be obtained ; and many
reasons were assigned for not granting it ; among the
rest, its giving them no power to lay taxes and raise money, especially on inhabitants not being of the company, and on strangers coming to or trading with them.
One of the chief acts of delinquency alleged in the

* William Smith's History of New York, p. 75.

writ of *scire facias*, issued against their former charter, was, their having *levied money of the inhabitants*.

1691.   King *William* and queen *Mary* granted a new charter, in which *Plymouth*, the *Main*, *Acadia* or *Nova Scotia*, and the tract lying between *Nova Scotia* and the *Main*, were annexed to and made a part of the *Massachusetts*. It was complained of, as being not much more than a shadow of the old; seeing that the appointment of the governor, lieutenant governor, secretary, and all the officers of the admiralty, was vested in the crown; that the power of the militia was wholly in the hands of his majesty's governor as captain general; that all judges, justices, and sheriffs, were to be nominated by the governor with the advice of the council; that the governor had a negative upon the choice of counsellors; that all laws enacted by the general assembly, were to be sent home for the royal approbation or disallowance; and that no laws, ordinances, elections, or acts of government whatsoever, were to be of any validity, without the consent of the governor signified in writing. The new charter, however, conferred on the inhabitants a number of very important privileges, and was to be preferred to the old in many respects. They were informed by the best civilians, that their religious liberties were for ever secured; and that they could be touched by no tax or law, but of their own making; which had a good effect in quieting them under the variations to which they objected.

1692.   The first act of the *Massachusetts* legislature, after the arrival of the charter, was a kind of Magna Charta, asserting and setting forth their general privileges, and this clause was among the rest, "*No aid, tax, tallage, assessment,*

*affessment, custom, loan, benevolence, or imposition whatso-
ever, shall be laid, affessed, imposed, or levied on any of his
majesty's subjects, or their estates, on any pretence whatever,
but by the act and consent of the governor, council, and representatives of the people assembled in general court.*" The
general court passed others favorable to liberty, which
were perused by the ministers of England at a distant
period; and with the preceding, disallowed of by the
regency in 1695. In December the reasons of this dif-
sent were transmitted to the governor and council. The
following extract from the letter sent by the committee
of plantations is subjoined, because of its being so extraordinary and decisive: " Whereas, by the act for securing the liberty of the subject, and preventing illegal
imprisonments, the writ of Habeas Corpus is required
to be granted, in like manner as is appointed by the
statute of 31 Charles II. in England, which privilege
has not as yet been granted in any of his majesty's plantations; it was not thought in his majesty's absence,
that the said act should be continued in force, and therefore the same hath been repealed."

The above extract makes this a proper place for mentioning, that the ancient colonists being destitute of personal security, for want of an Habeas Corpus act, were
in some provinces grievously oppressed. Edward Randolph, surveyor general during the reign of William III.
represented their condition to the board of trade March
1700; and among other beneficial regulations, he recommended " That it being the practice of governors
to imprison the subjects without bail, the Habeas Corpus act should be extended as fully to the colonies as it
is in England." It was accordingly soon after conferred

on Virginia by queen Anne. The council, in their address said upon the occasion, "We the council of Virginia acknowledge your majesty's late favor, in allowing us the benefit of the Habeas Corpus act, and in appointing courts of oyer and terminer, for the more speedy execution of justice, and relief from long imprisonments." The lower house in theirs, said, "We the burgesses now assembled, do beseech your majesty to accept our sincere thanks, for your many favors bestowed on your subjects of this colony. We shall not pretend to enumerate the particulars, nor can we omit mentioning these lately communicated to us by your majesty's royal instructions to your governor, wherein you have asserted to your subjects their legal rights and properties, by allowing them the Habeas Corpus act *."

The extension of the Habeas Corpus act to the plantations by Queen Anne, appears to have been only by instructions to the governors, and not by any act of parliament. By what prerogative could she extend that act to the colonists, were they not before entitled to its benefit? If entitled, it was unjust in any power to deny them the advantage of the act; and the royal favor to the Virginians consisted solely in the queen's *asserting to her subjects their legal rights and properties*, (as the burgesses expressed themselves) by giving suitable directions on the business. The high sense of colonial liberty exhibited by the *York* and *Massachusetts* general courts, was opposed by the *English* government.

1696. An act was passed by the parliament, declaring that "All laws, bye-laws, usages and customs, which shall be in practice in any of the plantations, repugnant to

* Chalmers's Political Annals.

any

any law made or to be made in this kingdom relative to the said plantations, shall be void and of none effect."

There might be no design on the part of the ministry of taxing any of the colonies; but about 1696, a 1696.
pamphlet was published, recommending the laying a
parliamentary tax on one of them. It was answered by
two others much read; which totally denied the power of
taxing the colonies, because they had no representation
in parliament to give consent. No answer, public or
private, was given to these pamphlets; no censure passed
upon them; men were not startled at the doctrine, as
either new, or illegal, or derogatory to the rights of
parliament *.

Though the parliament might not then claim the
right of taxing, they claimed the right of punishing disobedience to their laws, with the loss of charter privileges.
In the 11th of *William* III. an act was passed for the trial 1699.
of pirates in *America*, in which there is the following
clause, " Be it further declared, *that if any of the governors, or any person or persons in authority* there, shall
refuse to yield obedience to this act, such refusal is hereby
declared to be a *forfeiture* of all and every the *charters*
granted for the *government* or *propriety* of such plantation."

Severity is stamped upon the very face of the act, in
making the disobedience of a governor, the forfeiture of
a charter, meant to secure the liberties of thousands;
who might not have any the least power of preventing
such disobedience. The proprieties and charter colonies were so disinclined to admit of appeals to his majesty in council, and were thought so to thirst after in-

* Lord Camden's speech in April 1766.

H 3   depen-

dependence, that these and other objections against them
1701. were laid before the parliament, and a bill thereupon
brought into the house of lords for re-uniting the right
of government in those colonies to the crown : but better councils prevailed, and matters were left unaltered.
Some are for bringing as a precedent for the parliament's
raising a revenue from the colonies, what was passed in
1710. 1710, viz. " An act for establishing a general post-
office for all her majesty's dominions, and for settling a
weekly sum out of the revenues thereof, for the service
of the war and other her majesty's occasions." By this
act the postage of England, Scotland, Ireland, and
America were consolidated, to the end, that a general
post-office might be established through Great Britain
and Ireland, her colonies and plantations in North America and the West Indies, and all her other dominions,
in such manner as might be most beneficial to the people; and that the revenue arising from the said office
might be better improved. The consolidation made a
new act necessary ; and afforded the opportunity of advancing the rates of letters. The weekly sum amounted
to 700l. and was to be paid out of the revenue for 32
years: the payment was made perpetual in the third
year of her successor, having been, soon after granted,
appropriated by another act toward paying off, with interest at six *per cent*. the principal of 2,602,200l. which
government borrowed of the public. By the act, the
post-riders carrying the mail, were exempted from paying any thing for passing the ferries in North America,
and the ferryman was subjected to a penalty of five
pounds, if he did not convey them over within half an
hour after demand.

What-

Whatever power over the colonies, the parliament might exercise in the act, the diffimilarity between this and the fugar act, paffed in 1764, will not admit of the former's being quoted, with propriety, as a precedent for the latter. The colonifts were in no wife uneafy at it, and confidered not the American poftage in the light of an internal tax, defigned for the raifing of a revenue from them; for it was but a few comparatively who were affected by it; and thefe were accommodated in the conveyance of their letters, received a full equivalent for the poftage of them, and were not bound to fend them by the public poft, when they preferred a private conveyance.

In refpect to the readinefs of the colonies to co-operate with each other and the mother country, for the general good, they manifefted the fame as occafion required.

The *Maffachufetts* general court wrote to the feveral 1690, governors of the neighbouring colonies, defiring them to appoint commiffioners " to meet, advife, and conclude upon fuitable methods in affifting each other, for the fafety of the whole land." The governor of *New York* was requefted to fignify the fame to *Maryland*, and parts adjacent.

The commiffioners met on the 1ft of May, at *New* May *York*, and were ftiled a *Congrefs*, as may be concluded 1, Con- from the following paragraph in Mr. *Stoughton's* letter grefs, of October 20, 1693, to Lord *Nottingham* * ; " I crave leave further to acquaint your lordfhip, that the governor of *New York* having written unto his excellency the governor here, fignifying his appointment of a meeting at

* Hutchinfon's Hiftory, Vol. II. p. 74.

New York, upon the firft Wednefday of this month, of commiffioners from the feveral governments of *New England, Virginia,* &c. to concert and agree upon a certain *quota* of men and money, for the defence of *Albany,* &c. in obfervance of their majefties commands; it happened to be at fuch a time, and under fuch a conjuncture of affairs here, that no meet perfons could be procured to attend *that Congrefs.*" It does not appear, that there was any congrefs between the two periods. It may alfo be obferved, that the firft was procured at the motion of the *Maffachufetts* general court, formed, from the neceffity of the day, upon the vacated charter, before a new one was granted; and that the motion originated in the court, from zeal for the common fafety of the colonies, without any interpofition of their majefties command. We meet with no congrefs prior to what was thus procured.

1709.
Oct.
14.

At the defire of colonel *Vetch,* there was a congrefs of feveral governors, with fome of their council and affembly, to confult upon the intended expedition againft *Canada,* and to refolve on methods for fecuring the frontiers.

1711.
Oct.
31.

The *Maffachufetts* houfe of affembly, at the motion of lieutenant general *Nicholfon,* advifed, to a congrefs of her majefty's governors, attended with fuch perfons as the governments might appoint. The council appointed two, and the houfe three, out of their refpective bodies, to attend the governor to congrefs, which appears to have met afterward at *New London.*

But though the conduct of the *Maffachufetts,* in their exertions for the general good, was highly commendable,

able, their behaviour afterward, in their own colonial affairs, under governor *Shute*, was greatly cenfured.

The houfe of affembly attempted to take from colonel 1722. *Shute*, thofe powers in matters relative to the war, which belonged to him by the conftitution, and to veft them in a committee of the two houfes. They by degrees acquired, from the governor and council, the keys of the treafury; and no monies could be iffued, not fo much as to pay an exprefs, without the vote of the houfe for that purpofe; whereas, by the charter, all monies were to be paid out of the treafury, " by warrant from the governor, with advice and confent of the council."

The miniftry were greatly offended at the governor's being made uneafy; for colonel *Shute* was known at court and the offices of ftate, under the character of a very worthy gentleman, of a fingular good temper, fitted to make any people under his command happy. When, therefore, they found the contrary in the *Maffachufetts*, they concluded, that the people wifhed to have no governor from *Great Britain*, but wanted to be independent of the crown. The cry of the city of *London* ran exceedingly againft them; and a fcheme, that had been long planned for taking away the charter, had nearly been executed; but was fortunately fruftrated by the indefatigable pains of Mr. *Dummer*, their then agent. Their own council at home were obliged to a confeffion of their illegal proceedings. An explanatory charter 1725. was prepared, propofed, and accepted. Had it not been Jan. accepted, the defign was to have fubmitted to the confideration of the Britifh legiflature, " What further provifion may be neceffary to fupport and preferve his majefty's jetty's authority in the colony, and prevent similar invasions of his prerogative for the future *."

It had been usual to give instructions to the several governors, to recommend to the assembly, the establishing of a salary suitable to the dignity of their post; but the house had always declined complying, prudently apprehensive, that disagreeable consequences might ensue, from the independency of the governor on the people over whom he was placed. These instructions were renewed when governor *Burnet* was appointed to the chair, who adhering to them, and showing a fixed determination not to part with governmental rights, warm disputes followed between him and the house of representatives; whose treatment of him was so unwarrantable, that the 1729. council board, within a week after the affair, expressed their concern at the unbecoming and undutiful treatment given to his excellency, in the message of the house, on the sixth of December.

In divers instances, they showed such a disposition to encroach upon the prerogative, to wrangle with their governors, and to dispute with the crown, that the ministry, and other persons in public offices, as is natural for those who look for submissive compliance, were much irritated; and improved to the utmost, all advantages to excite prejudices against them.

It was suggested, that they were aiming at independence; and jealousies were raised in the minds of some, that there was danger of the colonies setting up for

* Hutchinson's History, Vol. II. p. 271, 290, 294, 321. and gov. Burnet's Speech to the Massachusetts general court, in the Massachusetts Records for 1728.

them-

themfelves. Neverthelefs, it was certain that fuch a
fcheme appeared to the whole country, wild and extravagant; becaufe of the univerfal loyalty of the people,
beyond what was to be found in any other part of the
Britifh dominions, together with the infancy of the colonies, and their being diftinct from one another in
forms of government, religious rites, emulation of
trade, and, confequently, their affections; fo that it was
not fuppofable, that they could unite in fo dangerous
an enterprife *.

However, when the *Maffachufetts* petitioned the houfe
of commons, praying that they might be heard by
counfel on the fubject of grievances, the houfe took that
opportunity of difcovering how jealous it was of the
kingdom's fupremacy, and uncontrollable authority over
the colony: for the commons having confidered the
matter, refolved " That the petition was frivolous and
groundlefs, a high infult upon his majefty's government,
and tending to *fhake off the dependency* of the faid colony
upon this kingdom, to which, *in law and right, they
ought to be fubject.*"

The colonies might object to fome acts paffed refpecting them, particularly—The act prohibiting the
cutting down of pitch and tar trees, not being within a
fence or enclofure—The act prohibiting the exportation
of hats made in the colonies, even from one colony to
another; and reftraining all makers of hats from taking
more than two apprentices at a time, or any for lefs than
feven years, and entirely from employing negroes in the
bufinefs—The act for the more eafy recovery of debts

---

* Maffachufetts Records for 1729 and 1731. Hutchinfon's Hiftory, Vol. II. p. 355, 360—363.

in

in his majefty's plantations and colonies in America, which made houfes, lands, negroes, and other real eftates affets for the payment of debts. It was paffed in 1732, upon the petition of the Englifh merchants trading to the colonies, who complained, that in Virginia and Jamaica, a privilege was claimed to exempt their houfes, lands, tenements, and negroes, from being extended for debt: the lords of trade at the fame time reprefented, that the affemblies of thofe colonies could never be induced to diveft themfelves of thefe privileges by any aft of their own. But whatever objections were made to the above acts, no general meafure was adopted to obtain their repeal. They continued in being; but the hatters act was difregarded; and methods were devifed for felling the prohibited trees, when the neighbourhood wanted a fupply. The operation of the act defigned for the benefit of creditors, was too often, as in other countries, weakened or evaded by the difhoneft debtor. Men of principle gave themfelves little concern about its exiftence, as they had nothing to fear from it, and knew that the fame was intended to prevent perfons being cheated out of their property.

The fugar colonifts combined together, and obtained an act againft the trade carried on from the Britifh northern provinces to the Dutch and French colonies, for foreign rum, fugar, and molaffes. The act paffed in 1733, and laid a duty of nine-pence a gallon on rum, fix-pence a gallon on molaffes, and five pounds on every hundred weight of fugar, that came not from the Britifh Weft-India iflands, and were brought into the northern colonies. It was profeffedly defigned as a prohibition from the foreign iflands; but did not anfwer.

It

It was found expedient, and for the general benefit, to admit of the molaffes, &c. being moftly run into the colonies, without infifting upon the duties, or making frequent feizures. The act unhappily produced an illegal fpirit of trading; but was continued by fubfequent ones down to 1761; when the duty on the molaffes was reduced to three-pence, to prevent its being run any longer. The act did not appropriate the monies to be raifed by the duties, fo that when, in length of time, there was a fum in the hands of the receiver worth remitting, a demur enfued as to the application of it.

The monies produced by this and other acts, were not confidered as real *taxes*, either by the colonies or the mother country. But fome perfons wifhed to have taxes impofed upon them, which would neceffarily produce many good pofts and places in *America* for courtiers; and during the war with *Spain*, which broke out in 1739, a fcheme for taxing the *Britifh* colonies was mentioned to Sir *Robert Walpole*. He fmiled, and faid, " I will leave that to fome of my fucceffors, who have more courage than I have, and are lefs friends to commerce than I am. It has been a maxim with me, during my adminiftration, to encourage the trade of the *American* colonies in the utmoft latitude; nay, it has been neceffary to pafs over fome irregularities in their trade with *Europe*: for, by encouraging them to an extenfive growing foreign commerce, if they gain 500,000l. I am convinced, that in two years afterward, full 250,000l. of their gains will be in his majefty's exchequer, by the labor and produce of this kingdom, as immenfe quantities of every kind of our manufactures go thither; and as they increafe in their foreign American

1739.

rican trade, more of our produce will be wanted. This is taxing them more agreeably to their own conſtitution and ours."

Had the ſcheme for taxing the colonies been attempted, it would have occaſioned a ferment, that muſt have prevented thoſe exertions in the common cauſe, which were given into by the *New Englanders*, eſpecially the *Bay-men*, ſo the inhabitants of the *Maſſachuſetts Bay* are frequently called.

War being declared againſt *Spain*, a requiſition of troops was made to the *Maſſachuſetts*, and a larger number raiſed and embarked on his majeſty's ſervice than was required, of whom, ſcarce one in fifty returned.

1744. Upon receiving the declaration of war with *France*, the general court, then ſitting, made immediate proviſion for raiſing forces for *Annapolis* in Nova Scotia: they happily arrived in ſeaſon, and were the probable means of ſaving the country. Divers times afterward, *Nova Scotia*, when attacked by the French, was relieved by the Bay-men; ſo that during that unproſperous war, poſſeſſion was always kept of it for the crown of Great Britain.

1745. But the moſt important ſervice to be mentioned, is the reduction of *Louiſburgh*. Governor *Shirley*'s heart was ſet upon effecting it. He prevailed upon the two houſes to lay themſelves under an oath of ſecrecy; and then communicated his plan of the expedition. A committee was appointed to conſider it, and were ſeveral days in deliberating. After mature conſideration, a majority diſapproved of the propoſal. The report was accepted, and the members of the court laid aſide all thoughts of the expedition. By the governor's influence probably, as well as with his approbation, a petition
from

from a number of merchants was prefented to the houfe of reprefentatives, praying a re-confideration of their vote, and their agreement to the governor's propofal. A fecond committee reported in favor of it. The report was debated in the houfe the whole day. It is remarkable, that Mr. *Oliver* * fell down, and broke his leg, while going to the houfe, with a full defign of oppofing the expedition. His prefence would have made a majority, and overfet it; but this accident occafioned his abfence; and upon the divifion in the houfe at night, the numbers were equal. The fpeaker, *Thomas Hutchinfon*, efq; † was called upon to give the cafting vote; which he did in favor of it, though he oppofed it when in the committee. He was, probably, prevailed upon thus to vote, that he might fecure the favor of the governor, and render himfelf the more popular.

The point being now fettled, there is an immediate Jan. union of both parties; and all are equally zealous in 25. carrying the defign into execution. Meffengers are difpatched as far as *Pennfylvania*, to entreat the junction of the feveral governments in the expedition. All excufe themfelves, except *Connecticut*, *New Hampfhire*, and *Rhode Ifland*. The firft agrees to raife 500 men, the other two 300 each. *Connecticut* and *Rhode Ifland* confent alfo, that their colony floops fhall be employed as cruifers.

The time for preparing is fhort. But the winter proves fo favorable, that all kinds of out-door bufinefs is carried on as well, and with as great difpatch, as at any other feafon. The appointment of a general officer is of the utmoft confequence. He muft be acceptable

* The prefent lieut. governor [1772.]　† The prefent governor [1772.]

to the body of the people; the inliftment depends upon
this circumftance. It is not eafy to find a perfon, thus
qualified, willing to accept. Colonel *Pepperrell* * has the
offer from the governor; but is rather preffed into the
fervice, than engages voluntarily. His example, in quit-
ing for the prefent his extenfive mercantile bufinefs, has
confiderable influence; and induces inferior officers, and
even private foldiers, to quit their fmaller concerns, for
the fervice of their country. Governor Wentworth, of
New Hampfhire, offers afterward to take the command
of the expedition. Two or three gentlemen of prudence and judgment, are confulted upon the occafion,
by governor Shirley, who finds them clearly of opinion,
that any alteration of the prefent command would be
attended with the greateft rifk, of entirely difgufting both
the Maffachufetts affembly and foldiers †. By the efforts
of a general exertion in all orders of men, the arma-

Apr.   ment is ready, fails, and arrives at *Canfo* the fourth of
4.   April. The *Bay-men* confift of 3,250 troops, exclufive
of commiffion officers. The *New Hampfhire* forces,
304, including officers, arrived four days before. The
Connecticut, being 516 inclufive, arrive on the twenty-
fifth. The 300 *Rhode Iflanders* do not arrive till the
place has furrendered.

Toward the end of the month, commodore *Warren*
arrives from the Weft Indies, with a fixty gun fhip, and
two of forty; and joins another of forty, which had
reached *Canfo* the day before, in confequence of his orders, received while under fail from *Portfmouth* in *New
Hampfhire* on her way to Britain. The men of war
fail immediately to cruife before *Louifburg*. The forces

---

* Grandfather of the prefent Sir William Pepperrell [1787.]
† Governor Shirley's Letter of February 16, 1744.

soon

soon follow, and land at *Chapeaurouge* bay the last day of April. The transports are discovered from the town early in the morning, which gives the inhabitants the first knowledge of the design.

The second day after landing, 400 men march round, behind the hills, to the north-east harbour, where they get about midnight, and fire all the houses and store-houses, until they come within a mile of the grand battery. The clouds of thick smoke, proceeding from the pitch, tar, and other combustibles, prevent the garrison's discovering the enemy, though but a few rods distant. They expect the body of the army upon them, and desert the fort, having thrown their powder into a well; but the cannon and shot are left, and prove of service to the Americans. A party, less than twenty, come up to the battery the next morning early; and seeing no signs of men, suspect a plot, and are afraid to enter. At length, an *Indian*, for a pint of rum, ventures in alone through an embrasure, and discovers the state of it to the rest, just as a number of French are relanding to recover possession. The army has near two miles to transport their cannon, mortars, &c. through a morass. This must be done by mere dint of labor. The hardiest and strongest bodies are employed, and the service performed, agreeable to the advice of major Ezekiel Gilman of Exeter, who having been used to draw the masts over the swamps, proposed making sleds to put the cannon, &c. upon, and then yoking the men together for draught. The men know nothing of regular approaches. They make merry with the terms, *zigzags* and *epaulements*; and taking advantage of the night, go on, void of art, in their own natural way.

VOL. I.   I   While

While the forces are bufy afhore, the men of war, and other veffels, are cruifing off the harbour, when the

weather permits; and on the eighteenth of May, capture a French fixty-four gun fhip, having 560 men on board, and ftores of all forts for the garrifon. This prize, with the arrival of other Britifh fhips, makes the commodore's fleet eleven by the twelfth of June, confifting of a 64, four of 60 guns, one of 50, and five of 40. It is given out, that an attack will be made by fea with the fhips, on the eighteenth, while the army do the like by land. Whether a general ftorm is really intended or not, the French feem to expect it, from the preparations on board the men of war, and do not incline to ftand it. On the fifteenth, a flag of truce is fent to the general, defiring a ceffation of hoftilities, that they may confider of articles for a capitulation. Time is allowed; but their articles are rejected by the general and commodore, and others offered, which are accepted by the French, and hoftages exchanged. The city is

delivered up on the feventeenth. But as it is a time to expect veffels from all parts to *Louifburgh*, the French flag is kept flying as a decoy. Two Eaft India, and one South Sea fhip, of the value of 600,000l. fterling, are taken by the fquadron, at the mouth of the harbour, into which they undoubtedly meant to enter.

The weather proved remarkably fine during the fiege: the day after the furrender, the rains began and continued ten days inceffantly, which would undoubtedly have proved fatal to the expedition, had not the capitulation prevented. It is not of material confequence for us to determine, whether the land or fea force had the greateft fhare in the reduction of *Louifburgh*. Neither

would

would have fucceeded alone. But there was, certainly, the ftrongeft evidence of a generous, noble, public fpirit, in the *New Englanders*, which firft inclined them to the undertaking, and of a firmnefs of mind in the profe-cution of it; for the labor, fatigue, and other hard-fhips of the fiege, were without parallel in all preceding American operations *. The paying of the charges of this expedition in 1748, leffens not the merit of the *New England* attempt; for they began it when they had no promife, and very little profpect of being reimburfed. Had it not fucceeded, they would not have been reim-burfed, and muft therefore have been involved in the greateft diftrefs. This they forefaw, and yet cheerfully ran the rifk for the public fervice. It would have coft the crown double the fum paid the New England go-vernments, to have fent an armament from Great Bri-tain for the reduction of the fame place. The colonies met with a heavy lofs, not eafily repaired, in the de-ftruction of the flower of their youth, by camp fevers, other ficknefles, the hardfhips and diftreffes of the fiege. Of how much importance Louifburgh was in the opi-nion of the French, appeared from their demanding two hoftages of the firft nobility in Britain, as pledges for its reftitution.

Should you hereafter read, " The leading men in the government of the *Maffachufetts*, having been guilty of certain mal-practices, for which they were in danger of

---

* Hutchinfon's Hiftory, Vol. II. p. 407—420. The above ac-count varies from Hutchinfon's, being corrected in fome inftances, from a manufcript copy of the Hiftory of the Reduction of Louifburgh, fent by Mr. Shirley to the duke of Newcaftle; and improved in others from information given me.

being

being called to an account, projected the expedition
againſt *Cape Breton*, in order to divert the ſtorm : and
proving ſucceſsful, the Engliſh nation was ſo overjoyed,
that they forgot every other idea in the general tranfport, ſo that the planners and conductors of the expedition, inſtead of being called to account for former
miſdemeanors, found themſelves careſſed and applauded"
—believe it not—eſpecially ſhould the writer give " this
public notice, I build nothing upon the preſent narration; and I only offer it (becauſe not corroborated by
ſufficient evidence) as a probable caſe, and as my own
opinion *." Should he be a D. D. you may think it
would have been well for him to have recollected the
complaint of *Jeremiah*, " I heard the defaming of
many ; report, *ſay they*, and we will report :" and ſo to
have been ſilent on the head of *Cape Breton*. Should
you judge it uncharitable to retort upon him ; yet you
may deem it juſt to remind him of his own, do you
find him uſing ſuch like expreſſions as theſe, " As I
never believed Dr. *Franklin* in any public matter, excepting in his electrical experiments, I was reſolved to
ſee with my own eyes, whether what he advanced was
true or not, having a ſtrong ſuſpicion that he fibbed de-
ſignedly, like Sir *Henry Wotton*'s embaſſador, *patriæ
cauſa* †."

But to return, the year after the reduction of Louiſ-
1746. burgh, Great Britain entertained the deſign of reducing
Canada, ; and requiſitions were made to the colonies,
from New Hampſhire to Virginia incluſive. It was
expected, that they ſhould raiſe at leaſt 5000 men ;

* See the Poſtſcript of Dean Tucker's humble addreſs.
† The Dean's letter to Edmund Burke, Eſq; p. 27.

they

they voted 8200; and the *Maſſachuſett's*, to the amount
of 3500, were ready to embark by the middle of July,
about ſix weeks from the firſt notice *. Though the
expedition was not proſecuted; this did not leſſen the
merit of the colonies, in preparing to ſecond the views
of the Britiſh government.

No ſooner were the diſtreſſes of war cloſed, by the 1748.
renewal of peace; than the coloniſts, particularly of
New England, were alarmed with the report of an *American epiſcopacy*; which it was the moſt earneſt deſire of
Dr. *Thomas Secker*, late archbiſhop of *Canterbury*, to
eſtabliſh. The Doctor, when biſhop of *Oxford*, in his
ſermon before the Society for propagating the goſpel, &c.
" began thoſe invectives againſt the coloniſts and their
religious character, which have been unwarily continued,
and were founded entirely upon miſinformations, and
miſrepreſentations of intereſted perſons, the miſſionaries
eſpecially, who found their account in abuſing better
chriſtians than themſelves †." This conduct had not
the leaſt tendency to reconcile them to the project, but
the direct contrary; and argued a ſecret bitterneſs of
ſpirit, which promiſed no great moderation, if the ſcheme
of epiſcopiſing ſucceeded. The talk of introducing
biſhops into America, was very warm among the epiſcopalians in Connecticut; and it is not an uncharitable
conjecture, that it originated from, or was promoted
by the zeal of biſhop Secker. During the height of
the converſation, a worthy divine, now at Rhode Iſland,
had the hopes of a biſhopric held out to him, to in-

* Hutchinſon's Hiſtory, Vol. II. p. 424.
† See a collection of letters and eſſays in favor of public liberty,
in three vols. printed for Wilkie, Vol. III. p. 34, 42.

I 3   duce

duce him to turn epifcopalian, though without effect. The colonifts had reafon to dread the introduction of epifcopacy, for it could not be thought, it fhould come unaccompanied with fuch a degree of civil power, as would at length trample upon the rights of other denominations. An extenfive and united hierarchy, however named, when armed with civil authority and in alliance with ftate power, is a dangerous engine, if under the direction of a crafty politician. The failure of the epifcopifing project, at this period, might be owing in a great meafure, to the part the *diffenting deputation* acted upon the occafion : for which the reprefentatives of the Maffachufetts-bay returned them their thanks, in a meffage figned by the fpeaker *. But though the colonies were relieved from this caufe of uneafinefs, they were laid under another, by the parliament's paffing an act, enacting, " That from and after the twenty-fourth of June, 1750, no *mill*, or *other engine*, for *flitting* or *rolling* of *iron*, or any *plating forge*, to work with a *tilt hammer*, or any *furnace* for *making fteel*, fhall be erected ; or, after fuch erection, continued *in any of his majefty's colonies in America.*"

The four New England colonies however, had no juft reafon to complain, when the power of parliament paffed an act " to regulate and reftrain paper bills of credit in faid governments, and to prevent the fame being legal tenders in payment of money ;" as they had made the act abfolutely neceffary, that fo Britifh creditors might be fecured from being defrauded by a legal tender of a depreciated and depreciating paper currency.

1750.

1751.

* See a fhort account of the proceedings of the deputation, p. 9.

The

The year after the peace, a grant of 600,000 acres
of the fineſt American land, in the neighbourhood of
the *Ohio*, was made out to certain noblemen merchants
and others, of *Weſtminſter London* and *Virginia*, who
aſſociated under the title of the *Ohio Company*. The
governor of Canada obtained early intelligence of it;
and was alarmed with the apprehenſion, that a ſcheme
was in agitation, which would for ever deprive the French
of the advantage ariſing from the trade with the *Twightwees*, and cut off the communication ſo beneficial to
the colonies of *Louiſiana* and *Canada*. He wrote therefore to the governors of *New York* and *Pennſylvania*,
acquainting them, that the Engliſh traders had en-
croached on the French territories, by trading with their
Indians; and that if they did not deſiſt, he ſhould be
obliged to ſeize them wherever they were found. This
was the firſt time that either French or Britiſh had pretended to any excluſive trade with any *Indians*, or even
the declared friends and allies of either; for it was ex-
preſsly ſtipulated by the treaty of *Utrecht*, that, on both
ſides, the two nations ſhould enjoy full liberty of going
and coming among the *Indians*, of either ſide, on account of trade; and that the natives of the Indian countries ſhould, with the ſame liberty, reſort as they pleaſed,
to the *Britiſh* or *French* colonies, for the purpoſe of
trade, without any moleſtation from either the Britiſh
or French ſubjects.

The *Britiſh Indian* trade had been carried on moſtly
with *Pennſylvania*, by the river *Suſquehanna*: a great part
of it was now to be diverted into another channel by the
Ohio company; who by opening a waggon-road through
the country, and building a truck-houſe at *Will's-creek*,

I 4 were

were providing for its being carried into *Virginia* by the
Patomak.   The Pennſylvania traders, jealous of the Ohio
company, were upon the watch to injure them, which
ſoon offered, when Mr. *Giſt* was employed by the company, in ſurveying the lands upon the *Ohio*, in order to
their procuring 600,000 acres of the beſt and moſt convenient for the Indian trade.   He carefully concealed
his deſign from the Indians, who were no leſs ſuſpicious
and inquiſitive ; and being jealous that he meant to
ſettle their lands, made uſe of threats.   They were not
pacified, till there was delivered to them a pretended
meſſage from the king of *Great Britain*.   The Pennſylvania traders, actuated by revenge, informed both French
and Indians, what was the ſervice on which he was employed ; and while he was on his progreſs, in the ſpring
1751. of 1751, ſome French parties with their Indians, put
the governor of Canada's menace into execution, and
1753. ſeized the Britiſh traders, who were trading among the
Twightwees, and carried them to a fort they were building on the ſouth-ſide of lake *Erie*.   The Britiſh alarmed
at the capture of their brethren, retired to the Indian
towns for ſhelter, and the *Twightwees*, reſenting the violence done to their allies, aſſembled to the number of
five or ſix hundred, and ſcoured the woods till they
found three French traders, whom they ſent to
Pennſylvania.   The French however, determined to
perſiſt ; and proceeded to build a ſecond fort, about
fifteen miles ſouth of the former, upon one of the branches
of the Ohio.   They alſo erected a fort at the conflux of
the *Ohio* and *Wabache* ; and thus completed their deſigned communication between the mouth of the *Miſ-
ſiſſippi* and the river *St. Lawrence*.   Nothing was done

by

by the Pennsylvania government, so that the French continued to strengthen themselves without interruption; and encouraged by the little notice taken of their violence, began to seize and plunder every British trader they found on any part of the *Ohio*.

Repeated complaints were made to lieutenant governor *Dinwiddie* of Virginia; and as the Ohio company, whose existence depended upon stopping the French encroachments and pretensions on that river, had great influence there, that colony was prevailed upon to act with some vigor.

The lieutenant governor having informed the house of burgesses, on the first of November, that the French had erected a fort on the Ohio, it was resolved to send somebody to Mr. *St. Pierre*, the French commandant, to demand the reason of his hostile proceedings, and to require him at the same time, to withdraw his forces. Major *Washington*, who was of age only on the eleventh of the preceding February, offered his service on this important occasion. The distance he had to go, was more than four hundred miles; two hundred of which lay through a trackless desert inhabited by Indians; and the season was uncommonly severe. Notwithstanding these discouraging circumstances, the major attended by one companion only, sat out upon this hazardous enterprise. He travelled from Winchester on foot, carrying his provisions on his back. Upon his arrival at the place of destination and delivering his message, the French commandant refused to comply, denied the charge of hostilities, and said that the country belonged to the king of France; that no Englishman had a right to trade upon any of its rivers; and

that

that, therefore, he would seize according to orders, and send prisoners to Canada, every Englishman that should attempt to trade upon the Ohio or any of its branches. Before major *Washington* had got back, or the Virginians had heard of the French commandant's answer, they sent out proper people, provided with materials for erecting a fort at the conflux of the *Ohio* and *Monongahela*, whom he met on his return. After excessive hardships and many providential escapes, during his long and tedious undertaking, he arrived safe at *Williamsburgh* and gave an account of his negotiation to the house of burgesses, the fourteenth of February following.

Ere the Virginians had finished their fort, the French came upon them, drove them out of the country, and erected a regular fort on the very spot where they had been at work. The consent of the Indian warriors had not been gained by the Virginians, or they would have supported the British against the French attack.

These proceedings of the French galled the British ministry. The Ohio company, whose schemes were now demolished, was their fondling. They could not submit to have their friends so treated; and therefore no sooner had they the news, than it was resolved to instruct the colonies to oppose the French encroachments by force of arms. The instructions were received at Virginia early in the spring of 1754. The Virginians applied to the other colonies for additional troops. Captain James Mackay with his independent company, upon the first order, marched with the utmost expedition from South Carolina to their assistance. Without waiting for two independent companies from New York, who were likewise ordered to assist them, the Virginians resolved

resolved by themselves with Mackay's company, to oppose the French encroachments; and sent off that and three hundred men raised by the colony, under the command of late major, but now colonel Washington. An engagement ensued between a party of French from fort *Du Quesne*, whom colonel Washington attacked and defeated, on the twenty-eighth of May; which put Mr. *de Villier* upon marching down against him with 900 men besides Indians, and attacking him on the third of July. Washington made so brave a defence behind a small incomplete entrenchment, called fort *Necessity*, that Villier seeing what desperate men he had to deal with, and desirous of saving his own, offered him an honorable capitulation; but the French officer was careful, in forming the articles, to throw the blame of the war upon the British, and to make it thought that they were the aggressors.

The lords commissioners for trade and plantations, had also recommended to the several colonies, to appoint commissioners to meet each other. Their lordships designed, that there should be a general league of friendship, between all the colonies and the Indians, in his majesty's name. The *Massachusetts* general court not only acceded to the proposal, but both houses desired his excellency, governor *Shirley*, " to pray his majesty, April that affairs which relate to the six nations and their al-¹⁰· lies, may be put under some general direction as his majesty shall think proper; that the several governments may *be obliged* to bear their proportions of defending his majesty's territories against the encroachments of the French, and the ravages and incursions of the Indians."

5   A ge-

July.   A general meeting of the governors and chief men from several of the colonies, was held at *Albany*. At this congress, the commissioners were unanimously of opinion, that an *union of all the colonies* was absolutely necessary for their common defence. The plan was, in short, " That a grand council should be formed of members to be chosen by the assemblies, and sent from all the colonies; which council together with a governor general to be appointed by the crown, should be empowered to make general laws, to raise money in all the colonies, for the defence of the whole." It was drawn up by Mr. *Hutchinson*; was accepted, and sent home. Had it been approved and established, *British America* thought itself sufficiently able to cope with the *French* without further assistance; several of the colonies, in former years, having alone withstood the whole power of the enemy, unassisted not only by the mother country, but by any of the neighbouring provinces. A *stamp act* was talked of among the commissioners, of which number was Mr. (now Dr.) *Franklin*, one of the three from Pennsylvania; and it was thought a proper mode of taxing; under the apprehension, that in its operation it would affect the several governments fairly and equally. The idea of a stamp act had been held out, so early as 1739, in two publications drawn up by a club of American merchants, at the head of whom were Sir *William Keith*, governor of Pennsylvania, Mr. *Joshua Gee* and many others. They proposed, for the protection of the British traders among the Indians, the raising a body of regulars, to be stationed all along the western frontier of the British settlements; and that the expence should be paid from the monies arising from a duty on stampt

paper

paper and parchment in all the colonies, to be laid on them by act of parliament. The congrefs plan was not agreeable to the views of miniftry; and another was propofed—" That the governors of all the colonies, attended by one or two members of their refpective councils, fhould affemble, concert meafures for the defence of the whole, erect forts where they judged proper, and raife what troops they thought neceffary, with power to draw upon the Britifh treafury for the fums that fhould be wanted; and the treafury to be re-imburfed by a tax laid on the colonies by act of parliament." When you are reminded, that the governors and councils were chiefly of the king's appointing, you will be apt to view the fcheme, as a moft fubtile and dangerous contrivance, to provide for favorites, to fap the liberties of the Americans, and eventually to chain them down to the moft abject flavery. Had the congrefs plan met with the countenance of miniftry, it might have been adopted after a while; though of that, it appeared, there could be no certainty; for when the governor laid it before the *Maffachufetts* affembly in October, the affembly determined, not to give it the leaft countenance. The minifterial plan was tranfmitted to governor *Shirley*, who was known to be for the Britifh parliament's laying the tax. It was communicated by him to Mr. Franklin, then at his native place Bofton, who foon returned it with a few fhort remarks, and the next day fent the governor the following letter, *viz.*

" Sir, *Wednefday morning, Dec.* 1754.

I mentioned it yefterday to your excellency, as my opinion, that excluding the people of the colonies from

all

all fhare in the choice of the grand council, would probably give extreme diffatisfaction, as well as the taxing them by an act of parliament, where they have no reprefentative. In matters of general concern to the people, and efpecially where burdens are to be laid upon them, it is of ufe to confider, as well what they will be apt to think and fay, as what they ought to think; I fhall therefore, as your excellency requires it of me, briefly mention what of either kind occurs to me on this occafion.

Firft, they will fay, and perhaps with juftice, that the body of the people in the colonies are as loyal, and as firmly attached to the prefent conftitution and reigning family, as any fubjects in the king's dominions :

That there is no reafon to doubt the readinefs and willingnefs of the reprefentatives they may choofe, to grant from time to time fuch fupplies for the defence of the country, as fhall be judged neceffary, fo far as their abilities will allow :

That the people in the colonies, who are to feel the immediate mifchiefs of invafion and conqueft by an enemy, in the lofs of their eftates, lives and liberties, are likely to be better judges of the quantity of forces neceffary to be raifed and maintained, forts to be built and fupported, and of their own abilities to bear the expence, than the parliament of England at fo great a diftance :

That governors often come to the colonies merely to make fortunes, with which they intend to return to Britain; are not always men of the beft abilities or integrity; have many of them no eftates here; nor any natural connections with us, that fhould make them heartily

tily concerned for our welfare; and might poffibly be fond of raifing and keeping up more forces than neceffary, from the profits accruing to themfelves, and to make provifion for their friends and dependants:

That the counfellors in moft of the colonies being appointed by the crown, on the recommendation of governors, are often of fmall eftates, frequently dependent on the governors for offices, and therefore too much under influence:

That there is, therefore, great reafon to be jealous of a power in fuch governors and councils, to raife fuch fums as they fhall judge neceffary, by draft on the lords of the treafury, to be afterward laid on the colonies by act of parliament, and paid by the people here; fince they might abufe it, by projecting ufelefs expeditions, haraffing the people, and taking them from their labors to execute fuch projects, merely to create offices and employments, and gratify their dependants, and divide profits:

That the parliament of England is at a great diftance, fubject to be mifinformed and mifled by fuch governors and councils, whofe united interefts might probably fecure them againft the effect of any complaint from hence:

That it is fuppofed to be an undoubted right of *Englifhmen*, not to be taxed but by their own confent given through their reprefentatives:

That the colonies have no reprefentatives in parliament:

That to propofe taxing them by parliament, and refufe them the liberty of choofing a reprefentative council, to meet in the colonies, and confider and judge of the

the neceffity of any general tax, and the quantum, fhows a fufpicion of their loyalty to the crown, or of their regard for their country, or of their common fenfe and underftanding, which they have not deferved:

That compelling the colonies to pay money without their confent, would be rather like raifing contributions in an enemy's country, than taxing *Englifhmen* for their own public benefit:

That it would be treating them as a conquered people, and not as true Britifh fubjects:

That a tax laid by the reprefentatives of the colonies might eafily be leffened, as the occafions fhould leffen; but being once laid by parliament, under the influence of the reprefentations made by governors, would probably be kept up, and continued for the benefit of governors, to the grievous burden and difcouragement of the colonies, and prevention of their growth and increafe:

That a power in governors to march the inhabitants from one end of the Britifh and French colonies to the other, being a country of at leaft 1,500 fquare miles, without the approbation or confent of their reprefentatives firft obtained, might occafion expeditions grievous and ruinous to the people, and would put them upon a footing with the fubjects of France in Canada, that now groan under fuch oppreffion from their governor, who for two years paffed, has haraffed them with long and deftructive marches to the Ohio:

That, if the colonies in a body may be well governed by governors and councils appointed by the crown without reprefentatives, particular colonies may as well, or better, be fo governed: a tax may be laid on them all

by

by act of parliament for support of government, and
their affemblies be difmiffed as an ufelefs part of the
conftitution:

That the powers propofed by the *Albany* plan of union,
to be vefted in a grand reprefentative council of the
people, even with regard to military matters, are not fo
great as thofe the colonies of *Rhode Ifland* and *Connecticut* are entrufted with by their charter, and have
never abufed : for by this plan, the prefident general is
appointed by the crown, and controls all by his negative;
but in thefe governments, the people choofe the governor, and yet allow him no negative:

That the Britifh colonies bordering on the French,
are properly frontiers of the Britifh empire; and the
frontiers of an empire are properly defended at the joint
expence of the body of the people in fuch empire. It
would now be thought hard, by act of parliament, to
oblige the cinque ports, or fea coafts of Britain, to
maintain the whole navy, becaufe they are more immediately defended by it; not allowing them at the fame
time, a vote in choofing the members of parliament:
and if the frontiers in America muft bear the expence
of their own defence, it feems hard to allow them no
fhare in voting the money, judging of the neceffity and
fum, or advifing the meafures:

That befides the taxes neceffary for the defence of
the frontiers, the colonies pay yearly great fums to the
mother country unnoticed; for taxes paid in Britain, by
the landholder or artificer, muft enter into and increafe
the price of the produce of land, and of manufactures
made of it; and great part of this is paid by confumers

in the colonies, who thereby pay a confiderable part of
the Britifh taxes.

We are reftrained in our trade with foreign nations;
and where we could be fupplied with any manufacture
cheaper from them, but muft buy the fame dearer from
Britain, the difference of price is a clear tax to Britain.
We are obliged to carry great part of our produce directly to Britain; and wherein the duties there laid upon
it leffen its price to the planter, or it fells for lefs than
it would in foreign markets, the difference is a tax paid
to Britain.

Some manufactures we could make, but are forbidden
and muft take of *Britifh* merchants; the whole price of
thefe is a tax paid to Britain.

By our greatly increafing the demand and confumption of Britifh manufactures, their price is confiderably
raifed of late years: their advance is clear profit to Britain, and enables its people better to pay great taxes;
and much of it being paid by us, is a clear tax to
Britain.

In fhort, as we are not fuffered to regulate our trade,
and reftrain the importation and confumption of Britifh
fuperfluities, (as Britain can the confumption of foreign
fuperfluities) our whole wealth centres finally among the
merchants and inhabitants of Britain; and if we make
them richer, and enable them better to pay their taxes,
it is nearly the fame as being taxed ourfelves, and
equally beneficial to the crown. Thefe kind of fecon-
dary taxes however, we do not complain of, though
we have no fhare in the laying or difpofing of them:
but to pay immediate heavy taxes, in the laying, appropriation,

propriation, and difpofition of which we have no part, and which, perhaps, we may know to be as unneceffary as grievous, muft feem hard meafure to *Englifhmen*; who cannot conceive, that by hazarding their lives and fortunes, in fubduing and fettling new countries, extending the dominion, and increafing the commerce of their mother nation, they have forfeited the native rights of *Britons*, which they think ought rather to be given them as due to fuch merit, if they had been before in a ftate of flavery. Thefe, and fuch kind of things as thefe, I apprehend, will be thought and faid by the people, if the propofed alteration of the Albany plan fhould take place. Then the adminiftration of the board of governors and councils fo appointed, not having any reprefentative body of the people to approve and unite in its meafures, and conciliate the minds of the people to them, will probably become fufpected and odious: dangerous animofities and feuds will arife between the governors and governed, and every thing go into confufion.

Perhaps I am too apprehenfive in this matter; but having freely given my opinion and reafons, your excellency can judge better than I whether there be any weight in them; and the fhortnefs of the time allowed me, will, I hope, in fome degree, excufe the imperfections of this fcrawl.

With the greateft refpect and fidelity, I have the honor to be, your excellency's moft obedient and moft humble fervant,

BENJAMIN FRANKLIN."

Thefe

These letters might be tranfmitted to, and might difpofe the miniftry to decline urging their plan of uniting and governing the colonies; but Mr. Shirley wrote to governor *Wentworth* of *New Hampfhire*, May 31, 1755—" I may affure your excellency, from every letter I have of late received from Sir Thomas Robinfon, I have reafon to think that his majefty hath a dependance upon a *common fund's* being raifed in all his colonies upon this continent, in proportion to their refpective abilities, for defraying all articles of expence entered into for their common defence; and that fuch an one muft, in the end, be either voluntarily raifed, or elfe affeffed in fome way or other." The miniftry difcovered a difpofition to raife a revenue in them, which

Nov. 6.

induced the *Maffachufetts* general court thus to inftruct their agent; " It is more efpecially expected, that you oppofe every thing that fhall have the remoteft tendency to raife a *revenue* in the plantations, for any public ufes or fervices of government:" he wrote to them the twenty-ninth of May following, " The inclinations I have reafon to think ftill continue for *raifing a revenue* out of the molaffes trade." The alarming ftate of public affairs might divert the miniftry from purfuing their inclinations.

It had been concluded to take effectual meafures for driving the *French* from the *Ohio*; and for the reduction of *Niagara*, *Crown Point*, and their forts in *Nova Scotia*. General *Braddock* was accordingly fent from Ireland to Virginia, with two regiments of foot; and when arrived, and joined by the reft of the forces deftined for that fervice, found himfelf at the head of about 2,200 men.

men. He had bravery, but wanted other qualifications to render him fit for the service to which he was appointed. His severity prevented his having the love of the regulars: his haughtiness, the love of the Americans; and what was worse, disgusted the Indians, and led him to despise the country militia, and to slight the advice of the Virginia officers. Colonel *Washington* earnestly begged of him, when the army was marching for fort *du Quesne*, to admit of his going before, and scouring the woods with his rangers, which was contemptuously refused. The general had been cautioned by the duke of *Cumberland*, to guard against a surprise; and yet he pushed on heedlessly with the first division, consisting of 1400 men, till he fell into an ambuscade of 400, chiefly Indians, by whom he was defeated and mortally wounded, on the ninth of July. The regulars were put into the greatest panic, and fled in the utmost confusion: the militia had been used to Indian fighting, and were not so terrified. The general had disdainfully turned them into the rear: they continued in a body, unbroken, and served under colonel *Washington* as a most useful rear-guard; covered the retreat of the regulars, and prevented their being entirely cut off.

1755. July 9.

Previous to this, and agreeable to the views of the British ministry, the *Massachusetts* assembly, who had never been remiss upon the prospect of a French war, raised a body of troops, which were sent to *Nova Scotia*, to assist lieutenant governor *Lawrence* in driving the French from their several encroachments within that province. The secrecy and dispatch used in this service was rewarded with success.

K 3

The

The expedition againſt Niagara was entruſted with governor Shirley; but failed through various cauſes.

Sir *William* (then colonel) *Johnſon* was appointed to go againſt Crown Point. The delays, ſlowneſs, and deficiency of preparations, prevented the ſeveral colonies joining their troops till about Auguſt. Meanwhile the active enemy had tranſported forces from *France* to *Canada*, marched them down to meet the provincials and attacked them; but, meeting with a repulſe, loſt ſi: hundred men, beſides having their general baroi *Dieſkau*, wounded and made priſoner.

The *Maſſachuſetts* the next year, raiſed a great armament to go againſt *Crown Point*; but Lord *Loudon* on his arrival, did not think it proper that the forces ſhould proceed. Afterward a temporary miſunderſtanding took place between his lordſhip and the general court; from his apprehending, that they thought a provincial law neceſſary to enforce a Britiſh act of parliament, and were willing to diſpute upon that ſubject. He determined to have no diſpute, but that the troops under his command ſhould be quartered agreeable to what he thought the public good required; and wrote to governor *Pownall*, 1757. " I have ordered the meſſenger to wait but 48 hours in Nov. 15. *Boſton*; and if, on his return, I find things not ſettled, I will inſtantly order into *Boſton* the three battalions from New York, Long Iſland, and Connecticut; and if more are wanted, I have two in the Jerſeys at hand, beſide three in Pennſylvania." Notwithſtanding this declaration, on December the ſixth, the legiſlature paſſed an act, which led him to conceive, that he was under an abſolute neceſſity of ſettling the point at once, and therefore he ordered the troops to march. The general
court

court finding how matters were going, did not venture upon extremities, but became pliable; so that his lord-ship wrote, December 26, " As I can now depend upon the affembly's making the point of quarters eafy in all time coming, I have countermanded the march of the troops." The general court were certainly terrified; and to remove all unfavorable impreffions, faid in the clofe of their addrefs to the governor, " The authority 1758. of all acts of parliament, which concern the colonies, 6. and extend to them, is ever acknowledged in all the courts of law, and made the rule of all judicial proceed-ings in the province. There is not a member of the general court, and we know no inhabitant within the bounds of the government, that ever queftioned this authority. To prevent any ill confequences that may arife from an opinion of our holding fuch principles, we now utterly difavow them, as we fhould readily have done at any time paft, if the had been occafion for it; and we pray that his lordfhip may be acquainted there-with, that we may appear in a true light, and that no impreffions may remain to our difadvantage." How-ever they might not queftion, whether the authority of acts of parliament, concerning and extending to the colonies, was made the rule of all *judicial* proceedings in the province; yet you are not to infer from their difavowal of the contrary principle, that they admitted the right of parliament, either to impofe internal taxes, or to control their colonial government.

When, happily for the Britifh nation, the great Mr. *Pitt* was placed at the head of the miniftry, the face of affairs was foon changed; the war was profecuted with unexampled fuccefs, and the enemy at length driven out

K 4

of

of *America*. But the frequent delays given to the raising of the neceffary fupplies, efpecially in the proprietary governments, through the refufal of their governors or councils, to admit that the eftates of the proprietors fhould be taxed, led Mr. *Pitt* to tell Mr. *Franklin*, that when the war clofed, was he in the miniftry, he fhould take meafures to prevent its being in the power of the colonies, to hinder government's receiving the fupplies that were wanted; and he added, that, was he not in the miniftry, he would advife his fucceffors to do it. What thefe meafures were, he did not mention. But 1760. toward the clofe of 1759, or the beginning of 1760, Mr. *Pitt* wrote to *Francis Fauquier* efq; lieutenant go-vernor of *Virginia*, and mentioned in his letter, that though they had made grants to the colonies, yet, when the war was over, they fhould tax them in order to *raife a revenue* from them. Mr. *Fauquier*, in his anfwer, ex-preffed his apprehenfion, that the meafure would occa-fion great difturbance. The anfwer might divert Mr. Pitt from his intention. Many months before, the pre-fent Lord *Camden* then Mr. *Pratt*, faid to Mr. *Franklin*, in a courfe of free converfation, " For all what you *Americans* fay of your loyalty, I know you will one day throw off your dependence upon this coun-try; and, notwithftanding your boafted affection to it, will fet up for independence." The other anfwered, " No fuch idea is entertained in the mind of the *Ameri-cans*; and no fuch idea will ever enter their heads, un-lefs you grofsly abufe them." " Very true, (replied Mr. *Pratt*) that is one of the main caufes I fee will happen, and will produce the event."

The

The colonies in general, and the Maſſachuſetts in particular, complied with the requiſitions of the miniſter, and ſhewed themſelves ready to ſupport his plans for the reduction of the French power. To aſſiſt and encourage their extraordinary exertions, the parliament granted them during the war, at different periods, no leſs than £. 1,031,666. 13s. 4d. But though the large importation of ſpecie annually, did not anſwer one half of their expences, it was ſtill of ſuch benefit to each government, that they cheerfully ſeconded the views of miniſtry. Upon application from admiral *Saunders*, the ſquadron employed againſt *Louiſburgh* and *Quebec*, was ſupplied by 500 ſeamen from the *Maſſachuſetts*; beſide, many were at ſeveral times impreſſed out of veſſels on the fiſhing banks. The colonies loſt by the war, 25,000 of their robuſt young men, excluſive of ſailors. The *Maſſachuſetts* continually raiſed the full number of troops aſſigned them: nor was it to be aſcribed to the peculiar addreſs of Mr. *Pownall*, who guided them with a ſilken cord, and by praiſing them plentifully, and flattering their vanity, did buſineſs with them in an eaſy manner; for it was the ſame, after he was ſucceeded 1760. by governor *Bernard*. Beſide their annual quota of Aug. men, in ſome years of the war they garriſoned Louiſ- 13. burgh and Nova Scotia, which gave the regular forces opportunity for retaining Canada. The whole coſt they were at upon theſe accounts, and for ſcouting companies ſent into the Indian country, and for two armed veſſels built and maintained for the protection of the trade, amounted to £.754,598. 10s. 10d½ ſterling. In this ſum, the expence of many forts and garriſons on the frontiers is not included. Add, that no eſtimate can be

made

made of the coft to individuals, by the demand of perfonal fervice. They that could not ferve in perfon,
who were much the greater number, when it came to
their turn, were obliged to hire fubftitutes at a high pre-
mium. They alfo who could not be impreffed, to
lighten the burdens of others, advanced largely for encouraging the levies. Moreover, the taxes were exceeding heavy. A Bofton gentleman, of reputation and
fortune, fent one of his rate bills to a correfpondent in
London, for his judgment on it; and had for anfwer, " That he did not believe there was a man in all
England, who paid fo much in proportion toward the
fupport of government." Such was the affeffment of
the town in one of the years, that if a man's income
was £.60 per annum, he had to pay two thirds or £.40,
and in that proportion whether the fum was more or
lefs; and if his houfe or land was valued at £.200 per
annum, he was obliged to pay £.72. He had alfo to
pay for his poll, and thofe of all the males in his houfe,
more than 16 years old, at the rate of 14*s*. 3*d*. each:
and to all muft be added, the part he paid of the excife
on tea, coffee, rum, and wine *. Other towns and colonies might not have been affeffed fo exorbitantly, but
fome muft certainly have been burdened with taxes.

The above ftatement of expences is thought to be more
correct than what gov. Bernard tranfmitted, in his letter
of Auguft 1, 1764, to the lords of trade, in which he
wrote, " From 1754 to 1762, the fums iffued amount
to £.926,000 fterling; out of which deduct, received
by parliamentary grant, £.328,000; and the ordinary

* Dr. Chauncy's thankfgiving fermon for the repeal of the ftamp-
act in a note.

expences

expences of government eftimated at £. 108,000, there remains £. 490,000, that is near £. 500,000 fterling expended by this province in the extraordinary charges of the war within eight years. An immenfe fum for fuch a fmall ftate! the burden of which has been grievoufly felt by all orders of men. Whereas if we compare this with the fouthern governments, Pennfylvania for inftance, which has expended little more than they have received from parliament, and Maryland which has expended fcarce any thing at all, we cannot fufficiently admire the inequality of the burden between one province and another. And when Pennfylvania has not been prevented by domeftic diffenfions, and have as it were done their beft, they have fent to the field only 2,700 men, when this province has fent 5,000—5,500, and one year 7,000. And notwithftanding the vaft fums this province has raifed, it has, by fevere taxations, kept its debt under."

The firft part of governor *Bernard*'s adminiftration was agreeable to the *Maffachufetts* general court. The two houfes, in anfwer to his fpeech, faid, " It gives us pleafure to fee, that the civil rights of the people are not in danger ; nor are we in the leaft degree fufpicious, that they ever will be under your excellency's adminiftration. The experience we have had of your excellency's difpofition and abilities, encourage us to hope for a great fhare of public happinefs under your adminiftration." The next year, the governor told them, at the clofe of the feffion, " The unanimity and difpatch with which you have complied with the requifitions of his majefty, require my particular acknowledgment." In his fpeech to the new court, he faid, " Every thing that

1761.
May

1762.
April
23.

May
27.

that has been required of this province, has been moſt readily complied with."

Both houſes, in their addreſs to him, expreſſed them-ſelves thus: " We congratulate your excellency upon that unanimity, which your excellency recommends, and which was never greater in the province than at this time." The governor at the cloſe of the ſeſſion, de-clared his great ſatisfaction in having obſerved, that the unanimity they aſſured him of, had fully evidenced it-ſelf throughout all their proceedings. But the lieutenant governor Mr. *Hutchinſon*, gained after a while too much aſcendency over him, and encouraged him in the purſuit of wrong meaſures, highly offenſive to the co-lony. He had indeed done him an irreparable injury, not long after his coming to the chair. Colonel *James Otis* (who was repeatedly returned for *Barnſtaple* in *Ply-mouth* county, notwithſtanding the ſtrenuous efforts which had been made to prevent it, on account of his ſiding with government) being a lawyer, had been pro-miſed by Mr. Shirley, when in the chair, to be made a judge of the ſuperior court, upon an opportunity's offer-ing. The firſt vacancy which happened, was filled up by the appointment of the ſecretary's ſon in law; for which Mr. Shirley apologized, by pleading a promiſe made to the ſecretary, and his having forgotten the former one. Mr. Otis was ſatisfied with a freſh aſſurance of the next vacancy, which was conſidered by him in the light of a governmental promiſe; and it was ex-pected that whenever a new vacancy happened, Mr. Otis would be appointed. There was no new vacancy till a ſhort time after governor Bernard entered upon his adminiſtration, when chief juſtice *Sewall* died. Upon
this

this death, Mr. *James Otis* the fon, of whom there will be a call to make frequent mention, expreffed himfelf as follows : " If governor Bernard does not appoint my father judge of the fuperior court, I will kindle fuch a fire in the province as fhall finge the governor, though I myfelf perifh in the flames." Mr. Hutchinfon however, hurried to Mr. Bernard, procured a promife, which being once given, the governor would not retract, and got himfelf appointed chief juftice, by which he gratified both his ambition and covetoufnefs, his two ruling paffions. The friends of government regretted the appointment, foreboding the evils it would produce. The governor loft the influence and fupport of colonel Otis. The fon quitted the law-place he held; would never be perfuaded to refume it, or to accept of another; joined himfelf to the party which was jealous that the views of adminiftration were unfavorable to the rights of the colony, and ftood ready to oppofe all encroachments; and foon became its chief leader. He fignalized himfelf, by pleading in a moft mafterly manner, againft granting *writs of affiftance* to cuftom-houfe officers. Thefe writs were to give them, their deputies, &c. a general power to enter any houfes, &c. that they would *fay they fufpected*. The cuftom-houfe officers had received letters from home, directing them to a more ftrenuous exertion in collecting the duties, and to procure writs of affiftance. The idea of thefe writs excited a general alarm. A ftrong jealoufy, of what might be eventually the effect of them upon the liberties of the people, commenced. They might prove introductory to the moft horrid abufes; which the meaneft deputy of a deputy's deputy might practife with impunity, upon
a mer-

a merchant or gentleman of the firſt character; and there would be the greater danger of ſuch abuſes, by reaſon of the immenſe diſtance of the ſcene of action from the ſeat of government. The voice of the complainant would not be heard three thouſand miles off, after the ſervants of government had deafened the ears of adminiſtration by miſrepreſentations. From this period may be dated, the fixed, uniform, and growing oppoſition, which was made to the miniſterial plans of encroaching upon the original rights and long eſtabliſhed cuſtoms of the colony. In 1761, the officers of the cuſtoms applied to the ſuperior court for ſuch writs. The great oppoſition that was made to it, and the arguments of Mr. *Otis*, diſpoſed the court to a refuſal; but Mr. *Hutchinſon*, who had obtained the place of chief juſtice, prevailed with his brethren to continue the cauſe till next term; and in the mean time, wrote to England, and procured a copy of the writ, and ſufficient evidence of the practice of the exchequer there, after which like writs were granted. But before this was effected, Mr. *Otis* was choſen one of the repreſentatives for *Boſton*, by the influence of the friends to liberty; whoſe jealouſies there and elſewhere, afterward increaſed apace, upon hearing that the Britiſh officers inſiſted frequently upon the neceſſity of regulating and *reforming*, as they ſtiled it, the colonial governments; and that certain travellers were introduced to particular perſons with a—

1762. " This is a gentleman employed by the earl of *Bute* to travel the country, and learn what may be proper to be done, in the grand plan of *reforming* the *American governments.*" It was underſtood, that their buſineſs was to make thorough obſervation upon the ſtate of the

country, that so the ministry might be enabled to judge
what regulations and alterations could safely be made in
the police and government of the colonies, in order to
their being brought more effectually under the government of parliament.   They were also as much as possible, to conciliate capital and influential characters, to
ministerial measures speedily to be adopted.   The British
ministry have been greatly mistaken, in supposing it is
the same in *America* as in their own country.   Do they
gain over a gentleman of note and eminence in the colonies, they make no considerable acquisition.   He takes
few or none with him ; and is rather despised, than adhered to by former friends.   He has not, as in Britain,
dependants who must act in conformity to his nod.   In
New England especially, individuals are so independent
of each other, that though there may be an inequality
in rank and fortune, every one can act freely according
to his own judgment.

But nothing, it may be, excited a greater alarm in
the breasts of those to whom it was communicated, than
the following anecdote, viz. The Rev. Mr. *Whitefield*,
ere he left *Portsmouth* in *New Hampshire*, on Monday
afternoon, April the second 1764, sent for Dr. *Langdon* 1764.
and Mr. Haven, the congregational ministers of the April
town, and upon their coming and being alone with 2.
him, said, " I can't in conscience leave the town without acquainting you with a secret.   My heart bleeds for
America.   O poor *New England !*   There is a deep laid
plot against both your civil and religious liberties; and
they will be lost.   Your golden days are at an end.   You
have nothing but trouble before you.   My information
comes from the best authority in *Great Britain*.   I was
allowed

allowed to fpeak of the affair in general, but enjoined
not to mention particulars. Your liberties will be loft*."
Mr. Whitefield could not have heard what the commons
did in the preceding month; his information muft have
been of an earlier date, and might have been communicated before he left Great Britain. Befide the general
defign of taxing the colonies, the plan was probably,
this in fubftance—Let the parliament be enaged to enter
heartily and fully into American matters; and then under its fanction, let all the governments be altered, and
all the councils be appointed by the king, and the affemblies be reduced to a fmall number, like that of New
York. After that, the more effectually to fecure the
power of civil government by the junction of church
influence, let there be a revifal of all the acts in the
feveral colonies, with a view of fetting afide thofe in
particular, which provide for the fupport of the minifters.
But if the temper of the people makes it neceffary, let
a new bill for the purpofe of fupporting them pafs the
houfe, and the council refufe their concurrence ; if that
will be improper, then the governor to negative it.   If
that cannot be done in good policy, then the bill to go
home, and let the king difallow it.   Let bifhops be introduced, and provifion be made for the fupport of the
epifcopal clergy.   Let the congregational and prefbyterian clergy, who will receive epifcopal ordination, be
fupported; and the leading minifters among them be
bought off by large falaries.   Let the liturgy be revifed
and altered.   Let epifcopacy be accommodated as much
as poffible to the caft of the people.   Let places of

* Dr. Langdon told it me in converfation; and afterward mentioned
it in his fermon preached before the convention of the minifters.

power,

power, truſt and honor be conferred only upon epiſco-palians, or thoſe that will conform. When epiſcopacy is once thoroughly eſtabliſhed, increaſe its reſemblance to the Engliſh hierarchy, at pleaſure.

Theſe were the ideas, which a certain gentleman com-municated to Dr. Stiles *, when they were riding toge-ther in 1765. The Doctor, after hearing him out, ex-preſſed his belief, that before the plan could be effected, ſuch a ſpirit would be rouſed in the people, as would prevent its execution. The good man groaned and re-plied, " If the commotions now exiſting prevail on the parliament to repeal the ſtamp-act, I am afraid the plan cannot be accompliſhed."

In reference to alterations in the civil line, Dr. Lang-don informed me, that governor *Wentworth* told him, the *Maſſachuſetts* and *New Hampſhire* were to be one govern-ment under one governor: the Doctor thought the de-ſign of joining *Rhode Iſland* with them was alſo men-tioned, though of this he could not be certain. The *New England* colonies would have ſuffered moſt by the propoſed alterations, while they deſerved it the leaſt, and were entitled for their ready exertions, to a return expreſſive of gratitude. Many of the common ſoldiers, who gained ſuch laurels, by their ſingular bravery on the plains of Abraham, when Wolfe died in the arms of victory, were natives of the Maſſachuſetts-bay. When Martinico was attacked in 1761, and the Britiſh force was greatly weakened by death and ſickneſs, the timely arrival of the New England troops, enabled the former to proſecute the reduction of the iſland to an happy iſſue. A great part of the Britiſh force being about to

* Now preſident of Yale College in Connecticut.

fail from thence for the Havannah, the New Englanders, whofe health had been much impaired by fervice and the climate, were fent off in three fhips, to their native country for recovery. Before they had completed their voyage, they found themfelves reftored, ordered the fhips about, fteered immediately for the Havannah, arrived when the Britifh were too much reduced to expect fuccefs, and by their junction ferved to immortalize afrefh, the glorious firft of Auguft, old ftile, in the furrender of the place on that memorable day : they exhibited, at the fame time, the moft fignal evidence of devotednefs to the parent ftate. Their fidelity, activity, and courage, were fuch as to gain the approbation and confidence of the Britifh officers *.

As to the religious part of the plan, recollect what has been already mentioned of archbifhop *Secker*; carefully perufe Dr. *Mayhew*'s noted anfwer to one of his publications, and what is related concerning him in the collection of papers above quoted; and you will fcarce doubt, " but that it was the metropolitan's intention to reduce all the Britifh colonies under epifcopal authority." Remember alfo, that the bifhop of *Landaff* in his fermon of 1766, affures us, that *the eftablifhment of epifcopacy* being obtained, " the *American* church will go out of its infant ftate; be able to ftand upon its own legs; and, without foreign help, fupport and fpread itfelf; and *then this fo-ciety will be brought to the happy iffue intended.*" Mr. Whitefield faid upon it, in his letter to Dr. *Durell*, " fuppofing his lordfhip's affertions true, then I fear it will follow, that a fociety, which fince its firft inftitution

* From Brooke Woodcock efq. of Saffron Walden, who ferved at the taking of Belleifle, Martinico, and the Havannah.

hath

hath been looked upon as *a society for propagating the gospel*, hath been all the while rather *a society for propagating episcopacy in foreign parts*."

This letter will close with a few more articles of information. Among the original instructions to *Benning Wentworth* esq; governor of *New Hampshire*, signed June 30th 1761, the 27th says, "You are not to give your assent to, or pass any law imposing duties on negroes imported into *New Hampshire:*" some of the colonies were for discouraging the introduction of negroes; for which purpose they wished to lay a duty upon them. The 69th contains the following direction, "No school-master to be henceforth permitted to come from *England* without the licence of the bishop; and no other person now there, or that shall come from other parts, shall be admitted to keep school without your licence first obtained."

A law passed in the *Massachusetts* entitled, "An act to incorporate certain persons, by the name of *The society for promoting Christian Knowledge among the Indians in North America*; but was disallowed at the court of *St. James*'s the 20th of May 1763. Mr. *Jasper Mauduit* in his letter to Mr. *Bowdoin* of April 7, 1763, writes, "So long ago as the 10th of December, I was told at the plantation office, that this act was opposed by the archbishop and the society for propagating the gospel. Mr. *Pownall* told me, that the bill would not pass; that the lords would not dispute the laudableness of the design, but there were political reasons for not confirming it; that the people might apply the money to oppose the missionaries of the church of England. I answered, I wished that the society for propa-

margin: 1762 Feb.

L 2   gating

gating the gofpel had employed their miffionaries more among the Indians, than they had hitherto done in *North America.*" From what paffed, the real reafons for difallowing the bill may be gathered.

L·E T T E R   III.

Roxbury, Dec. 24, 1772.

1763. MR. *Ifrael Mauduit,* the *Maffachufetts* agent, gave early notice of the minifterial intentions to tax the colonies; but the general court not being called together till the latter end of the year, inftructions to the agent, though folicited by him, could not be fent in feafon.

1764. The houfe of reprefentatives came to the following ·refolutions—" That the fole right of giving and granting ·the money of the people of that province, was vefted in them as their legal reprefentatives; and that the impofition of duties and taxes by the parliament of Great Britain, upon a people who are not reprefented in the houfe of commons, is abfolutely irreconcileable with their rights."—" That no man can juftly take the property of another without his confent; upon which original principle, the right of reprefentation in the fame body which exercifes the power of making laws ·for levying taxes, one of the main pillars of the *Britifh ·conftitution,* is evidently founded."

Thefe

Thefe refolutions were occafioned by intelligence of what had been done in the Britifh house of commons. It had been there debated in March, whether they had a *right* to tax the *Americans* they not being reprefented, and determined unanimoufly in the affirmative. Not a fingle perfon prefent ventured to controvert the *right*. Soon after, the fugar or molaffes act was paffed : and April " it is certainly true, that till then, no act avowedly for 5. the purpofe of revenue, and with the ordinary title and recital taken together, is found in the ftatute book. All before ftood on *commercial* regulation and reftraints*." It is ftiled " an act for granting certain duties in the Britifh colonies and plantations in America, for continuing amending and making perpetual an act paffed in the fixth year of George the fecond, (entitled an act for the better fecuring and encouraging the trade of his majefty's colonies in America) for applying the produce of fuch duties, &c." From its perpetuating the fugar act of George II. it is called the fugar or molaffes act. It runs thus, " Whereas it is expedient, that new provifions and regulations fhould be eftablifhed in improving the revenue of this kingdom, and for extending and fecuring the navigation and commerce between Great Britain and your majefty's dominions in America—And whereas it is juft and neceffary, that a *revenue* be raifed in *America* for defraying the expences of defending, protecting, and fecuring the fame—We the commons, &c. toward raifing the fame, give and grant unto your majefty after the 29th of September 1764, upon clayed fugar, indigo and coffee of foreign produce—upon all wines except French—upon all

* Mr. Burke's fpeech on American taxation, April 19, 1774.

wrought

wrought filks, Bengals and ftuffs mixed with filk of
Perfia, China, or Eaft-India manufacture—and all cal-
licoes painted, printed, or ftained there (certain fpecified duties)—upon every gallon of molaffes and firups,
being the produce of a colony not under the dominion
of his majefty, the fum of three-pence—the monies
arifing, after charges of raifing, collecting, &c. are to
be paid into the receipt of his majefty's Exchequer—
fhall be entered feparate, and be referved to be difpofed
of by parliament, toward defraying the neceffary expences of defending &c. the Britifh colonies." The
wording of the act might induce the colonies to view
it as the beginning of forrows; and they might fear
that the parliament would go on in charging them with
fuch taxes as it pleafed, for fuch military force as it
fhould think proper.   This ill profpect feemed to
the Americans, boundlefs in extent, and endlefs in duration.

They objected not to the *parliament's right of laying
duties to regulate commerce:* but the *right of taxing them*
was not admitted.   The minifterial plan, fent to Mr.
Shirley in 1754, occafioned much converfation on the
fubject, and the common opinion was, that the parliament could not tax them, till duly reprefented in that
body, becaufe it was not juft, nor agreeable to the nature of the Englifh conftitution.   But though few or
none were willing to admit the *right;* the generality
were cautious how they denied the *power,* or the obligation to fubmit on the part of the Americans, when
the power was exercifed.   Even Mr. *Otis* tells us, "We
muft and ought to yield obedience to an act of parliament,

ment, though erroneous, till repealed *." " The power of parliament is uncontrollable, but by themfelves, and we muft obey. There would be an end of all government, if one or a number of fubordinate provinces fhould take upon themfelves, fo far to judge of the juftice of an act of parliament, as to refufe obedience to it. If there was nothing elfe to reftrain fuch a ftep, prudence ought to do it, for forcibly refifting the parliament and the king's laws is high treafon. Therefore let the parliament lay what burthens they pleafe upon us, we muft, it is our duty to fubmit, and patiently to bear them, till they will be pleafed to relieve us †." He went fo far as to publifh, " It is certain that the parliament of Great Britain has a juft and equitable right, power and authority, to impofe taxes on the colonies, internal and external, on lands as well as on trade ‡." " The fupreme legiflative reprefents the whole fociety or community, as well the dominions as the realm. This is implied in the idea of a fupreme power; and if the parliament had not fuch an authority, the colonies would be independent §." But the two laft quotations were extorted from him, through fear of being called to an account for the part he had acted, or for what he had before advanced in print, converfation, or debate. His firft pamphlet, *The rights of the* BRITISH *colonies,* which had been twice read over in the houfe of affembly within the fpace of five days, though guarded by fome expreffions, had a ftrong tendency to excite a powerful oppofition to minifterial plans; efpecially where he fays, " I cannot but obferve

---

* Otis's Rights of the Britifh Colonies, p. 57.   † Ibid. p. 59.
‡ His Vindication of the Britifh Colonies, p. 4.   § Ibid. p. 21.

here,

here, that if the parliament have an equitable right to tax our trade, it is indisputable, that they have as good a one to tax the lands and every thing else. There is no foundation for the distinction some make in England, between an internal and external tax on the colonies *." These expressions could not but spread a general alarm through the country, and inflame every planter against parliamentary taxation. The house had so high an opinion of this pamphlet, that they ordered it to be sent over to Mr. *Mauduit* with a letter, wherein they instructed him to use his endeavours to obtain a repeal of the sugar act, and to exert himself to prevent a stamp act, or any other impositions and taxes, upon this and the other American provinces. They do not appear to have made any particular objection to the term *revenue* introduced into the sugar act; but to have confined their objections to the laying on of the duty, when they were not represented.

The act disgusted the more, because of its being so unseasonable. The duties were to be paid in specie, while the old means of procuring it were cut off. The ministry, resolved to prevent smuggling, obliged all sea officers stationed on the American coasts, to act in the capacity of the meanest revenue officers, making them submit to the usual custom-house oaths and regulations for that purpose. This proved a great grievance to the American merchants and traders. Gentlemen of the navy were unacquainted with custom-house laws. Many illegal seizures were made. No redress could be had but from Britain; which it was tedious and difficult to obtain. Beside, the *American* trade with the *Spaniards*,

* Otis's Rights of the British Colonies. p. 63.

by

by which the Britiſh manufactures were vended in
return (for gold and ſilver in coin or bullion, cochi-
neal, &c. as occaſion ſerved) was almoſt deſtroyed inſtantly, by the armed ſhips under the new regulations. The trade was not literally and ſtrictly according to law, but highly beneficial; and a thorough
ſtateſman would have declined employing his own
navy in cruſhing it. The trade alſo from the northern colonies with the *French Weſt-India* iſlands was
nearly ſuppreſſed. Theſe irritating meaſures ſtrength-
ened the oppoſition to the ſugar act.

The *Maſſachuſetts* aſſembly, who were the firſt repre- June
ſentative body that took the act into conſideration, or- 13.
dered, that Mr. *Otis* and four others of the houſe ſhould
be a committee in the receſs of the court, to write to
the other governments, and acquaint them with the inſtructions voted to be ſent to their agent; and that the
ſaid committee, in the name and behalf of the houſe,
ſhould deſire the ſeveral aſſemblies on the continent to
join with them in the ſame meaſures. The committee
attended to the buſineſs: and the end propoſed by it
was anſwered: committees were moreover appointed by
divers other colonies to correſpond with the ſeveral aſſemblies, or committees of aſſemblies on the continent. Thus
a new kind of correſpondence was opened between the colonies, tending to unite them in their operations againſt
miniſterial encroachments on their privileges; and which
proved of great advantage to them afterward.

At the next ſeſſion a committee was appointed to con- Oct.
ſider the ſtate of the province, as it might be affected, 24.
by certain duties and taxes laid and propoſed to be laid
by acts of parliament upon the colonies. The conſequence
was, a committee of the council and houſe to prepare an
addreſs

address to the parliament. The lieutenant governor, Mr. *Hutchinson*, who was of the council, was chairman, but declined drawing up any. Several were proposed, which expressed in strong terms an exclusive right in the assembly to impose taxes. He urged the indecency and bad policy, when they had the resolutions of the house of commons before them, of sending an address asserting, in express words, the direct contrary. Many days having been spent upon the business, at the desire of the committee, he drafted an address, which considered the *sole power* of taxation as an indulgence of which they prayed the continuance, and it was *unanimously* agreed to. The petition does not intimate the least denial of the right of parliament to tax them; but sets forth the impolicy of the laws and the hardships brought upon the petitioners, and prays that they may be relieved from the burdens brought upon them by the sugar act; that the privileges of the colonies relative to their internal taxes, which they have so long enjoyed, may be still continued; or that the consideration of such taxes as are proposed to be laid upon the colonies, may be referred, until the petitioners, in conjunction with the other governments, can have an opportunity to make a full representation of the state and condition of the colonies, and the interest of Great Britain with regard to them. The proceeding of the general court was approved of out of doors, until the copy of the *New York* address was received, which was so high, that many of the friends of liberty were mortified at their own conduct; and if possible would gladly have recalled their own doings *.

* Mr. Hutchinson's letter of March 8, 1766.

The

The Maſſachuſett's petition was forwarded by gover- Nov.
nor Bernard, and accompanied with a letter to lord ¹⁸·
Halifax; in which he wrote, " Maſſachuſetts is the only
one of the old colonies, that I know of, that enjoys a
ſpecie currency.   This reflects great honor upon the
province itſelf, as it is a great inſtance of their prudence,
who took hold of a ſingular opportunity to deſtroy their
paper money, which other colonies who had it equally
in their power neglected.   But I fear, that if the great
ſums, which are expected to be raiſed in America are
to be tranſported to Great Britain, there will ſoon be an
end of the ſpecie currency of the Maſſachuſetts; which
will be followed by a total diſcouragement for other
provinces to attempt the ſame in future.   In which caſe,
perpetual paper money, the very negative power of
riches, will be the portion of America."   After arguing
againſt the duties, from America's being unable, for
want of a ſufficient ſpecie currency, to pay them without being drained of their ſpecie, as it would require a
dead ſtock of three years value of the annual income
of the revenues, he added, " If due care be taken to
confine the ſale of manufactures and European goods
(except what ſhall be permitted) to Great Britain only,
all the profits of the American foreign trade will neceſſarily centre in Great Britain; and therefore if the firſt
purpoſe is well ſecured, the foreign American trade is
the trade of Great Britain.   The augmentation and diminution, the extenſion and reſtriction, the profit and
loſs of it all, finally comes home to the mother country.
It is the intereſt of Great Britain, that the trade to both
the Spaniſh and French Weſt Indies ſhould be encouraged as much as may well be, and the Britiſh Weſt

8   Indies

Indies fhould be taught that equitable maxim, *live and let live.*" It appeared to be the decided opinion of the governor, that the fending home the produce of the duties and taxes propofed, would take from the Americans the means of trade, and render it impracticable for them to make remittances to Great Britain.i

The *Virginia* council and houfe of burgeffes petitioned the king, prefented a memorial to the houfe of lords, and remonftrated to the houfe of commons. *New York, Rhode Ifland,* &c. petitioned. The *New York* petition was conceived in fuch ftrong terms, and deemed fo inflammatory, that their agent could not prevail on any one member of the houfe to prefent it.

The colonies denied the *parliamentary right of taxation* many months before any member of the Britifh parliament uttered a fingle fyllable to that purpofe: and the American oppofition to the ftamp-act was fully formed before it was known by the colonifts, that their caufe was efpoufed by any man of note at home, as *Britain* is ftiled.

Befide the colonial proceedings related above, it muft be noted, that the inhabitants of feveral places met and agreed, not to buy any clothing (they could do without) which was not of their own manufacturing. Divers affociations alfo were formed, all of whom refolved to confume as few Britifh manufactures as poffible.

The raifing of a revenue from the molaffes trade, and a fund to defray the expences of defending the colonies, were in contemplation nine years before *; but the refolutions taken by the houfe of commons, in the be-

* Mr. agent Bollan's letters of that date to the Maffachufett's general court.

ginning

ginning of this year, might be forwarded by Mr. *Huske*, an *American*, a native of *Portsmouth* in *New Hampshire*, who a short time before obtained a seat in parliament. Instead of standing forth a firm advocate for the country which gave him birth, he officiously proposed to the house, laying a tax on the colonies, that should annually amount to five hundred thousand pounds sterling, which he declared they were well able to pay: and he was heard with great joy and attention *. He or some other, recollecting that a stamp act was talked of by the commissioners at Albany, in 1754, might suggest that mode of taxing, for whatever was thought, *the stamp-act was not originally Mr. Grenville's* †.

The disposition to tax the *Americans*, unless they would tax themselves equal to the wishes of the ministry, was undoubtedly strengthened by the reports of their gaiety and luxury, which reached the mother country: it was also said, that the planters lived like princes, while the inhabitants of *Britain* labored hard for a tolerable subsistence. The officers lately returned, represented them as rich, wealthy, and even overgrown in fortune. Their opinion might arise from observations made in the American cities and towns during the war, while large sums were spent in the country, for the support of fleets and armies. American productions were then in great demand, and trade flourished. The people, naturally generous and hospitable, having a number of strangers among them, indulged them-

* Mr. Sayre's letter to captain Sears of New York, dated London 7th of February, 1764.

† Mr. Jackson's letter to lieutenant governor Hutchinson, December 26, 1765.

felves in many uncommon expences. When the war was terminated, and they had no further apprehenfion of danger, the power of the late enemy in the country being totally broken—*Canada*, and the back lands to the very banks of the *Miffiffippi*, with the *Floridas*, being ceded to *Great Britain*—it was thought they could not well make too much of thofe who had fo contributed to their fecurity. Partly to do honor to them, and partly, it is to be feared, to gratify their own pride, they added to their fhow of plate, by borrowing of neighbours, and made a great parade of riches in their feveral entertainments. The plenty and variety of provifion and liquors, enabled them to furnifh out an elegant table at a comparatively trifling expence.

Mr. *Grenville*'s intended ftamp-act was communicated to the American agents. Many of them did not oppofe it. Half their number were placemen, or dependent on the miniftry. Mr. *Jofeph Sherwood*, an honeft quaker, agent for *Rhode Ifland*, refufed his affent to America's being taxed by a Britifh parliament. Mr. *Mauduit*, the Maffachufetts agent, favored the raifing of the wanted money by a ftamp duty, as it would occafion lefs expence of officers, and would include the Weft India iflands. But the fcheme was poftponed, and the agents authorized to inform the American affemblies, that they were at liberty to fuggeft any other way of raifing monies; and that Mr. Grenville was ready to receive propofals for any other tax, that might be equivalent in its produce to the ftamp-tax. The colonies feemed to confider it as an affront, rather than a compliment. He would not have been content with any thing fhort of a certain fpecific fum, and proper funds

for

for the payment of it. Had not the fums been anfwerable to his wifhes, he would have rejected them; and
he would fcarce have been fatisfied with lefs than
300,000l. per annum, which was judged abfolutely neceffary to defray the whole expence of the army propofed for the defence of America: he might rather have
expected that it fhould amount to what Mr. *Hufke* had
mentioned. No fatisfactory propofals being made, he
adhered to his purpofe of bringing forward the ftamp-
bill, though repeatedly preffed by fome of his friends to
defift, while he might have done it with honor. *Richard Jackfon* efq; had been chofen agent for the Maffachufetts; he with Mr. *Ingerfoll*, Mr. *Garth*, and Mr.
Franklin, lately come from Philadelphia, waited on Mr.
Grenville, the fecond of February, 1765, by defire of
the colonial agents, to remonftrate againft the ftamp-
bill, and to propofe that in cafe any tax muft be laid
upon America, the feveral colonies might be permitted
to lay the tax themfelves. At this interview Mr. *Jackfon* opened his mind freely on the fubject; and Mr.
Franklin, as muft be fuppofed, mentioned that he had
it in inftruction from the affembly of *Pennfylvania*, to
affure the miniftry, that they fhould alway think it their
duty to grant fuch aids to the crown, as were fuitable
to their circumftances, whenever called for in the ufual
conftitutional manner. Mr. Grenville however, perti-
nacioufly adhered to his own opinions; and faid, that
he had *pledged his word for offering the ftamp-bill to the
houfe*, and that the houfe would hear their objections,
&c. &c.

The bill was brought in; and on the firft reading,
Mr. *Charles Townfend* fpoke in its favor. He took notice

1765.
Feb.
2.

tice of several things that colonel *Barre* had said in his speech against it; and then concluded with the following or like words: " And now will these *Americans*, children planted by our care; nourished up by our indulgence, until they are grown to a degree of strength and opulence; and protected by our arms; will they grudge to contribute their mite, to relieve us from the heavy weight of that burden which we lie under?"

On this colonel *Barre* rose, and after explaining some passages in his speech, took up Mr. *Townsend*'s concluding words in a most spirited and inimitable manner, saying, " *They planted by* YOUR *care!* No, your oppressions planted them in America. They fled from your tyranny, to a then uncultivated and unhospitable country, where they exposed themselves to almost all the hardships to which human nature is liable; and among others, to the cruelties of a savage foe, the most subtle, and I will take upon me to say, the most formidable of any people upon the face of God's earth; and yet, actuated by principles of true English liberty, they met all hardships with pleasure, compared with those they suffered in their own country, from the hands of those that should have been their friends.——*They nourished up by* YOUR *indulgence!* They grew by your neglect of them. As soon as you began to care about them, that care was exercised in sending persons to rule them, in one department and another, who were, perhaps, the deputies of deputies to some members of this house, sent to spy out their liberties, to misrepresent their actions, and to prey upon them—men, whose behaviour on many occasions, has caused the blood of those *sons of liberty* to recoil within them—men promoted to the

highest

higheſt ſeats of juſtice; ſome who to my knowledge
were glad, by going to a foreign country, to eſcape being
brought to the bar of a court of juſtice in their own.——
They protected by YOUR *arms!* They have nobly taken
up arms in your defence; have exerted a valor, amidſt
their conſtant and laborious induſtry, for the defence of
a country, whoſe frontier was drenched in blood, while
its interior parts yielded all its little ſavings to your emo-
lument.——And believe me, remember I this day told
you ſo, that ſame ſpirit of freedom, which actuated that
people at firſt, will accompany them ſtill——but prudence
forbids me to explain myſelf further.——God knows, I
do not at this time ſpeak from motives of party heat; what
I deliver are the genuine ſentiments of my heart. However ſuperior to me in general knowledge and experience the reſpectable body of this houſe may be, yet I
claim to know more of America than moſt of you,
having ſeen and been converſant in that country.——The
people, I believe, are as truly loyal as any ſubjects the
king has; but a people jealous of their liberties, and
who will vindicate them, if ever they ſhould be violated
——but the ſubject is too delicate—I will ſay no more."
Theſe ſentiments were thrown out, ſo entirely without
premeditation, ſo forcibly and ſo firmly; and the breaking off was ſo beautifully abrupt, that the whole houſe
ſat awhile amazed, intently looking without anſwering a
word.

The London merchants trading to America, being
much alarmed on account of their outſtanding debts,
petitioned againſt the ſtamp-act. Their petition was
offered at the ſecond reading of the bill. The rule of
the houſe, never to receive petitions againſt money bills,

VOL. I. M was

was urged.   General *Conway* obferved, that it appeared undeniable, that the practice was by no means invariable; at beft it was but a practice of convenience, from which they ought, in the prefent inftance, to vary.   The miniftry publicly declared, " *That it was intended to eftablifh the power of Great Britain to tax the colonies.*" They were induced to make a point of it, becaufe moft of the petitions from thence, denied in the ftrongeft terms, the right of Britain to impofe taxes.   It was evident that the minifterial forces would prevail, the petition of the London merchants was therefore withdrawn.   After that, the others from the colonies were offered, but rejected upon the plea taken from the rule of the houfe.   During the debate upon the bill, in this ftage of it, " general *Conway* denied the *right* of parliament to tax the *Americans*, in the moft peremptory manner ; and urged, with great vehemence, the many hardfhips, and what he was pleafed to call, abfurdities that would follow from the contrary doctrine and practice *."   Alderman Beckford alfo difputed the right of parliament, according to Mr. Ingerfoll's letter.

The fupporters of the ftamp-act infifted much upon the colonies being *virtually* reprefented ; and mentioned *Leeds, Halifax, Birmingham, Manchefter,* &c. as enjoying a *virtual reprefentation.*   Whoever had a recourfe to a *virtual reprefentation* of the colonies, in vindication of the parliament's taxing them, therein acknowledged, that there ought not to be taxation without reprefentation.   But the difference between *Leeds, Halifax,* &c. and the *American* colonies, is as wide as the *Atlantic.* The landholders of thofe towns enjoy a real reprefenta-

* Mr. Ingerfoll's letter of March 6, 1765.

tion,

tion, if their freeholds yield a certain annual income.
Many of the inhabitants have a choice in the election
of members, in one place or another. The general interests of the freeholders and tenants, electors and non-
electors, are so interwoven, that all are liable to be
equally affected by the same common taxes. The one
pays the same duty on his sugar, tea, coffee, and choco-
late, as the other. The relative connection between
them, produces what may be called, with a kind of propriety, a *virtual representation*; answering, though in a
lower degree, to what the family of a freeholder or freeman enjoys. But was all the soil in the British colonies
a man's freehold, it would not give him a single vote
for any one member of parliament. There is not an
individual in them, who should he cross the Atlantic,
would have a right to vote in any election, by virtue of
any privileges enjoyed in America. He must be a free-
holder of Britain, or a freeman of some British city,
borough, or corporation, and have a British qualification, before he can elect or be elected. The interests
of *America* and *Britain* are not interwoven, as are those
of British electors and non-electors. If the British parliament impose taxes on the Americans, Britons do not
bear with them, their part and proportion in the said
taxes. The former are burdened, that the latter may
be eased. The monies raised have the nature of a tribute, exacted from a conquered people in a slavish dependence; and not of a tax voluntarily granted by the
voice of freemen, through their own elected representatives, paying scot and lot with themselves for the support of government. Beside, the British parliament are
so far removed from America, that they cannot obtain

M 2   that

that full information refpecting the colonies, which ought alway to accompany the exercife of a taxing power.

When the queftion upon the bill, in its laft ftage, was brought to a vote, there were about 250 for, and 50 againft it. In the houfe of lords, fo ftrong was the unanimity, that there was not a fingle fyllable uttered againft the bill; and on the twenty-fecond of March, it obtained the royal affent. The night after it was paffed, Dr. *Franklin* wrote to Mr. *Charles Thomfon* *, " the fun of liberty is fet; you muft light up the candles of induftry and œconomy." Mr. *Thomfon* anfwered, he was apprehenfive that other lights would be the confequence, and predicted the oppofition that followed.

Mar. 22.

The framers of the ftamp-act flattered themfelves, that the confufion which would arife upon the difufe of writings, would compel the colonies to ufe the ftamp-paper, and therefore to pay the taxes impofed. Thus they were led to pronounce it, *a law which would execute itfelf.* Mr. Grenville however appears to have been apprehenfive, that it might occafion diforders; to prevent or fupprefs which, he projected another bill, which was brought in the fame feffion, whereby it was to be made lawful for military officers in the colonies, to quarter their foldiers in private houfes. This feemed intended to awe the people into a compliance with the other act. Great oppofition being made to it, as under fuch a power in the army, no one could look on his houfe as his own, that part of the bill was dropt; but there ftill remained a claufe, when it paffed into a law, to oblige the feveral affemblies to provide quarters for the foldiers, and to furnifh them with firing, bedding, candles, fmall beer, rum, and fundry other articles, at

* Since the fecretary of Congrefs.

the

the expence of the feveral provinces; which continued
in force when the ftamp-act was repealed. It equally
militated with the other againft the American principle,
*That money is not to be raifed on Englifh fubjects without
their confent.*

Whatever might be urged, government was under no
neceffity of adopting the mode of taxing the colonies,
for their defence and the fecuring of the new ceded countries. Though after the general peace, an Indian war
might be continued or renewed, that was no reafon for
continuing Britifh forces in America. The colonifts
were better able to deal with them than the regulars.
The new ceded countries required no great number of
troops to fecure them. The colonies were at hand to
fupport the Britifh garrifons in cafe affiftance was wanted; and they had repeatedly fhowed their readinefs upon
former occafions. The idea of a dangerous enemy upon
the American continent was at an end: and the Britifh
adminiftration muft have been inexcufable, had they not
guarded againft the transferring of one from Europe.
It was become futile to exclaim—" Shall it depend upon
the refolutions of a Philadelphia affembly, whether our
fellow fubjects fhall arm in defence of liberty and property? Does the fate of a whole continent bear any
proportion to an almoft imperceptible encroachment
upon the important privilege of an American, deliberating for a year or two, whether he will pay fix-pence
in the pound to fave himfelf and family from perdition?"
The danger of perdition was a mere bugbear, which
might frighten the ignorant into an apprehenfion, that
it was abfolutely neceffary to maintain an army in America, for the expence of which the colonies fhould be

M 3   made

made to answer : but the Americans knew better than to startle at the spectre. Had no more troops been stationed upon the American continent than circumstances called for, the ministry might have obtained all the aids it was reasonable for the colonies to have given, by the old mode of requisition. From the time that they were first considered as capable of granting aids, the constant mode of obtaining them, was by *requisition from the crown*, through the governors to the several assemblies : and the ministers, from *Charles* II. to the present king, most effectually recognised the distinction between parliamentary superintendence and taxation, in their requisitions to the colonies to raise men and money by acts of assembly. Had this happy method been continued, all the money that could have been justly expected from them in any manner, might have been procured without the least breach of that harmony, which so long subsisted between the colonies and the mother country : and it was not acting wisely to thwart unnecessarily the prejudices of the Americans. But the imposition of taxes upon them might be introductory to, or a part of the plan for overturning their civil and religious liberties, alluded to by the Rev. Mr. *Whitefield*, before even the sugar-act had passed.

The stamp-act having passed, the colony agents waited upon Mr. Wheatley by desire, who told them, that Mr. Grenville did not think of sending from Great Britain stamp officers, but wished to have discreet and respectable persons appointed from among the inhabitants ; and that he would be obliged to them to point out to him such persons. Thus the agents were drawn in to nominate. Dr. Franklin recommended Mr. *Hughes*

to

to be chief diftributor of ftamps in *Pennfylvania*, and Mr. *Cox* in the *Jerfeys*; and being confulted by Mr. *Ingerfoll*, advifed him to accept, adding, *go home and tell your countrymen to get children as faft as they can*—thereby intimating his opinion of the oppreffion the colonifts were under, and of their prefent inability to make effectual refiftance; but that they ought, when fufficiently numerous, to fhake off the yoke and recover their liberty. It is apparent from the recommendations, and the appointments made in confequence of the nominations, that the agents were far from thinking, that fuch difturbances would have been occafioned by the ftamp-act, or they would have fpared their friends. They certainly expected the act would have gone down, and the ftamp-papers have been ufed. But it was the reverfe.

A general difcontent through the *Maffachufetts* difcovered itfelf immediately on the firft advice of the act's having paffed; but there was no other expectation among the bulk of the people, than that the act would be fubmitted to, and the duty paid; and feveral who afterward oppofed it violently, made intereft with the diftributor, that they or their friends might obtain appointments. The newfpapers indeed, groaned for the lofs of liberty; however, nothing extravagant appeared in them: but the friends to the claims of the colonies, pleafed with colonel Barre's fpeech, and what he had pronounced the Americans, affumed to themfelves the title of—SONS OF LIBERTY.

In Connecticut, the inhabitants were quite inattentive to the fatal confequences that the act might draw after it in fome diftant period. The judges themfelves, feveral of whom were of the council, appeared perfectly

M 4   fecure, secure, and were no ways alarmed. The Rev. Mr. *Stephen Johnson* of *Lyme*, vexed and grieved with the temper and inconfiderateness of all orders of people, determined if poffible to roufe them to a better way of thinking. He confulted a neighbouring gentleman, an Irifhman by birth, who undertook to convey the pieces he might pen to the *New London* printer, fo fecretly as to prevent the author's being difcovered. Three or four effays were publifhed upon the occafion. The eyes of the public began to open, and fears were excited. Other writers engaged in the bufinefs, while the firft withdrew, having fully anfwered his intention. The congregational minifters faw further into the defigns of the Britifh adminiftration than the bulk of the colony; and by their publications and converfation, increafed and ftrengthened the oppofition. It became fo confiderable, that when governor *Fitch* propofed that he and the counfellors fhould be fworn agreeable to the ftamp-act, colonel *Trumbull* * went out and refufed even to witnefs to the tranfaction. Others followed this fpirited example, and only four of the council remained.

In *Virginia* a general difpofition appeared to fubmit to the ftamp-act: but *George Johnfton* and *Patrick Henry* efqrs. confulted together; and afterward, at the clofe of the feffions, when there was but a thin houfe, many members being abfent preparing to return home, Mr. Henry brought in a number of refolves. They were as follows, viz. " Whereas the honorable houfe of commons in *England*, have of late drawn into queftion how far the general affembly of this colony hath power to enact laws for laying of taxes and impofing duties, pay-

* Now governor Trumbull.

able

able by the people of this his majefty's moft ancient colony—for fettling and afcertaining the fame to all future times, the houfe of burgeffes of this prefent general affembly, have come to the following refolves:

Refolved, That the firft adventurers, fettlers of this his majefty's colony and dominion of *Virginia,* brought with them and tranfmitted to their pofterity, and all other his majefty's fubjects fince inhabiting in this his majefty's faid colony, all the liberties, privileges, franchifes and immunities, that have at any time been held, enjoyed, and poffeffed by the people of *Great Britain:*

Refolved, That by two royal charters, granted by king *James* I. the colonifts aforefaid are declared and entitled to all liberties, privileges, and immunities of denizens and natural fubjects, to all intents and purpofes, as if they had been abiding and born within the realm of *England:*

Refolved, That his majefty's liege people of this ancient colony have enjoyed the right of being thus governed by their own affembly, in the article of taxes and internal police; and that the fame have never been forfeited, or any other way yielded up, but have been conftantly recognifed by the king and people of *Britain.*

Refolved, therefore, That the general affembly of this colony, together with his majefty or his fubftitutes, have in their reprefentative capacity, the only exclufive right and power to lay taxes and impofts upon the inhabitants of this colony; and that every attempt to veft fuch power in any other perfon or perfons whatfoever, than the general affembly aforefaid, is illegal, unconftitutional, and unjuft, and hath a manifeft tendency to deftroy *Britifh* as well as *American* liberty:

Refolved,

Refolved, That his majefty's liege people, the inhabitants of this colony, are not bound to yield obedience
to any law or ordinance whatever, defigned to impofe
any taxation whatfoever upon them, other than the laws
or ordinances of the general affembly aforefaid:

Refolved, That any perfon who fhall, by fpeaking or
writing, affert or maintain, that any perfon or perfons,
other than the general affembly of this colony, have any
right or power to impofe or lay any taxation on the
people here, fhall be deemed an enemy to this his majefty's colony."

Upon reading thefe refolves, the *Scotch* gentlemen in
the houfe, cried out treafon, &c. they were however
adopted. The next day, fome old members got them
revifed, though they could not carry it to reject them.
As revifed they ftand thus on the printed journals of the
houfe of burgeffes.

Thurfday, May 30, 1765.

May
30.

Refolved, That the firft adventurers, &c. &c. as
above:

Refolved, That by two royal charters, &c. &c.

Refolved, That the taxation of the people by themfelves, or by perfons chofen by themfelves to reprefent
them, who can only know what taxes the people are
able to bear, or the eafieft method of raifing them, and
muft themfelves be affected by every tax laid on the
people, is the only fecurity againft a burdenfome taxation; and the diftinguifhing characteriftic of *Britifh* freedom; without which the ancient conftitution cannot exift;

Refolved, That his majefty's liege people of this his
moft ancient and loyal colony have, without interruption,
enjoyed

enjoyed the ineftimable right of being governed by fuch laws, refpecting their internal polity and taxation, as are derived from their own confent, with the approbation of their fovereign or his fubftitute; and that the fame hath never been forfeited or yielded up, but hath been conftantly recognifed by the kings and people of *Great Britain.*"

Lieutenant governor Farquier diffolved the houfe of June burgeffes upon being made acquainted with their re- 1. folves.

A manufcript of the unrevifed refolves foon reached *Philadelphia*, having been fent off immediately upon their paffing, that the earlieft information of what had been done might be obtained by the fons of liberty. From thence the like was forwarded on the feventeenth of June. At *New York* the refolves were handed about with great privacy : they were accounted fo treafonable, that the poffeffors of them declined printing them in that city. The *Irifh* gentleman alluded to above, being there, inquired after them, and with much precaution was admitted to take a copy. He carried them to *New England*, where they were publifhed and circulated far and wide in the newfpapers, without any referve, and proved eventually the occafion of thofe diforders which afterward broke out in the colonies. Till they appeared, it was thought that the *Rhode Iflanders* would fubmit. Murmurs indeed were continually heard; but they feemed to be fuch as would die away. The Virginia refolutions gave a fpring to all the difgufted; and they began to adopt different meafures.

The *Maffachufetts* affembly had hit upon a wife and quiet mode of feeking redrefs, before ever they could

be

be acquainted with what had been done in Virginia. It was projected and brought on by Messrs. *Otis*'s, father and son. They were visiting at *James Warren*'s esq; of Plymouth, a son and brother in law, he having married Miss *Otis*. The state of public affairs, and how to get rid of the burdens coming upon the colonies, were the subjects of conversation. Congresses had often been held, and though there was no precedent of any one's being called, but at the instance of persons authorized or employed by the ministry, excepting the first congress we read of, which was proposed by the *Massachusetts* general court in 1690; yet no reasonable objection could be made against holding one upon the present emergency, notwithstanding it might want the sanction of administration. It was agreed to forward the meeting of a congress as a proper method for obtaining the removal of American grievances. The matter was moved in the house of assembly; the consequence

June 6.

was, an agreement that " It is highly expedient, there should be a meeting, as soon as may be, of committees from the houses of representatives or burgesses in the several colonies, to consult on the present circumstances of the colonies, and the difficulties to which they are and must be reduced, and to consider of a general address—to be held at New York the first Tuesday of October." Within two days, a letter was drafted to be sent to the several speakers; and at the close of a fortnight, *James Otis*, jun. *Oliver Partridge*, and *Timothy Ruggles* esqrs. were chosen the committee for the Massachusetts. The governor, in his account to the lords of trade, said, " It was impossible to oppose this measure to any good purpose; and therefore the friends of

govern-

government took the lead in it, and have kept it in their hands. Two of the three chosen are fast friends to government, prudent and discreet men, such as I am assured will never consent to any improper applications to the government of Great Britain." Lieutenant governor *Colden* designedly prorogued the meeting of the *New York* assembly, till after the time appointed for the congress; but the committee ordered, by the vote of the house of the eighteenth of October 1764, to be a committee during the recess, to write to and correspond with the several assemblies or committees of assemblies on the continent, did by virtue of that order, meet in congress; and the house afterward approved of their conduct, on the twentieth of November; and moreover resolved, " that for the obtaining relief from the operation and execution of the stamp-act, and other acts for levying duties and taxes on the colonies, humble petitions be prepared to the king, the house of lords, and the house of commons, as nearly similar to those drawn up by the congress as the particular circumstances of the colony will admit."

The assemblies of *Virginia*, *North Carolina*, and *Georgia* were prevented, by their governors, having the opportunity of sending committees to congress. *The Massachusetts-bay, Rhode-Island and Providence Plantations, Connecticut, New York, New Jersey, Pennsylvania, the Delaware Counties, Maryland* and *South Carolina*, had their respective committees present at the place appointed; and Mr. *Ruggles* was chosen chairman. The petition to the house of commons being finished was signed; though only by members from six colonies; the committees from *Connecticut, New York,* and *South Carolina,*

not

not having been fufficiently empowered. Mr. *Ruggles* took leave of the members, Thurfday evening the twenty-fourth of October, and came off the next morning without figning; for which he was afterward cenfured by the *Maffachufetts* affembly. Mr. *Otis* was upon the point of trefpaffing in like manner; but was prevented by the influence of Mr. *Thomas Lynch* of the *South Carolina* committee. The congrefs diffolved on October the twenty-fifth, having finifhed the bufinefs, to which they had been appointed. The colonies that could not fend committees, fhowed as opportunities offered; their approbation of what had been done, by forwarding to their agents petitions to the like purpofe with that of congrefs. *New Hampfhire* had excufed their not fending to congrefs, from the then fituation of their governmental affairs; but the fpeaker laying before the affembly the proceedings of congrefs, on November the twenty-fecond, they voted unanimoufly; " That this houfe do fully approve of and heartily join in the refolves and feveral petitions agreed to by the faid general congrefs; and that the fpeaker, with two others (all whofe names are mentioned) be empowered to fign the fame in behalf of this houfe, if not too late; if the general petitions are forwarded, in that cafe the faid petitions to be fairly engroffed, that they fign them in behalf of the houfe, and forward them with duplicates to *Barlow Trecothick* and *John Wentworth* efqrs. who are appointed fpecial agents for the houfe, and are empowered and defired to prefent the faid petitions, *&c.*" The committee wrote to thefe agents, on December the fixth, and concluded with faying, " We in this province have not been fo boifterous and irregular as fome others, not

Oct.
25.

becaufe

becaufe we were infenfible of our diftreffes; but becaufe we thought the prefent method moft likely to obtain relief."

The *Virginia* refolves having had their full operation, and the fpirits of the people being highly inflamed, the colonial difturbances break out upon the following occafion. Meffrs. *John Avery*, jun. *Thomas Crafts, John Smith, Henry Welles, Thomas Chace, Stephen Cleverly, Henry Bafs*, and *Benjamin Edes*, to manifeft their abhorrence and deteftation of thofe perfons, who they fuppofed were endeavouring to fubvert the Britifh conftitution, to enflave the colonies, and to alienate the affections of his majefty's moft faithful fubjects in America, provide and hang out early in the morning of Auguft the fourteenth, upon the limb of a large old elm, toward the entrance of Bofton, over the moft public ftreet, two effigies, one of which by the labels, appears to be defigned for the ftamp officer; the other is a jack boot, with a head and horns peeping out of the top. Not only the ufual paffengers pafs under it, but the report fpreads and draws great numbers from every part of the town, and the neighbouring country. The affair is left to take its own courfe, an enthufiaftic fpirit diffufes itfelf through the body of the fpectators. In the evening the pageantry is cut down, and carried in funeral proceffion, the populace fhouting, *liberty and property for ever—no ftamps*, &c. &c. They direct their way to a new building, lately erected by Mr. *Oliver*, which they pull down, falfely fuppofing it to be defigned for the ftamp-office. They go on to his houfe, before which they behead his effigy, breaking at the fame time all the windows next the ftreet. They then repair to

Aug. 14.

Fort Hill, on the afcent to which ftands his houfe, where they burn his effigy. After this they return to attack his premifes; and many of them with clubs, ftaves, &c. go to work on the garden, fences, barns, &c. Mr. Oliver had prudently retired, leaving a few friends behind to keep poffeffion of the dwelling: thefe committing fome flight indifcretions, the populace are fo enraged, that they force themfelves into the lower part of it, break the windows and deftroy the furniture.

15. They difperfe about midnight. The next day Mr. Oliver, fearful of what may otherwife happen, declares that he has written to England, and refigned. The mob affemble again at night: and, after fome expreffions of joy for the refignation, proceed to the lieutenant governor's, Mr. *Hutchinfon*'s houfe, which they befiege for an hour, though in vain, infifting repeatedly upon knowing whether he had not written in favor of the ftamp-act: at length, through the influence of fome difcreet perfons, they withdraw, and finifh their evening's entertainment at a bonfire.

26. Eleven days after, the diforders grow more enormous and alarming. In the evening a number of perfons, difguifed and armed with clubs, fticks, &c. collect in King-ftreet, in confequence of a preconcerted plan. They go firft to Mr. *Paxton*'s, marfhall of the court of admiralty and furveyor of the port; being affured by the owner of the houfe, that Mr. Paxton had quitted it with his beft effects; and being invited by him to the tavern to drink a barrel of punch, they accept the offer, and the houfe is faved. Having finifhed the punch, they proceed to and attack the houfe of Mr. *William Story*, deputy regifter of the court of admiralty; break the windows;

windows; force into the dwelling; ftrip the office of the
books and files belonging to the faid court; burn and
deftroy them, with many other papers; injure and ruin
a great part of his furniture.

It is the opinion of fome, that the firft movers in the
affair meant mainly an affault upon the houfe of the
deputy regifter, who, by various mal-practices, had
made himfelf highly obnoxious to perfons doing bufinefs at his office. But mobs once raifed, foon become
ungovernable by new and large acceffions, and extend
their intentions far beyond thofe of the original inftiga-
tors. Crafty men may intermix with them, when they
are much heated, and direct their operations quite differently from what was at firft defigned.

How far the fcheme of the prefent mob extended,
when it firft collected, is hard to fay; but upon leaving
Mr. *Story*'s, they proceed to the houfe of Mr. *Benjamin
Hallowell*, comptroller of the cuftoms for Bofton; and
to the repetition of fimilar exceffes to what have been
juft committed, add the drinking and deftroying of
liquors in the cellars, the taking away of wearing apparel, the breaking open of defk and drawers, and the
carrying off of thirty pounds fterling in money. Many
being now inflamed with liquor, and numbers having
joined them, they become more riotous, and are ready
for any mifchief. They hurry away to Mr. *Hutchinfon*'s houfe with the rage of madmen. He fends off
his children; bars his doors and windows; and means
to remain; but is foon under the neceffity of withdrawing, firft to one houfe, then to another, where he continues till four in the morning; by which time, one of
the beft finifhed houfes in the colony has nothing re-

maining but the bare walls and floors. Gentlemen of the army, who have feen towns facked by an enemy, declare they never before faw an inftance of fuch fury. The rioters carry off about nine hundred pounds fterling, befide plate, family pictures, houfhold furniture of every kind, and the apparel of the lieutenant governor, his children and fervants. They alfo empty the houfe of every thing whatfoever, except a part of the kitchen furniture; and fcatter or deftroy all the manufcripts and other papers he has been collecting for thirty years back, befides a great number of public papers in his cuftody. The lofs of papers is irreparable.

27.   The next dav it was ftrongly reported, by the enemies of Dr. *Jonathan Mayhew*, that he approved of thefe doings; and had, indeed, encouraged them, in a fermon preached the preceding Lord's day on *Gal.* v. 12, 13. This led him to write immediately to Mr. Hutchinfon; and in his letter he condoled with him, " on account of the almoft unparalleled outrages, committed at his houfe the preceding evening;" and faid, " God is my witnefs, that, from the bottom of my heart, I deteft thefe proceedings; and that I am fincerely grieved for them, and have a deep fympathy with you, and your diftreffed family on this occafion. I did, indeed, exprefs myfelf ftrongly, in favor of civil and religious liberty, as I hope I fhall ever continue to do; and fpoke of the ftamp act as a great grievance, like to prove detrimental, in a high degree, both to the colonies and the mother country; and I have heard your honor fpeak to the fame purpofe. But, as my text led me to do, I cautioned my hearers very particularly, againft the abufes of liberty; and expreffed my hopes,

that

that no perfons among ourfelves had encouraged the
bringing of fuch a burden on their country, notwithftanding it had been ftrongly fufpected. In truth, Sir,
I had rather lofe my hand, than be an encourager of
fuch outrages as were committed laft night. I do not
think my regard to truth was ever called into queftion,
by thofe that knew me ; and therefore hope your honor
will be fo juft as to give intire credit to thefe folemn
declarations."

This fame day the fuperior court began its term.
The chief juftice, Mr. *Hutchinfon*, attended in his only
fuit, and necefFarily without thofe enfigns of office, fo
wifely calculated to procure regard to authority; while
the other gentlemen of the bench and bar appeared in
their refpective robes. The court refufed to do any
bufinefs, and adjourned to the fifteenth of October, to
fhow their refentment of the infult offered the lieutenant
governor, as well as their fenfe of the anarchy to which
the government was reduced. Half a dozen of the
dregs of the people, who, being taken up, refufed to
difcover the ringleaders, were committed. Three broke
jail and fled, againft one of whom a bill was found:
againft the other three in cuftody none was found; for
it was not thought fafe to profecute. The temper of
the public would not admit of it, without hazarding
further difturbances; and for that reafon, one, who was
capitally charged with being a principal in the riot, and
fecured, was finally difmiffed by the juftices.

Various caufes might contribute toward the outrageous
attack upon the houfe and property of Mr. Hutchinfon. As long back as 1748, the currency having depreciated to about an eighth of its original value, he,

N 2 being

being then fpeaker of the houfe, projected and carried
through a bill for abolifhing it, and fubftituting gold
and filver in its place, which made him extremely obnoxious to feveral, who had lived by fraud, and were
much diffatisfied with the alteration. They then threatened him with deftruction; and, retaining their rancour,
are fuppofed to have been aiders and abettors, if not
actors in the riot.—A certain gentleman of great integrity, and who fills a place in the judicial department,
with much credit and to the fatisfaction of the public,
has expreffed a ftrong apprehenfion, that the mob was
led on to the houfe, by a fecret influence, with a view
to the deftruction of certain papers, known to be there,
and which, it is thought, would have proved, that the
grant to the New Plymouth company on Kennebec
river, was different from what was contended for by
fome claimants. The papers were never found afterward.—But Mr. *Hutchinfon* had certainly difgufted the
people exceedingly, by promoting the fuperior court's
granting writs of affiftance; and by fhowing himfelf fo
ftrenuous in fupporting government, when become odious, by the meafures adopted for obliging the colonies
to pay taxes in compliance with Britifh acts of parliament.—He was alfo ftrongly fufpected of having forwarded the ftamp-act, by letters written upon the occafion. Thefe circumftances, co-operating with the general difpofition in the people to tumult, produced by a
prevailing perfuafion, that they were deprived of the
liberties of Englifhmen, will account for the exceffive
outrages againft him in particular. But their enormity,
was alarming. No one knew who might be the next
facrifice. The town of Bofton therefore, befide con-
demning

demning them the next day, unanimoufly voted, " That the felect men and magistrates be defired to ufe their utmoft endeavours to fupprefs the like diforders for the future:" and for fome time, the magiftrates and private gentlemen, the cadet and other companies, kept watch at night to prevent further violences.

In juftice to Mr. *Hutchinfon* it muft be obferved, that from his letters to Meffrs. *Bollan*, *Jackfon*, and others, it appears, that he then confidered parliament's taxing the colonies as inconfiftent with the rights of the colonifts, and as a mere act of power, without regard to equity. He was at the trouble of writing a pamphlet in 1764, containing *A brief ftate of the claim of the colonies, and the intereft of the nation with refpect to them.* This, when he had difguifed it fo as that it might not be fufpected to come from America, he fent to Mr. Jackfon the agent, who was either to fupprefs or publifh it; and he afterward expreffed a furprife at his not having done the latter. The following are extracts from it.

" The right to new acquired countries, according to the conftitution of England, two hundred years ago, was allowed to be in the crown. The crown from time to time difpofed of thefe countries, not only to their own fubjects but to foreign princes: particularly *Acadie* and *Nova Scotia*, when begun to be fettled by Britifh fubjects, were ceded to *France*, although France had no better claim to them than to New England: and *Surinam* was fold to, or exchanged with the *Dutch*." He might have adduced in proof of James I. being of opinion, that he had a perfonal right to alienate at pleafure new acquired territory, his granting, in September 1621, *Nova Scotia*, which he could not inherit but as king of

England, to Sir *William Alexander* of Menftry, afterward Lord Stirling, under the feal of Scotland; and
his erecting it into a palatinate, to be holden as a fief
of the crown of Scotland.   Under the fame feal, and
in the fame words, the grant was confirmed by Charles I.
in June 1625.   The legality of thefe grants appear not
to have been queftioned at the time, which indicates that
the prevailing opinion of the Englifh correfponded then
with that of their fovereigns.

Mr. Hutchinfon goes on to mention, " *American*
lands in their natural ftate are of no value : there is not
any colony which has not coft more to make it capable
of rendering profit than it is now worth."

" In the trading towns, in fome of the colonies the laft
war, one fourth part of the profit of the trade was annually paid to the fupport of the war, and other public
charges.   In the country towns, a farm which would not
rent for twenty pounds a year, paid ten pounds taxes.
Was it from parental affection to the colonifts, and to fave
them from French vaffalage, that Great Britain was at
fuch expence; or was it from fear of lofing the advan-
tageous trade fhe had carried on with her colonies?"

" When there is peace in Europe, what occafion is
there for any national expence in America ?"

" It cannot be gcod policy to tax the Americans ; it
will prove prejudicial to the national interefts.   The advantages propofed by the increafe of the revenue, are
fallacious and delufive.   You will lofe more than you
will gain.   Britain reaps the profit of all their trade, and
of the increafe of their fubftance."

" Your commerce with the colonies will be enough
for you, fhould you have no commerce elfewhere, if
                                                              you

you encourage the colonies to increafe the confumption of your manufactures for fifty years to come, as they have done for fifty years paft; and with no more than reafonable encouragement they will infallibly do it, and in much greater proportion."

Though the difturbances began in *Bofton*, yet they were not confined to the *Maffachufetts*. They broke out in the other colonies; and fo near to the fame time, as to excite fufpicions, that it was not wholly the effect of accident, but partly of a preconcerted defign. *Rhode Ifland* and *Providence* Plantations fhowed themfelves among the foremoft in their oppofition to the ftamp-act.

A gazette extraordinary was publifhed at *Providence*, Aug. with *Vox populi*, *Vox Dei*, in large letters for the fron- 24. tifpiece; and underneath, *Where the Spirit of the Lord is, there is liberty*. The publication had a tendency to prepare the people for action. Effigies were alfo exhibited; and in the evening, cut down and burnt by the populace.

About nine in the morning, the people of *Newport* 27. in *Rhode Ifland* brought forth three effigies, meant for Meffrs. *Howard*, *Moffatt*, and *Johnfton*, in a cart with halters about their necks, to a gallows near the townhoufe, where they were hung; after a while cut down, and burnt amid the acclamations of thoufands.

By the next day there was time enough to hear of 28. what had been done at *Bofton*. The people collected, or rather were muftered afrefh, and befat the houfe of Mr. *Martin Howard* jun. a lawyer of reputation, and a writer in defence of the parliament's right to tax the colonies. They deftroyed every thing, and left only a fhell. They paffed on to Dr. *Thomas Moffatt's*, a phy-

fician,

sician, one who had warmly supported in conversation the same right, and behaved in like manner. They intended doing it to Mr. *Augustus Johnston*, but desisted upon persuasion ; and on his coming to town, and giving it under his hand that he would not accept the office of distributor of the stamps, unless the public were satisfied, they became quiet. Messrs. Howard and Moffatt hastened on board a ship of war for personal safety.

The commotions in *Connecticut* were not equally violent : but Mr. *Ingersoll* was the subject of exhibition in divers places.

Aug. 22.   They had their pageantry at *Norwich*, which they committed to the flames, when the day closed.

26.   They had the same at *Lebanon*; but before they executed and burnt, they had the parade of a mock trial.

27.   The next day there was a repetition of the like, excepting the trial. At length the resentment against the stamp-distributor became so general and alarming, that he resigned his office.

A like resignation takes place in *New York*, some time in August. It becomes a necessary point of prudence, from the spirit which the citizens discover. The stamp-act is treated with the most indignant contempt, by being printed and cried about the streets, under the title of, *The folly of* ENGLAND *and ruin of* AMERICA. Toward the end of October the stamp papers arrive ; and Mr. M'Evers having resigned, lieutenant governor *Colden* takes them into *Fort George.* Some extraordinary preparations for securing them having displeased the inhabitants, joined to the dislike they have entertained to

Nov. 1.   *Colden*'s political sentiments, and its being the day for the stamp-act to take place, numbers are induced to

assemble

assemble in the evening. They proceed to the fort walls; break open his stable; take out his coach; and, after carrying it through the principal streets of the city in triumph, march to the common, where a gallows is erected; on one end of which they suspend his effigy, having in his right hand a stamped bill of lading, and in the other, a figure for the devil. After hanging a considerable time, they carry the whole, with the gallows intire, the coach preceding, in procession to the gate of the fort; from whence it is removed to the bowling-green, under the muzzles of the guns; where a bonfire is immediately made, and all, coach included, are consumed amid the exultations of some thousands of spectators. They go from hence to major *James's* house, before known by the name of *Vaux-hall*, which is genteely furnished; contains a valuable library and many curiosities, and has a handsome garden belonging to it. They strip it of every article, make another bonfire, and consume the whole, beside destroying the garden; and all because of his being a friend to the stamp-act.

The next morning a paper is privately drawn up, and given to a man to read from the balcony of the coffee house, to and about which the citizens are used to frequent: it sets forth the necessity of being peaceable, and calls upon the inhabitants to turn out with their arms upon any alarm, and quell all riotous proceedings. The effect it appears to have upon being heard, is frustrated by captain *Isaac Sears*, who formerly commanded a privateer, and is bitterly set against the stamp-act. Having been secretly informed in the morning what is to be done, he is present, and tells the populace, who collect about him, " The intention of the proposal that has

Nov. 2.

been

been read, is to prevent our having the ſtamp papers;"
and adds, " but we will have them within four and
twenty hours." He then flouriſhes his hat, and cries,
" Huzza, my lads." They immediately comply in
loud ſhouts. He turns to ſeveral gentlemen preſent, and
ſays, " Your beſt way, as you may now ſee, will be to
adviſe lieutenant governor *Colden* to ſend the ſtamp
papers from the fort to the inhabitants." In the evening the mob aſſemble, and inſiſt upon his delivering
them into their hands. He hopes to ſatisfy them, by
declaring he will do nothing in relation to the ſtamps,
but leave it to Sir Henry Moore to do as he pleaſes on
his arrival. The people are not contented; they will
have the ſtamps, or attempt taking them away by force;
which muſt probably be attended with much bloodſhed.
After repeated negotiation, it is agreed, that they ſhall be
delivered to the corporation; which is accordingly done,
and they are depoſited in the city hall, to general ſatisfaction. Ten boxes of the like, which arrive afterward,
meet with a worſe fate, being committed to the flames.

The deſtruction of major *James*'s houſe, (for it was
reduced to a ſhell) convinced the gentlemen, who were
ſtanding up for the rights of the colonies, that it was
neceſſary to have leaders to manage the mob. It was
therefore contrived to call the people together.

Nov.
6.
They met in the fields; and it was propoſed, that a
committee be appointed to open a correſpondence with
the other colonies. This was a meaſure of ſo ſerious
and important a nature, as to endanger the property and
lives of the committee, eſpecially ſhould the ſtamp-act
be enforced and carried through; and therefore there
was no one, for more than half an hour, who would
venture

venture to accept. Mr. *James De Lancey*, who had joined the popular fide, in order to fecure a feat in the affembly at the next general election, was nominated; but declined, pleading his being upon the committee to converfe with the lawyers, on their proceeding to bufinefs without ftamps, inftead of fufpending it, as they appeared to intend. At length, however, captain Sears with four others offered, and were approved.

They agreed among themfelves to fign all the letters with their feveral names, and to open a correfpondence with all the colonies. The *Philadelphians* were requefted to forward their enclofed letters to the more fouthern ftates, and the *Boftonians* to forward thofe for *New Hampfhire*.

Here we fee another fet of correfponding fons of liberty originated, to ftrengthen the oppofition of the colonies to parliamentary taxation.

The commotions beyond *New York* did not terminate in fimilar exceffes to what had happened there, at *Newport*, and *Bofton*; but the exhibition of effigies in the day, the burning them at night, and other marks of difpleafure, induced the ftamp officers to refign. Some did it with a better grace than others. Mr. *George Mercer*, diftributor for *Virginia*, arrived in the evening at *Williamfburgh*. The people immediately urged him to refign. The next day he declined acting, in fo genteel a manner, that he had the repeated acclamations of all prefent. At night the town was illuminated, the bells were fet a ringing, and all was joy and feftivity.

At *Philadelphia*, upon the appearance of the fhips, Oct. having on board the ftamps, all the veffels in the har- 5. bour hoifted their colours half ftaff high; the bells were

muffled

muffled and continued to toll till evening; and every countenance added to' the marks of fincere mourning. A large number of people, chiefly of the prefbyterian perfuafion, and of the proprietary party, with *William Allen* efq; the chief juftice's' fon at their head, affembled and endeavoured to procure the ftamp diftributor's refignation. It had been for fome time warmly talked of, that he ought to refign. Mr. *Hughes* was obnoxious to both the prefbyterian and the proprietary party; but particularly hateful to the latter, as it was his *intereft, affiduity and influence,* in the *Pennfylvania* houfe of affembly, that enabled the province to fend home Dr. *Franklin* to prefent their petitions, for a change of government from proprietary to royal—a change highly difagreeable to each party. The body of quakers feemed difpofed to pay obedience to the ftamp-act, and fo did part of the church of *England,* and of the baptifts not under proprietary influence. But no pains were fpared to engage the *Dutch* and lower clafs of people in the oppofition; and though Mr. *Hughes* held out long *, yet he found it neceffary at length to comply.

Mr. *Hood,* ftamp diftributor for *Maryland,* that he might avoid refigning, fled to *New York,* and obtained protection in the fort. Upon Sir *Henry Moore*'s arrival he left the fort, and went to *Long Ifland.* A number of the freemen croffed over unexpectedly; furprifed him; obliged him to fign a paper, declaring his abfolute and final refignation; and then took him before a magiftrate, to whom he read the paper, and afterward made oath to the matter therein contained.

* Mr. Hughes's letters of October and November 1765.

At

At *Boston* they took care to keep up the spirit of liberty, though they avoided former violences. A new political Sept. paper appeared under the significant title of " The ²¹· Constitutional Courant, containing matters interesting to *liberty*, and no ways repugnant to *loyalty*; printed by *Andrew Marvel*, at the sign of the *Bribe refused*, on *Constitution Hill, North America*." It wore a more significant head piece—a snake cut into eight pieces, the head part having N E the initials of *New England* affixed to it, and the rest the initials of the other colonies to *South Carolina* inclusively, and in order, N Y, N J, P, M, V, N C, S C. The device accompanying them was I O I N or D I E.

The morning of the day when the stamp-act took Nov. place, was ushered in with the tolling of bells. The ¹· large old elm (which since the fourteenth of August, when the riots began, had been adorned with an inscription, and obtained the name of *liberty tree*, as the ground under it had that of *liberty hall*; and which gave rise to other trees being so called, upon an appropriation to popular purposes by the sons of liberty) was decorated with two effigies. They were cut down at three o'clock, amid the acclamations of thousands; carried about town, then to the gallows upon the Neck; there hung up again; after a while cut down; torn in pieces and scattered. The people repaired home; and the evening passed away quietly. But a transaction took place afterward, not much to the credit of the town.

Mr. *Oliver* was called upon by a letter from (as it Dec. was improperly signed) *the true sons of liberty*, to make ¹⁶· a public resignation of his office on the morrow, under liberty tree. He desired a gentleman to interpose, and procure

procure him at leaft leave to refign at the town-houfe ;
but after feveral confultations, nothing more could be
obtained than a promife of having no affront offered,
and a propofal to invite the principal perfons of the
town to accompany him.   He was obliged to repair to
liberty tree; there to read his declaration in the prefence
of more than two thoufand people ; and then to fwear
to it before a juftice, on the fpot for that purpofe.   The
cool, firm, and judicious fons of liberty, muft condemn
this procedure toward the fecretary, as mean, revenge-
ful, and cruel.   It was torturing his feelings afrefh, as
upon a ftage, in the moft confpicuous manner, after
having been terrified into a refignation four months before ; and when it might be expected, that the bitternefs
of the refentment againft him was ended.

The oppofition to the ftamp officers was not confined
to the continent.   The people of St. *Kitts* obliged the
diftributor and his deputy to refign.   *Barbadoes* fubmitted to the act.   *Jamaica* in general cleared out with
ftamps ; but *Kingfton*, as before, without.   Upon the
continent, *Canada* and *Halifax* fubmitted.

The general fear that individuals were under, either
of diftributing or ufing ftamps, was increafed in one
government by the following paper, pafted up at the
door of every public office, and at the corner of the
ftreets—

Pro Patria.

The firft man that either diftributes or makes ufe of
ftamped paper, let him take care of his houfe,
perfon, and effects.

We dare   Vox Populi.

The

The public refentment was kept alive and lively by the contemptuous treatment which the ftamp-act itfelf met with, being openly burnt in feveral places with the effigies of the officers; and by caricatures, pafquinades, puns, bon mots, and fuch vulgar fayings fitted to the occafion, as by being fhort, could be moft eafily circulated and retained, while, being extremely expreffive, they carried with them the weight of a great many arguments.

The refignation of the officers, and the want of perfons, either to undertake the delivery of ftamps, or to receive and ufe them, neceffarily laid the colonifts under a legal inability for doing bufinefs, according to parliamentary law. They however ventured upon it, and rifked the confequence. The veffels failed from the ports as before; excepting that, in fome inftances, a certificate was given that the perfon appointed to diftribute ftamp'd papers in the province, refufed to deliver them, which certificate being handed by the mafters to the naval officer, they were admitted to give bond in his office, and to pafs through the other offices without ftamps. The *Rhode Ifland* and *Providence* Plantations kept their courts open the whole time, even when they were fufpended in the other colonies. Toward the end of November, it was agreed in *Maryland* and *Virginia* to proceed on bufinefs in the ufual manner without ftamps. In the Maffachufetts the popular party fo far prevailed, that the houfe of affembly refolved, January the twenty-third 1766, "That the fhutting up the courts of juftice is a very great grievance; and that the judges, juftices, and all other public officers in this province ought to proceed as ufual." But when the fuperior

rior

rior court opened, on the eleventh of March, the parties
concerned evaded the profecuting of bufinefs. The
lawyers in a body waited, as ufual, upon the judges, on
the firft day of the term, before they went into the court.
The chief juftice, Mr. Hutchinfon, not being prefent at
this meeting, Mr. Peter Oliver faid he attended according to his duty, and that he underftood it would be expected that he and his brethren fhould proceed in bufinefs
in defiance of the late act of parliament: fuch proceeding, he added, was contrary to his judgment and opinion; and if he fubmitted to it, it would be only for
felf-prefervation, as he knew he was in the hands of the
populace: he therefore previoufly protefted, that all fuch
acts of his, if they fhould happen, would be acts under
durefs. To which the other judges affenting, it was
propofed to each of the lawyers fingly, *Do you defire
that bufinefs fhould proceed contrary to the act of parliament?* Every one of them anfwered in the negative,
even Mr. Otis himfelf. But they faid, it would be proper to try a caufe or two to quiet the people: accordingly one caufe, which had been at iffue before the
ftamp-act took place, was tried, and all other civil bufinefs was poftponed to the middle of April.

Though the violent and riotous proceedings, which
have been noticed, were feverely cenfured by many; and
numbers in all the colonies, might feem inclined to fubmit
to the ftamp-act, yet the right of impofing it was univerfally condemned, and the colonial rights as univerfally
acceded to by the moft peaceably difpofed. The refolutions of the *Pennfylvania* affembly, which met at *Philadelphia* in September 1765, were paffed *nemine contra-
dicente*; and left upon their minutes, " as a teftimony
of

1765.
Sept.

of the zeal and ardent defire of that houfe, to preferve
their ineftimable rights, which as *Englifhmen* they poffeffed ever fince the province was fettled, and to tranfmit
them to their lateft pofterity." They " refolved, That
the only legal reprefentatives of the inhabitants of this
province, are the perfons they annually elect to ferve as
members of affembly—Refolved therefore, That the
taxation of the people of this province by any other perfons whatfoever, than fuch their reprefentatives in affembly, is unconftitutional, and fubverfive of their moft
valuable rights—Refolved, That the laying of taxes
upon the inhabitants of this province, in any other manner, being naturally fubverfive of public liberty, muft,
of neceffary confequence, be utterly deftructive of public
happinefs *." There might not be fo many quakers in
the houfe as ufual; the times probably occafioned a
larger choice out of other denominations; but there muft
have been feveral, and thefe we find acquiefced. Thefe
refolutions are as much oppofed to the claims of the
Britifh parliament, as are thofe of the *Maffachufetts* affembly, paffed October the twenty-ninth. Indeed the
latter dwell more upon the unalienable effential rights of
mankind, of which thefe cannot be divefted, confiftent
with the law of God and nature, by any law of fociety;
and they evidently mark it out, in their opinion, as one
of thofe rights, that no man can juftly take the property
of another without his confent. They alfo refolved,
that a reprefentation in parliament of the inhabitants of
their province, fuch as the fubjects in Britain actually
enjoy, is impracticable for the fubjects in America †.

* See the Gentleman's Magazine, Vol. XXXV. p. 538.   † Ibid.
Vol. XXXVI. p. 94.

But both affemblies, though their expreffions differed, agreed in refolving, that the extenfions of the court of admiralty within the provinces, is a moft violent infraction of the right of trials by juries. The refolves of the *Maryland* and *Connecticut* affemblies, paffed, the one September the twenty-eighth, and the other November the firft, breathed the fame fpirit *.

Oct. 31.
But we have now to attend to a judicious meafure, purfued by the *New York* merchants, the more effectually to obtain a repeal of the ftamp-act. They refolved to direct their correfpondents not to fhip any more goods till it was repealed; and that they would not fell any goods upon commiffion, which fhould be fhipped from Britain, after the firft of January, unlefs upon that condition. They were the foremoft in adopting the nonimportation agreement; and recommended the like conduct to the *Maffachufetts* and the neighbouring provinces in trade.

Nov. 7.
The merchants and traders of *Philadelphia* had a general meeting, and entered into a fimilar agreement. Some quakers, who would not fign the combination, thought it prudent to be governed by the fame reftriction; and gave directions that the goods ordered fhould not be fent, unlefs the ftamp-act was repealed.

Dec. 9.
It was not till December the ninth that the merchants and traders of *Bofton* refolved upon a non-importation. Government may deem fuch combinations illegal, as they are apt to do all that are oppofed to their own meafures; but furely the cafe of communities is bad indeed, if they have not a right voluntarily to agree among

* Gentleman's Magazine, Vol. XXXVI. p. 94 and 95.

themfelves,

themfelves, merely to fufpend buying till they can obtain their own terms, when equitable.

The peaceable line purfued in thefe agreements, had
not been attended to by all who oppofed the ftamp-act.
They therefore, for their own fafety, had a recourfe to
another, which might have drenched the country with
blood, had not the repeal prevented. The way had been
prepared by the publication of a fyftem of politics,
which appeared originally in the New York papers, the
principal point of which was, that the colonies are no
otherwife related to Great Britain but by having the fame
king. The effays meant to propagate and fupport this
fyftem made their firft appearance in the New York
prints, but moft probably fome of the manufcripts were
fent from Bofton. The New York fons of liberty
had, at length, a meeting, wherein they refolved, that
they would go to the extremity with lives and fortunes
to prevent the ftamp-act. This fpirit produced the following agreement between them and the fons of liberty
in Connecticut.

" Certain reciprocal and mutual agreements, concef- Dec.
fions and affociations made, concluded and agreed upon 25.
by and between the fons of liberty of the colony of
New York of the one part, and the fons of liberty of the
colony of *Connecticut* on the other part, this twenty-fifth
day of December, in the fixth year of the reign of our
fovereign Lord *George* the Third, by the grace of God,
of *Great Britain*, *France* and *Ireland* king, defender of
the faith, and in the year of our Lord one thoufand feven
hundred and fixty-five.

The aforefaid parties taking into their moft ferious
confideration the melancholy and unfettled ftate of *Great*

Britain

Britain and her *North American colonies,* proceeding as they are fully perfuaded, from a defign in her moft infidious and inveterate enemies, to alienate the affections of his majefty's moft loyal and faithful fubjects of *North America* from his perfon and government—Therefore to prevent as much as in us lies the diffolution of fo ineftimable an union, they do, in the prefence of *Almighty God,* declare that they bear the moft unfhaken faith and true allegiance to his majefty King *George* the Third— that they are moft affectionately and zealoufly attached to his royal perfon and family, and are fully determined to the utmoft of their power, to maintain and fupport his crown and dignity, and the fucceffion as by law eftablifhed; and with the greateft cheerfulnefs they fubmit to his government, according to the known and juft principles of the BRITISH CONSTITUTION, which they conceive to be founded on the eternal and immutable principles of juftice and equity, and that every attempt to violate or wreft it, or any part of it from them, under whatever pretence, colour or authority, is an heinous fin againft God, and the moft daring contempt of the people, from whom (under God) all juft government fprings. From a facred regard to all which, and a juft fenfe of the impending evils that might befal them, in confequence of fuch a dreadful diffolution, They do hereby voluntarily, and of their own free will, as well for the fupport of his majefty's juft prerogative and the Britifh conftitution as their own mutual fecurity and prefervation, agree and concede to affociate, advife, protect, and defend each other in the peaceable, full and juft enjoyment of their inherent and accuftomed rights as Britifh fubjects of their refpective *colonies,* not in the

least

leaft defiring any alteration or innovation in the grand bulwark of their liberties and the wifdom of ages, but only to preferve it inviolate from the corrupt hands of its implacable enemies—And whereas a certain pamphlet has appeared in America in the form of an act of parliament, called and known by the name of the *Stamp-Act*, but has never been legally publifhed or introduced, neither can it, as it would immediately deprive them of the moft invaluable part of the Britifh conftitution, viz. the trial by juries, and the moft juft mode of taxation in the world, that is, of taxing themfelves, rights that every Britifh fubject becomes heir to as foon as born. For the prefervation of which, and every part of the Britifh conftitution, they do reciprocally refolve and determine to march with the utmoft difpatch, at their own proper cofts and expence, on the firft proper notice, (which muft be fignified to them by at leaft fix of the fons of liberty) with their whole force if required, and it can be fpared, to the relief of thofe that fhall, are, or may be in danger from the *ftamp-act*, or its promoters and abettors, or any thing relative to it, on account of any thing that may have been done in oppofition to its obtaining—And they do mutually and moft fervently recommend it to each other to be vigilant in watching all thofe who, from the nature of their offices, vocations or difpofitions, may be the moft likely to introduce the ufe of ftamped papers, to the total fubverfion of the Britifh conftitution and American liberty; and the fame, when difcovered, immediately to advife each other of, let them be of what rank or condition foever; and they do agree, that they will mutually, and to the utmoft of their power, by all juft ways and means, endeavour to

O 3   bring

bring all such betrayers of their country to the most condign punishment—And further, they do mutually resolve to defend the liberty of the press in their respective colonies from all unlawful violations and impediments whatever, on account of the said act, as the only means (under divine Providence) of preserving their lives, liberties and fortunes, and the same in regard to the judges, clerks, attornies, &c. that shall proceed without any regard to the *stamp-act*, from all pains, fines, mulcts, penalties, or any molestation whatever—And finally, that they will, to the utmost of their power, endeavour to bring about, accomplish, and perfect the like *association* with all the *colonies* on the continent for the like salutary purposes and no other."

The opposition to the stamp-act raged apparently more in New York and Connecticut than in the Massachusetts; but the association being agreed upon, was sent by express to the sons of liberty at *Boston*, and received Sunday the second of February 1766. On its receipt, letters were forwarded to a few individuals; and on the sixth of February, a circular letter to the several towns in the colony, containing the association, and the desire of the first original associators to accomplish the like association, with a request to be informed of the sentiments and dispositions of the people in such towns. A letter was also sent on the same subject, to the sons of liberty at *Portsmouth* in *Hampshire* colony. They met; and in their answer of February the eighth, testified their approbation of the measure already taken, and their determination to oppose the execution of the stamp-act, &c.

The

The *Boston* sons of liberty accepted the proposal of uniting themselves to *New York* and *Connecticut*; and in their letter to the brotherhood at *Norwich*, proposed to commence a continental union, of which the latter greatly approved in their answer of February the tenth.

On February the thirteenth, the sons of liberty at *Bos-* 13. *ton* wrote a *circular letter* to *New Hampshire, Connecticut* and *New York*; and before the month was ended, the *New Yorkers* sent circular letters as far as *South Carolina*, urging a *continental union*.

Most of the towns in the *Massachusetts*, having been applied to, signified " their determination to march with their whole force to the support of the British constitution, and consequently the relief of those that shall or may be in any danger from the stamp-act or its abettors."

It is not to be supposed, that the disorderly proceedings, above related, were chargeable solely on the dregs of the colonies. The sons of liberty at New York, who held regular meetings, were said to be directed by much greater persons than any that appeared among them. The mobs consisted not of mere rabble; but were composed much of independent freemen and freeholders, so that some of the first people in the provinces were intimidated, and left the cause of the parliament without proper support. Merchants, assemblymen, magistrates, &c. united directly or indirectly in the riots, and without their influence and instigation the lower class of inhabitants would have been quiet; but great pains were taken to rouse them into action. At *Boston* such was the protection and countenance given to the rioters, that some of the principal ringleaders walked the streets

with

with impunity, no officer daring to attack them, no attorney general to profecute them, no witnefs to appear againft them, and no judge to fit upon them. But when the enormities are faid to have originated from the Prefbyterians and Congregationalifts, the charge muft be imputed to malevolence, or to grofs ignorance, or a mixture of both. The gentlemen on the fide of government, who were upon the fpot, in their letters written at the time, placed them to the account of the *Virginia* refolves. Mr. *Hutchinfon* tells his correfpondent, " Nothing extravagant appeared in the papers till an account was received of the *Virginia* refolves." Mr. *Hughes* writes, " the fire began in *Virginia:*" governor *Bernard*, " the publifhing the *Virginia* refolutions proved an alarum bell to the difaffected:" another, in his letter to Mr. Secretary *Conway*, from *New York*, " the refolves of the affembly of *Virginia* gave the fignal for a general outcry over the continent." The *Virginians* are epifcopalians, and if there is either blame or merit, in exciting that fixed and fpirited oppofition to the ftamp-act, which followed upon their refolves, let them be credited for the fame : to them belongs the honor or difgrace ; and folely to particular colonies the difgrace of the feveral enormities committed in them. The bulk of the people at *Bofton* are congregationalifts ; at *New York*, the prefbyterians, including the Dutch and foreign focieties, may poffibly be fully equal to, or even exceed the epifcopalians. At *Newport* all denominations are equally encouraged, and enjoy no afcendency over each other, and therefore might be equally concerned, the peaceable quakers excepted. At *New York* the moft violent actors were epifcopalians ; at *Bofton*, congregationalifts ; though

though here they were joined by a number of episco-
palians, and there by a number of presbyterians.

People in *Britain* were differently affected by the difturbances in the colonies. This party was for supporting the authority of parliament at all adventures, and
for enforcing the stamp-act, if needful, with the point
of the sword; that for quieting the colonies by the repeal of it. Happy for them, Mr. *Grenville* and his
party had thrown themselves out of place on a difference as to the regency bill; so that the marquis of
Rockingham and others in opposition, who were better 1765.
inclined to the Americans, came into office. The mar- July
quis and his friends did not come to a resolution di-   10.
rectly to repeal the act. The main lines of their own
plan were not marked out, nor the repeal determined
upon, until a little before the meeting of parliament.
But the choice of the measure, and of the principle to
proceed upon was made before the session. The papers
relative to American affairs were produced to the
house of commons: and it was a kind of plan on all
sides, to maintain the authority of parliament, and by
that very authority to give the colonies every relief the
nature of the case required. But the great commoner
Mr. *Pitt*, who neither communicated, nor connected
himself with any one, came to the house and declared,
that parliament had *no right* to tax the colonies; and
said also, *I am glad America has resisted.* He hereby
deranged matters; threw the opposition into a rage;
and reduced the ministry to a necessity of accompanying the repeal, with the declaratory bill, expressive of
the *right* of parliament to *bind* the colonies *in all cases
whatever.*

1766.   Mr. *Grenville* moved, that the ftamp-act fhould be enforced, and was fupported by 134, but oppofed by 274. The merchants and manufacturers joined their efforts with miniftry to obtain a repeal. They were alarmed at the non-importation agreement, and the confufions which exifted, as being neceffarily prejudicial to their own interefts, and tending to the deftruction of commerce. The miniftry did not fail to encourage petitions, complaining of hardfhips brought on by the great decay of trade to the American colonies; and alfo inftructions to members from the trading and manufacturing towns. The petition of congrefs was not admitted: the members not being called together by the authority of the crown, though a futile was yet a prevailing argument againft its admiffion. But the repeal was grounded on the other petitions; and after a fix weeks inquiry into *American* affairs, was moved for, with the greateft propriety, by general *Conway*, the fecretary, who had oppofed the ftamp-bill at the fecond reading, and denied the right of parliament to tax the Americans. The debate, which enfued, was warm, interefting and long. But, by three o'clock in the morning, " the houfe, by an independent noble fpirited and unexpected majority, in the teeth of all the old mercenary *Swifs* of the ftate, in defpite of all the fpeculators and augurs of political events, in defiance of the whole embattled legion of veteran penfioners and practifed inftruments of court, gave a total repeal to the ftamp-act, and (if the fcheme of taxing the colonies had been totally abandoned) a lafting peace to the whole empire *." The motion was carried by 275, againft 167. The cyder counties

Feb. 22.

* Mr. Edmund Burke's fpeech, April 19, 1774.

fupsupported it; for they expected a repeal of the duty on cyder; and obtained it in April. It has been said, that had not the ministry bartered the stamp-act against the repeal of the cyder duty, they would not have succeeded *. This however must be a false charge, if the former marked paragraph is strictly true. During the debate, " the trading interest of the empire, crammed into the lobbies of the house of commons, with a trembling and anxious expectation, and waited, almost to a winter's return of light, their fate from the resolution of the house. When, at length, that had determined in their favor, and the doors thrown open, showed them the figure of their deliverer, in the well earned triumph of his important victory, from the whole of that grave multitude there arose an involuntary burst of gratitude and transport. They jumped upon him, like children on a long absent father. They clung about him as captives about their redeemer. All *England* joined in his applause. Nor did he seem insensible to the best of all earthly rewards, the love and admiration of his fellow citizens. *Hope elevated and joy brightened his crest* †."

The ministry had certainly great difficulties to encounter: the principal originated in the colonies, and were caused by the intemperate proceedings of the various ranks of men within them. " Their violence awakened the honor of parliament, especially after Mr. *Pitt*'s speech, and thereby involved every friend of the repeal into the imputation of betraying its dignity. This is so true, that the act could not have been repealed, had not men's minds been in some measure sa-

---

* Political Memoirs, printed 1783.   † Mr. Burke's speech.

tisfied

tisfied with the *declaration of right* *." All the *Scotch* members, save two, voted against the repeal. Mr. Bollan, who informed lieutenant governor Hutchinson of it by letter, omitted mentioning the names of the gentlemen.

The bill having passed the house of commons, went up to the house of lords. Lords *Bute* and *Strange* publicly declared, that his majesty's wish was not for a repeal. The marquis of *Rockingham* and Lord *Shelburne* went together to the king, and told what was reported. They were informed, that his majesty had expressed his desire that it should be enforced; but if it could not be done peaceably and without bloodshed, it was his sincere desire and intention, that it should be totally repealed. The dukes of York and Cumberland, the lords of the bed-chamber, and the officers of the household, were for carrying fire and sword to America. Most of the bench of bishops joined them. Instead of ascribing that to a sanguinary disposition, to which their profession was opposed; let it be imputed to the painful prospect of being hindered eventually, from establishing the English hierarchy within the American colonies. There were in the house of lords, proxies included, for the repeal 105, against it 71.

Mar. 19.

On Wednesday, March the nineteenth, his majesty went to the house of peers, and passed the bill for repealing the American stamp-act; as also that for securing the dependency of the colonies on the British crown. On this occasion the American merchants

---

* The London merchants letter to John Hancock esq: and others, dated February 28.

made

made a moſt numerous appearance, to expreſs their gratitude and joy; ſhips in the river diſplayed their colours; houſes at night were illuminated all over the
city, and every decent and orderly method was obſerved, to demonſtrate the juſt ſenſe they entertained of his
majeſty's goodneſs, and the wiſdom of parliament, in
conciliating the minds of the people on this critical occaſion.   An expreſs was diſpatched immediately to Falmouth, with letters to the different provinces, acquainting them with the news of the repeal; that ſo their fears
might vaniſh, and give place to joy and exultation.

LETTER IV.

Roxbury, April 14, 1773.

MR. *Samuel Adams*'s name will occur frequently in
the courſe of our correſpondence; be it noted
therefore, that the firſt time of his being returned for
Boſton, and ſerving as a repreſentative, was upon an
election occaſioned by the death of *Oxenbridge Thacher*
eſq.   The deceaſed belonged to the band of patriots;
but when he happened to think differently from Mr.
Otis jun. in the houſe of aſſembly, the latter treated him
in ſo overbearing and indecent a manner, that he was
obliged at times to call upon the ſpeaker to interpoſe
and protect him.   The ſtate of affairs required a particular

1765.
Sept.
27.

ticular attention to the political fentiments of the perfon who fhould be chofen. The inhabitants, in fixing
upon Mr. S. Adams, made choice of a member, who
was zealoufly attached to the rights of the Maffachufetts in particular, and the colonies in general; and but
little to his own perfonal interefts. He was well qualified to fecond Mr. Otis, and learned in time to ferve
his own public views by the influence of the other. He
was foon noticed by the houfe, chofen, and continued
their clerk from year to year, by which means he had
the cuftody of their papers; and of thefe he knew how
to make an advantage for political purpofes. He was
frequently upon important committees, and acquired
great afcendency, by difcovering a readinefs to acquiefce
in the propofals and amendments of others, while the
end aimed at by them, did not eventually fruftrate his
leading defigns. He fhowed a pliablenefs and complai-
fance in thefe fmaller matters, which enabled him in the
iffue to carry thofe of much greater confequence; and
there were many favorite points, which the fons of liberty in the *Maffachufetts* meant to carry, even though
the ftamp-act fhould be repealed.

1766.   Mr. *Pitt*'s declaration againft the parliament's right
to impofe *internal taxes,* and his faying *I am glad America has refifted,* were feized with eagernefs by the popular leaders in the colonies. They praifed and idolized
him for the fame, without regarding what he had declared, in favor of the authority of parliament in all
cafes of *external taxation,* and for enforcing all laws for
that purpofe; and notwithstanding his having faid, " If
obedience be refufed, I would not fuffer a horfe-nail to
be made in the plantations." Their fpirits were elated,

and

and they took encouragement from his declaration, to fortify themselves in their own sentiments upon American liberty.

It is impossible to express or describe the extraordinary joy, with which the body of the Americans received the news of the repeal, though the power of the vice-admiralty courts remained unabridged, and the declaratory act was added. The latter was considered by some, as passed merely to save appearances, while contemned by others, whose wisdom would have been more evident, had they repressed their contempt, whatever was their opinion. In regard to the former, " the judges of the vice-admiralty courts in the colonies had had assigned them, by acts of parliament, a jurisdiction for the recovery of penalties upon the laws of revenue and trade, without juries for near a century past *." Had a prudent and moderate temper taken possession of all parties at this period, it had been happy; but they were so much heated in some colonies, as to be determined upon opposing each other.

When the choice of members for *Boston*, to represent the town in the next general court, was approaching, Mr. *John Rowe*, a merchant, who had been active on the side of liberty, in matters of trade, was thought of by some influential persons. Mr. *Samuel Adams* artfully nominated a different one, by asking with his eyes looking to Mr. *Hancock*'s house, " Is there not another *John*, that may do better?" The hint took. Mr. *John Hancock*'s uncle was dead, and had left him a very considerable fortune. Mr. *Samuel Adams* judged, that the fortune would give credit and support to the cause of

* The lords protest against the repeal of the stamp-act.

liberty;

liberty; that popularity would pleafe the poffeffor; and that he might be eafily fecured by prudent management, and might make a confpicuous figure in the band of patriots.

Meffrs. *James Otis* jun. *Thomas Cufhing, Samuel Adams,* and *John Hancock,* (who had never been of the houfe before) were returned for *Bofton.* The town of *Plymouth* made choice alfo of a new reprefentative, the high fheriff of the county, *James Warren* efq; a gentleman of real abilities, and who efpoufed the fide of liberty upon principle. The government wifhed to have him on their fide, and played off both threats and promifes: however he was immoveable.

May 28. The general court met according to charter. The houfe of affembly chofe Mr. *Otis* fpeaker. Governor *Bernard* negatived, inftead of adopting the conciliating meafure of accepting him. The acceptance might have foftened and induced him to have dropped the plan of leaving out of the council, in the new election, the crown officers and juftices of the fuperior court; but the refufal confirmed him in it, and by irritating the houfe enabled him to execute it the more eafily. The crown officers were the lieutenant governor and fecretary, Meffrs. *Hutchinfon* and *Oliver*; the others held only provincial commiffions. The oppofition affigned as the reafon for leaving them out, that they might redrefs a grievance long complained of by their conftituents, a dangerous union of legiflative and executive powers in the fame perfons. But the true ones probably were, the fufpicions and diflike they entertained of and to their political fentiments, and Mr. *Otis*'s having been negatived. Mr. *Bernard* retaliated, and excepted againft the

fix

fix counfellors chofen in the room of the others. Thus
the animofity was increafed. Had he negatived two
or three only, there might have been an opening for
healing the breach; but now it was otherwife. The
liberty party gained ftrength, and it was ordered by the June
affembly, "That the debates of this houfe be open, [12.]
and that a gallery be erected for the accommodation of
fuch as fhall be inclined to attend them." A gallery
was prepared with the utmoft expedition, and finifhed
in a few days. It was viewed as a great acquifition to
the common caufe; and certainly ferved a double purpofe. The admiffion of the people at large, to hear
the debates, and to watch the members, reftrained fome
from fpeaking with their ufual freedom in fupport of
governmental meafures; and encouraged others to indulge themfelves in all that animated language, and
thofe folemn proteftations of difinterefted zeal for the
rights and privileges of their country, which are fo
taking with men of honeft minds and plain underftand-
ings. But you are not to fuppofe that thefe proteftations were always true on this fide of the Atlantic, any
more than on yours. Many joined the banners of
liberty, and violently oppofed the governor and governmental meafures, becaufe of the reftraints they
were under from the laws of trade, the danger they
were in of fuffering by them, and his perfifting to give
thefe laws all the fupport in his power. The oppofition had great advantage in the political conteft, by
branding all the fupporters of government as friends to
the ftamp-act, though they knew to the contrary. Both
fides were fenfible that the act was merely financial,

VOL. I. P without

without any regard to the political state of America, or any purpose to remove one of its difficulties.

10.   The house were unanimous in voting, that thanks should be returned to the duke of *Grafton* and other noblemen, to Mr. *Pitt* and other gentlemen, who had been active and aiding in the repeal of the stamp-act. However, when his majesty's recommendation to make up the losses of the sufferers in the late unhappy times, came before them from the governor with these words, " The justice and humanity of this requisition is so forcible, that it cannot be controverted; the authority with which it is introduced, should preclude all disputation about complying with it;" they objected to the manner in which it was proposed, as being " derogatory to the honor of the house, and in breach of the privileges thereof," and unreasonably declined making compensation; whereas their privileges might have been preserved uninjured, by a vote to relieve the sufferers upon their own application, out of dutiful respect to the mild representation of his majesty, and out of humanity and generosity to the sufferers.

When a compensation was first talked of, it was the general opinion, that it ought to be made, but that it was due from Boston only, and not the province in general. This thought probably determined the Boston members to oppose making the compensation even out of the treasury; a way in which it might have been done, had they and their friends joined the friends of government. But had the money been ordered out of the treasury, a subsequent motion might have charged it upon Boston, which as the tax bill was to be past at that time, would have been easily effected. The interest

of

of the town induced its members to employ every circumstance to prevent the compensation's being voted at present. After a while repeated advices were received, that the honor of parliament was engaged to see the compensation made, and that they would certainly take it in hand, if the provincial assembly refused. It was obvious, that the parliament could enforce payment from a sea-port. The people of Boston grew uneasy, that the money was not paid. A town-meeting was called: the abovementioned expedient was proposed and approved of, and their representatives were directed to use their influence, that compensation might be granted upon those principles, and the money be paid out of the treasury.

Mr. *Hutchinson* and the other sufferers petitioned for Sept relief *. Their petitions were considered; and on the question being put, " Whether shall compensation be made out of the province treasury?" it passed in the negative. A bill however, was finally admitted for making compensation, which was to be transmitted to the several towns, for the sentiments of the constituents.

It passed to be engrossed, yeas 53, nays 35; but not Dec. without the house's resolving, " That it is under a full 5. persuasion, that the sufferers have no just claim or demand on the province."—A needless resolve, tending to excite disgust in many, without answering any important purpose. The act granted compensation to the sufferers; and a free and general pardon, indemnity and oblivion to the offenders in the late times. It was disallowed at home, on account of the assembly's having

* Mr. Hutchinson's loss was 2396l. 3s. 1d¼. Mr. Oliver's 129l. 3s. Mr. Hallowell's 289l. 0. 1½d. Mr. Story's, 50l. 11s. 6¾d, all sterling.

incor-

incorporated an act of pardon with an act of compenfation, without having obtained his majefty's previous
confent to fuch act of pardon.   The fufferers however
received the compenfation, and the offenders were not
profecuted.

Nov.   In *Virginia* a bill paffed the houfe of burgeffes, for
7.   erecting a ftatue to his majefty, as an acknowledgment
for repealing the ftamp-act, and alfo an obelifk to commemorate thofe worthy patriots who diftinguifhed themfelves in bringing about that happy event.   And at
Dec. *New York*, an act was paffed for making reftitution to
the feveral perfons therein named, for loffes fuftained
in the late commotions.   But when the affembly was
applied to, for carrying into execution the act of parliament of the preceding year, for quartering his majefty's troops, they faid in their addrefs to the governor,
Sir *Henry Moore*, "According to the conftruction put
on it here, it is required, that all the forces, which fhall
at any time enter this colony, fhall be quartered during
the whole year, in a very unufual and expenfive manner: by marching feveral regiments into this colony,
this expence would become ruinous and infupportable;
and therefore we cannot, confiftent with our duty to
our conftituents, put it in the power of any perfon (whatfoever confidence we may have of his prudence and integrity) to lay fuch a burden on them:" and fo juftified
their declining to provide for the troops.

Before clofing the account of 1766, be it obferved,
that the people of *Connecticut* failed not to fhow their
refentment againft their late governor's having qualified,
agreeable to what the ftamp-act enjoined.   There was
a meeting of gentlemen at *Hartford*, for concerting a
plan

plan for the choice of a new governor and counfellors, in the room of thofe, who with him had taken the oath required. Matters were fo managed at this meeting, that when the election came on, Mr. *Pitkin* was chofen governor, and colonel *Trumbull*, deputy governor. But the epifcopalians, almoft to a man, voted for Mr. *Fitch*; and by thus making a party with adminiftration, againft the claims and rights of their colony, rendered themfelves obnoxious.

The *Maffachufett's* houfe of affembly continued their oppofition to the lieutenant governor, Mr. *Hutchinfon*, and refolved, "That he not being elected a counfellor, has by the charter, no right to a feat at the council board, with or without a voice, while the commander in chief is in the province." March the fifth the council determined the fame; but in their meffage to the houfe, expreffed their furprife at what had been done without them, and at its not being mentioned to the board till February the twenty-fourth. Mr. *Hutchinfon* afterward did not attempt to be prefent. Lord Shelburne, in anfwer to what was tranfmitted to him, by the governor upon the affair, wrote in September " the admiffion of the lieutenant governor lies after all in the breaft of the council only, as being the proper judges of their own privileges, and as having a right to determine whom they will admit to be prefent at their deliberations." Thefe proceedings of the *Maffachufett's* and *New York* affemblies, thought to be, in name at leaft, two of the moft confiderable in the colonies, were afcribed to an unreafonable perverfenefs of temper; and exafperated the friends of America, by expofing them, however unjuftly, to the imputation of facrificing the

1767. Jan. 31.

P 3   interefts

interefts of Great Britain to thofe of America.   They
alfo encouraged the Anti-Americans to refume the plan
of taxing the colonies; and Mr. *Charles Townfend* pawn-
ed his credit to them, for effecting it, and became chan-
chellor of the Exchequer.   But, three of the miniftry
oppofed in the council, taxing the Americans afrefh;
and it would have been a blefling had their opinion
prevailed.

May   The chancellor of the Exchequer moved for leave to
15. bring in bills, for granting a duty upon paper, glafs,
painters colours, &c. in the Britifh American colonies; for fettling falaries on the governors, judges, &c.
in North America; and for taking off the duty on teas
exported to America, and granting a duty of three-
pence a pound on the importation in America.   Two
bills were at length framed, the one for granting duties
in the Britifh colonies in America, on paper, glafs,
painters colours, tea, &c. the other for taking off the
duty of a fhilling a pound on all black and Singlo tea,
and for granting a drawback on teas exported to Ireland
and America.   The firft received the royal affent June
the twenty-ninth; the laft July the fecond.   The preamble to the firft act expreffes, that the duties are laid,
"for the better fupport of government, and the adminiftration of the colonies."   The colonifts deemed it unneceffary, unjuft, and dangerous to their moft important rights.   There is a claufe in it, enabling the crown,
by fign manual, to eftablifh a *general civil lift*, throughout every province in *North America*, to any indefinite
extent, with any falaries penfions or appointments, to
any unlimited amount, even to the produce of the laft
farthing of the American revenue.   The point was now
carried,

carried, which had been the object of every minister since the reign of Charles II. viz. *the establishment of a civil list in America independent of the assemblies.* Mr. *Richard Jackson* spoke in the house of commons against that part of the bill, and was supported only by Mr. *Huske,* and no other member. He was convinced, that though the judges ought to be independent, both of crown and people, yet mischiefs might arise from the independency of governors on the people, much greater than could arise from their dependence; and that it was not fit, that such persons as governors usually are, should be independent of the people, and dependent upon the crown for their governments. The act provides, that, after all such ministerial warrants under the sign manual, as *are thought proper and necessary,* shall be satisfied, the residue of the revenue shall be at the disposal of the parliament. But who can suppose, that such warrants will ever be satisfied, till ministers have provided for all their friends and favorites? May it not be said upon the plan of this act, " the mockery of an American revenue proves at last to be the crumbs that fall from the minister's table—the residue indeed, of a royal warrant, countersigned by the first lord of the Treasury * ?"

An account being received of *New York*'s having refused to provide for quartering the troops, Mr. *Grenville* and his adherents raised such a clamor against America, that it was thought necessary to bring in a bill " for restraining the assembly of *New York* from passing any act, till they had complied with the act of parliament for the furnishing his majesty's troops with the neces-

May 27.

* Mr. Hartley's letters.

saries

faries required by that act;" and it had the royal affent the fecond of July. The taking away in this manner from the province of *New York* all the powers of legiflation, till they fhould comply with the former act, occafioned a general alarm among the Americans. They now faw that their own colonial parliaments, as they confidered them, were to be bound to what the Britifh miniftry might deem their good behaviour, by the acts of a Britifh parliament. Nothing could be more grating to the fons of liberty in every province. It was the club of power which, while it knocked down the *New York* affembly, threatened every other with the like, if not pliable.

A plan of a board of commiffioners for the American department, in order to eafe the old board of commiffioners of part of its burden through increafing bufinefs, had been in contemplation. It was intended to be placed in London, in order to be near the treafury, the ultimatum of revenue matters. Mr. *Paxton* thought to be the moft plaufible and infinuating of mankind, though not the moft fincere, having left Bofton and gone to Britain, had free accefs to the chancellor of the exchequer, Mr. *Charles Townfend*. It is faid, that he whined, cried, profeffed, fwore, and made his will in favor of that great man; and then urged the neceffity of an *American board of commiffioners*, and his having a feat at it. He might forward the bufinefs. Be that as it may, the chancellor brought in a bill for eftablifhing a cuftom-houfe and a board of commiffioners in America, which alfo paffed into an act at the fame time with the former. Mr. Paxton, for his own convenience and pleafure, might procure the fixing the board at Bofton; but of all

June 3.

places

places it was the moft improper. The people were of all others the moft jealous of infringements on their liberties; and were the leaft fuited to fee crown officers living among them in great ftate, upon what they could not but deem, from the mediocrity of their own circumftances, large falaries, payable from the revenue, to be raifed from the colonies. The board fhould have been placed at *New York*. Smuggling was as prevalent there as at Bofton. The inhabitants had been long ufed to crown officers with fplendid appearances; the commanders of his majefty's troops refided much among them; numbers of them lived in a higher ftile than the Boftonians; befide, there the commiffioners would have had forces at hand to have fupported them, and have met with greater affiftance from the fervants of a royal government and their connections. The timing alfo, as well as the placing of the board, was rather unfortunate; for it fupplied the Americans with the opportunity of propagating, that it was appointed merely to enforce the new duties. By this means the people were inflamed, and the appointment was pronounced unconftitutional and oppreffive. The duties were to take place after the twentieth of November; and in the beginning of that month, three of the commiffioners, *Henry Hulton, William Burch*, and *Charles Paxton* efqrs. arrived at Bofton: the other two, *John Temple* and *John Robinson* efqrs. were in America before. As to the expence of the board of cuftoms, including the whole, it was a thoufand pounds lefs than that of the four furveyors general, and the office connected with them at London. The chancellor had been inftrumental in reviving thofe American animofities, which the repeal of the ftamp-

act

act had quieted; but did not live to fee the fatal confequences which have followed, as he died the fourth of
September.

Oct.
28.

A few gentlemen at a private club in *Boſton*, having
fuggeſted a non-importation agreement, the thought
was improved upon, till at length the inhabitants, at a
town meeting, agreed upon meaſures to promote induſtry, œconomy, and manufactures; thereby to prevent the unneceſſary importation of *European* commodities. They alſo voted, that a ſubſcription paper ſhould
be prepared, and a committee appointed to procure
ſubſcriptions to it; by which the parties engaged to encourage the uſe and conſumption of all articles manu-
factured in any of the Britiſh American colonies; and
after the thirty-firſt of December following, not to purchaſe certain enumerated articles imported from abroad.

The failure of expected ſucceſs from theſe meaſures,
and an apprehenſion of diſagreeable conſequences from
an ineffectual oppoſition, were probably the motives that
Nov.
20.
induced Mr. *Otis*, at a ſubſequent town-meeting, to
make a long ſpeech on the ſide of government, wherein
he aſſerted the king's right to appoint officers of the
cuſtoms, in what number and by what denomination he
pleaſed; and that as to the new duties, it would be
very imprudent in the town to make an oppoſition to
them, when every town in the province, and every other
province in America ſeemed to acquieſce in them and
Dec.
be contented. But the propoſed meaſures were afterward approved of and adopted at *Providence* and *Newport*.

1768.
Jan.
The *Connecticut* towns and *New York* followed the example. Still the buſineſs labored without being productive

ductive of any important effects. This engaged the attention of one captain Malcolm, a fmall trader, who about eighteen months before had made himfelf famous by a violent and fuccefsful refiftance with fword and piftol, to the cuftom-houfe officers, when endeavouring to fearch his houfe for uncuftomed goods, under the authority of a writ of affiftance. Having, about the middle of February, fafely run the cargo of a fchooner from Fyall, confifting of about fixty pipes of wine, he within two or three days procured a meeting of fome merchants and traders, at which he prefided. Nothing was determined upon more, than the calling of a general meeting of the merchants on Friday, March the fourth. This may be ftiled the firft movement of the merchants againft the new acts of parliament. The refult of this meeting was, that a fubfcription for not importing any Englifh goods, except for the fifhery, for eighteen months, fhould be prepared and carried round the town. It met with no great encouragement, and many declined fubfcribing. On this, all engines were fet to work; fome were threatened and made afraid for their perfons and houfes; others for their trade and credit. By fuch means the fubfcription was filled. But the merchants of New York and Philadelphia declining to concur in the meafure, thofe of Bofton were obliged to give it up for the prefent. However they renewed it within a few months, as you will learn below.

The *New England* fpirit of patriotifm and œconomy was greatly approved of at *Philadelphia*; and it was faid, that "If America is faved from its impending danger, New England will be its acknowledged guardian." Periodical pieces were publifhed at Bofton, on the nature and

I

extent

extent of Britiſh parliamentary power. Hints were thrown out about independency: and intimations given, that freemen were not to be governed any more than taxed but by their own conſent, in real or virtual repreſentatives. The power of Britiſh legiſlation over the Americans was queſtioned, and virtually denied. Matters were brought to this length, by broaching anew a diſpute that ſhould never have been moved again; and which might happily have lain dormant for half a century or more, had no freſh attempt been made to tax the Americans. Before the ſtamp-act, they allowed the mother country a certain prerogative over them. They acquieſced in the parliament's right to make many acts, binding them in divers internal matters, and regulating their trade. They did not reaſon neither then nor immediately after the repeal, " if the parliament has no right to tax us *internally*, they have none to tax us *externally*, or to make any other law to bind us." They admitted the diſtinction between internal and external taxation, and between raiſing money from the regulation of trade, and raiſing it for the purpoſes of a revenue. The wiſdom of parliament ſhould have abode by their conceſſions, and have adopted and confirmed their diſtinction. But being obliged to enter afreſh the field of political controverſy, great numbers began to think, that the want of repreſentation in parliament freed them abſolutely from any obedience to the power of the Britiſh legiſlature; and that there was no real, and only a nominal difference between internal and external taxation, agreeable to what was infifted upon by the party oppoſing the repeal of the ſtamp-act. *John Dickinſon* eſq; began ſo early as in November 1767 to employ his

pen

pen againſt the acts which had been paſſed, in a ſeries of *Letters from a Farmer in Pennſylvania to the Inhabitants of the Britiſh Colonies.* They amounted to twelve; and in them he ably maintained the rights of the coloniſts. He cloſed with a poſtſcript in theſe words: " Is there not the greateſt reaſon to hope, if the univerſal ſenſe of theſe colonies is immediately expreſt by *reſolves* of the aſſemblies in ſupport of their rights, by *inſtructions* to their agents on the ſubject, and by *petitions* to the crown and parliament for redreſs, that thoſe meaſures will have the ſame ſucceſs now that they had in the time of the ſtamp-act?" The inhabitants of Boſton were ſo ſenſible of the eminent ſervice he did to the common cauſe, that they wrote to him upon the occaſion. In his anſwer, April the eleventh, he ſaid, " Never will my heart become inſenſible till inſenſible of all worldly things, of the unſpeakable obligation I owe to the inhabitants of the *Maſſachuſetts Bay,* for the vigilance with which they have watched over, and the magnanimity with which they have maintained, the liberties of the *Britiſh* colonies on this continent." It was probably owing to Mr. *Dickinſon*'s publications, that the *Pennſylvania* aſſembly, early in February, before they knew what meaſures the *Maſſachuſetts Bay,* or any other colony, would purſue, took into conſideration the act impoſing duties on paper, glaſs, &c. and gave poſitive inſtructions to their agents, to unite with other agents in applying to parliament and praying relief.

It may be juſtly concluded, from governor *Bernard*'s letters to lord Shelburne, that the Maſſachuſetts aſſembly were inclined to bury in oblivion the diſcords occaſioned by the ſtamp-act, and to eſcape other ſubjects of

future

future controverfy, had not the late chancellor unhappily revived the animofities. " The houfe, (fays
the governor) from the time of opening the feffion to
this day, has fhewn a difpofition to avoid all difpute
with me; every thing having paffed with as much good
humor as I could defire, except only their continuing
to act in addreffing the king, remonftrating to the fecretary of ftate, and employing a feparate agent. It is
the importance of this innovation, which induces me to
make this remonftrance at a time when I have a fair
profpect of having, in all other bufinefs, nothing but
good to fay of the proceedings of the houfe *."

" They have acted in all things, even in their remonftrance, with temper and moderation: they have avoided
fome fubjects of difpute, and have laid a foundation for
removing fome caufes of former altercation †."

" I will make fuch a prudent and proper ufe of the
letter as, I hope, will perfectly reftore the peace and
tranquillity of this province, for which purpofe confiderable fteps have been made by the houfe of reprefentatives ‡."

Jan.
21.
The *Maffachufetts* houfe of reprefentatives, in a debate upon the " expediency of writing to the affemblies
of the other colonies upon the continent, with refpect to
the importance of joining with them," put a queftion
on the propofition of writing letters, defiring thofe affemblies to join them, which was negatived for this very
reafon, becaufe containing the propofition of joining.
The houfe thought exceptions might be taken at it, as
having a tendency to form combinations; and that it
might be confidered at home as the appointing another

* January 21, 1768.   † January 30.   ‡ February 2.

congrefs.

congrefs. It is an excellent rule of the houfe, that no
vote fhall be re-confidered, unlefs the number of members prefent equals the number at its paffing. When
they had the fame number, eighty-two, which makes a Feb.
full houfe, a motion was made for re-confidering the 4.
vote againft applying to the other colonies; and the vote
of re-confideration was obtained by a large majority.
The fame day a committee was appointed to prepare a
letter to be tranfmitted to the feveral houfes of reprefentatives and burgeffes upon the continent, to inform
them of the meafures the houfe had taken with regard
to difficulties they were apprehenfive would arife from
the operation of feveral acts of parliament for levying
duties and taxes on the American colonies. The committee, after deliberating a week, reported the letter, 11.
which being read in the houfe, was accepted almoft
unanimoufly, in the prefence of eighty-three members.
It began thus: " Sir, the houfe of reprefentatives of
this province have taken into their ferious confideration
the great difficulties that muft accrue to themfelves and
their conftituents, by the operation of feveral acts of
parliament impofing duties and taxes on the American
colonies." It then related the meafures they had taken
in petitioning the king making reprefentations to the
miniftry, &c. and concluded with, " the houfe is fully
fatisfied that your affembly is too generous and enlarged
in fentiment, to believe that this letter proceeds from
an ambition of taking the lead, or dictating to the other
affemblies. They freely fubmit their opinion to the
judgment of others, and fhall take it kind in your
houfe to point out to them any thing further that
may be thought neceffary. This houfe cannot conclude
without

without expreffing their firm confidence in the king, our common head and father, that the united and dutiful fupplications of his diftreffed American fubjects will meet with his royal and favorable acceptance."

Peter Gilman efq; fpeaker of the *New Hampfhire* affembly, wrote, by order of the houfe, in anfwer to the Maffachufetts circular letter—" The fentiments contained in it are highly approved, and the communication kindly received and gratefully acknowledged. The time of the houfe's exiftence in that relation is near expiring; they can't engage for their fucceffors, and can only exprefs their fatisfaction in the Maffachufetts proceedings, and declare their hopes, that the next affembly will heartily concur in fentiments on this affair, and purfue the fame method." The letter ran in the higheft recommendatory ftrain of the Maffachufetts-Bay affembly; and concluded with, " What remains for us at prefent is to offer our daily prayer to the Governor and Lord of the univerfe, to avert the impending evil, and to make way for the full eftablifhment of Britifh liberty in every branch of it, and to quiet every colony in all the enjoyment of all their civil and religious rights and privileges." For thefe courtly expreffions, with which the houfe declined doing any thing in the bufinefs, the next affembly was rewarded with courtly commendations. The governor, *John Wentworth* efq; in a meffage of October the twentieth, communicated the copy of the following extract of a letter from Lord *Hillfborough*, of July the ninth : " It is his majefty's pleafure that you fhould affure his faithful fubjects in *New Hampfhire*, that his majefty has nothing more at heart than to promote their welfare and happinefs, whofe cheerful obedience

dience to the laws of this kingdom, and steady resolution in refusing to accede to the measures and proposals
which have been urged with so much indecent warmth
in other colonies, cannot fail to recommend them to his
royal favor and countenance." The assembly however,
nine days after, petitioned the king, and mentioned that
his royal predecessors granted them a power of legislation, limited to the approbation or disallowance of the
crown, with the powers and privileges essential to British
liberty, of raising internal taxes by their own representatives. The petition was most profoundly humble; and
so softly worded, that it could not offend the most delicate ear of the highest parliamentary prerogative man.
By some accident or contrivance, it was not sent till an-
tiquated and out of season. Mr. *Wentworth* had gained
an ascendency over the people of his government, by
which he kept them from entering into any such spirited
measures for the redress of grievances as would be offensive to ministry. The other colonies adopted a different line of conduct. The *Virginia* house of burgesses
applauded the *Massachusetts* representatives for their attention to American liberty; took notice of the act
suspending the legislative powers of *New York*; and
said, " If the parliament can compel the colonies to
furnish a single article to the troops sent over, they may
by the same rule, oblige them to furnish clothes, arms,
and every other necessary, even to the pay of the officers
and soldiers, a doctrine replete with every mischief, and
utterly subversive of all that is dear and valuable." The
council concurred with them in all their proceedings;
and their agent was enjoined to consult the agents of
the other colonies, and to co-operate with them in ap-

plying

plying for redrefs. Moft of the affemblies upon the continent, as they had opportunity, approved of the doings of the Maffachufetts, and harmonized with them in refolves and petitions. But an account of their doings

April
22.

had not reached Great Britain long, ere Lord *Hillfborough* wrote to governor *Bernard* upon the occafion. For want of fuller and jufter information, or of due attention to the governor's expreffions, the proceeding which originated the circular letter, was mentioned—" as unfair, contrary to the real fenfe of the affembly, and procured by furprife; and therefore" upon this miftaken principle, the governor was inftructed, " fo foon as the general court is again affembled, to require of the houfe of reprefentatives, in his majefty's name, to refcind the refolution which gave birth to the circular letter from the fpeaker, and to declare their difapprobation of, and diffent to that rafh and hafty proceeding." In cafe they refufed to comply, he was immediately to diffolve them, and to tranfmit to his lordfhip an account of their tranf-

June
21.

actions. The houfe was informed of what was required; and three days after, of what they were to expect if unpliable. Their refolution not being returned within fix days of the laft part of the information, the governor fent them word he could wait no longer, which haftened the bufinefs in which they were engaged.

30.

A committee of the houfe reported a letter to Lord *Hillfborough*, fetting forth the feveral votes and refolutions which paffed in the laft houfe of reprefentatives, relating to the circular letter; and fhowing that the whole of thefe matters was tranfacted in the height of the feffion in a full houfe, and by a large majority. The letter was approved of by 93 out of 105 members
present,

prefent, and ordered to be tranfmitted to his lordfhip.
The houfe agreed alfo upon a meffage to the governor,
in which they faid, " It is to us incomprehenfible that
we fhould be required, on the peril of a diffolution of
the general court, to refcind a refolution of a former
houfe, when it is evident, that that refolution has no
exiftence but as a mere hiftorical fact. Your excellency
muft know, that the refolution is, to fpeak in the language of the common law, not now executory, but to
all intents and purpofes executed. If, as is moft probable, by the word refcinding is intended the paffing a
vote, in direct and exprefs difapprobation of the meafure taken by the former houfe as illegal, inflammatory,
and tending to promote unjuftifiable combinations againft
his majefty's peace, crown and dignity, we muft take
the liberty to teftify and publicly declare, that we take
it to be the native, inherent, and indefeafible right of
the fubject, jointly or feverally, to petition the king for
the redrefs of grievances; provided alway, that the
fame be done in a decent, dutiful, loyal and conftitutional way, without tumult, diforder and confufion.—If
the votes of the houfe are to be controlled by the direction of a minifter, we have left us but a vain femblance
of liberty.—We have now only to inform you, that this
houfe have voted *not to refcind*, and that on a divifion
on the queftion, there were ninety-two nays, and feventeen yeas." The meffage was firm, patriotic, and fpirited; and in fome parts allufively fevere upon the governor; but every where decently expreffed. The re-
fcinders were governmental receivers or expectants.
They had, or looked for a reward, for their crouching

July compliance. The next day the governor paffed fome
1. neceffary acts, and then diffolved the affembly. It is
fcarce conceivable how a new affembly of reprefentatives
could think themfelves capable of being more grofsly
infulted, than by being made accountable for the proceedings of a diffolved and dead one, and by being
punifhed with immediate deftruction for not declaring
themfelves of oppofite fentiments to their predeceffors.
Mr. *Otis* in his fpeech againft refcinding faid, " When
Lord Hillfborough knows that we will not refcind our
acts, he fhould apply to parliament to refcind theirs.
Let Britain refcind their meafures or they are loft for ever."
His fpeech by the patriotic enthufiafts was extolled to
the fkies ; and by the governmental ones, was declared
to be the moft violent, infolent, abufive, treafonable de-
clamation, that perhaps was ever delivered. While the
matter of refcinding was under confideration, the houfe
received an anfwer from *Virginia*, and one from *New
Jerfey*, which, though not fo very high as the other, was
far from being unfavorable. They had alfo intelligence,
that they might expect the like from other affemblies :
thefe circumftances probably increafed the majority againft
refcinding. Had it not been for the mandate to refcind,
the feffions might have terminated profperoufly and
peaceably : for Mr. *Otis*, though he had diftinguifhed
himfelf by carrying the objections to the authority of
parliament to the greateft length, had retracted all his
former opinions, in a fet fpeech at the opening of it.
He faid, he had fully informed himfelf of the relation
between Great Britain and her colonies ; and was convinced that the power of parliament over her colonies

was

was abfolute, with this qualification, that they ought
not to tax them until they allowed them to fend reprefentatives; and that if the colonies had reprefentatives,
the power of parliament would be as perfect in America
as in England. He then argued for an American reprefentation. This furprifed the affembly, and induced
a member on the fide of government to charge the oppofition with the intention of making an American reprefentation neceffary, by denying the authority of parliament over them becaufe not reprefented. The anfwers of the other party were thought to ftrengthen the
fufpicion. Upon which Mr. Timothy Ruggles point-
edly faid, that as they were determined to have reprefentatives, he begged leave to recommend to them a
merchant, who would undertake to carry their reprefentatives to England for half what they would fell for
when they arrived there. But the beft argument to
have filenced any of the oppofition, who might intereft-
edly hanker after an American reprefentation, would
have been to have repeated the refolve of the houfe on
the 29th of October 1765—" A reprefentation in parliament of the inhabitants of the province, fuch as the
fubjects in Britain actually enjoy is impracticable for the
fubjects in America." The day before Lord *Hillſborough*
wrote to Mr. *Bernard* upon the bufinefs of refcinding,
a circular letter was written to the governors of the refpective provinces, to accompany a copy of that of the
Maſſachuſetts, in which his lordfhip faid, " It is his
majefty's pleafure, that you fhould immediately, upon
the receipt hereof, exert your utmoft influence to defeat
this flagitious attempt to difturb the public peace, by
prevailing upon the affembly of your province to take

Q 3

no notice of it, which will be treating it with the contempt it deferves." He then added a clofing paragraph meant to influence the affemblies into a compliance. The circular letter was in fome inftances received in time, but produced a very different effect from what was intended. The *New York* affembly had felt the weight of the parliament's high difpleafure, and been bereaved of legiflative power, till they fhould comply with the billetting act. In the beginning of the year, they voted the fum wanted to the general, for the purchafe of falt, pepper and vinegar, inftead of paffing an act conformable to the parliament's act, which vote was accepted. But when they met at the clofe of the year, after having completed a petition to his majefty, another to the lords, and a remonftrance to the commons, they proceeded to confider the circular letters from the affemblies of *Maffachufetts-Bay* and *Virginia*, and unanimoufly agreed to anfwer them in the moft refpectful manner. They then entered into fome very fpirited refolves in favor of liberty and the rights of their conftituents; and appointed a committee to correfpond and confult, with any other his majefty's fubjects out of the colony, either individually or collectively, on any matter or thing whatfoever, whereby the rights or privileges of the houfe or its conftituents might be affected. Thefe doings occafioned their being diffolved.

We are now entering upon another interefting period.

It had been the common practice for the tide waiter, upon the arrival of a veffel, to repair to the cabin, and there to remain drinking punch with the mafter, while the failors and others upon deck were employed in landing the wines, molaffes, or other dutiable goods. The

com-

commiffioners of the cuftoms were determined that the laws of trade fhould be executed.

Upon the arrival of Mr. *Hancock*'s floop *Liberty*, *Nathaniel Barnard* mafter, from *Madeira*; the tidefman, *Thomas Kirk*, went on board in the afternoon. Captain *Marfhall*, in Mr. *Hancock*'s employ, followed; and about nine in the evening, made feveral propofals to *Kirk*, which being rejected, captain *Marfhall*, with five or fix others, laid hold of, overpowered, and confined him below for three hours, in which time the wine was taken out, before entry had been made at the cuftom-houfe or naval office. *Marfhall* threatened *Kirk*, in cafe of difcovery. The captain wrought fo hard in unloading the floop, that his fudden death, that night, while in bed, before affiftance could be obtained, was generally believed to have been owing to fome injury received from his uncommon exertions. The next morning the mafter entered, as it is faid, four or five pipes, and fwore that was the whole of his cargo. It was refolved to feize the floop for a falfe entry's being made; though it was thought by many that no one would undertake the bufinefs.

Mr. *Jofeph Harrifon* the collector, and Mr. *Benjamin* June *Hallowell* the comptroller, repaired to Hancock's wharf. 10. Mr. *Harrifon* objected to the unfeafonablenefs of the time, being between fix and feven, when the lower ciafs of people were returning from their day labor. The feizure however was made before fun-fet, fo as to be perfectly legal. Mr. *Harrifon* thought the floop might lie at the wharf, after clapping the broad arrow upon her; but Mr. *Hallowell* judged it would be beft to move her under the guns of the *Romney*, and made fignals for her

boats

bo: to come afhore. The people upon the wharf cried
out. " There is no occafion, fhe will lie fafe, and no
officer has a right to remove her ;" but the mafter of
the man of war cut her moorings and carried her off.
Every mean was ufed to interrupt the officers in the
execution of their bufinefs, and numbers fwore that they
would be revenged. A mob was foon collected, which
increafed to a thoufand or two, chiefly of fturdy boys
and negroes. The minds of the people were inflamed
by the feizure and removal of the veffel. They had
been before irritated, by the captain of the man of war's
preffing fome feamen belonging to the town ; add to
that, their averfion to the board of commiffioners, the
popularity of the owner, and the name of the floop—
thefe of courfe excited their refentments, and wrought
them up into a combuftible body. Captain Malcolm,
who was deeply engaged in running the wines, headed a
number of men after the feizure, and was very active in
attempting to prevent the floop's being removed. Mr.
Harrifon was pelted with ftones, bricks, and dirt, and
received feveral blows with fticks, particularly one on
the breaft, fo that it was with difficulty he could keep
from falling ; he was afterward confined to his bed from
the injuries he had received. Mr. *Hallowell*, Mr. *Irving*,
infpector of imports and exports, and the collector's fon
were fharers in the treatment. They all efcaped with
the utmoft hazard of their lives. Mr. *Hallowell* was confined to his houfe under the care of a furgeon from
wounds and bruifes. Mr. *Richard Harrifon*, the collector's fon, was thrown down, dragged by the hair of his
head, and otherwife treated barbaroufly. Mr. *Irving*
was beaten with clubs and fticks ; had his fword broken

to pieces, and received a few flight wounds. The mob proceeded to the houfes of the collector and comptroller, broke their windows, and thofe of Mr. *Williams* infpector general, then dragged the collector's boat through the town, and burnt it on the common. This was on Friday evening. Saturday and Sunday evenings are facred; and the commiffioners *Hulton, Burch, Paxton* and *Robinfon* efqrs. remained pretty eafy : during the outrages, to avoid infults, they retired from their own to neighbours houfes. But receiving information, that further riots were intended, and the governor telling them, he could not protect them, and that there would be no fafety for them in Bofton, confidering the temper of the people; on Monday morning early, they fent a card to the governor, to let him know that they were going on board the Romney, and defired his orders for their reception at the caftle, which he readily gave. They repaired firft on board the man of war, and then proceeded from thence to the caftle. The collector and comptroller, and moft of the other officers of the cuftoms withdrew, either then or afterward. On 13. the Monday morning large numbers of people were gathered together, and to appearance regularly formed into parties, under their different leaders, in feveral parts of the town. If they meant any thing againft the commiffioners, they were difappointed by their having withdrawn. In the afternoon printed tickets were put up, notifying a meeting of the fons of liberty the next day at ten o'clock. This prevented all mifchief in the evening. At the appointed time, thoufands of the lower 14. clafs met; but the day being rainy, numbers adjourned to Faneuil hall, and there agreed to fend the conftables

about

about to notify a legal town meeting for the afternoon. Little elfe was done at this meeting, but the appointing a committee to wait upon the governor with a petition, the receiving his anfwer, writing a letter to a friend, and voting fuch inftructions as they thought proper to their reprefentatives. The common talk was, that the removal of the floop was an affront to the town, as it contained an infinuation that fhe would not have been fafe if left at the wharf in cuftody of a cuftom-houfe officer. It was afferted, and very truly, that there had been no refcue lately; but an invincible reafon exifted for it, as no feizure had been lately made. When captain Malcolm, more than a year and half back, oppofed, in an armed manner, the officers in attempting to fearch his houfe, fuch a number of people affembled about it, when he had got the officers out and fhut his gates againft them, that they were glad to retreat without doing their bufinefs. This defiance of the law paffed unnoticed and unpunifhed, fo that the officers never afterward attempted to make a feizure, although informations were not wanting, until the prefent time, when they were ordered by their fuperiors. About a month after, a fchooner was feized for having thirty hogfheads of molaffes on board, and was left at the wharf in cuftody of two cuftom-houfe officers. July the eighth at night, thirty men boarded her, confined the officers to the cabin, and carried off the molaffes, The towns-people were diffatisfied that their declarations concerning the floop Liberty, that fhe would have been fafe if left at the wharf, fhould be fo foon falfified. The felect men fent for the mafter, and ordered him to return the molaffes directly, under pain of the difpleafure

of

of the town. It was immediately done, and the molaffes put on board again, the day after it was conveyed
away.

The day before the town meeting of June the fourteenth, a committee of both houfes was appointed to
inquire into the ftate of the province. When they made
their report, in fpeaking of the affair on Friday the 30.
tenth, they faid, " The feizure occafioned a number of
people to be collected, who from the violence and un-
precedentednefs of the procedure in carrying off the
veffel, &c. took occafion to infult and abufe the officers
and to commit other diforders, &c,—Refolved, that
though the extraordinary circumftances of faid feizure
may extenuate the criminality, yet being of a very criminal nature and of dangerous confequence, the two
houfes declare their utter abhorrence and deteftation of
them, and refolve that the governor be defired to direct
the attorney general to profecute all perfons concerned
in the faid riot, and that a proclamation be iffued, offering a reward for making difcovery, fo as the rioters
or abettors may be brought to condign punifhment."
Neither rioters nor abettors had any thing to fear from
either proclamation or profecution; and knew themfelves to be perfectly fafe, notwithftanding the report;
but the politicians faw it was expedient to fay fomething
to fave appearances, and well-meaning perfons might
join them, in the fimplicity of their hearts, believing
that the others intended their words fhould be productive of the events to which they feemingly pointed. At
the fitting of the fuperior court in Auguft, the grand
jury was found to have among them feveral of the abettors of the Bofton rioters, and particularly the famous
captain

captain Malcolm, a circumstance that necessarily quashed all informations and prosecutions, as it strongly foreboded their issue.

The council in a letter to Lord *Hillsborough* insinuated, that the commissioners had concerted a plan, with the design of raising a disturbance by the seizure of the sloop Liberty. The insinuation must be placed to the ill will they bore to the commissioners, more than to any thing beside. On the twenty-ninth of July, they said, " The commissioners were not obliged to quit the town; there never had been any insult offered to them; their quitting the town was a voluntary act of their own; we do not apprehend there was any sufficient ground for their quitting it." But it appears from a manuscript in Mr. *Hutchinson*'s hand writing, that the commissioners applied, December the nineteenth, to each of the judges of the superior court separately, for their opinions upon four questions; and that after having conferred together, they were unanimously of opinion,

" That from the spirit which had been excited in the populace against all the commissioners of the customs, Mr. *Temple* excepted, they could not have remained long in safety at Boston, after the seizure of the sloop Liberty, but would have been in great danger of violence to their persons and properties from a mob, which at that time it was generally expected would be raised for that purpose:

" That government was insufficient to restrain, suppress or punish the several mobs which had been assembled since the fourteenth of August 1765; and that at the time of the commissioners retiring to the castle, there

was

was no probability that the fame authority could have had any greater force :

" That they could not have returned to town, and executed their commiffion with fafety, at any time after they withdrew, before the arrival of his majefty's troops :

" And that they knew of no better meafure that they could have taken, than retiring to Caftle William."

Mr. *Temple* was excepted, for he was not obnoxious to the populace, being averfe to the eftablifhment of the board of commiffioners, which leffened both his falary and power. He wifhed the diffolution of it, and to be reftored to his former place of furveyor general of the cuftoms. Though the reft of the commiffioners could not have returned to have executed their commiffion with fafety, they might moft probably have returned and been fafe, had they declined executing the fame, which however was not to be expected. They continued at, but were not confined to the caftle. They rode about the country at pleafure, without any interruption from the people.

The commiffioners wrote to general Gage, colonel June
Dalrymple, and commodore Hood, defiring troops to [15.]
fupport them in their office. Whatever this application might contribute toward the fending of them, yet it certainly did not give rife to it. Meafures had been taken to procure them long before. Mr. *Paxton*, when in London the preceding year, told Mr. *Bollan* repeatedly, that Mr. *Hutchinfon* and fome other of his friends were of opinion, that ftanding troops were neceffary to fupport the authority of the government at Bofton; and that he was authorized to inform him of this their opinion. Moft probably he was authorized to inform others
alfo.

also. Mr. *Bollan* was against sending troops, and when
there was a talk of doing it, endeavoured to prevent
it, and freely related to a gentleman of considerable influence, what some of the principal merchants said, that
they who should send over the standing troops, would
certainly be cursed to all posterity *. But the disposition of some to try the experiment was strengthened by
a letter from the commissioners to the lords of the treasury received before the riot happened; and rendered
efficacious upon the arrival of governor *Bernard*'s letters
at the secretary's office, especially that of March, giving an aggravated detailed account of a terrible difturbance on the joyous anniversary of the repeal of the
stamp-act; which general *Gage*, in his of October to
Lord *Hillsborough*, declared, from the best intelligence he
could procure, to have been trifling. When the matter
came to be considered, it was agreed to send troops to
June
8.
Boston. Accordingly, Lord *Hillsborough* in his secret
and confidential letter to general *Gage*, wrote, " I am
to signify to you his majesty's pleasure, that you do
forthwith order one regiment, or such force as you shall
think necessary, to Boston, to be quartered in that town,
and to give every legal assistance to the civil magistrate,
in the preservation of the public peace, and to the officers of the revenue, in the execution of the laws of
trade and revenue; and as this appears to be a service
of a delicate nature, and possibly leading to consequences
not easily foreseen, I am directed by the king to recommend to you to make choice of an officer for the command of those troops, upon whose prudence, resolution,
and integrity, you can entirely rely." And on the

* Mr. Bollan's letter to Mr. Hutchinson, August 11, 1767.

eleventh,

eleventh, he informed the governor, that his majefty, from the reprefentation made by him and the commiffioners of the cuftoms, had directed one regiment at leaft to be ftationed in Bofton, and to garrifon, and (if neceffary) to repair the caftle; and had ordered a frigate, two floops, and two cutters to repair to, and remain in the harbour of Bofton for fupporting and affifting the officers of the cuftoms in the execution of their duty. His lordfhip's letter to Gage being dated two days before the riot occafioned by the feizure of the floop Liberty, the order contained in it could not poffibly be founded on fuch riot; though the riot, with the fubfequent tranfactions of the town, might be related as a reafon in the refolves afterward drawn up, exhibiting the neceffity of fending a military force to Bofton. But perfons in office are liable to fall into miftakes, through the multiplicity and hurry of bufinefs, and for want of due confideration, or better intelligence. In this way you may account for his lordfhip's figning a circular Sept. letter, to the governor and council of *Rhode Ifland*, to 2. the following purpofe—" Gentlemen, the king having obferved, that the governors of his colonies have, upon feveral occafions, taken upon them to communicate to their councils and affemblies, either the whole or parts of letters from his majefty's principal fecretary of ftate, I have it in command to fignify, that it is his majefty's pleafure, that you do not upon any pretence whatever communicate to the affembly, any copies or extracts of fuch letters, unlefs you have his majefty's particular directions." This was foon publifhed in the *Providence* Gazette after being received. That colony choofes its own governor annually, and he has neither

right

right nor power to withhold from the assembly copies of any such letters. Upon another occasion his lordship gave orders to the governor of *Pennsylvania*, in case the assembly did not act conformable to what was expected, immediately to dissolve them; whereas it is the inherent privilege of that house, to sit on their own adjournments; and the governor has no power to dissolve them.

Nov. 3.
    A month after the arrival of the troops at *Boston*, Mr. *Hancock* was served with a precept for 9000 l. sterling, by the marshal of the court of Admiralty. The marshal having arrested him, demanded bail for 3000 l. Five other gentlemen were arrested for the like sum. He and the five others gave bail. The commissioners prosecuted the supposed owner, and each person they imagined concerned in unloading the wines, for the value of the whole cargo and treble damages. The vessel seized was restored after a long detention; and the suits in the court of Admiralty dropped, March the twenty-sixth, 1769, by a declaration from the king's advocate, that his majesty would prosecute no further. It was idle to think of supporting the prosecution by sufficient evidence. Want of inclination or fear would prevent witnesses appearing, and corruption would procure counter-evidence from men of no principle, who would justify themselves from the prosecution's being built upon acts of parliament, to which they supposed the colonies owed no obedience; and would plead, as in too many instances is done at home, that it is not he who takes, but he who imposes the oath, who is chargeable with the crime of swearing falsely. The law would not allow the prosecuted any costs or damages. In this case
the

the allowance would have been unreasonable; the innocence of the parties could not have been urged in its behalf.

The colonists could not overlook the good effects produced by the former non-importation agreement; and were earnest for playing off the same engine against the new attempts of ministry, to saddle them with the payment of taxes. About the beginning of April, several gentlemen of *Boston* and *New York*, wrote to others at *Philadelphia*, in order to learn, whether they would unite with them, in stopping the importation of goods from *Great Britain*, until certain acts of parliament should be repealed, which were thought to be injurious to their rights, as freemen and British subjects. A numerous meeting of merchants followed, when an address was read to them. It set forth the claims of the colonies, and then went into an enumeration of grievances, which the colonists had long borne, and seemed willing to forget, had they not been alarmed afresh by the late proceedings of the ministry. The address remarked, that, in the act obliging the several assemblies to provide quarters for the soldiers, &c. a power is granted to every officer, upon obtaining a warrant from any justice (which warrant the justice is empowered and ordered to grant, without any previous oath) to break into any house by day or by night, under pretence (these are the words of the act) of searching for deserters. It pointed out to them the danger they were in, of having erected over them a despotic government, to rule them as slaves. It called upon them to deliberate, by what means they might defend their rights and liberties, and obtain a repeal of the obnoxious acts. It

VOL. I.   R   urged

urged them to join in the meafure propofed by their brethren of *Bofton* and *New York*; and clofed with " *United we conquer, divided we die.*" The *Pennfylvania* merchants agreed with the other colonies in opinion, that the revenue acts were unconftitutional; but declined adopting the non-importation agreement, as they believed it to be premature. They knew that multitudes in Great Britain would fuffer much by a fufpenfion of trade with her, whenever it fhould be carried into execution; and judged that it ought not to be made ufe of, but as the laft and moft certain remedy, when petitions proved ineffectual. They faw clearly, that the acts were manifeftly injurious to the Britifh trade, and hoped the parliament would therefore find it expedient to repeal them; and were willing to allow a proper time for the repeals being effected. Thefe reafons induced them to refufe complying with the folicitations of their neighbours. But the merchants and traders of Philadelphia agreed upon a memorial, wherein they ftated their grievances, which was tranfmitted to their mercantile friends in London; on whofe affiftance they relied for an application to government for relief; and this they hoped to obtain as to fome of the chief, though it might not be all the articles of complaint.

But the *Bofton* merchants and traders, having been drawn in, partly by their connections with the politicians and the fear of oppofing the popular ftream, agreed upon a new fubfcription paper, wherein they engaged as follows—" We will not fend for or import from Great Britain, either upon our own account, or upon commiffions, this fall, any other goods than what are already ordered for the fall fupply."—" We will

Aug. 1.

not

not fend for or import any kind of goods or merchandife from Great Britain, &c. from the firft of January
1769, to the firft of January 1770, except falt, coals,
fifh-hooks and lines, hemp and duck, bar-lead and fhot,
wool-cards and card wire."—" We will not purchafe of
any factor or others, any kind of goods imported from
Great Britain, from January 1769 to January 1770."—
" We will not import, on our own account, or on
commiffions, or purchafe of any, who fhall import from
any other colony in America, from January 1769 to
January 1770, any tea, glafs, paper or other goods,
commonly imported from Great Britain."—" We will
not, from and after the firft of January 1769, import
into this province any tea, paper, glafs, or painters colours, until the act impofing duties on thofe articles
fhall be repealed." The fubfcription paper was carried
about town ; and, at length, generally figned ; though
feveral refpectable merchants remained non-fubfcribers.
The fame month the *Connecticut* and *New York* merchants came into fimilar agreements ; and thofe of *Salem*,
the beginning of September. Some merchants had undoubtedly the forefight to provide for an abftinence
from importation for a year, by unufually large orders.

A report having been fpread, that governor *Bernard*
had intimated his apprehenfions, that one or more regiments were to be daily expected at *Bofton*, a meeting
of the inhabitants was called, and a committee appointed to wait on him, to know the grounds of his apprehenfions, and to pray him to iffue precepts forthwith
for convening a general affembly. He acknowledged
his having received thofe informations which produced
fuch apprehenfions, but faid they were of a private na-

Sept.
12.

R 2

ture.

ture. The calling of another affembly he told them
could not be complied with, till his majefty's commands
were received. The anfwer being reported, it was re-
13. folved, " That the freeholders, and other inhabitants of
the town of Bofton, will, at the peril of their lives and
fortunes, take all legal and conftitutional meafures to
defend all and fingular the rights, liberties, privileges,
and immunities granted in their royal charter." It was
alfo declared to be the opinion of thofe prefent, " That
a fuitable number of perfons to act for them as a committee in convention, with fuch as may be fent to join
them from the other towns, fhould be now chofen, in
order that fuch meafures may be confulted and advifed,
as his majefty's fervice, and the fafety of the province
may require." It was then voted, " That the felect
men of Bofton fhould write to the felect men of the
other towns, to acquaint them with the foregoing refolutions, and to propofe, that a convention be held at
Faneuil Hall in Bofton, on the twenty-fecond inftant."
It was afterward voted, " That, as there is an apprehenfion, in the minds of many, of an approaching war
with France, thofe inhabitants who are not provided, be
requefted to furnifh themfelves forthwith with arms."

22.   The *convention*, confifting of committees from ninety-
fix towns and eight diftricts, met as propofed; and after
conference and confultation, petitioning the governor,
declaring that they only confidered themfelves as private
perfons, making loyal profeffions, expreffing their averfion to ftanding armies, to tumults and diforders, their
readinefs to affift in fuppreffing riots and preferving the
peace, and recommending patience and regard to good order, they broke up and went home on Thurfday the twenty-ninth.

ty-ninth. Advice was received the day before, that the men of war and tranfports from Halifax, with fome hundreds of troops, were fafe arrived at Nantafket harbour, a few miles below Caftle William. Two days before the convention clofed, they difpatched a letter to Mr. *De Berdt*, containing a reprefentation of what had taken place, with fuch papers and inftructions as were judged moft fuitable to the circumftances of their affembly.

When the news was firft received of troops being ordered to Bofton, broad hints were thrown out that they fhould never land; and to ftrengthen the appearance of an intention to oppofe them, a barrel was placed upon the beacon, fuppofed to be a tar barrel, to have been fired to call in the country upon the troops appearing, which was afterward found to be an empty nail barrel. Many of the deputies came down to the convention, with inftructions and difpofitions to prevent the Boftonians involving the province in the fatal confequences of their own furious devices. Numbers were from the beginning, fenfible of the impropriety and danger of their proceeding, and defirous by a moderate conduct, to correct the one and waid off the other. The governor's meffage to them after their addrefs was high, and might tend to keep fome of them in awe, as the troops were thought to be at no great diftance. When Mr. *Otis* joined them, inftead of being violent, he was quite moderate; and when Mr. *Samuel Adams* attempted to launch out in the fame free and unreftrained language, to which he was accuftomed in the houfe of reprefentatives, he was prefently filenced.

The convention having finifhed in the above manner, the perfons juft named affumed to themfelves the mo-

deration

deration of thofe whom they called together for very different purpofes. The governor himfelf was not always wholly ignorant of what was going forward among the fons of liberty. He kept up an acquaintance with fome of them; and by that mean, at times, procured ufeful intelligence, while he gave his informers the ftrongeft affurance, that their names fhould not be quoted, nor any communication be made of it, which could make them fufpected. Too much occafion was given for this paragraph, which foon after appeared in the New York Journal.—" I blame the Boftonians for having given fome room for the idle reports of their defigning to oppofe the landing of the troops, by the ridiculous puff and bombaft (for which our eaftern brethren have always been too famous) of warning every man to provide himfelf with a good firelock, ammunition, &c. under the difingenuous jefuitical pretence of the profpect of a French war, full as abfurd and hypocritical as is the pretence of a military eftablifhment in America for its protection and defence."

When the troops from Halifax were daily expected, the governor would have prevailed upon the council to have provided quarters for them in Bofton; but they refufed, and in anfwer to what he advanced, faid, "The troops are by act of parliament, to be quartered no where elfe but in the barracks, until they are full; there are barracks enow at the caftle to hold both the regiments; and it is therefore againft the act to bring any of them into town." However, the orders of general Gage to lieutenant colonel *Dalrymple* were pofitive to land one of them at Bofton. But in the interim captain Montrefor, the engineer, arrived with letters of a fubfequent date, from gen. Gage for the governor and the colonel, wherein the general mentioned, that it being reported and believed from a number of private letters and the publications, that the people in and about Boston had revolted, he had therefore fent the captain to affift the forces, and enable them to recover and maintain the castle, and fuch other posts as they could fecure. Upon this the colonel altered his plan, and concluded to land both regiments at Boston without lofs of time. The fleet therefore was immediately put into motion, and by the next morning commanded the whole town. Every thing being fully prepared, near upon fourteen* ships of war lying with their broadfides to the town, having fprings on their cables, and their guns ready for firing inftantly upon the place, in cafe of the leaft oppofition; about one o'clock at noon, October the firft, the troops Oct. began landing, under cover of the ships cannon, with- 1. out moleftation; and having effected it, marched into the common, with muskets charged, bayonets fixed, drums beating, fifes playing, &c. making, with the train of artillery, upward of 700 men. In the evening, the felect men were required to quarter the two regiments in town, but abfolutely refufed. One of the regiments however, being without their camp equipage, was humanely permitted to enter *Faneuil-hall* and its chambers, about nine o'clock at night, that fo the men might enjoy a temporary shelter. The next being Lord's day, the town or state houfe was opened in the evening, by

---

* The Launcefton of 40 guns, the Mermaid of 28, Glafgow 20, Beaver 14, Senegal 14, Bonetta 10, and feveral armed fchooners, befides the Romney of 60 guns, and the other ships which had been fome time in the harbour.

order

order of the governor, for the reception of the troops, who took poffeffion of all the chambers, except the one appropriated for the meeting of the council. He certainly ftretched his authority in feveral points; but particularly in thus acting. This ftep was an infult not only to the town, as it was a great annoyance to the gentlemen and merchants, who had been accuftomed to make the lower floor their exchange, but to the whole colony, as the reprefentatives chamber was now poffeffed by the foldiery. After the quarters of the troops were fettled, the main guard was pofted directly oppofite to, and not twelve yards from the ftate houfe, with two field pieces pointed to it. It was with no fmall indignation that the people beheld the reprefentatives chamber, court-houfe, and Faneuil-hall—feats of freedom and juftice—occupied by troops; and guards placed at the doors, and the council paffing through the guards in going to their own chamber. They refented alfo the common's being covered with tents, and alive with foldiers; their marchings and counter-marchings to relieve the guards; the town's being a perfect garrifon, and the inhabitants being challenged by the fentinels, as they paffed and re-paffed. Perfons devoutly inclined, complained much of being difturbed at public worfhip on the fabbaths, with drums beating, and fifes playing, to which they had never been accuftomed in the Maffachufetts. Quarters being obtained for the troops, the council were required to provide barrack provifions for them, agreeable to act of parliament; but refolutely declined going into any meafure which might be conftrued into a fubmiffion to the faid act. The oppofition of the council to the quartering of, and providing for the troops,

was

was so encouraged and strengthened by Mr. *James Bowdoin*, who was one of them, that Mr. *Hutchinson*, in his letter of November 6, ascribed the whole to his management. It was thought that the peaceable landing of the troops was not what some of the ministry either expected or desired; and that they were in hopes, that the folly and rage of the town and colony would have led them into an hostile opposition, and thereby have afforded an opportunity for giving them some naval and military correction. Under this apprehension, the gentleman, who delivered the first dispatches from governor Bernard, containing the account of the troops having landed, &c. narrowly watched the countenance and conduct of the person who read them, and was confirmed in such opinion. But had he not possessed that opinion, it might not have been excited by what he observed. The sentiments of the military differed so extremely from those of the Bostonians, who were unjustly viewed as rebelliously inclined, that it was not to be wondered at that they were insulted and abused, and that quarrels should ensue, though they did not proceed soon to a dangerous height. Undoubtedly the inhabitants could not be continually blameless: there would necessarily be some rash and imprudent persons among such multitudes; but the greatest rashness and imprudence lay in the sending of troops on a service, which could have been effectually and better executed by a naval force properly stationed and employed. Ships of war might have possessed the harbour till the commissioners could have executed their office with safety.

The committee of merchants in *London* paid a due attention to the memorial sent them by the merchants and

and traders of *Philadelphia*, and took pains to obtain relief from the grievances therein complained of, though without effect. The department to which they applied, afforded little hopes of redrefs in a way that might put an end to the differences that had arifen between Great Britain and her American colonies. The act impofing duties on glafs, paper, &c. was acknowledged to be inexpedient; but it was added, " Such has been the unjuftifiable conduct of fome in America, that the prefent juncture is not a proper feafon for a repeal." Adminiftration was firmly refolved to oppofe it with their utmoft ftrength, while it fhould be infifted on by threats on the part of the colonifts, for in that light they confidered the fteps which had been taken by them to obtain redrefs. It was faid, " If a proper difpofition appears in the colonies, and their merchants, in a fucceeding feffion, fhall think proper to petition parliament on the principle of inexpediency only, there is every reafon to believe that no part of adminiftration will object to the repeal." But the minifter did not declare what was the proper difpofition he expected. No fooner were the *Philadelphians* apprifed, by the receipt of this information, that no hope remained of a repeal in that feffion, than they unanimoufly entered into the very agreement, which fome months before, when propofed to them, they had declined: and it was their opinion, that as the agreement had been formed on mature deliberation, the people of the province would firmly adhere to it. Of this they gave notice to the committee of 1769. merchants in *London*, by letter of April 8, 1769. In April 8. that letter, remarking upon the information they had received, they wrote—" It would become perfons in power

power to confider, whether even the unjuftifiable behaviour of thofe who think themfelves aggrieved, will
juftify a perfeverance in a matter confeffed to be wrong.
Certain it is, that the wifdom of government is better
manifefted, its honor and authority better maintained
and fupported, by correcting the errors it may have
committed, than by perfifting in them, and thereby
rifking the lofs of the fubjects affections. We are apprehenfive that perfons in power are greatly abufed, and
that the people of America have been grofsly mifreprefented, otherwife the fteps which they have taken to
obtain redrefs, could never be looked upon as threats.
Threats they never intended; but as all the American
colonies were equally affected, it was thought that their
joint petitions would have more weight; and for this
end the feveral affemblies communicated their fentiments to each other. This ftep, to the inexpreffible
furprife of all America, is reprefented as " a flagitious attempt, a meafure of a moft dangerous and factious tendency, &c." The diffolution of affemblies that followed, and the meafures purfued to enforce the acts in
America, awak ned the fears, and exafperated the minds
of the people to a very great degree. They therefore
determined not only to defeat the intent of the acts, by
refraining from the ufe of thofe articles on which duties
were laid, but to put a ftop to the importation of goods
from Great Britain. This is the only threat we know
of; and if this is fufficient to engage the miniftry to
oppofe a repeal of the acts, we apprehend the miniftry
muft, by a change of meafures, endeavour to regain the
affections of the people before they can be induced to
alter their determination."

" The

" The Americans confider themfelves as Britifh fub-
jeds, entitled to all the rights and privileges of freemen.
They think there can be no liberty without a fecurity
of property; and that there can be no property, if any
can, without their confent, deprive them of the hard-
earned fruits of their labor. They know that they
have no choice in the election of the members of parliament; and from their fituation, never can have any.
Every act of parliament therefore, that is made for
raifing a revenue in America, is in their opinion, depriving them of their property without their confent,
and confequently is an invafion of their liberty."

" If then the acts cannot be repealed while the
miniftry objects, and if to remove the objections the
Americans muft give up their fentiments, we muft candidly confefs we have little hopes of a repeal ever taking
place; much lefs is it to be expected, that the merchants will prefume to petition parliament on the principle of inexpediency only, when every affembly on the
continent are applying for a repeal on the principle of
right."

" Happy had it been for both countries if the idea
of raifing taxes in America had never been ftarted;
however, if the acts complained of are repealed, and
no other of the like nature are attempted hereafter, the
prefent unhappy jealoufies will, we believe, quickly fubfide, and the people of both countries in a fhort time,
return to their ufual good humor, confidence, and
affection."

If miniftry thought that the refolves of the houfe of
lords, the preceding December, would have put a ftop
to non-importation agreements and the fpirited exertions

5   of

of the colonists, they foon found themfelves much miftaken. It can fcarce be imagined, but that fome of the
Philadelphia gentlemen had received the account of fuch
refolves; for the above letter was in anfwer to London
ones of January 4th and 26th, and yet they proceeded
as has been related.

The refolves cenfured the votes, refolutions, and proceedings of the houfe of reprefentatives of *Maffachufetts*
of January and February; as alfo the declarations, refolutions and proceedings in the town of *Bofton*. They
pronounced the election of deputies to fit in convention,
and the meeting of fuch convention, daring infults offered to his majefty's authority, and audacious ufurpa-
tions of the powers of government. The lords then
ordered an humble addrefs to be prefented to his majefty; in which they exprefled their fatisfaction in the
meafures his majefty had purfued; gave him the ftrongeft
affurances, that they would effectually fupport him in
fuch further ones as might be found neceffary to maintain the civil magiftrates, in a due execution of the laws,
within the Maffachufetts-bay; and befeeched him to
direct the governor to take the moft effectual methods
for procuring the fulleft information, touching all treafons
committed within that government fince the 30th of
December 1767, and to tranfmit the fame, with the
names of the perfons moft active in the commiffion of
fuch offences; in order that his majefty might iffue a
fpecial commiffion for hearing and determining the faid
offences, within the realm, purfuant to the ftatute of the
35th year of *Henry* VIII.

The refolutions and addrefs were fent down to the
houfe of commons for their concurrence. Colonel *Barre*
oppofed

oppofed them; and directing himfelf to the miniftry, faid, " Away with thefe partial refentful trifles, calculated to irritate, not to quell or appeafe, inadequate to their purpofe, unworthy of us! Why will you endeavour to deceive yourfelves and us? You know that it is not this place only that difputes your right, but every part. They tell you, that you have no right from one end of the continent to the other. My fentiments of this matter you well know. Confider well what you are doing. Act openly and honeftly. Tell them, you will tax them; and that they muft fubmit. Do not adopt this little, infidious, futile plan. They will de-

Feb. 9. fpife you for it." However, on the ninth of February, they were agreed to and returned with fome amendments; and the addrefs was ordered to be prefented by both houfes. The *Maffachufetts*, with becoming firmnefs, conftantly afferted their rights, which drew down upon them minifterial vengeance. They had no general affembly when the refolves and addrefs reached America, the laft having been diffolved for refufing to comply with the mandate to refcind, and the time appointed by charter for calling another not being arrived. But the *Virginia* houfe of burgeffes entered upon the fubject.

May 16. They met on the eighth of May, and on the fixteenth took into ferious confideration the ftate of the colony, being alarmed at the diftrefs in which all America was likely to be involved. They came to feveral neceffary refolutions, copies of which they gave their fpeaker, with particular directions to tranfmit them without delay, to the fpeakers of the feveral houfes of affembly on the continent; whofe concurrence in the like was requefted.

The

The refolves exprefs, " That the fole right of impofing taxes on the inhabitants of the colony, is now,
and ever hath been legally and conftitutionally vefted in
the houfe of burgeffes, with confent of the council, and
of the king, or his governor for the time being—That
it is the privilege of the inhabitants to petition their fovereign for redrefs of grievances, and that it is lawful
to procure the concurrence of his majefty's other colonies in dutiful addreffes, praying the royal interpofition
in favor of the violated rights of America—That all
trials for treafon, mifprifion of treafon, or for any felony
or crime whatfoever, committed by any perfon refiding
in faid colony, ought to be in and before his majefty's
courts within faid colony ; and that the feizing any perfon refiding in the colony, fufpected of any crime whatfoever, committed therein, and fending fuch perfon to
places beyond the fea to be tried, is highly derogatory
of the rights of Britifh fubjects, as thereby the ineftimable privilege of being tried by a jury from the vicinage, as well as the liberty of producing witneffes on
fuch trial, will be taken away from the party accufed."
Thefe refolutions were followed by a humble addrefs
to his majefty, befeeching his royal interpofition to quiet
the minds of his loyal fubjects in the colony, and to
avert thofe dangers and miferies, which will enfue from
feizing and carrying beyond fea the inhabitants of America to be tried in any other manner, than by the ancient
and long eftablifhed mode of proceeding.

The next day Lord *Bottetourt* fent for them, and faid, May
" Mr. fpeaker and gentlemen of the houfe of burgeffes, 17.
I have heard of your refolves, aud augur ill of their
effects. You have made it my duty to diffolve you,

and

and you are diſſolved accordingly." The gentlemen
who compoſed the houſe, being reduced by the diſſo-
lution to private perſons, repaired immediately to another place, that ſo they might conſider what meaſures
were proper to be taken, and choſe the late ſpeaker
Peyton Randolph eſq; moderator.

8.   They entered into an aſſociation unanimouſly [which
they ſubſcribed and recommended to all merchants,
gentlemen, traders and others] againſt importing any
goods taxed, and many other articles; againſt wines,
againſt importing and purchaſing negroes, &c.

The next month, the *Maryland* gentlemen and merchants entered into a non-importation agreement ſimilar
to the *Virginian.*

The *South Carolinians* followed the example.

The inhabitants of *Charleſtown* broke off all commerce with the *Rhode Iſlanders* and *Georgians,* whom they
charged with having acted a moſt ſingularly infamous
part, from the beginning of the preſent glorious ſtruggle
for the preſervation of American rights. This had its
effect, and *Georgia* came into the non-importation
agreement September the nineteenth; *Providence* October the tenth; but *Rhode Iſland* not till the thirtieth.

Oct.   The *North Carolina* aſſembly came to the like reſolutions with the *Virginia* houſe of burgeſſes, for which
governor *Tryon* diſſolved them. Upon that, the gentlemen who had compoſed it, repaired to the court houſe,
choſe the late ſpeaker moderator, and came to a reſolution for an aſſociation againſt importing, &c. conformable to what had been done elſewhere. Thus the
non-importation agreement became general, and was
forwarded by the very means applied for its prevention.

Meet-

Meetings of the affociators were regularly held. Committees were appointed to examine the cargoes of all veffels arriving from Britain; and regular votes and refolutions of cenfure were paffed in thofe meetings, upon fuch as refufed to concur in the affociations, and their names publifhed in the news-papers as enemies to their country. The decrees of thofe committees met with a refpect and obedience denied to the conftitutional authority of government. In fome cafes goods imported from Britain were locked up in warehoufes, under the care of the committees, and in a few inftances returned. *Portfmouth*, the only feaport in *New Hampfhire*, never came into the non-importation agreement. Governor *Wentworth* had addrefs enough to prevent it, and keep all quiet. There are few private fchools in that colony, and the bulk of the people are very illiterate. If a perfon can write a note of hand, read a chapter, and cypher to the rule of three, he paffes for a man of learning. Men, whofe capacities remain fmall for want of ufe and improvement, and who have little knowledge, are liable to be duped by thofe who poffefs fuperior rank and abilities. The affociations were as general, and in common as well obferved as could be reafonably expected, confidering the difadvantages and loffes they neceffarily occafioned to many. But it is not to be thought, that there were no collufions; that all the goods belonging to the profeffing fons of liberty, which were ftored, remained in the warehoufes, without being conveyed out upon particular occafions, and to ferve certain purpofes; that all, who had given their names or honors not to import, did not privately order fome of the prohibited articles to pleafe themfelves, families or neighbours; that when, fome months afterward, the zeal of the daughters of liberty, in feveral of the colonies, profcribed the drinking of tea, and ren-. dered the difufe of it a univerfal fafhion, all were fo true to their engagements, as not to fip their green or bohea in fecret, or under a new name; and that all who affociated or agreed to the ftoring of their goods, did it voluntarily and without compulfion. The fear or appearance of a mob often produced a compliance in perfons, who would have gladly retained their goods till they could have turned the fame into cafh; and brought them to own, that they were willing that they fhould be ftored, juft as they would have been willing at fea to have thrown them overboard to efcape perfonal fhipwreck. The committees had the arts of perfuafion; and in fome places their moft powerful arguments for reducing the obftinate were not known to be ufed by them.

The importer is fent for, and defired to come into the agreement; he declines; he muft fell; his liveli- hood depends upon it. Arguments are ufed for his complying, and he is urged, foothed and entreated; but it avails nothing. He is determined at all hazards to difpofe of his goods as purchafers offer. Some of the mobility, or their leaders, are told, that the im- porter cannot be prevailed upon. In a day or two he finds himfelf furrounded; in danger of an affault; is terrified; inquires the reafon; and upon learning it, hurries to the committee; begs their interpofition; complies with what was before defired of him; hopes
that.

that they will reſtore him to the good graces of his fellow townſmen or citizens, and thanks them for their
promiſed aſſiſtance, not in the leaſt ſuſpecting the depth
of their contrivance. Every committee however, had
not this prudent forecaſt, whereby to accompliſh their
deſigns without expoſing their own characters.

We have hitherto omitted recording the tranſactions
of the *Maſſachuſetts* aſſembly in the preſent year, the
Virginia houſe of burgeſſes demanding a prior attention,
but now proceed to them.

The general court being called together according to May
charter, a committee from the houſe of repreſentatives 31.
remonſtrated to his excellency, " That an armament by
ſea and land inveſting this metropolis (*Boſton*,) and a
military guard with cannon pointed at the door of the
ſtate houſe where the aſſembly is held, are inconſiſtent
with that dignity and freedom, with which they have a
right to deliberate, conſult, and determine. They expect that your excellency will, as his majeſty's repreſentative, give effectual orders for the removal of the above-
mentioned forces by ſea and land out of this port, and
the gates of this city during the ſeſſion of the ſaid aſſembly." The governor returned for anſwer, " Gentlemen, I have no authority over his majeſty's ſhips in
this port, or his troops within this town."

He negatived eleven of the perſons elected to form June
the council.   1.

The houſe in a meſſage to him declared—" The uſe 13.
of the military power to enforce the execution of the laws,
is, in the opinion of this houſe, inconſiſtent with the
ſpirit of a free conſtitution, and the very nature of government.

vernment. This military force is uncontrollable by any authority in the province: it is then a power without any check here, and therefore it is fo far abfolute. What privilege! what fecurity then is left to this houfe!"

It was not urged, whatever the cafe might admit; " The governor is the king's *locum tenens*, and his office entire. The chief civil and military authority being by the Britifh and our conftitution infeparable, the king cannot fever them. An independent military tends to the utter overthrow of the civil power. The operations of the great feal, which is *clavis regni*, cannot be controlled by the privy feal, the king's fignet, fign manual, or fignification of his pleafure by his fecretary; in other words, our charter cannot be infringed by any of thefe."

The houfe firmly declined doing bufinefs furrounded with an armed force, fo that the governor the next day adjourned the court to *Cambridge*.

July 6. His excellency fent a meffage to them, with the accounts of the expenditures already incurred by quartering his majefty's troops, defiring funds to be provided for difcharging the fame, and requiring a provifion for the further quartering the forces in Bofton and Caftle Ifland, according to act of parliament.

7. The houfe of affembly, as though they meant by it to defpife the parliamentary refolves, no lefs than maintain their own privileges, paffed a number of refolves, and among them the following:

" That a general difcontent on account of the revenue acts, an expectation of a fudden arrival of a military power to enforce faid acts, an apprehenfion of the troops being quartered upon the inhabitants, the general

ral court diffolved, the governor refufing to call a new one, and the people almoft reduced to a ftate of defpair, rendered it highly expedient and neceffary for the people to convene by their committees; to affociate, confult, and advife the beft means to promote peace and good order; to prefent their united complaints to the throne; and jointly to pray for the royal interpofition in favor of their violated rights. Nor can this procedure poffibly be illegal, as they exprefsly difclaimed all governmental acts:

" That the eftablifhment of a ftanding army in this colony, in time of peace, is an invafion of natural rights:

" That a ftanding army is not known as a part of the *Britifh* conftitution:

" That fending an armed force into the colony under pretence of affifting the civil authority, is highly dangerous to the people, unprecedented and unconftitutional."

The laft is the fame with that of *Virginia.*

The governor called upon them to anfwer, whether 12. they would or would not make provifion for the troops.

The houfe by meffage, after remarking upon the 15. mutiny or billetting act, anfwered, " As we cannot confiftently with our own honor or intereft, much lefs with the duty we owe to our conftituents, fo we never fhall make any provifion of funds for the purpofes in your feveral meffages." Upon that the governor prorogued them to the tenth of January to meet at Bofton.

South Carolina affembly, no lefs than the *Maffachufetts,* ventured to difobey the mutiny act, and adopted fimilar refolutions to thofe of *Virginia.* The *Maryland* lower

houfe

houfe entered partly into fimilar ones, but the laft was omitted, and the firft more ftrongly expreffed. The *Delaware* Counties early followed the lead of *Virginia*, and adopted their laft refolve *verbatim*; and toward the clofe of the year, the *New York* affembly concurred in their refolves with Virginia.

The propofal of parliament for tranfporting perfons from *America* in order to trial in *Great Britain*, purfuant to the ftatute of *Henry* VIII. excited a general alarm through the continent. The procedure they recommended was not wholly without precedent. The cafe of Culpeper has been already related (p. 76.) Under queen Anne, in 1710, the ringleaders of an unnatural contention in *Antigua*, wherein the governor was murdered, were brought to Great Britain, tried, and many of them convicted and executed upon this ftatute. Precedents however, will never reconcile fenfible men to practices which, though legal, are fraught with cruelty, and liable to the moft horrid abufes. Befide, the ftatute was become obfolete.

The *Virginia* houfe of burgeffes, in their addrefs to his majefty, expreffed themfelves with propriety upon this fubject, " When we confider, that by the eftablifhed laws and conftitution of this colony, the moft ample provifion is made for apprehending and punifhing all thofe who fhall dare to engage in any treafonable practices againft your majefty, or difturb the tranquillity of government; we cannot, without horror, think of the unufual, and permit us, with all humility, to add unconftitutional and illegal mode, recommended to your majefty, of feizing and carrying beyond the fea, the inhabitants of America fufpected of any crime, and of
trying

trying fuch perfons in any other manner, than by the
ancient and long eftablifhed courfe of proceedings; for
how truly deplorable muft be the cafe of a wretched
American, who having incurred the difpleafure of any
one in power, is dragged from his native home and his
deareft domeftic connections, thrown into a prifon, not
to wait his trial before a court, jury or judges, from a
knowledge of whom he is encouraged to hope for
fpeedy juftice, but to exchange his imprifonment in his
own country for fetters among ftrangers. Conveyed to a diftant land, where no friend, no relation will
alleviate his diftreffes, or minifter to his neceffities, and
where no witnefs can be found to teftify his innocence,
fhunned by the reputable and honeft, and configned to
the fociety and converfe of the wretched and abandoned, he can only pray, that he may foon end his mifery
with his life."

We have been reviewing the noble and animated proceedings of the *Virginians* and others, in behalf of liberty; and cannot but regret, that the exiftence of flavery and its effects among them, fhould adminifter the
leaft occafion for any one's writing concerning them.—
" The laft refolves of the Virginia burgeffes deferve a
very hard name. It is indeed laughable, to fee a few
diffipated bafhaws, tyrants over a parcel of wretched
negro flaves, meet together and give themfelves airs
againft Great Britain upon the fubject of liberty—this
applies to all the fouthern colonies. The fpirit of independency in *New England* is more confiftent and characteriftic of the people, but *Virginia* a... the *Carolinas* are
but *petii maitres* in the bufinefs *."

* Mr. M. H's letter to Mr. Hutchinfon,

It

It is time to crofs the Atlantic, and advert to what was doing in *Britain*. An attempt in the houfe of commons, to bring on a repeal of the obnoxious act before the feffion clofed, proved ineffectual. It was objected from every quarter, that it was not a proper time. Lord *North*'s language upon the occafion was, " However prudence or policy may hereafter induce us to repeal the late paper and glafs act, I hope we fhall never think of it, *till we fee* AMERICA *proftrate at our feet.*" When the feffion was over, the miniftry, with a view, it might be, of foothing the Americans into a better temper, managing their refpective affemblies, and bringing them to retract their refolutions and open the trade as before, gave out, that at the next feffion the American grievances fhould be redreffed; and Lord *Hillfborough* wrote

May
13.
a circular letter to every colony, mentioning " their intention to propofe, in the next feffion of parliament, taking off the duties upon glafs, paper and colours, upon confideration of fuch duties having been laid contrary to the true principles of commerce;" and affuring each, that his majefty's minifters, " at no time entertained a defign, to propofe to parliament, to lay any further taxes on America, for the purpofe of raifing a revenue." Lord *Bottetourt*, following the directions he had received, fo to explain meafures as might re-eftablifh mutual confidence and affection between Great Britain and her colonies, made the matter known to the *Virginia* houfe of burgeffes in a fpeech, and then declared, " It is my firm opinion, that the plan which I have ftated to you will certainly take place, and that it will never be departed from. I fhall exert every power with which I am or ever may be legally invefted,

in

in order to obtain and maintain, for the continent of America, that fatisfaction which I have been authorized to promife this day, by the confidential fervants of our gracious fovereign, who to my certain knowledge rates his honor fo high, that he would rather part with his crown, than preferve it by deceit." The houfe in their addrefs to him, expreffed their hope and confidence in a manner that implied. fear and diftruft; but willing to make the beft improvement of what his lordfhip faid, clofed with—" We efteem your lordfhip's information, not only as warranted, but even fanctified by the royal word." The conduct of miniftry contained the idea of a public renunciation of all further future taxation of America for a revenue; and the houfe appeared to view it in that light.

But the circular letter was far from fatisfying the American fons of liberty in general. The evident exception of the duty on tea, and the profeffed defign of repealing upon commercial principles, excited their apprehenfions, and confirmed them in the opinion, that the ground of prefent grievances was not to be abandoned, but to be referved for a future opportunity of making frefh effays for the impofition of internal taxes. The merchants and traders therefore, of *Bofton*, foon after the knowledge of it, called a meeting, and unanimoufly voted, that the taking off the duties on the articles of glafs, paper, and colours, would by no means relieve the trade from the difficulties it was under. They then confirmed their former agreement, to fend for no goods contrary thereto, unlefs the revenue acts were repealed.

Though

Though the teſtimony of the *Pennſylvania* aſſembly, againſt the reſolves of parliament, and in favor of the Virginia reſolves, the repeal of all the revenue acts, and a redreſs of all grievances, was wanting; yet the *Philadelphia* committee of merchants, whoſe character and influence in the preſent buſineſs weighed more than that of the aſſembly, failed not to expreſs their minds fully to the committee in *London*, long after the circulatory letter was a matter of notoriety.   They thus Nov. wrote—" Though we are not favored with an anſwer to 25. our letter of the eighth of April laſt, yet as the liberty of America is at ſtake, and the minds of the people here are much agitated, and as the continuation of the unhappy diſpute between the parliament and the colonies muſt not only affect your and our intereſt, but the general intereſt and happineſs of both countries, we think it our duty to apply to you again, and earneſtly requeſt you would uſe your beſt endeavours with thoſe in the adminiſtration, to reſtore tranquillity, and re-eſtabliſh the colonies in the enjoyment of their ancient rights and privileges. We are very ſenſible, that the proſperity of the colonies depends upon their union and connection with Great Britain.   In this ſentiment all the Americans concur, yet they cannot bring themſelves to think, that for this reaſon they ought to be diveſted of liberty and property. Yet this muſt be the caſe, if the parliament can make laws to bind the colonies in all caſes whatever—can levy taxes upon them without their conſent, diſpoſe of the revenues thus raiſed without their control, multiply officers at pleaſure, and aſſign them fees to be paid, without, nay, contrary to and in direct violation of acts of aſſembly regularly

passed

paſſed by the colonies and approved by the crown—can enlarge the powers of admiralty courts, divert the uſual channels of juſtice, deprive the coloniſts of trials by a jury of their countrymen, in ſhort, break down the barriers which their forefathers have erected againſt arbitrary power, and enforce their edicts by fleets and armies. To ſuch a ſyſtem of government the Americans cannot tamely ſubmit; not from an impatience of ſubordination, a ſpirit of independence, or want of loyalty to their king; for in a quiet ſubmiſſion to juſt government, in zeal, affection and attachment to their king, the people of the colonies dare to vie with any the beſt of their fellow ſubjects; but from an innate love of liberty and the Britiſh conſtitution.

In our laſt we intimated our fears, that the miniſtry were greatly abuſed, and the people of America groſsly miſrepreſented, by ſome who did not wiſh well either to Great Britain or the colonies. The letters of one of our American governors, (Bernard) and the memorials of a board lately erected among us, not to mention other documents laid before the public, evince that our fears were but too well grounded. From theſe it is apparent, that every ſly art has been uſed to incenſe the miniſtry againſt the colonies; every argument that malice could invent has been urged to induce them to overturn the ancient foundations of liberty. Nay, to compaſs their baſe ends, they have declared in expreſs terms, and taken uncommon pains, to make the miniſtry believe, that " there has been a long concerted and extenſive plan of reſiſtance to the authority of Great Britain in all the provinces, and that a ſeizure made

made at Boston had haftened the people there to the commiffion of actual violence fooner than was intended."

In juftice to the province where we refide, and indeed to all America, we beg leave to affure you, that fuch reprefentations are without any juft foundation, and that nothing can be a greater deviation from truth. Though at the fame time we confefs, that the ends accomplifhed by thefe and fuch like infamous flanders and vile arts, have given a general alarm, and caufed a univerfal uneafinefs in the minds of the Americans. They now fee a rod of power held over their heads; they begin to feel the feverities of a court, that by its late enlarged jurifdiction, is empowered to break in upon the proceedings of the common law courts; and they have anxious fears for the exiftence of their affemblies, which they confider as their laft and only bulwark againft arbitrary power. For if, fay they, laws can be made, money levied, government fupported, and juftice adminiftered, without the intervention of affemblies, of what ufe can they be? They are no effential member of the conftitution. And being ufelefs and uneffential, is there not reafon to fear they will quickly become difagreeable, and then be wholly laid afide? And when that happens, what fecurity have we for freedom, or what remains for the colonifts, but the moft abject flavery?

Thefe are not the reafonings of politicians; but the fentiments and language of the people in general. For with great truth we may fay, in no country is the love of liberty more deeply rooted, or the knowledge of the rights inherent in freemen, more generally diffufed, and the principles of freedom and government better underftood, than among the Britifh American colonies.

For

For this reaſon we think ourſelves obliged to inform you, that though the merchants have confined their agreements to the repeal of the act laying a duty on tea, paper, glaſs, &c. yet nothing leſs than a repeal of all the revenue acts, and putting things on the ſame footing they were before the late innovations, can or will ſatisfy the minds of the people. The fleets and armies may overawe our towns; admiralty courts and boards of com-miſſioners, with their ſwarms of underlings, may by a rigorous execution of ſevere unconſtitutional acts, ruin our commerce, and render America of little uſe to the people of Britain; but while every farmer is a free-holder, the ſpirit of liberty will prevail, and every at-tempt to diveſt them of the privileges of freemen muſt be attended with conſequences injurious to the colonies and the mother country.

In a matter of ſo great importance you will excuſe this freedom. We conſider the merchants here and in England as the links of the chain that binds both coun-tries together. They are deeply concerned in preſerving the union and connection. Whatever tends to alienate the affections of the coloniſts, or to make them averſe to the cuſtoms, faſhions and manufactures of Britain, hurts their intereſt. While ſome therefore, from am-bitious views and ſiniſter motives, are laboring to widen the breach, we whoſe private intereſt is happily connected with the union, or which is the ſame, with the peace and proſperity of both countries, may be allowed to plead for an end to theſe unhappy diſputes; and that by a repeal of the offenſive acts, the cauſe of jealouſy and uneaſineſs may be removed, tranquillity reſtored, har-

mony

mony and mutual affection re-eftablifhed, and trade return to its ufual channel."

The names of the committee on the back of the draft
from which the above has been copied, were, *Alexander
Hufton*, *John Rhea*, *John Cox*, *John Gibfon*, *Jofeph Swift*,
James Meafe, *J. M. Nefbit*, *William Weft*, *Robert Morris*,
Charles Thomfon, *Daniel Benezet*, *William Fifher*, *George
Roberts*, *Samuel Howell*, and *Thomas Mifflin*.

The ftationing of troops in *Bofton* might afford greater
perfonal fecurity to the commiffioners than what they
could otherwife have enjoyed, and might induce them
or their underlings to exceed the bounds of their commiffion or of prudence, but could not prevent fmuggling,
or protect informers from infult and abufe. Even
fkippers, bound to different parts of the colony, had
their veffels ftopt and libelled for having uncleared articles of trifling confequence on board. Perfons who
ventured to lodge informations, when difcovered, were
often fubject to a treatment, which gave them a ridiculous appearance, and laid them under a difficulty to
clear themfelves of the drefs impofed upon them. They
were ftripped, well tarred, and then covered with fea-
thers. The punifhment took fo with the lower clafs of
people, that afterward it was not confined to informers,
but was alfo applied by them to others who offended
their dread majefty. There was a degree of intemperance and indifcreetnefs on the part of the commiffioners
and cuftom-houfe officers, which tended to irritate;
whereas the utmoft lenity and forbearance were requifite
in order to general tranquillity. Mr. *Eliot* at *New York*,
where fmuggling was as prevalent as at Bofton, found

it

it neceſſary to wink at many irregularities that he might prevent diſturbances and ill humor among the body of merchants. The commiſſioners expreſſed their diſſatiſ-faction, and wanted him to alter his line of conduct: he ſtated the caſe to a friend at home, and by his in-fluence was ſecured from ſuch like directions in future. They tranſmitted to Britain ſuch repreſentations of Mr. *Otis* jun. as provoked him to inſert a publication in the Boſton gazette, which brought on an affray at the coffee houſe between him and Mr. *Robinſon,* one of the com-miſſioners, from the latter's attempting to pull the other by the noſe, becauſe of ſome expreſſions in the ſaid publication. Mr. Robinſon being in danger of coming off with the worſt, ſeveral of the company fell upon Mr. Otis; ſome of whom held him while others ſtruck him with canes or different weapons. A friend paſſing along, obſerved what was doing, preſſed in and reſcued Mr. Otis, though he himſelf ſuffered conſiderably from the aſſailants. The noiſe ſoon drew multitudes about the houſe, when Mr. Robinſon and his aſſociates pru-dently retreated by means of a back door *. This pro-cedure of the revenue officers (for no military one was preſent) opened a large field of altercation, and multi-plied quarrels, which were before too frequent between the king's officers and the leaders of oppoſition.

Governor *Bernard* could carry nothing in the govern-mental way through the preſence of the troops, but was continually loſing ground, and growing more and more obnoxious to the inhabitants; ſo that he was abuſed in

* Mr. Otis afterward proſecuted Mr. Robinſon for the aſſault, and the law gave heavy damages againſt him; but Mr. *Otis* generouſly for-gave him upon an acknowledgment of the offence.

ſcurrilous

fcurrilous publications, for which the Boston gazette was notorious. They were craftily calculated for the meridian where they firſt appeared, and ſuited the too levelling diſpoſition of the *Bay-men*; after the politicians had encouraged a ſpirit of licentiouſneſs, in order to weaken the force of government, and counteract the deſigns carrying on againſt their liberties: but their want of decency offended many of the ſons of liberty in the other colonies. Heavy threats were alſo thrown out againſt the governor's perſonal ſafety. Of theſe however he was regardleſs; and being aſked by a friend, how he could venture to walk about alone at his country ſeat, only five miles from the centre of Boſton, and whether he was not afraid, he anſwered, " No, they are not a blood-thirſty people."

At length it was thought proper to recall him, as ſaid, to lay before his majeſty the true ſtate of the province: this he ſignified to the aſſembly in the month of June. Before they were prorogued, they embraced the occaſion for drawing up a petition to his majeſty, in which, after complaints of him, they entreated that he might be for ever removed from the government of the province. When his letters, written home in confidence, came to be expoſed to public view, it would have argued great weakneſs to have continued him, unleſs it was deſigned to adopt his plans, and ſupport him by force at all adventures. Governor Bernard was too open, and had too little command of his temper; and ſuffered his reſentment to get the better of what ought to have been his political judgment. Every governor ſhould diveſt himſelf of reſentment, eſpecially in his public capacity, as his own happineſs, and that of the governed require it.

Men

Men of fpirit may be drawn, when they will not be forced. Sir Francis, inftead of aiming his cenfures at individuals, directed them againft whole bodies. Thus he charged the council with fervility to the populace, the pleafing of whom, he faid, was the rule of their conduct; and alfo both houfes of the general affembly exprefsly, in his fpeeches, with oppugnation againft the royal authority, declaring that they had left gentlemen out of the council, only for their fidelity to the crown. Such charges ftrengthened the hands of thofe whom he moft oppofed, by touching the honor of the whole. Had they been true, they fhould have been fuppreffed, or mentioned only in private; but though the fubftance of them was even true, when applied to individuals, it might be otherwife when applied to the body, the majority of whom might act upon different principles. Political leaders frequently throw out motives, by which to catch and conduct the well-intentioned, differing from thofe by which they themfelves are actuated. Sir Francis did not poffefs thofe mollifying arts which the ferment of the times required; and was more ready to aggravate diforders than to apologize for them. It was common for him in his official letters, to ftile the oppofition the faction, even while he owned that it comprehended the majority of the affembly. A parental governor would have thrown in many hints to have leffened the difpleafure of perfons in power, on account of offences committed at three thoufand miles diftance, under an enthufiaftic attachment to the caufe of liberty, at a period when divers outrages were perpetrated at home, by mobs in various parts of the kingdom. He evidenced too great an inclination to make the worft of every thing; and at times hearkened to and tranfmitted the ftrangeft rumors. He was a principal inftrument in bringing the troops to Bofton. It was a favorite meafure with him and the lieutenant governor, long before it was executed. While he profeffed himfelf a friend to the province, he was endeavouring to undermine its conftitution, and to obtain an effential alteration in the charter, through an appointment of the council by the king, inftead of its continuing in the election of the general court, where the reprefentatives of the people neceffarily carried it, whenever they united.

Toward the end of June, he had the faireft opportunity of getting the troops removed from the Maffachufetts, but oppofed the meafure. General Gage defired general Mackay to confult with him concerning the neceffity of continuing the troops at Bofton, and to procure his opinion in writing, whether his majefty's fervice required that troops fhould remain there any longer, and what number, whether one or two regiments. It is impoffible to exprefs his furprife at the propofition. The knowledge of it, fo far as it reached, occafioned a confternation among the civil officers of government, its friends, and the importers of goods from Great Britain. Gage, in a letter, requefted his opinion, and affured him he fhould not publifh it, or make it known on this fide the Atlantic. He immediately anfwered, that he had no hefitation to declare his opinion, that it would be detrimental to his majefty's fervice to remove any of the two regiments remaining; and that it would be quite ruinous to the caufe of the crown to draw all the troops out of Bofton: but that he was inclined to think, that a regiment in town, and ano-

ther

ther at the caftle, might be fufficient. He had time enough in which to have ripened a plan with the court for the removal of the troops, to the joy of the country, and with fafety to the civil officers and fupporters of government. But he too early, for his own peace and the happinefs of his government, deviated from the line of conduct, marked out for him by Lord Halifax, immediately after his appointment, when it was recommended to him to fee and converfe with governor Pownall, of whom his lordfhip wrote in the fame letter, " It is impoffible to purfue a better plan of government than what he directed himfelf by." However, his conduct was fo agreeable to the miniftry, that a title was fecured him. He was created a baronet March the twentieth 1769; and his majefty took upon himfelf the whole expence of paffing the patent, which added greatly to the honor done him, as it was a favor feldom or ever before granted. Sir Francis, during his eleven years refidence in America, made very little advance in his eftate. The Bofton fons of liberty had great advantages againft him, from the early intelligence procured by the fuppofed author of Junius Americanus, and forwarded for fafety under an unfufpected coarfe paper cover, to Mr. Thomas Bromfield, glover, at Bofton. Sir Francis was aftonifhed to find, that the contents of his letters from miniftry were known by them as foon as by himfelf. When he embarked from the caftle on board the Rippon man of war for Great Britain, Auguft the firft, few lamented his departure. Even his friend, the lieutenant governor Mr. *Hutchinfon*, regretted not his recall; by it he gained an opening for fucceeding to the chair,

T 2

ro

to which he had been long looking, and was in hopes of being advanced.

Boston and *New York* entered into the non-importation agreement fo early as Auguft the preceding year: before the prefent was out they began to be embarraffed, and numbers grew weary of their engagement. Advantage was taken of thefe circumftances. The *Britifh* officers, either of their own thought or through hints from home, offered merchants the liberty of having their goods directed to them as though intended for the army; and many were got in under that cover, efpecially at *New York.* Several perfons imported into *Bofton* and fold freely, without its being particularly noticed, while a few only were called to an account and expofed in the newfpapers. This occafioned an alarm; and the people 1770. affembled at Faneuil-hall, in confequence of a notifica-
Jan.
23. tion, upon the bufinefs of preventing the non-importation agreements being rendered abortive.

Mr. *Theophilus Lillie,* obferving the grofs partiality which prevailed in fuffering fome to fell, while a few others were profcribed, determined upon felling his goods alfo. To point him out as inimical to the agreement, and a perfon whofe fhop was to be fhunned, a piece of pageantry was placed before the door. Mr. *Richardfon,* attempting to remove it, was driven into his houfe by a number of boys, and there attacked by ftones through the windows. Provoked, rather than endangered by the Feb. affault, he fired and killed *Chriftopher Snider,* a lad of
22. eleven years old, who was recorded in the public prints as the firft martyr to the noble caufe of liberty. The boy was buried with the greateft refpect imaginable, according to the cuftom of the country; and fuch was

the

the number of people following the corps, that the foot proceffion extended a full quarter of a mile. The event tended rather to promote than injure the non-importation agreement. Boys, fmall and great, and undoubtedly men, had been and were encouraged, and well paid by certain leaders, to infult and intimidate thofe who had avowedly counteracted the combination, and ftill perfevered. The lieutenant governor in April, attempted prevailing upon a merchant of the firft eftate and character, to promote an affociation, in oppofition to the non-importation agreement, but to no purpofe; and received for anfwer, " Until parliament makes pro-vifion for the punifhment of the confederacies, all will be ineffectual, and the affociates will be expofed to po-pular rage." Another meeting was called to determine whether the goods already arrived and thofe expected, fhould be fent back to Britain. A gentleman having received a letter from a member of parliament, in which it was faid, that fhipping back 10,000l. of goods will do more than ftoring 100,000l. and the fame being communicated, the fcale, when upon a balance, was turned, and all the importers belonging to the town fub-mitted to fend their goods back; and in May many were re-fhipped on board captain *Scott.* The leaders gave out that it was done voluntarily: and yet the major part of the merchants wifhed to fee the trade free from re-ftraint; but having in the height of their zeal, called in the populace as their fervants to intimidate thofe who refufed to join in the combination, they were now forced to fubmit to them as their mafters, under the influence of a few of the merchants, who ftill adhered to their firft plan. Several of the laft importers begged with tears,

that

that they might be allowed to houfe their goods, but it was not granted. One who had been pretty fturdy, had a committee of tradefmen fent him, with an axe-man, a carpenter, at their head, who told him that there were a 1000 men waiting for his anfwer, and if he did not comply, there was no faying what would be the confequences. The ftrength of the argument prevailed; and a day or two after the paper publifhed that he complied voluntarily. The *Boftonians* moreover refolved to leave off all trade with the *Newport* people, becaufe of their duplicity, and breaking through the non-importation agreement. The next month *Hartford* followed the example of Bofton. But about the fame time, the *New Yorkers*, by dexterous management, were brought to agree to import " every thing, except fuch articles as are, or may hereafter be, fubject to duty for the purpofe of raifing a revenue in America." Government gained a party in the committee of merchants, who took advantage of the charges brought againft *Bofton* of importing large quantities of goods; and Mr. *Hancock* was complained of for fuffering them to be brought in his veffels. By thefe means they prepared the minds of the people for the execution of the plan they had concerted. They did not call a meeting of the citizens, in which the vote of the populace, procured by the arts of individuals, might prevail; but went through the feveral wards, and took the fenfe of the principal inhabitants feparately, when it appeared that the majority were for importing. Upon the receipt of letters from *Philadelphia* and *Bofton*, the fenfe of the inhabitants was again taken, and turned out as before. They were feverely cenfured by the Philadelphians for their defection, and

and by others alfo. The letter of the committee to the merchants at Bofton, informing them what agreement they had adopted, was contemptuoufly torn to pieces. When thofe *Yorkers*, who were in the intereft of government, began to concert their plan, they refted on af- furances of what would be done in parliament, and knew not, for certain, that the duties on glafs, paper, and colours, had been taken off; but the news of the obnoxious act being fo far repealed, reached the con- tinent before they had fully perfected the bufinefs on the tenth of July *.

The *New Yorkers* were in general faithful, while their non-importation agreement lafted; more fo, it was thought, than the *Boftonians*. Thefe fuffered much in their reputation among the fons of liberty at New York and Philadelphia, for the large quantities of goods found by fome of the newfpaper publications, to have been imported into Bofton. Some of the inhabitants were defirous of rolling away much of the reproach, by point- ing out, that a confiderable part of the goods charged to the fcore of Bofton, belonged to *Salem, Marblehead*, and other ports; but when the non-importation agree- ments were ended, it was omitted, and thus they con- tinued to lie under greater difgrace than really belonged to them. While the New York plan was carrying on, a trial was made by about a dozen perfons, to frighten the gentlemen who were inclined to import from fo doing, but it failed; the populace had been fecured.

The king gave his affent to the act for repealing the April duties on glafs, paper, and colours. The tea duty was [12.]

* The date of the committee's letter to the Philadelphians, after taking the fenfe of the inhabitants a fecond time.

pro-

profeſſedly continued as a pepper-corn rent, for the point of honor, and as a badge of ſovereignty over the colonies. The miniſtry might alſo mean to uſe it in ſome future period, for deeper purpoſes than could be then fathomed. They intended in the beginning of the ſeſſion to bring in a bill againſt American aſſociations; but the violence of party was ſuch, that it was thought the times would not admit of it. The ſtrong oppoſition made to miniſterial meaſures at home, was certainly helpful to the cauſe of the colonies, and encouraged them to go thoſe lengths which they would otherwiſe have ſcarce ventured upon. This however was not to be charged to the anti-miniſterialiſts, as an evil for which they were anſwerable. Let miniſters attempt at any time, to make unjuſtifiable inroads upon the liberties of Britiſh ſubjects, their opponents are bound in duty, as the guardians of the public, to uſe all warrantable efforts to diſconcert them; and the miſchief which follows is to be placed to the account of thoſe who render the oppoſition a neceſſary meaſure.

The news of a partial repeal did not ſatisfy the colo-niſts. But they attempted in vain to keep up the non-importation agreement after the defection of New York. The Boſton merchants at length, in a meeting held at the coffee-houſe in October, unanimouſly voted to alter it, and adopt the ſame plan of importing with that of the New Yorkers. It appeared to be the ſenſe of the one and the other, and alſo of the Philadelphians, that no tea ſhould be imported; and that if any was brought into the ſeveral ports, it ſhould be ſmuggled to avoid paying the duty. The *Virginia* houſe of burgeſſes, in a petition to his majeſty, expreſſed their exceeding great

concern

concern and deep affliction upon finding that the several acts impofing duties, for the purpofe of raifing a revenue in America, were continued; and faid, " A partial fufpenfion of duties, and thefe fuch only as were impofed upon Britifh manufactures, cannot remove the too well grounded fears and apprehenfions of your majefty's fubjects, whilft impofitions are continued on the fame articles of foreign fabric, and entirely retained upon tea for the avowed purpofe of eftablifhing a precedent againft us." The prefent year was marked by a different fcene of blood than what offered in February, which could not be introduced in the order of time, without breaking the thread of the preceding narration.

Outrages had been committed by the foldiers; and frequent quarrels had happened between them and the inhabitants of Bofton, who viewed the military as come to dragoon them into obedience to ftatutes, inftructions and mandates, that were thoroughly detefted. Each day gave rife to new occurrences which augmented the animofity. Reciprocal infults foured the tempers, and mutual injuries imbittered the paffions of the oppofite parties. Befide, fome fiery fpirits, who refented the indignity of having foldiers quartered among them, were continually exciting the towns people to quarrel with the troops. Not only fo, but a pompous newfpaper account of a victory obtained by the inhabitants of New York over the foldiers there, in an affray, undoubtedly excited the refentment of the military at Bofton, and exultations among their opponents, and thus increafed the ferment. Every thing tended to a crifis; and it is rather wonderful that it did not exift fooner, when fo many circumftances united to haften its approach. The

lieutenant

lieutenant governor did not attend to these things properly; and was not sufficiently careful to prevent consequences, by strongly urging the officers to keep their men in the barracks as much as possible, and to maintain the strictest discipline. He was desirous of recommending himself both to them and the commissioners, and therefore was very cautious left he should offend either.

At length a private of the twenty-ninth regiment, Mar. passing along in the morning near Mr. John Gray's rope 2. walk, being provoked by insulting words, resented it; and being overpowered, went off, but soon returned with a dozen soldiers, between whom and the rope-makers an affray ensued, which terminated in the defeat of the former; who in the afternoon, armed themselves with clubs, and were on their way to renew the action, but were stopped. On this many of the towns people were so enraged, that they determined upon fighting it out with the soldiers on the Monday. The Rev. Dr. *Eliot* was told of the determination on the Saturday; and was also informed, that the bells were to be rung to assemble the inhabitants together; so that when on the Monday evening he heard them ring, he was not alarmed with an apprehension of its being on account of a fire's breaking out in the town, which is generally the case *. It does not appear that any militia were called in before the firing upon the people, or that any regular plan was formed for compelling the troops to move from the town: it is absurd to think, on the other hand, that there was a settled plot for employing the soldiers to massacre

* The Doctor's account to me, when discoursing upon what is called the *massacre*.

the

·the inhabitants. But from the characters, principles, and politics of certain persons among the leaders of the opposition, it may be feared, that they had no objection to a rencounter, that by occasioning the death of a few, might eventually clear the place of the two regiments. That some design was on foot, which might be attended with danger in the execution, may be gathered from lieutenant colonel Marshall's saying, when giving evidence for the crown—" The bells were ringing, and the people began to collect as they do at the cry of fire, and I began to think it was fire. I had a mind to go out, but I had a reluctance, because *I had been warned not to go out that night* ;" meaning in which the men were shot *.

Between seven and eight o'clock at night, unusual numbers are met coming from the south end of the town with sticks in their hands, and serious consequences are apprehended from it. About the same time, parties amounting in the whole to near two hundred, several with great sticks or clubs, proceed from the north end, some of whom say, " let us go to the south end and join our friends there, and attack the damned scoundrels, and drive them out of the town ; they have no business here." More people than common, with large sticks, are observed running from all quarters toward King-street. The north end parties collect in and about Dock-square, and attack several soldiers belonging to Murray's barracks about nine o'clock : upon an officer's coming up, these are ordered to their barracks, and when got in, with much difficulty, are immediately confined. The mob follow the officer to the gate, and provoke the soldiers by the most abusive language, and

* The trial of the soldiers, p. 52.

Mar.
5.

dare

dare them to come out. They are hardly reſtrained by their officers from doing it. While theſe things are tranſacting, ſome are calling *town-born turn out,* twenty or thirty times over; others cry *fire, fire,* in different places, the more effectually to draw people out of their houſes, and to increaſe their numbers; and ſoon after the nine o'clock bell has ceaſed, the bells are ſet a ringing, which thoſe who are not better informed, imagine to be the alarm of fire.

Upon the ſoldiers being reſtrained to the barracks, the mob are deſired by one or more conſiderate perſons, to return home. A few comply, but the generality have ſomething further to engage their attention. Numbers employ themſelves in tearing up the ſtalls of the market-place in Dock-ſquare, for the purpoſe they expreſs while calling out, " Damn the dogs, where are they now? Let us go and kill that damned ſcoundrel of a ſentry, and then attack the main-guard." The body of the mob when they have finiſhed their repeated attacks upon the barracks, are addreſſed in the ſtreet by a tall large man in a red cloak and white wig. After liſtening to what he has to offer in the ſpace of three or four minutes, they huzza for the main-guard, and ſay, " We will do for the ſoldiers." They ſeparate into three diviſions, and take different routs for King-ſtreet, one through the Main-ſtreet. A party, who have collected at Oliver's-dock, bend their courſe toward the ſame point. In the mean time, the ſentry before the Cuſtom-houſe is aſſaulted while upon duty. A boy comes up, and pointing to him, ſays, " There is the ſon of a bitch that knocked me down." About twenty young fellows, eighteen years old, call out, " kill him, kill him,

knock

knock him down." Their behaviour obliges him to load his gun. They pelt him with fnow-balls, pieces of ice, and any thing that offers, and halloo "fire and be damned." They advance upon him; oblige him to retreat; he mounts the fteps, and knocks at the door for admiffion. Meeting with no relief in this way, more perfons collecting in the ftreet, and his danger increaf-ing, he calls out to the main-guard, within hearing, for protection. Captain Prefton, the officer of the day, being told that the ringing of the bells is the fignal for affembling the inhabitants to attack the troops, repairs to the main-guard; and learning the fituation of the fentry, fends off a corporal and fix men to protect both him and the king's cheft in the cuftom-houfe. The foldiers march off with their pieces unloaded, and the captain follows to prevent diforder. Ere they have formed, that part of the mob, which comes through the Main-ftreet, and appears to be headed by the mu-latto Attucks, and to contain a number of failors, upon coming to the town houfe, exclaim—" Damn the raf-cals, this will never do; the readieft way to get rid of thofe people, is to attack the main-guard, ftrike at the root, this is the neft." The foldiers are pelted while going to defend their comrade; and, when upon their ftation, are ferved as was the fingle fentry, have fnow-balls, large pieces of ice, fticks, and other things thrown at them, and are obliged to load for their own fafety. The reproachful language with which they are abufed, exclufive of a plenty of oaths and execrations, is, "Come on you rafcals, you lobfter fcoundrels, you bloody-backs, you cowards, you daftards for bringing arms againft naked men; fire if you dare; fire and be damned,

we

we know you dare not," and much more to the fame purpofe. The reafon for faying, " you dare not fire," is probably to be found in the doctrine lately advanced, " that foldiers, while on duty, may upon no occafion whatever fire upon their fellow fubjects, without the order of a civil magiftrate." The mob prefs in upon the foldiers; advance to the points of the bayonets; are defired to keep off; and are treated with cautious attention. This may be owing to apprehenfions of danger to themfelves in cafe of a contrary conduct. The fhouts, huzzas, threats, fcreams, and almoft yells of the mob, with the ringing of the bells to increafe the general confufion, may juftly alarm them; but their precaution foon avails nothing. While they are pufhing off the people, without once leaving their ftation or attempting to follow them, the Mulatto, and about a dozen perfons, feveral in failors habits, come down to the fpot, give three cheers, furround the foldiers, and ftrike their guns with clubs, crying out to the others, " Do not be afraid of them, they dare not fire; kill them; kill them; knock them over." The Mulatto aims a blow at captain Prefton, ftrikes down one of the guns, feizes the bayonet with his left hand, and fhows a hardy difpofition anfwering to the threats which have been uttered. At this inftant, there is a confufed cry of " damn your bloods, why don't you fire," and partly from perfons behind the captain. Firing fucceeds. Montgomery, whom the Mulatto has affaulted, after recovering his legs, and relieving his gun by a fudden twitch, is the firft that fires, and his affailant falls. After fix or eight feconds, another fires, the other five follow in quick fucceffion. It is agreed, that only feven out

of

of the eight foldiers difcharge their pieces, and that
no one fires twice. Three perfons are killed; five
are very dangeroufly wounded, and a few flightly.
Moft are either paffengers going through the ftreet, or
unaffifting fpectators. It is well that no more are killed,
confidering that there were from fifty to a hundred about
the foldiers. They ran off at the firing, but foon affemble again to take away the dead and wounded.

The whole town is immediately in the greateft commotion. Their drums beat to arms, and there is a
conftant calling out " to arms, to arms, turn out with
your guns." The townfmen affemble in the next ftreet,
to the amount of fome thoufands. The lieutenant governor repairs to captain *Prefton*, and upon coming up
afks him, " how came you to fire upon the people without the orders of a civil magiftrate ?" The captain begins to apologize for what had happened, by faying,
" *we were infulted* ;" and is about adding more, but recollecting the impropriety of the place, ftops fhort, and
afks Mr. *Hutchinfon* to walk up into the guard room,
where he means to finifh what he has begun ; but the
lieutenant governor goes to the council chamber. The
captain's words are obferved by fome gentlemen, who
attend Mr. Hutchinfon, and are confidered as conceding
to the implied charge of having given direction to fire ;
and are remembered to his difadvantage. Mr. Hutchinfon cannot avoid expofing himfelf in the midft of the
enraged inhabitants, upon whom he prevails to difperfe
till morning. It having been a clear moon light night,
perfons have been enabled to diftinguifh what paffed.

The next morning the people collect in vaft bodies. The Mar.
lieutenant governor fummons a council. Before any 6.

debate

debate commences, lieutenant colonel *Dalrymple*, and lieutenant colonel *Carr* attend, being informed, that they may if they will. The town meets in full affembly, and choofe a committee, who, while the bufinefs is largely difcuffing in council, wait upon the lieutenant governor and deliver him a meffage, declaring, " It is the unanimous opinion of the meeting, that nothing can rationally be expected to reftore the peace of the town, and prevent blood and carnage, but the immediate removal of the troops." Colonel Dalrymple fignifies to Mr. Hutchinfon, his readinefs to place the 29th regiment, which has rendered itfelf in a fpecial manner obnoxious, in the barracks at the caftle.

In the afternoon the lieutenant governor receives another meffage, acquainting him, that it is the opinion of the meeting, confifting of near three thoufand people, that nothing but a total and immediate removal of the troops will fatisfy. Mr. *Samuel Adams*, one of the committee, in his venerable grey locks, and with hands trembling under a nervous complaint, tells colonel *Dalrymple*, " If you can remove the 29th regiment, you can alfo remove the 14th; and it is at your peril if you do not;" and continues talking to him, in fuch a refolute tone and with fuch ftrong implications, as nearly to communicate the trembling to the colonel. Mr. *Hutchinfon* wifhes to get clear of the council, but finds it impoffible; and therefore lays the matter before them. Several declare their apprehenfions of more bloodfhed, unlefs the troops are removed. Mr. *Royal Tyler* in his zeal for effecting it, fays to him, " It is not fuch people as formerly pulled down your houfe, who conduct the prefent meafures. No; they are people of

4   the

the best characters among us, men of estates, men of religion. They have formed their plan for removing the troops out of town; and it is impossible they should remain in it. The people will come in from the neighbouring towns; there will be ten thousand men to effect the removal of the troops, who will probably be destroyed by the people, be it called rebellion, or occasion the loss of our charter, or be the consequence what it may." When Mr. *Tyler* said, *they have formed their plan*, it was not to be understood, that the plan was formed prior, but subsequent to the bloodshed of the preceding evening. His representations might be aggravated: even when there is not a natural cast for hyperbole, persons inflated by passion, will imperceptibly have a recourse to the figure. Mr. Hutchinson tells the council, " Nothing shall ever induce me to order the troops out of town." They, upon that, unanimously advise him to request colonel Dalrymple to order them to the castle. To the colonel he says, " I have nothing to do with it, it lies wholly with you." While they are pressing him, the people are informed, that the colonel is ready to remove the regiments, if the lieutenant governor will only join in desiring it. He inclines to stand out, and to leave it with the colonel and council to settle, as they can agree about the business. He deliberates till near night, dreading lest any one measure he may adopt, shall lessen him in the opinion of the ministry and endanger his advancement. At length the secretary, Mr. *Oliver*, perceiving how artfully matters are managed, whispers him in the ear, " You must either comply or determine to leave the province." This prevails; he complies with the advice of the council; and the general ferment begins to fubfide. The troops however, are not removed fo early as is expected by the town; they continue till the next Monday; and upon the colonel's being afked the reafon, he mentions that it lies at the door of the lieutenant governor, who fhuffles with the colonel, in hope that fome occurrence will exift, which may exempt him from being charged with occafioning the removal of the troops by the interpofition of his advice.

Mean while captain Prefton and his party are committed to jail. One of the wounded men dies. It is determined to bury the four perfons * in one vault, and Mar. in a peculiarly refpectful manner. The generality of the 8. fhops in town are fhut. All the bells of *Boflon*, *Charleftown*, and *Roxbury*, are ordered to toll in the moft doleful tone. The corpfes form a junction in King-ftreet, where they fell when the foldiers fired. Hence they proceed in orderly fucceffion through the main ftreet, followed by an immenfe concourfe of people, fo numerous as to be obliged to go in ranks of fix a-breaft, and the whole clofed by a long train of carriages belonging to the principal gentry of the town. Thus are they diftinguifhed and honorably attended to the place of interment, with unparalleled pomp, not on account of perfonal merit, but to exprefs the vehement indignation of the inhabitants againft the flaughter of their brethren, by the Britifh foldiery quartered among them, in violation, as they imagine, of their civil liberties.

Samuel Gray, Samuel Maverick, James Caldwell, and Crifpus Attucks. Samuel Gray was a journeyman, and wrought in the rope-walks belonging to Mr. John Gray the rope-maker.

8   Captain

Captain Prefton's trial begins. Mefirs. John Adams Oɑ. and Jofiah Quincy are his council. They are warm in ²⁴· the caufe of liberty, and offend feveral of their own party by undertaking the defence of the prifoner; but faithfully employ their diftinguifhed abilities in his behalf. The trial does not finifh till the thirtieth. While carrying on, Mr. Quincy pufhes the examination and crofs-examination of the witneffes to fuch an extent, that Mr. Adams, in order to check it, is obliged to tell him, that if he will not defift, he fhall decline having any thing further to do in the caufe. The captain and his friends are alarmed, and confult about engaging another counfellor; but Mr. Adams has no intention of abandoning his client. He is fenfible that there is fufficient evidence to obtain a favorable verdiɑ from an impartial jury; and only feels for the honor of the town, which he apprehends will fuffer yet more, if the witneffes are examined too clofely and particularly, and by that mean more truth be drawn from them than what has an immediate conneɑion with the foldiers firing, by or without the orders of the captain. When the trial is ending, judge Lynde, toward the clofe of his fpeech fays, " Happy I am to find, after fuch ftriɑ examination, the conduɑ of the prifoner appears in fo fair a light; yet I feel myfelf deeply affeɑed, that this affair turns out fo much to the difgrace of every perfon concerned againft him, and fo much to the fhame of the town in general." The jury return their verdiɑ—Not guilty.

On Tuefday commences the trial of William Wemms, Nov. James Hartegan, William M'Cauley, Hugh White, ²⁷· Matthew Killroy, William Warren, John Carrol, and

U 2 Hugh

Hugh Montgomery, foldiers in the 29th regiment, for the murder of Crifpus Attucks, Samuel Gray, Samuel Maverick, James Caldwell, and Patrick Carr, the laft of whom did not die till ten days after he was wounded. The foldiers have the fame council that was engaged for their captain. The trial is continued from day to day, Sunday excepted, till Wednefday December the fifth. Attempts were made to prejudice the people againft the prifoners, one efpecially in a certain weekly paper the day before the trial began. The publication included an infult on the fupreme court, and expreffed the greateft malignity of heart. To counteract the baneful effects of all fuch proceedings, Mr. Quincy, in his addrefs to the juftices and jury, obferves—" We muft fteel ourfelves againft paffions, which contaminate the fountain of juftice. Let it be borne deep upon our minds, that the prifoners are to be condemned by the evidence *here in court* produced againft them, and by nothing elfe. Matters heard or feen abroad, are to have no weight; in general they undermine the pillars of juftice and truth. As though a feries of *ex parte* evidence was not enough, all the colours of the canvafs have been touched in order to frefhen the wounds, and by a tranfport of imagination, we are made prefent at the fcene of action. The prints exhibited in our houfes, have added wings to fancy, and in the fervor of our zeal, reafon is in hazard of being loft. The pomp of funeral, the horrors of death have been fo delineated, as to give a fpring to our ideas, and infpire a glow incompatible with found, deliberate judgment. In this fituation, every paffion has alternately been predominant. They have each in turn fubfided in degree, and they

have

have fometimes given place to defpondence, grief, and
forrow. How careful fhould we be, that we do not
miftake the impreffions of gloom and melancholy, for
the dictates of reafon and truth! How careful left borne
away by a torrent of paffion, we make fhipwreck of
confcience!

" Many things yet exift fufficient to keep alive the
glow of indignation. I have aimed at fecuring you
againft the catching flame. I have endeavoured to difcharge my duty in this refpect.—What fuccefs will follow thefe endeavours, depends on you, gentlemen. If
being told of your danger, will not produce caution,
nothing will. If you are determined in opinion, it is
in vain to fay more; but if you are zealous inquirers
after truth; if you are willing to hear with impartiality,
to examine and judge for yourfelves, enough has been
faid to apprize you of thofe avenues, at which the enemies of truth and juftice are moft likely to enter, and
moft eafily to befet you."

When the evidence in favor of the prifoners is finifhed, Mr. Quincy refumes his addrefs.—" I ftated to you,
gentlemen, your duty in opening this caufe. I pointed
out the dangers to which you were expofed. How much
need was there, that you fhould fufpend your judgment
till the witneffes were all examined! How different is
the complexion of the caufe? Will not all this ferve to
fhow every honeft man the little truth to be attained in
partial hearings? This trial ought to have another effect,
it fhould ferve to convince us all of the impropriety,
nay, injuftice, of giving a latitude in converfation upon
topics likely to come under a judicial decifion; the
criminality of this conduct is certainly inhanced, when

fuch

such loose sallies and discourses are so prevalent as to be likely to touch the life of a citizen. In the present case, how great was the prepossession against us! and I appeal to you, gentlemen, as to what cause there now is to alter our sentiments."

In the course of pleading, he is under a necessity of saying, " And here, gentlemen, I must first tell you by what law the prisoners are *not* to be tried or condemned. And they most certainly are *not* to be tried by the *Mosaic* law: a law we take it, especially designed for the government of a peculiar nation, who being in a great measure under a theocratical form of government, its institutions cannot, with any propriety, be adduced for our regulation in these days. It is with pain therefore, I have observed any endeavour to mislead our judgment on this occasion, by drawing our attention to the precepts delivered in the days of Moses: and by disconnected passages of scripture, applied in a manner foreign to their original design or import, there seems to have been an attempt to touch some peculiar sentiments, which we know are thought to be prevalent; and in this way we take it, an injury is like to be done, by giving the mind a bias it ought never to have received, because it is not warranted by our laws."

" We have heard it publicly said of late, oftener than formerly, *Whosoever sheddeth man's blood, by man shall his blood be shed.* This is plainly, gentlemen, a general rule, which like all others of the kind must have its exceptions—a rule, which if taken in its strict literal latitude, would imply, that a man killing another in self-defence, would incur the pains of death—a doctrine that certainly never prevailed under the *Mosaical* institution;

tution; for we find the *Jews* had their six cities of refuge, to which the man-flayer might flee from the
avenger of blood." Let it be obferved, en paffant, that
as it was ordained that the man-flayer fhould abide in
the city of refuge till the death of the high prieft, fo
every perfon to efcape fuch confinement and reftraint,
would be extremely careful left he fhould prove the
cafual occafion of another's death; and would not venture upon gratifying a fettled or fudden evil difpofition,
by needlefsly flaying a fellow creature, becaufe it would
pafs for chance-medley. But to go on in company with
Mr. Quincy. " And fo, that *the* MURDERER *fhall flee
to the pit*, comes under the fame confideration. And
when we hear it afked, as it very lately has been, " Who
DARE ftay him?" I anfwer, if the laws of our country
ftay him you ought to do likewife; and every good
fubject *dares* to do what the law allows. But the very
pofition is *begging the queftion*; for the queftion now in
iffue is, whether either of the prifoners is *a murderer* in
the fenfe of our laws: what is murder and what not, is
a *queftion of law* arifing upon facts ftated and allowed."

" Again, " you fhall take no fatisfaction for the life of
a *murderer*, who is *guilty of death*." Here again is a
begging the queftion; and moreover the words *guilty of
death*, if rightly confidered, muft be one of thofe general
rules which always have their exceptions. But in the
margin of our great bible, we find them rendered *faulty
to die*. Againft a pofition of this kind we have no objection. If we have committed *a fault*, on which our
laws inflict the punifhment of *death*, we muft fuffer.
But what fault we have committed, you are to inquire:
or rather you, gentlemen, are to find the *facts proved*

in court againſt us, and the judges are to ſee and conſidet what the law pronounces touching our offence, and what puniſhment is thereby inflicted as a penalty."

Mr. John Adams, in his pleadings, produces from the beſt authorities, thoſe rules of law which muſt govern all caſes of homicide, and particularly that which is before the court; and then conſiders the evidence to ſee whether any thing has occurred that may be compared to the rules of law. He enters into a minute conſideration of every witneſs produced on the crown ſide; and endeavours to ſhow from the evidence on that ſide, that the aſſault upon the party was ſufficiently dangerous to juſtify the priſoners; at leaſt, that it was ſufficiently provoking to reduce to manſlaughter the crime even of the two, who are ſuppoſed to be proved guilty of having killed. He then proceeds to conſider the teſtimonies of the witneſſes for the priſoners; and concludes with—— " I will enlarge no more on the evidence, but ſubmit it to you, gentlemen.——Facts are ſtubborn things; and whatever may be our wiſhes, our inclinations, or the dictates of our paſſions, they cannot alter the ſtate of facts and evidence: nor is the law leſs ſtable than the fact. If an aſſault was made to endanger their lives, the law is clear, they had a right to kill in their own defence. If it was not ſo ſevere as to endanger their lives, yet if they were aſſaulted at all, ſtruck and abuſed by blows of any ſort, by ſnow-balls, oyſter-ſhells, cinders, clubs, or ſticks of any kind; this was a provocation, for which the law reduces the offence of killing, down to manſlaughter, in conſideration of thoſe paſſions in our nature, which cannot be eradicated. To your candor

candor and juftice I fubmit the prifoners and their caufe."

"The law, in all viciffitudes of government, fluctuations of the paffions, or flights of enthufiafm, will preferve a fteady undeviating courfe : it will not bend to the uncertain wifhes, imaginations, and wanton tempers of men. To ufe the words of a great and worthy man, a patriot, and an hero, an enlightened friend of mankind, and a martyr to liberty, I mean ALGERNON SIDNEY, who from his earlieft infancy fought a tranquil retirement under the fhadow of the tree of liberty, with his tongue, his pen, and his fword, " The law (fays he) no paffion can difturb. 'Tis void of defire and fear, luft and anger. 'Tis *mens fine affectu*; written reafon ; retaining fome meafure of the divine perfection. It does not enjoin that which pleafes a weak, frail man, but without any regard to perfons, commands that which is good, and punifhes evil in all, whether rich or poor, high or low. 'Tis deaf, inexorable, inflexible." On the one hand it is inexorable to the cries and lamentations of the prifoners ; on the other it is deaf, deaf as an adder to the clamors of the populace."

The judges, when fumming up the evidence to the jury, and giving their opinions of the conftructions of law upon the evidence, apply themfelves to the removing of thofe bad impreffions, which may poffibly have been made upon the jury by the mifconftruction of fcripture paffages. Says one of them—" In the courfe of this year you doubtlefs have heard much of the law given to the *Jews*, refpecting homicide, as well as of the precept given to Noah, that *whofo fheddeth man's blood, by man fhall his blood be fhed.* Whence it has been inferred,

I   ferred,

ferred, that whofoever *voluntarily* kills another, whatever the inducement or provocation may be, is a *murderer*, and as fuch ought to be put to death. But furely not only the avenger of blood, and he who killed a thief breaking up a houfe in the night, were exceptions to that general precept, but alfo he who killed another in his own defence. Even the Jewifh doctors allowed this, and that juftly; becaufe the right of felf-defence is founded in the law of nature." It appears upon the trial, that the facts related above, under the fifth of March, are well attefted. There are no lefs than *thirty-eight* witneffes to prove a defign to attack the foldiers, fix of whom the council for the king have produced. Nigh *thirty* witneffes have fworn to words of provocation uttered againft the prifoners, as daring them to fire, and threatening to kill them: and *twenty-five* have witneffed to *ice*, *fnow-balls*, *fticks*, &c. being thrown at them, ten of whom are witneffes for the crown. There is evidence that Patrick Carr, one of the deceafed, repeatedly declared, and confirmed the fame but a few hours before he died—that he went with a defign againft the foldiers; that he thought they were abufed and would have fired before; that he forgave and did not blame the man, whoever he was, that fhot him; that he blamed himfelf for going to the riot, and might have known better, for he had feen foldiers called to quell riots, but never faw any bear half fo much before. The jury withdraw for about two hours and a half. Upon comparing the evidence, they cannot be convinced that the foldiers were not too hafty in firing. Was there evidence of all having fired, they would convict all of manflaughter; but it is agreed on all hands, that no

more

more than feven guns were fired, confequently one is
innocent, and they choofe that the guilty fhall efcape
rather than one innocent perfon be convicted *. They
return into court and agree, that as to Wemms, Hartegan, M'Cauley, White, Warren and Carrol, they are
not guilty, on which they are immediately difcharged.
As to Killroy and Montgomery, they agree that they
are not guilty of murder, but of manflaughter. Both
pray the benefit of clergy, which is allowed; each is
burnt in the hand, in open court, and difcharged. The
trial has been long, but the iffue of it, as well as of that Dec.
of the captain's, may be brought in proof of the inte- 5.
grity of Bofton juries, venturing to give upright verdicts
in defiance of popular opinions.

Edward Manwaring efq; John Munroe, gentleman, 12.
Hammond Green, boat-builder, and Thomas Greenwood, laborer, were tried for being prefent, aiding,
affifting, &c. William Warren in the murder of Crifpus
Attucks. The whole evidence confifted in one witnefs's
declaring that he faw two flafhes from the cuftom-
houfe, one from the balcony, the other from a chamber
window, and a perfon in the balcony with a gun or
piftol in his hand; and in the teftimony of a French
boy, fervant to Mr. Manwaring, who fwore to his being
at the cuftom-houfe when the foldiers fired, and to a
ftory of perfons firing out of the chamber window. The
falfhood of the whole evidence was immediately detected
by a number of the moft creditable witneffes, fo that
the jury acquitted the prifoners without going from their
feats.

* Lieutenant governor Hutchinfon's letter of December 10, 1770.

In

In the pleadings upon the trials (of the foldiers efpecially) Mr. John Adams difcuffed the fubject of homicide fo largely, and fhowed fo fully by what a variety of
circumftances it was reduced to manflaughter, that the
popular leaders perceived the neceffity of altering their
plan of oppofition to the military, and from thence-
forward promoted a particular attention to the militia
and the manual exercife, that the country might be
qualified for repelling arms by arms, whenever the fame
fhould be requifite for the prefervation of their liberties.

The ferment occafioned by the minifterial meafures
did not fubfide in the *New York* colony any more than
in the *Maffachufetts*.

About the middle of January and at night, the *liberty-
pole* was cut down by the foldiery, which enraged the
inhabitants, and produced much difturbance and riot
afterward between them and the troops. The foldiers
pofted up papers about the city againft the fons of
liberty, which occafioned a confiderable affray. The
oppofition foon expreffed their determination to perfevere, by erecting a new *liberty-pole*, ftrongly fecured with
iron to prevent its being demolifhed. The *May-poles*
in different parts of the continent had changed their
names, or given place to *liberty-poles*, after the exhibition
upon the liberty-tree at Bofton during the ftamp-act.
The conduct of the foldiers was probably owing to the
meafures which had been taken the preceding month,
in order to prevent the affembly's granting money for
the fupport of the troops. The affembly had in their
former feffion, voted to fupply his majefty's troops
quartered in the colony, which gave great umbrage.
To quiet the people they made a unanimous declaration,
that

that it fhould be the laft fupply they would ever grant, until their grievances were redreffed, and it gave fatis-faction. But the houfe in the prefent feffion, paffed a vote for a further fupply of 2000l. which greatly inflamed the minds of the inhabitants. Two papers were publifhed upon the occafion: the one addreffed *to the betrayed inhabitants of the city and colony of* NEW YORK, and figned A SON OF LIBERTY: the other figned LEGION, defiring the inhabitants to meet in the fields. The papers were voted *falfe, feditious,* and *infamous* libels by the affembly, who defired the lieutenant governor to iffue out proclamations, offering rewards for the difcovery of the authors, 100l. for the firft, and 50l. for the laft. A ftripling who had been journeyman to the printer of the firft, but difcharged for bad behaviour, allured by the proffered reward, lodged a complaint againft his late mafter, who was terrified into a difcovery of Mr. *M'Dougall* as the publifher. Mr. *M'Dougall* was by the chief juftice's warrant brought before him, and upon Feb. refufing to give bail was committed to jail. In confe-8. quence of the fecond paper, about fourteen hundred inhabitants met, and appointed Mr. *John Lamb* to propound queftions relative to the vote of the affembly. After explaining it, the queftion was put, " Do you approve of the vote?" *No,* was the anfwer. He proceeded, " Are you for giving money to the troops, on any confideration whatfoever?" It was again *No.* There were but about half a dozen for the affirmative upon either of the queftions. He then afked, " Will you appoint a committee to communicate the whole of this tranfaction to your members?" *Yes,* was the word. They then appointed for the committee, Meffrs. *Ifaac Sears,*

Sears, Casper Wistar, Alexander McDougall, Jacobus Van Zandt, Samuel Broome jun. *Erasmus Williams,* and *James Van Vaurk.* The meeting in the fields, and the transactions at it, were several weeks before the discovery and commitment of Mr. *McDougall.* Mr. *Lamb* was called before the house to answer for his conduct; but in the mean time the committee wrote to the speaker, acknowledging themselves, in every respect, parties with him, and answerable for each step that had been taken, and ready to defend their conduct in a constitutional manner. When Mr. *Lamb* appeared before the assembly, he told them that he had assembled with the rest of his fellow citizens, and had proposed *questions,* which as a citizen, a freeman, and an *Englishman,* he had a right to do, and was surprised to hear it controverted. The house finding that they had to do with men of sense and resolution, who were determined upon supporting the rights of their countrymen and fellow citizens, gave up the point and dismissed them. Their vote of 2000 l. for the troops soon passed into a law: but the deficiency demanded by the lieutenant governor as arrears, amounting to upward of 1000 l. was left unpaid. Had there been a provision for the arrears, the compliance with the mutiny act would have been formal and complete. That matters were carried so far must be attributed to an extraordinary and sudden coalition in the assembly between politicians, who had long been at mortal variance.

April The grand jury found a bill against captain *McDougall,* but the trial was put off; and he was bailed out of jail. When the house met again toward the close of the year, he was ordered to attend at their bar. The

speaker

speaker afked him whether he was the author or publifher of the addrefs, &c. He declined anfwering, and
affigned his reafons. It was refolved, that in his reply
he denied the authority of the houfe, and was therefore
guilty of a high contempt. On his refufing to afk
pardon of the houfe, he was ordered into cuftody, and
the fpeaker iffued his warrant to the jail keeper of the
city to receive and keep him prifoner, until he fhould
be difcharged by due courfe of law. He remained in
jail till the affembly was prorogued on the 25th of the
following February 1771, when he was enlarged after a
confinement of near three months. It was not till March
the 27th that he was difcharged from his recognizance,
by the fupreme court then fitting at *New York*, (without
having been brought to a trial) after having been under
bonds for near twelve months, and fuffered twenty and
three weeks actual imprifonment. He was the firft fufferer
for liberty after the commencement of the united efforts
of the American fons, to fruftrate the minifterial plans
for encroaching upon, and eventually fubverting their
long claimed and enjoyed rights and privileges. This
honor belongs to a gentleman born in Scotland, and who
is indeed, what he figned himfelf, *A Son of Liberty*. He
bore his imprifonment with fortitude; but the difagree-
ablenefs of it was much leffened, and the difgrace of it
wholly removed, as the citizens of the higheft and beft
characters, ladies and gentlemen, reforted to the place of
his confinement. His character as well as his caufe was
good; fo that the moft virtuous efpoufers of the latter,
were neither afraid nor afhamed, by their repeated vifits,
to afford him their public countenance.

The

The *Massachusetts* again demands your attention.

May 31.
The new general court met at *Cambridge*; the house remonstrated against being held there, or at any other place than *Boston*; and by a majority of 96 out of 102, voted it to be a very great grievance, and resolved not to do business out of *Boston*; on which the lieutenant governor prorogued them.

July 25.
They met again, but the assembly refused to do business; and in their message to Mr. *Hutchinson*, insisted upon the right of the people to appeal to heaven in disputes between them and persons in power, when there is an abuse of power; but they softened what they advanced, by saying " We would, however, by no means be understood to suggest, that this people have occasion at present to proceed to such extremity;" and yet they afterward added, " these and other grievances and cruelties, too many to be here enumerated, and too melancholy to be much longer borne by this people, we have seen brought upon us by the devices of the ministers of state." They were prorogued afresh.

Sept. 26.
They met a third time. The lieutenant governor told them, that the garrison at the castle in the pay of the province was to be withdrawn by order of his majesty, and the fortress to be garrisoned by his regular forces. His orders were to deliver the possession of the fort to such officer as general *Gage* should direct to take the command of it. The information excited a suspicion in the assembly, who despaired of obtaining a removal to Boston by persisting in a refusal to do business; the leaders therefore procured this vote:

29.
" Resolved, that next Wednesday (October 3) be observed by the two houses as a day of prayer, to seek the

Lord

Lord for his direction and blessing," which went up to
the council, and was unanimously concurred. Men of
a profane cast are too prone to ridicule religion, because
of its being thus made a stalkinghorse to serve the purposes of politicians. Would they confine their wit and
satire to the parties offending, the correction would be
proper. But let not the well-intentioned and undesign-
ing children of devotion, be charged with hypocritical
canting, because they are imposed upon and duped by
the subtilty of guides, who, like most thorough-paced
politicians, can change themselves into angels of light,
that they may perfect their devices.

The house resolved to proceed to business from absolute necessity, protesting against the restraint the general court was held under to do it out of *Boston*. A
few days after, they sent to the lieutenant governor to
know whether he held the command of the *Castle*. " If
the custody and government of that fortress," said they,
" is now lodged with the military power, independent
of the supreme civil magistrate within this jurisdiction,
it is so essential an alteration of the constitution as must
justly alarm a free people." His answer was so worded,
as to leave the assembly, in general, ground for concluding, that the military in the castle were dependent
upon himself the same as were the provincials. When
he delivered it up, he repaired thither, sent for the
keys, and upon colonel *Dalrymple*'s coming into the state
room with his officers, gave them to him, and lodged
with him the custody and government of the fort;
but retained some trifling appearances of superior command. He soon learnt however, that he could not

Vol. I.   X   come

come at a flag when in want of it, or even oars for a boat, without applying to general *Gage.*

Nov. 6. The representatives resolved, that the merchants having receded from their non-importation agreement, &c. they would difcourage prodigality, extravagance, and the ufe of foreign fuperfluities; and promote induftry, frugality, and their own manufactures in the feveral towns they reprefented.

7. They appointed a committee of correfpondence to communicate intelligence to the agent and others in Great-Britain, and to the fpeakers of the feveral affemblies through the continent, or fuch committees as they have appointed or may appoint.

Before the lieutenant governor prorogued them, he obferved to them, that fince they had difcovered a refolution to remove unneceffary obftacles, they had done more bufinefs, notwithftanding all the inconveniencies from the place of holding the court, which they had infifted upon, than he remembered to have been done in the like fpace of time, fince he had fhared in public affairs.

1771. April 3. The following fpring feffion produced nothing very material, but afforded him the pleafing opportunity of acquainting the general court, in form, of his being appointed captain general and commander in chief over the province. The council prefented a congratulatory addrefs; and expreffed their fatisfaction at his appointment. Upon the queftion in the houfe of affembly, whether to appoint a committee to prepare an addrefs, there was a negative. The houfe however, afterward requefted the removal of the general court to *Bofton,* which was not granted.

I

They

They met, as the year before, at *Cambridge*. In three May weeks the affembly protefted againft his excellency's 29. convening them there, and afterward appointed a committee of correfpondence.

The governor informed the houfe, that by his ma- July jefty's inftruction, he was forbidden giving his confent 4. to fuch an act as fubjects the officers of the crown to be taxed, by the affeffors in the towns where they refide, for the profits which they receive from their commiffions, although their offices have no relation to the province, fo that the tax-bill muft be qualified.

The houfe, by meffage, expreffed their furprife and 5. alarm at the reafon affigned for his not affenting to the tax-bill, and faid, " We know of no commiffioners of his majefty's cuftoms, nor of any revenue his majefty has a right to eftablifh in *North America*. We know and feel a tribute levied and extorted from thofe, who, if they have property, have a right to the abfolute difpofal of it."

Had it been known, how infignificant the taxes were which the officers of the crown were required to pay, it is hard to conceive how wifdom could have dictated fuch inftruction, and have ventured to give a frefh difguft to thofe, who were already too much irritated. However, the governor's inftructions did not oblige him to confine the general court to *Cambridge*, and he might have removed them to *Bofton*; but by fhowing a firmnefs in oppofing their defires, while they protefted againft the reftraint they were under, he meant to recommend himfelf to the miniftry. By the fame intention he was induced, in a great meafure, to refufe his confent to the grants made to Mr. *Bollan* and Mr. De

X 2   Berdt's

Berdt's executors by this affembly, as he had done in refpect to thofe made by the preceding. Thefe refufals ferved to keep up the animofity.

The difpofition to import goods into the Maffachu-fetts, in defiance of the laws of revenue and trade, and to fupport fuch practices by open violences 'upon the officers, whofe duty it was to carry the laws into execu-tion, broke out upon many occafions; and as ufual, the magiftrates declined giving their affiftance and fup-port, being in principle oppofed to fuch laws, as fun-damentally defective in point of rectitude. The like difpofition to import goods prevailed in the other colo-nies; but there was no call to go into the like open violences.

Dec. 3.   Mr. Otis jun. was carried off in a poft-chaife, bound hand and foot, his reafoning powers being wholly de-ranged. This calamity, which fomewhat leffens the weight of oppofition to minifterial meafures, is to be imputed, not to any effects of the affray with Mr. Ro-binfon, but rather to the high tone given to his animal frame by the ftrength of his paffions, and a failure in the point of temperance. The fons of liberty would have fuftained an exceffive lofs, had this event taken place in the early ftage of the oppofition; but the times had brought fo many able perfons of fimilar fentiments into the general court, who had been in training for years, and were converfant with the political management of public bufinefs, that the plans of the Maffachufetts anti-governmental party fuffered no derangement.

An opportunity now offers of mentioning, that Sir Alexander Gilmour baronet, and George Dempfter efq; were the gentlemen who fo nobly diftinguifhed them-

felves

felves by voting for the repeal of the ftamp-act, while all the other Scotch members prefent voted againft it. [See p. 204 at the top.]

After what has been written and tranfmitted, you will judge yourfelf under an obligation to return me fpeedy information of all that is doing in Great Britain, relative to the American colonies.

———————

LETTER V.

Roxbury, June 25, 1773.

THE annual elections of the *Maffachufetts* were in 1772. favor of the friends to colonial liberty; but the ftate of Mr. *Otis*'s mind neceffarily occafioned his being left out of the lift of the *Bofton* reprefentatives.

The general court ftill met at *Cambridge*, but the go- May vernor adopted a conciliating meafure, in declining to 28. negative Mr. *Hancock*, who was again chofen one of the council. He had been repeatedly chofen, and till now as repeatedly negatived; he declined however, taking his feat at the board, choofing to remain in the affembly as one of the Bofton members.

Mr. *Hutchinfon* acquainted the houfe, in anfwer to a June meffage, that his majefty had made provifion for his 13. fupport; and then, after requiring the opinion and advice of the council, upon their oaths, whether he might now remove the general court to Bofton, confiftent with

X 3   the

the fignification of his majefty's pleafure to him, and receiving their unanimous opinion and advice in the affirmative, adjourned them to meet at Bofton. He might have afked and received that very advice long before.

A committee having been appointed to confider the matter of the governor's fupport being provided for by the king, reported and obferved, " That the king's July providing for the fupport of the governor is a moft dan-
10. gerous innovation. It is a meafure whereby not only the right of the general affembly of this province is re-fcinded, but the higheft indignity is thrown upon it. It is an infraction of the charter in a material point, whereby a moft important truft is wrefted out of the hands of the general affembly." And the houfe, the fame day, de-clared by a meffage to the governor, " That the mak-ing provifion for his excellency's fupport, independent of the grants and acts of the general affembly, and his excellency's receiving the fame, is an infraction upon the rights of the inhabitants granted by the royal char-ter."

The payment of the governors by the crown, is not relifhed by the colonies, as it makes them entirely de-pendent upon that, and wholly independent of the peo-ple, and provincial affemblies; and as it deftroys the mutual check which each branch of the legiflature ought to have upon the others, and that balance of power which is effential to all free governments. It will be a new fource of complaint. On the other hand, the af-fair which has happened in the *Rhode Ifland* government will prove a frefh provocation to miniftry, and tend to fix them in their plans refpecting the colonies.

Lieu-

Lieutenant *Dudington* the commander of the late armed schooner the *Gaspee*, had been remarkably affiduous in supporting the laws against smuggling, and in searching after contraband goods, by which he had given great offence. He had also brought upon himself the resentments of many, by firing at the *Providence* packets (employed in transporting goods and passengers from thence to *Newport*, and *vice versa*,) in order to oblige the masters to take down their colours, and by chasing them even into the docks when it had been refused. The *Providence* packet coming up as usual with colours flying and company on board, probably a party of pleasure, as is frequent in the summer season, and refusing to take them down, the lieutenant fired a shot, which being disregarded he chased. It was near upon or quite high water. The packet stood in with the land as close as consisted with safety, designing that the *Gaspee* should be run a-ground in the chase. The design succeeded. The Gaspee was soon fast, and could not stir, the tide having done flowing. The packet proceeded to town. The situation of the Gaspee and resentment against the commander, excited the thought of attacking and destroying her. Mr. *John Brown*, a considerable merchant of *Providence*, was the principal in the business. Captain *Whipple* was immediately employed to beat up for volunteers, and a number offered and engaged to go upon any service for which they were wanted. Several whale boats were procured and filled with armed men. Mr. Brown accompanied them in the expedition. Captain Whipple, as they proceeded, observed to Mr. Brown, that he might lose his life, and that he had a family, and therefore he required that care should be

June 9.

taken

taken of them in cafe of his death.   Mr. Brown engaged
to do it fhould that happen.   About two o'clock in the
morning, they boarded and carried the fchooner, as fhe
lay a-ground about feven miles below Providence.   Mr.
Brown was himfelf the firft on board.   The lieutenant
was wounded.   He and the crew were put on fhore, and
every thing valuable belonging to him, was taken out
and faved for him ; after which the Gafpee, with all her
ftores, was burned.

Though a reward of five hundred pounds, together
with a pardon, if claimed by an accomplice, has been
offered by proclamation for difcovering and apprehending any of the perfons concerned ; yet the commiffioners appointed to try the matter, have tranfmitted accounts to miniftry, that *they can obtain no evidence*.   If
any one had wifhed to give evidence, that he might get
the reward ; yet the thought that he fhould rifk his life,
or be obliged to fly the country and become a perpetual
exile, would naturally have overcome fuch propenfity.
It was too hazardous to turn informer.   Some who were
fecured, in expectation that they would give intelligence,
were affifted by the populace in making their efcape,
before any thing material could be learnt from them by
the commiffioners.

Governor *Hutchinfon* and his adherents having been ufed
to reprefent the party in oppofition, as only an uneafy
factious few in Bofton, while the body of the people were
quite contented ; Mr. *Samuel Adams* was thereby induced to
vifit Mr. *James Warren* of *Plymouth*.   After converfing
upon the fubject, the latter propofed to originate and
eftablifh committees of correfpondence in the feveral
towns of the colony, in order to learn the ftrength of

3   the

the friends to the rights of the continent, and to unite
and increase their force. Mr. Samuel Adams returned
to Boston, pleased with the proposal, and communicated
the same to his confidents. Some doubted whether the
measure would prosper, and dreaded a disappointment
which might injure the cause of liberty. But it was concluded to proceed. The prime managers were about
six in number; each of whom when separate, headed a
division; the several individuals of which, collected and
led distinct subdivisions. In this manner the political
engine has been constructed. The different parts are
not equally good and operative. Like other bodies, its
composition includes numbers who act mechanically, as
they are pressed this or that way by those who judge for
them; and divers of the wicked, fitted for evil practices when the adoption of them is thought necessary to
particular purposes, and a part of whose creed it is,
that in political matters the public good is above every
other consideration, and that all rules of morality when
in competition with it, may be safely dispensed with.
When any important transaction is to be brought forward, it is thoroughly considered by the prime managers. If they approve, each communicates it to his
own division; from thence, if adopted, it passes to the
several subdivisions, which form a general meeting in
order to canvass the business. The prime managers being known only by few to be the promoters of it, are
desired to be present at the debate, that they may give
their opinion when it closes. If they observe, that the
collected body is in general strongly against the measure
they wish to have carried, they declare it to be improper: is it opposed by great numbers, but not warmly,
they

they advife to a re-confideration at another meeting, and prepare for its being then adopted; if the oppofition is not confiderable, either in number or weight of perfons, they give their reafons, and then recommend the adoption of the meafure. The principal actors are determined upon fecuring the liberties of their country, or perifhing in the attemp...

The news of his majefty's granting falaries to the juftices of the fuperior court, afforded them a fair opportunity for executing the plan of eftablifhing committees of correfpondence through the colony. The moft fpirited pieces were publifhed, and an alarm fpread, that the granting fuch falaries tended rapidly to complete the fyftem of their flavery.

Nov.
2.
A town meeting was called, and a committee of correfpondence appointed, to write circular letters to all the towns in the province, and to induce them to unite
19.
in meafures. The committee made a report, containing feveral refolutions contradictory to the fupremacy of the Britifh legiflature. After fetting forth, that all men have a right to remain in a ftate of nature as long as they pleafe, they proceed to a report upon the natural rights of the colonifts as men, chriftians and fubjects; and then form a lift of infringements and violations of their rights. They enumerate and dwell upon the Britifh parliament's having affumed the power of legiflation for the colonies in all cafes whatever—the appointment of a number of new officers to fuperintend the revenues—the granting of falaries out of the American revenue, to the governor, the judges of the fuperior court, the king's attorney and folicitor general. The report was accepted; copies printed, and fix hundred
circu-

circulated through the towns and districts of the province, with a pathetic letter addressed to the inhabitants, who were called upon not to doze any longer, or sit supinely in indifference, while the iron hand of oppression was daily tearing the choicest fruits from the fair tree of liberty. The circular letter requested of each town a free communication of sentiments on the subjects of the report, and was directed to the select men, who were desired to lay the same before a town meeting, which has been generally practised, and the proceedings of the town upon the business have been transmitted to the committee at Boston. This committee have their particular correspondents in the several towns, who upon receiving any special information, are ready to spread it with dispatch among the inhabitants. It consists of twenty-one persons, of heterogeneous qualities and professions. The governor, in expectation of exciting prejudice, and fixing a stigma upon them, their connections and proceedings, has written to a gentleman in power, "Strange that a government, which within a century would suffer no person to be free of the commonwealth who was not one of their church members, should now take for their leaders men, who openly contemn all religion, and should join deacons and atheists in one trust; and that they should be instigated to this by some of the clergy, who make the highest pretences to devotion; and yet the spirit of political party produces all this." He would gladly receive them all into his own arms, and be devoutly thankful for them, were they to change sides and join in supporting his administration. But he has unwarily acknowledged, that the government, or the great body of the people in
their

their legiflative and ruling capacity are in the oppofition, which therefore cannot confift merely of a few factious leaders; and he appears not to have recollected, that men of oppofite principles and characters will unite heart and hand, in keeping off a general calamity, which will involve them all in one and the fame ruin. The towns in general have chofen committees of correfpondence, and refolved in a ftile agreeable to the wifhes of the Boftonians. But the refolutions have not been alway drawn up by the townfmen. An inhabitant of *Peterfham* applied to that worthy and difinterefted fon of liberty, Mr. *Quincy,* whom you will recollect to have been of the council for captain Prefton and the foldiers, for his affiftance, and was furnifhed with the following draft intended for Bofton, excepting the introduction and the paragraphs marked with a ftar, which were added by fome other perfon.

1773.
Jan.
4.

At a meeting of the freeholders and other inhabitants of the town of *Peterfham* in the county of *Worcefter,* duly affembled according to law, held by adjournment on the 4th of January 1773, the committee chofen the 30th *ult.* made the following report, *viz.* " The town having received a circular letter from the town of *Bofton,* refpecting the prefent grievances and abominable oppreffions under which this country groans, have thereupon taken into their moft ferious confideration, the prefent policy of the Britifh government and adminiftration, with regard to *Great Britain* and thefe colonies; have carefully reviewed the mode of election, and the quality of the electors of the commons of that ifland; and have alfo attentively reflected upon the enormous and growing influence of the crown, and that bane of

all

all free states, a standing army in the time of peace; and in consequence thereof are fully confirmed in opinion, that the ancient rights of the nation are capitally invaded, and the greatest part of the most precious and established liberties of *Englishmen* utterly destroyed :— And whereas the parliament of Great Britain, by various statutes and acts, have unrighteously distressed our trade, denied and precluded us from the setting up and carrying on manufactures highly beneficial to the inhabitants of these territories; restricted and prevented our lawful intercourse and commerce with other states and kingdoms; have also made laws and institutions touching life and limb, in disherison of the ancient common law of the land; and moreover have in these latter times, robbed and plundered the honest and laborious inhabitants of this extensive continent of their property, by mere force and power; and are now draining this people of the fruits of their toil, by thus raising a revenue from them, against the natural rights of man, and in open violation of the laws of God.

This town in union with the worthy inhabitants of Boston, now think it their indispensable duty to consider of the premises and the present aspect of the times, and to take such steps as upon mature deliberation, are judged right and expedient, and hereupon this town

Resolved, That, with a governor appointed from Great Britain (especially at this day) during pleasure, with a large stipend, dependant upon the will of the crown, and controlled by instructions from a British minister of state, with a council subject to the negative of such a governor, and with all officers civil and military subject to his appointment or consent, with a castle in the hands

of

of a ftanding army, ftationed in the very bowels of the
land; and that amazing number of placemen and dependants, with which every maritime town already
fwarms, no people can ever be truly virtuous, free, or
brave:

Refolved, That the parliament of Great Britain, ufurp-
ing and exercifing a legiflative authority over, and ex-
torting an unrighteous revenue from thefe colonies, is
againft all divine and human laws. The late appointment of falaries to be paid to our fuperior court judges,
whofe creation pay and commiffion depend on mere will
and pleafure, completes a fyftem of bondage, equal to
any ever fabricated, by the combined efforts of the in-
genuity, malice, fraud and wickednefs of man:

* Refolved, That it is the opinion of this town, that
a defpotic arbitrary government is the kingdom of this
world, as fet forth in the New Teftament, and is dia-
metrically oppofite to the eftablifhment of Chriftianity
in a fociety, and has a direct tendency to fink a people
into a profound ftate of ignorance and irreligion; and
that, if we have an eye to our own and pofterity's happinefs (not only in this world, but the world to come)
it is our duty to oppofe fuch a government:

* And further refolved, That the depriving the colonies of their conftitutional rights, may be fitly compared to the difmembering the natural body, which
will foon affect the heart; and it would be nothing unexpected for us to hear, that thofe very perfons, who
have been fo active in robbing the colonies of their conftitutional rights, have alfo delivered up the conftitution of our mother country into the hands of our
king:

There-

Therefore refolved, That it is the firft and higheft focial duty of this people, to confider of, and feek ways and means, for a fpeedy redrefs of thefe mighty grievances and intolerable wrongs; and that for the obtaining of this end, this people are warranted, by the laws of God and nature, in the ufe of every rightful art and energy of policy, ftratagem and force.

* And while we are thus under thefe awful frowns of divine Providence, and involved as this people are in heavy calamities, which daily increafe in number and feverity, it is highly becoming towns and individuals to humble themfelves before Almighty God, ferioufly to commune with their own hearts, and feek carefully with tears, for the caufes of the prevailing diftreffes of the land; and while it is apparent, that priftine piety and purity of morals, have given place to infidelity, diffipation, luxury, and grofs corruption of mind and morals, there is a loud call for public humility, lamentings and reformation; and it is at this time eminently incumbent on one and all, to feek at the throne of the Great God for thofe fpecial and remarkable interpofitions of divine Providence, grace and mercy, which have fo often faved New England from both public and private diftrefs and mifery: and as there is great reafon to believe, that in paft times we have too much depended upon the exertions of worldly wifdom and political devices, it becomes us in our prefent melancholy fituation, to rely no longer on an arm of flefh, but on the arms of that all-powerful God, who is able to unite the numerous inhabitants of this extenfive territory, as a band of brothers in one common caufe—who can eafily give that true religion, which fhall make us his people indeed; that
spirit

spirit, which shall fit us to endure temporal hardships for the procurement of future happiness; that spirit of valor and irresistible courage, which shall occasion our aged and our youth to jeopard their lives with joy, in the high places of the field, for his name and service sake, for the preservation also of this goodly heritage of our fathers, for the sake of the living children of our loins, and the unborn millions of posterity.

* We believe that there are very many, who in these days have kept their integrity and garments unspotted, and hope that God will deliver them and our nation for their sake. God will not suffer this land, where the gospel hath flourished, to become a slave of the world; he will stir up witnesses of the truth; and in his own time spirit his people to stand up for his cause, and deliver them. In a similar belief, that patriot of patriots the great *Algernon Sidney* lived and died, and dying breathed a like sentiment and prophecy, touching his own and the then approaching times, a prophecy however not accomplished until a glorious revolution.

Approved of by vote of the town, without contradiction.

SYLVANUS HOW, per order.

The governor, instead of over-looking in his speech, the proceedings of the towns, has been induced by them to broach the dispute about the supremacy of the parliament; and has fallen into the snare, which probably some of the politicians laid for him, expecting to get the majority of the general court to declare against it. He designed to recommend himself to the ministry by obtaining a victory; but they will not thank him for increasing their embarrassments.

The

The council in their anfwer, faid, " The ftamp-act Jan.
with fome preceding and fucceeding acts of parliament, 25.
fubjecting the colonies to taxes without their confent,
was the original caufe of all the uneafinefs that has happened fince, and has occafioned alfo an inquiry into the
nature and extent of the authority by which they were
made."

This was the truth. When the ftamp-act took place,
" fome people, under the notion of zeal for liberty,
ran into the moft exceffive licentioufnefs, and were guilty
in one place and another of the moft lawlefs, unjuft, and
tyrannical proceedings; fuch as pulling down and deftroying houfes, abufing perfons, endangering men's
lives, deftroying their property, breaking windows, delivering prifoners out of the hands of juftice, putting
many into great fear, all contrary to the laws of the
province : but there was nothing of this kind before *."
Let me add, that in all my refearches, not an inftance
has occurred to me of the mob's having been the death
of a fingle individual, though they might have proceeded to the moft criminal lengths alfo, had they not
been gratified or diverted from their purfuits. But before that fatal act, there was not a more loyal, orderly,
and peaceable people, than the Americans in general,
through the whole Britifh empire. All ranks and conditions gloried in their connection with Great Britain;
rejoiced in her friendfhip and protection; and triumphed
in her profperity.

Toward the clofe of their anfwer, the houfe of affembly expreffed a concern at their having been reduced by
the fpeech to the unhappy alternative, either of appear-

* The Rev. Mr. Whitney's difcourfes on the public faft.

ing by their filence to acquiefce in the governor's fentiments as to the fupremacy of parliament, or of freely
difcuffing the point. The houfe might be concerned;
but the leaders were pleafed with the opportunity. The
governor replied; and the houfe in their rejoinder told
him, " Although the colony may have fubmitted *fub
filentio* to fome acts of parliament, that they conceived
might operate for their benefit, they did not conceive
themfelves bound by any of its acts, which they judged
would operate to the injury of individuals." The people at large believe, that the houfe has the beft of the
argument, and are confirmed in their oppofition to the
claims of parliament.

The houfe voted the ufual falaries to the judges of
the fuperior court early in the feffion. The governor
delayed giving his affent to the grants; which produced
a meffage to him requefting his making known the difficulty that prevented his affenting; to this it was anfwered, that he had received information, that his majefty had been pleafed to order falaries to be allowed to
the juftices of the fuperior courts, &c. By this anfwer
Feb. the houfe gained the opportunity of fending a fecond
meffage, in which they expreffed their refentment at the
many attempts made, effectually to render null and void
thofe claufes in their charter, upon which the freedom
of their conftitution depends; and faid that they were
more and more convinced, that it had been the defign
of adminiftration to introduce an arbitrary government
into the province. They declared at the clofe, their
impatience to know, " that the juftices will utterly refufe ever to accept of fupport in a manner fo juftly obnoxious to the people of the province, it being repug-

nant

nant to the charter, and utterly inconfiftent with the
fafety of the rights, liberties, and properties of the people." To add the greater weight to their fentiments,
and make them the more regarded by all perfons, they
came to feveral refolves refpecting the falaries and the Mar.
judges: among the reft, " that their dependence on the ³·
crown, efpecially while they hold their commiffions during pleafure, tends to the fubverfion of juftice and
equity, and to introduce oppreffion and defpotic power:
and that while they hold during pleafure, any who fhall
accept of and depend upon the pleafure of the crown
for his fupport, independent of the grants of the general
court, will difcover that he is an enemy to the conftitution, and has it in his heart to promote the eftablifhment
of an arbitrary government in the province."

The meafures purfued on each fide the Atlantic are
not calculated to promote harmony.

LETTER VI.

London, Auguſt 7, 1773

FRIEND G.

YOU will receive from me, without further application, regular accounts of what is doing on this
fide the Atlantic, in relation to the colonies.

The burning of the *Gaſpee* fchooner near Providence,
has given the chief rife to " An act for the better fe-

curing his majefty's dock yards, magazines, fhips, ammunition, and ftores." If the button of a marine's coat, the oar of a cutter's boat, or the head of a cafk belonging to the fleet, are included under the comprehenfive term *ftores*, then according to the act, a perfon wilfully and malicioufly deftroying, or aiding and affifting in deftroying the fame, is to fuffer death on being convicted. But what will affect you more than all the reft is, that the act is extended to the colonies, and fubjects a perfon to a trial at the pleafure of his majefty, his heirs or fucceffors, in any fhire or county in Great Britain. Your own feelings will furnifh you with the beft comment on this new extenfion of parliamentary power.

The fupporting of the authority of parliament was the only caufe affigned by the minifter himfelf, for retaining the tea duty, at the very time when he acknowledged it to be as anti-commercial a tax, as any of thofe which he had repealed upon that principle. It now appears that government had fomething more in contemplation.

The Eaft India Company, feeling the bad effects of the colonial fmuggling trade (occafioned by the retention of the duty) in the large quantities of tea which remained in their warehoufes unfold, requefted the repeal of the three-pence per pound in America, and offered that, upon its being complied with, government fhould retain fix-pence in the pound on the exportation. Thus the company prefented the happieft opportunity which could have offered, for honorably removing the caufe of difference with America. Here was an opening for doing right, without infringing the claims on either fide. The company afked, and their fituation required relief.

It

It could not be alleged, that it was done at the instance of American discontent. The minister was requested and intreated, by a gentleman of great weight in the company, and a member of parliament, to embrace the opportunity; but it has been rejected. New contrivances have been set on foot to introduce the tea, attended with the three-penny duty, into all the colonies. Various intrigues and solicitations have been used to induce the chairman and deputy chairman, to undertake this rash and foolish business. It has been protested against as contrary to the principles of the company's monopoly: but the power of ministry has prevailed; and the insignificant three-penny duty on tea is doomed to be the fatal bone of contention between Great Britain and America. A bill has been passed into an act, for May enabling the company to export their own teas. In con- 10. sequence of it, they have adopted the system, and are become their own factors. They have come to a resolution of sending 600 chests of tea to *Philadelphia*, the like quantity to *New York* and *Boston*, beside what is designed for other places: several ships are accordingly freighted for different colonies, and agents appointed for the disposal of the commodity.

The several colonies will undoubtedly consider the scheme as calculated merely to circumvent them into a compliance with the revenue law, and thereby to open the door for an unlimited taxation; for if taxation can be established in this instance, it will be extended to others. Consequences will not fail to convince the minister, that it would have been far more eligible to have repealed the duty, than in this way to attempt its establishment.

Y 3

blifhment. It will be needlefs for me to affure you, that
you may upon all occafions, command the affiftance of

Your, &c.

N. B. Some of the captains have refufed to take the
tea on board.

———————————

L E T T E R VII.

Roxbury, March 28, 1774.

BEFORE you have an account of the American
proceedings in refpect to the teas of the Eaft-
India Company, you muft be prefented with fome matters of an earlier date.

1773.
May
14.

The Boftonians perfifted in difcovering on every occafion, a determined oppofition to minifterial meafures.
Twelve days before the election day the town refolved,
" That if the council apply for Faneuil-hall for to
dine in on the anniverfary election day, the felect men
fhall not grant it but upon the exprefs conditions, that
neither the commiffioners of the cuftoms, nor their at-
tendants, nor the officers of the army and navy, ftationed
here for the purpofe of enforcing unconftitutional acts
of parliament by military execution, be invited." It
has been an eftablifhed cuftom for the governor, council,
and many other gentlemen, to dine there on that day:
but

but the refolve prevented an application, and occafioned their dining elfewhere, with the commiffioners and officers.

Whether the votes of *Boston* fent to *Virginia*, as the patriots fay, or their own private letters might or might not lead to it, the houfe of burgeffes refolved, in the beginning of March, to maintain an intercourfe with the fifter colonies. They therefore appointed a committee of eleven perfons, " whofe bufinefs it fhould be to obtain the moft early and authentic intelligence of all fuch acts and refolutions of the Britifh parliament, or proceedings of adminiftration, as may relate to or affect the Britifh colonies, and to keep up and maintain a correfpondence and communication with their fifter colonies." They then refolved, " That their fpeaker tranfmit to the fpeakers of the different affemblies their refolutions to be laid before their affemblies, and requefting their appointing committees." Nothing could be more acceptable to the *Maffachufetts* affembly. It was the firft particular bufinefs they entered upon when they met. They came to feveral refolves, and were careful in the firft to fpeak highly in praife of *Virginia*. They appointed a committee of fifteen members, and directed them " to prepare a circular letter to the fpeakers, requefting them to lay the fame before their refpective affemblies, in confidence that they will comply with the wife and falutary refolves of the houfe of burgeffes of Virginia." *Connecticut, Rhode Ifland, Maryland,* and *New Hampfhire,* entered into fimilar meafures: but the anfwer ordered by the *New Hampfhire* affembly, to be given to the fpeakers of *Virginia* and *Rhode Ifland,* was guardedly expreffed; they gave affurance, that their fifter colonies might rely upon

May 28.

Y 4 their

their sincerely joining them in every constitutional plan for securing the rights of America. The institution of these committees tends greatly to unite the colonies, and to render them more alert and formidable in resisting the encroachments of ministry. They by this mean become early prepared to meet new and unexpected occurrences; and are drawn in to look upon themselves as jointly interested in each others safety, and public concerns.

An event has happened in the *Massachusetts*, which has excited on the part of the people, the utmost indignation and animosity; on the side of the governor and others, the greatest confusion.

The agent, Dr. *Franklin*, has by some means yet unknown, obtained and sent over to Mr. Bowdoin a number of letters, to be communicated by him after perusal, to a few trusty gentlemen, viz. the honorable James Pitts, Mr. Thomas Cushing, Mr. Samuel Adams, Dr. Winthrop, Dr. Chauncy, and Dr. Cooper: it is added, they are to be returned and put into the place whence they were taken. The letters are signed *Tho. Hutchinson, And. Oliver, Ch. Paxton, Thomas Moffat, Robert Auchmuty, Nath. Rogers, George Rome*. Though they were partly private and confidential, they were designed to procure public coercive measures; and tended to incense the mother country against her colonies, and by the steps recommended, to widen the breach, which they have undoubtedly effected. Their contents were the subject of conversation and solicitous inquiry: till at length Mr. *Sam. Adams* acquainted the assembly, that he had perceived the minds of the people to be greatly agitated with a prevailing report, that letters of an extraordinary

June 2.

traordinary nature had been written, and sent to England, greatly to the prejudice of this province—that he had obtained certain letters, which with the consent of the gentleman from whom he had received them, might be read in the house under certain restrictions, namely, that the said letters be neither printed nor copied in whole or in part: the proposal was considered, and they were read under the said restrictions. A committee of the whole house afterward reported, " that the tendency and design of said letters was to overthrow the constitution of this government, and to introduce arbitrary power into the province;"—Yeas 101, Nays 5.

The restrictions under which the letters were communicated, were invalidated by contrivance; and in a week's time, Mr. *Hancock* acquainted the house, that he June had received copies of certain letters, which he sup- 9. posed were copies of the letters before the house, and moved that they might be compared. The next day, 10. one of a committee appointed to consider some means whereby the house might be honorably and fully possessed of the letters, reported, " That Mr. S. Adams had acquainted him, that having conversed with the gentleman from whom he received the letters, he was authorised to inform the house, that the said gentleman consented (as he found that copies of said letters were already abroad, and had been publicly read) that the house should be fully possessed of them, to print, copy, or make what use of them they pleased, relying on the goodness of the house, that the original letters be returned, they retaining attested copies for their use." Mr. S. Adams being called upon, declared the same. At length the assembly resolved to petition the king to
remove

June remove governor *Hutchinson* and lieutenant governor
16   *Oliver* for ever from the government of the province.
22   They agreed alfo to furnifh the council with the original
letters upon the exprefs condition, that the board would
by no means fuffer them to go out of their hands. The
council complied with the infulting ftipulation aimed at
the governor; and upon his requiring the letters for
examination, refufed to deliver them into his hands, but
fent a committee to open them before him, that he
might examine the hand-writing. To this indignity he
24   was obliged to fubmit, as well as to the mortification
of acknowledging the fignature. After which they refolved, " that the removal of the governor and lieutenant governor will be promotive of his majefty's fervice."

The *Bofton* committee of correfpondence, that they
might add weight to the doings of the general court,
inclofed the governor's letters and alfo the refolves of the
houfe, in a fpirited circular letter, and fent them to the
feveral town clerks through the province to be communicated to their refpective towns.

The houfe of affembly in their petition and remonftrance to his majefty, charged the governor and lieutenant governor with being betrayers of their trufts and
of the people they governed, and with giving private,
partial, and falfe information; declared them enemies to
the colony; and prayed for juftice againft them and for
their fpeedy removal. So prevalent was the refentment,
that thefe charges with many others. were carried through
by a majority of 82 to 12.

To enter now upon the fubject of the TEA. While
the bill for allowing the Eaft-India Company to export

it

it was in parliament, letters from Britain infinuated into the minds of the colonifts, that a plan was laid to bring them into a fnare ; that a noble refiftance on this occafion would free them from the flavery intended for them; that if this opportunity was loft they would never have another; and that if they fuffered the fhips to land the tea and the duty to be paid, they would rivet their own chains. The Britifh merchants have been alarmed with the thought of the loffes, which muft neceffarily accrue to themfelves from the exportations of the company, and from the fales going through the hands of confignees ; and have contributed to the ftrengthening of that refiftance to which the people were already inclined, through their prevailing jealoufy at the refervation of the tea duty when the other duties were repealed. The united oppofition of the colonies was to be fecured ; but the event was precarious. The *Boftonians* were much fufpected by the fons of liberty in the other provinces, on account of the many goods which were imported into the town during the general non-importation agreement, and afterward of the teas contrary to the agreement refpecting that article. *New York* and *Philadelphia* had kept to the agreement, and had run all the teas that the market demanded : but there had been imported into *Bofton*, from the beginning of 1768 to the end of laft year, not lefs than 2714 chefts, by more than a hundred different perfons. Mr. Hutchinfon and his fons were confiderable importers. It was evident that the body of merchants could not be depended upon. Mr. *Thomas Mifflin* of Philadelphia being at Bofton, put it therefore to the fons of liberty, when the teas were expected,

expected, " Will you engage that they shall not be landed ? If so I will answer for Philadelphia." They pledged
their honor.

Oct.   The inhabitants of *Philadelphia* assembled and unani-
2. moufly entered into various resolves, in which they censured
the resolution of the East India company to send out
their tea to America, subject to the payment of duties
on its being landed, as an open attempt to enforce the
ministerial plan, and a violent attack upon the liberties
of America; and declared it to be the duty of every
American to oppose this attempt, and that whoever
should directly or indirectly countenance it, was an enemy
to his country.   They then fixed upon a committee to
wait on the gentlemen reported to be appointed to receive and sell the tea, and to request their resigning.
Within three days the whole number resigned; Messrs.
Whartons and *Brown* without making the least difficulty;
the other two not, till the treatment they met with (on
appearing at the coffee-house) for the shuffling answer
they had given, convinced them that it was not safe
trifling with the public opinion.   Since this meeting,
the Boston sons of liberty have assured by letter the sons
of liberty at Philadelphia, that no tea shall be landed.

At *New York*, when captain *Sears* and captain *M'Dougall* heard that the tea was to be sent, they concluded
that an opposition to it was necessary, and agreed upon
contriving to unite the tea-smugglers, the merchants,
and the sons of liberty in that service; and that captain
M'Dougall should write against the design of introducing and vending the tea agreeable to the ministerial plan,
but should remain concealed as the author.   A few of
each

each class were called together, and the mode of opposition settled.   Publications, tending to spread and increase the alarm of imminent danger to the liberties of
the country, appeared periodically.   As the time approached for the arrival of the tea ships, the publications
became more spirited and threatening.   An hand bill Nov.
addressed to the friends of liberty and commerce was 5.
circulated through the city, calculated to provoke resentment against all the encouragers of the tea-plan.
Afterward written papers were stuck up at the coffee- 8.
house and other places, menacing destruction to any person who should accept a commission for the sale of the
East India company's teas, or be an accessary.   In rather more than a week, there was published a paper 18.
signed *Legion*, addressed to the stated pilots of the port,
and all others whom it might concern, directing them
how to proceed in reference to any tea ship, and requiring
them at their peril, to bring her no further than the
Hook.   In another paper, signed the *Mohawks*, the tea
ship is said to be laden with fetters, forged for them in
Great Britain, and every vengeance is denounced against
all persons, who dare in any manner to contribute to the
introduction of these chains.   In December, the *London*, captain *Chambers*, and the tea ship arrived on the
same day ; the former came up directly to the wharf,
the other remained at the *Hook*, and was watched till she
returned, by a vessel stationed there for the purpose.   On
her arrival a committee waited on the consignees, who
agreeable to a former promise assured them, that they
would neither receive nor sell the tea, as it came liable
to an *American duty*.   Captain Chambers ventured to
bring seventeen chests on a private account, which were
                                                taken

taken and thrown overboard into the harbour. Had the company's ſhip came to the wharf, ſhe would probably have been burnt, for captain *Sears* and five others had determined upon it, and provided themſelves with combuſtibles for the purpoſe.

At *Philadelphia*, printed papers were diſperſed, warning the *Delaware* pilots not to conduct any of the tea ſhips into harbour, as they were only ſent for the purpoſe of enſlaving and poiſoning all the Americans; and at the ſame time plainly intimating, that it was expected they would apply their knowledge of the river, under the colour of their profeſſion, ſo as effectually to ſecure their country from ſuch an imminent danger.

In moſt places, the conſignees were obliged to relinquiſh their appointments, and to enter into engagements not to act in that capacity; and no other perſons daring to receive the cargoes conſigned to them, the captains of the New York and Philadelphia ſhips, from theſe circumſtances, and the knowledge of the riſk they ran from the determined reſolution of the people, concluded upon returning directly to Great Britain, without entangling themſelves by any entry at the cuſtom-houſes. But it was otherwiſe in the *Maſſachuſetts*.

Methods were taken to ſpirit up the people at large by fugitive pieces, hand bills, reſolves of town meetings, the mutual intercourſe of committees and the like. At length, ſome hundreds of the inhabitants of *Boſton* and the neighbouring towns, meet at *Liberty-tree*, agreeable to a notification iſſued the day before, " for to hear the conſignees reſign and ſwear that they will reſhip any teas, that may by the *Eaſt-India* company be aſſigned to them." The conſignees are in general obnoxious

Nov. 3.

noxious to the public by reason of their near and intimate connections with the governor, on whose support
they depend. They are not terrified into an appearance at the place proposed; but meet together by
agreement at the store of Mr. *Clark*, who is one of them,
in King-street. A committee is appointed by the af-
sembly to wait upon them with a message, to which they
pay no regard. The people, who attend the committee
as spectators, upon this force open the doors of the ware-
house, and enter with great violence; and then attempt
getting up stairs into the comptinghouse, but are driven
back. The sons of liberty not having succeeded in this Nov.
procedure, a town-meeting of the freeholders and other 5.
inhabitants is called. A large number is collected;
and it is agreed to adopt the resolves of the citizens of
Philadelphia. A committee is chosen to wait upon the
consignees, who decline complying with the request of
the town by letters, which, though decent, are the next
day voted daringly affronting, when the meeting is immediately dissolved. Some of the sons of liberty are
fearful of pushing the matter too far, lest the town, and
then the colony, should be drawn into a quarrel with
Great Britain. To such it is said, " It must come to
a quarrel with Great Britain and the colony, sooner or
later; and if so, what can be a better time than the
present? Hundreds of years may pass away before the
parliament will make such a number of acts in violation
of the British constitution as it has done of late years,
and by which it has excited so formidable an opposition
to the measures of ministry. Beside, the longer the
contest is delayed, the more administration will be
strengthened. Do not you observe, how the government

ment at home are increasing their party here, by sending over young fellows to enjoy appointments, who
marry into our first families and so weaken the oppofition ? By such like means, and by multiplying pofts and
places, and giving them to their own friends, or applying them to the corruption of their antagonifts, they
will increafe their own force fafter in proportion than the
force of the country party will increafe by population.
If then we muft quarrel, ere we can have our rights
fecured, now is the moft eligible period.   Our credit
alfo is at ftake; we muft venture, and unlefs we do, we
fhall be difcarded by the fons of liberty in the other colonies, whofe affiftance we may expect upon emergencies, in cafe they find us fteady, refolute and faithful."
They conclude to venture onward.

18.   A new town-meeting is called, and a new committee
appointed to wait upon the confignees to know, whether they will refign their appointment ; to which they
anfwer, " It is out of our power to comply with the requeft of the town."   This anfwer may be built upon
folemn engagements not to refign; otherwife it is hard
to conceive how it fhould be more out of their power,
than the power of the Philadelphia confignees, who have
refigned fix weeks ago.   It is a managed affair between
19.   them and the governor, who calls a council for advice
upon meafures proper for preferving the peace, and for
fupporting the authority of government.   While the
council are debating, a petition of the confignees is
prefented, praying leave to refign themfelves and the
property committed to them, to his excellency and their
honors as the guardians of the people.   After debate
the further confideration is poftponed to the 23d, then

to

to the 27th, then to the 29th, when the council make a 29.
few obfervations, decline complying with the petition,
and advife his excellency to renew his orders to the juftices and others, to exert themfelves for the fecurity of
his majefty's fubjects, the prefervation of peace and
good order, and for preventing all offences againft the
law.   About this time the confignees, confifting of the
governor's fons, coufins, and particular friends, remove
to the caftle for perfonal fafety.   The day before the
laft meeting of the council, captain *Hall* in the *Dartmouth*, came to an anchor near the caftle, having on
board one hundred and fourteen chefts of tea; and on
the day of their meeting, comes into the harbour.   On
the fame day a notification is pofted up in all parts of
the town, inviting every friend to his country to meet
at nine o'clock, to make a united refiftance to the moft
deftructive meafure of adminiftration.   The meeting of
the people of Bofton and the neighbouring towns is continued by adjournment to the next day, when it is de- 30
termined, that the tea fhall be returned.   Faneuil-hall
being too fmall for the affembly, they adjourn to the
Old South Meeting-houfe, and confirm the former
determination by voting, " that the tea fhall not be
landed, that no duty fhall be paid, and that it fhall be
fent back in the fame bottom."   They further vote,
" that Mr. *Rotch*, the owner of the veffel, be directed not to enter the tea at his peril, and that captain
Hall be informed, at his peril not to fuffer any of the tea
to be landed."   They alfo appoint a watch of twenty-
five men to be a guard upon the Dartmouth, lying at
Griffin's wharf.   A letter is received from the confignees,
offering to ftore the teas till they can write and receive

VOL. I.   Z   further

further orders; but the propofal is rejected. Mr. *Green-leaf*, the sheriff, appears and begs leave to read a proclamation from the governor, which requires the people forthwith to disperse and to surcease all further proceedings. He is allowed to do it; and, upon finishing, there is a loud and general hiss. The people afterward vote, " that captain *Bruce*, on his arrival, do conform to the votes respecting Hall's veffel; that no tea from Great Britain be landed or fold till the act impofing the duty is repealed; that the captain of the prefent watch be defired to make out a lift for the next night, and fo on, until the veffels leave the harbour; that fhould the watch be molefted, the inhabitants be alarmed by the tolling of the bells at night, and the ringing of them in the day; that fix perfons be appointed to give notice to the country towns, upon any important occafion; that every veffel arriving with tea have a proper watch, and that their brethren in the country be defired to afford their affiftance on the firft notice." They determine to carry their votes and refolves into execution at the rifk of life and property; thank their brethren in the neighbouring towns, and then diffolve the meeting.

After the diffolution, the committee of correfpondence for the town of Bofton hold their meetings, and invite the like committees of the adjacent towns to join them; feveral do it; the whole jointly affume the direction of all that relates to the teas of the Eaft India company. They keep a conftant military watch of twenty-five men every night, generally with fire arms, to prevent the tea being privately landed. The veffels belonging to captains *Bruce* and *Coffin*, are upon their arrival ordered to Griffin's wharf.

The

The people of Boston and the neighbouring towns, Dec. that have agreed to act in concert with Boston, meet at 14. the Old South Meeting-house, and conclude upon ordering Mr. *Rotch* to apply immediately for a clearance for his ship. Mean while the governor receiving intimation that she would be sent to sea, and that it might not be through the ordinary channel by the castle, acquaints admiral *Montague* and desires him to take the proper precautions, on which the admiral orders the Active and King Fisher to be fitted for sea, and to fall down and guard the passages out of the harbour. The governor likewise renews in writing his orders to colonel *Leslie*, to suffer no vessel, coasters excepted, to pass the fortress from the town without a permit signed by himself. A sufficient number of guns are loaded on this special occasion.

The assembly are acquainted, that the collector cannot give Mr. *Rotch* a clearance, until the vessel is discharged of dutiable articles. Mr. *Samuel Phillips Sa-* 16. *vage*, of *Weston*, is chosen moderator. The number assembled from town and country is thought to be some thousands. Upon the present crisis several gentlemen deliver their sentiments; and Mr. *Josiah Quincy* jun. his to the following purpose;—" It is not, Mr. Moderator, the spirit that vapors within these walls that must stand us in stead. The exertions of this day will call forth events, which will make a very different spirit necessary for our salvation. Whoever supposes, that shouts and hosannas will terminate the trials of the day, entertains a childish fancy. We must be grossly ignorant of the importance and value of the prize for which we contend; we must be equally igno-

rant

rant of the power of thofe who have combined againſt us; we muſt be blind to that malice, inveteracy, and infatiable revenge, which actuate our enemies public and private, abroad and in our boſom, to hope that we ſhall end this controverſy without the ſharpeſt, the ſharpeſt conflicts—to flatter ourſelves that popular reſolves, popular harangues, popular acclamations, and popular vapor, will vanquiſh our foes. Let us conſider the iſſue. Let us look to the end. Let us weigh and conſider, before we advance to thoſe meaſures, which muſt bring on the moſt trying and terrible ſtruggle this country ever ſaw."

About three o'clock in the afternoon the queſtion is put, " will you abide by your former reſolutions with reſpect to not ſuffering the tea to be landed ?" It paſſes in the affirmative, *nem. con.*

Mr. *Rotch* is ordered to make a proteſt, and procure a paſs for his veſſel. He waits upon the governor at Milton, who offers to give him a letter to the admiral for protection, which he declines, fearing in that caſe the rage of the people, and being in no concern about his ſhip, as that is not the object of reſentment, but the tea. He intimates to the governor, that ſome of the leaders of the people wiſh the ſhip to go down and be ſtopped at the caſtle, " for then they will be rid of the affair, and may ſay they have done all in their power." While Mr. Rotch is abſent, the ſpeakers in the meeting keep the people together by engaging their attention till he returns, which is before ſix o'clock, when he informs the body, that upon applying to the governor for a paſs, he received for anſwer, " I cannot give you a paſs conſiſtent with the laws and my duty to the king,

unleſs

unlefs the veffel is properly qualified from the cuftom-
houfe." Upon this there is a great deal of difputing,
when a perfon difguifed like an Indian, gives the war-
whoop in the front gallery, where there are few if any
befides himfelf. Upon this fignal it is moved and voted
that the meeting be immediately diffol-ed. The people
crowd out and run in numbers to Griffin's wharf. At
the fame inftant, a number of perfons, chiefly mafters
of veffels and fhip-builders from the north end of the
town, about feventeen, though judged to be many more
as they run along, crofs Fort-hill, dreffed as Indians,
and repair to the tea fhips; and in about two hours hoift
out of them and break open 342 chefts of tea, and
difcharge their contents into the falt water. They are
not in the leaft molefted. The multitude of fpectators
upon and about the wharf, ferves as a covering party.
The whole bufinefs is conducted with very little tumult,
and no damage done to the veffels or any other property: when finifhed, the people return quietly to their
own towns and habitations.

Prior to the deftruction of the tea, captain *Loring* in
a brig, being the fourth and laft veffel on the Eaft-India
Company's account, was caft afhore at Cape Cod; and
what tea was faved, has been conveyed to the caftle.

The arrival of the tea-fhips firft at Bofton, the confignees refufing to refign, though they had the example
of others to induce them, and the governor's refolution
to pay no regard to the voice of the public, brought on
the deftruction of the tea. The fons of liberty were
fenfible, that if it was landed and ftored, it would fome
how or other obtain a fale; and that the virtue of the
people, to decline buying and ufing a commodity to

Z 3   which

which they were so attached from love and habit, was
too precarious a ground on which to risk the salvation of
their country. They have been obliged, but with the
utmost reluctance, to venture upon a desperate remedy.
Many of their friends, who are not acquainted with circumstances or do not attend to them, may be ready to
censure them severely. But had the tea been landed,
the union of the colonies in opposing the ministerial
schemes would have been dissolved; and it would have
been extremely difficult ever after to have restored it.
The fulfilment of their solemn declaration, that the tea
should not be landed, though in a way which would not
have been chosen had any other effectual one offered,
has secured them the good opinion and confidence of
their co-patriots in other parts. The governor has that
influence with the consignees, that he could undoubtedly
have prevailed on them to resign; but he has encouraged
them to the contrary: and therefore what he has written,
" It has been absolutely out of my power to prevent
the destruction of the tea, without conceding to the unreasonable demands of a lawless set of men, and thereby
giving government up and rendering myself obnoxious
to my sovereign," will scarce be admitted as a sufficient
justification. Sovereigns themselves, upon special emergencies, wisely give place to the opinions and wishes of
their subjects; but are often disgraced and forced into
difficulties, through the want of like wisdom in their
representatives. Had the governor given a pass for the
ship in the present instance, he would not have been
viewed by considerate persons, as breaking either the
laws or his oath. Cases offer, when statute laws and
oaths of office are required to give place to the supreme

law

law of society, the safety of the community. Had he looked back to the time of the stamp-act, he would probably have found many precedents of ships having permits from his predecessor in office, Sir Francis Bernard, to pass the castle without being duly qualified for want of stamps; and yet the granting them did not render Sir Francis obnoxious to his sovereign. But the truth was, Mr. *Hutchinson* had repeatedly urged government at home to be firm and persevering; this was a favorite topic on which he was often insisting; he himself therefore could not think of yielding: and then he would not believe that the people were determined at all adventures to perfect their engagements; but expected that when the critical moment came, they would desist. Whereas when that moment came, and the tea on board the Dartmouth, captain Hall, was in danger of being seized and secured by the custom-house officers, who might have been supported by admiral Montague, the sons of liberty projected the destruction of it in the manner above related: and in order to make short work of the whole business, and prevent their repeating the preceding formalities, they did not confine their operations to the tea on board the Dartmouth, but extended them to the teas brought in afterward by captains *Bruce* and *Coffin*.

Some expect that the destruction of the tea will issue in the destruction of the charter, which will make the inhabitants of the colony furious beyond expression. One gentleman, apprehensive of the fatal consequences that will follow upon the parliament's meddling with the charter, the great darling of the people, has written freely and fully upon the subject to his correspondent,

an influential member in the house. Another, being defirous of learning the real fentiments of the more moderate party, and of fuch as have not plunged themfelves
into the politics of the day, has converfed with feveral
of them; but has difcovered in them the warmeft indignation and the higheft refentment at the thought of
being deprived of their charter.   A major in the militia
(whom Mr. Hutchinfon honored with the commiffion,
for his good conduct as foreman of the jury on the trial
of the foldiers for killing the perfons on the 5th of
March 1770) told him, " Sir, you know that I am a
friend to government and wifh to fupport it; but if there
is an attempt to take away our charter, I will fight up
to my knees in blood in defence of it."   The gentleman has perceived fuch a fpirit to predominate among
all the people, that he has judged it right to communicate his knowledge to Sir Francis Bernard, and to acquaint him with his apprehenfions as to the fatal confequences which will follow upon the adoption of violent
meafures.   He has written alfo to another friend upon
the fubject, in hope that the intelligence will get to the
miniftry, and prove beneficial to the public, by preventing harfh proceedings.   At Charleftown the Carolinians have unloaded the tea, and ftored it in cellars,
where it cannot be ufed, and where it will finally perifh.

Let me pafs from hence to relate the doings of the
Maffachufetts affembly refpecting the judges, which you
will probably pronounce intemperate.

The houfe being informed, that each of the judges
refufed to take more than one half of the fum granted
them the laft year, which they confidered as implying
on the part of the judges, a determination to accept of
their

their support from the crown, resolved, " That it is the incumbent duty of the judges explicitly to declare, whether they are determined to receive the grants of the general assembly or to accept of their support from the crown; and their delaying any longer to let the public know their determination, will discover that they have little or no regard for the peace and welfare of the province : and in such case it will be the indispensable duty of the commons of this province to impeach them before the governor and council." Four of the judges, 1774. Feb. in the beginning of February, acquainted the house that they had received their whole salary granted them by the general court, and not any part of the grant made by the crown, and that they were determined still to receive the grants of the general assembly; which was pronounced satisfactory. But the chief justice, *Peter Oliver* esq; sent them a letter informing them, That 3. since being upon the bench seventeen years, he had suffered above three thousand pounds sterling; that he had been encouraged not to resign with the hope of a support, but had never .been relieved; that he had taken his majesty's grant from the 5th of July 1772 to the 5th of January 1774, and that without his majesty's leave he dare not refuse it.

The house resolved, " That Peter Oliver hath, by his 11. conduct, proved himself an enemy to the constitution of this province, and is become justly obnoxious to the good people of it; that he ought to be removed from the office of chief justice; and that a remonstrance and petition to the governor and council for his immediate removal be prepared"—yeas 96—nays 9.

The

Feb. 24.　The houſe propoſed to exhibit articles of impeach-ment, in their own name and the name of all the in-habitants of the province, againſt the chief juſtice. His excellency excepted to the proceedings of the houſe as unconſtitutional; for which reaſon he could not give them any countenance.

Mar. 1.　They prepared articles of high crimes and miſde-meanors againſt the chief juſtice, to preſent to his ex-cellency and the council, in which they ſaid, " The ſalary and hopes of augmentation muſt have the effect of a continual bribe, and expoſe him to a violation of his oath. His accepting hath betrayed the baſeneſs of his heart and the luſt of covetouſneſs, in breach of his engagements to rely ſolely on the grants of the aſſembly, neceſſarily implied and involved in his accepting ſaid office. By receiving a grant out of the revenue unjuſtly extorted from the American colonies, he hath, as far as lay in his power, put a ſanction on and eſtabliſhed the ſaid revenue, counter-acted the reaſonable petitions of the people to his majeſty, and in defiance of the known ſenſe of the body of this people, hath wickedly endea-voured to increaſe the diſcontent and jealouſies of this people and the grievance aforementioned."

9.　It was reſolved, " That the houſe have done all that in the capacity of repreſentatives can be done for the removal of Peter Oliver; and it muſt be preſumed, that the governor's refuſing to take any meaſures therein is becauſe he alſo receives his ſupport from the crown."

It is not to be thought, that the leading gentlemen in theſe proceedings expected to obtain the removal of the chief juſtice: but by the help of them, they rendered

　　　　　　　　　　　　　　　　　　　　　..him

him and the governor more and more obnoxious to the
body of the people; added to the dignity and importance of the houſe in the eyes of the repreſentatives, by
placing them upon an apparent level with the houſe of
commons in Britain; and preſerved the general animoſity againſt miniſterial meaſures from falling into a
decline.

The real, genuine ſentiments of the profeſſed patriots
may be deſired; let me therefore mention, that theſe
are divided in wiſh and opinion. The great body of
them through the ſeveral colonies and even in this, aim
at no more than the removal of all the innovations ſince
the expiration of the war. They want to have matters
revert back to the ſtate in which they were when the
peace commenced; and to be fixed in that ſtate. They
wiſh moſt ardently to continue in union with Great
Britain; and abhor the thought of a ſeparation. They
judge that it would be neither ſafe nor beneficial; that
it is infinitely more eligible to have the protection of
the mother country, and to remain under her ſhadow;
and that no greater happineſs can be enjoyed by them,
than a thorough reſtoration of harmony and affection
between them and the parent ſtate, ſo as to obliterate
the remembrance of all paſt animoſity. But there are
a few in this colony who hanker after independency,
and will be likely to bend their whole influence for the
obtaining of it, whenever there is the leaſt opening to
encourage their efforts. At the head of theſe we muſt
place Mr. *Samuel Adams*, who has long ſince ſaid in
ſmall confidential companies—" The country ſhall be
independent, and we will be ſatisfied with nothing ſhort
of it." At one time his influence was ſmall, owing to
                                                    defects

defects in pecuniary matters, especially as collector of the taxes for Boston, in which office he served for years. He was accountable to the town for between one and two thousand pounds; but a great part of it had never been gathered. What with not pressing the payment of the taxes in time, as is too generally the case; not calling when the money happened to be ready and other casualties, no inconsiderable sum was lost. His necessities probably (for he appears to be addicted to no extravagances) urged him to supply himself, time after time, from the cash in hand, without attending to the accumulation of the balance against him, till called upon to settle. The town had several meetings upon the business; at length, by the exertion of his friends, a majority was obtained for the relinquishment of the demand upon him. Since his first election into the house in 1765, his influence has been gradually increasing, until he has obtained a great ascendency in directing the town of Boston, and the house of representatives, and consequently the council. His abilities and policy will foster the idea of independency, by the aids of those very severities the ministry may adopt, in order to compel the colonies into a submission to parliamentary authority in all cases whatever.

LET

LETTER VIII.

London, July 2, 1774.

THE letters sent over to the Massachusetts by Dr. Franklin have produced a duel between Mr. *Whateley* the banker, brother to the late secretary to the treasury, and *John Temple* esq; in which the former was dangerously wounded. This has led the doctor to inform the public, that both the gentlemen are totally ignorant and innocent, as to the transaction and its circumstances about which they fought. He declares that he alone was the person who obtained and transmitted to Boston the letters in question, and says—" Mr. W. could not communicate them, because they were never in his possession; and for the same reason they could not be taken from him by Mr. T." The doctor justifies his own conduct, and concludes with telling the world, he " thought it his duty to transmit them to his constituents." But if they were sent over to be communicated to a few confidential gentlemen only, instead of being addressed to the speaker of the assembly, or one of the committee appointed to correspond with him, with orders to lay them before the house, how were they *transmitted to his constituents?* There is something mysterious in this business, which it is apprehended will not bear a discovery at present. It is suspected that the letters were procured out of some public office; and that
Mr.

Mr. Temple is not so perfectly ignorant of all circumstances as the doctor's language seems to express.

**1774.
Jan.
29.** The merits of the petition, presented some time ago by the doctor as agent for the Massachusetts, praying for the removal of the governor, came on to be heard before the privy council. It is reported, that Mr. *W——* *——*, wandering from the proper question before their lordships, poured forth such a torrent of virulent abuse on Dr. *Franklin* as scarce ever before took place in judicial proceedings. His reproaches appeared to some present to be incompatible with the principles of law, truth, justice, propriety and humanity. And it was thought it would have redounded more to the honor of their lordships, had they seemed to enjoy less the lashes which the doctor underwent; and had they expressed their dissatisfaction by reducing the orator to the remembrance of the exalted characters before whom he uttered such language. The petition was dismissed, and the doctor is displaced from the office of deputy postmaster general for the colonies. The philosopher may recollect in some future day the liberties taken with him before the privy council on the twenty-ninth of January, and take ample revenge on British ministers and courtiers.

**Mar.
7.** A message from his majesty, on account of the late disturbances in America, was presented to both houses. Particular mention was made of the outrage committed by the people at Boston. Matters are now brought to a crisis, and ministry are bent upon vigorous, spirited measures. To prevent opposition from the merchants, the public papers were filled with writings on the subject, which painted the misconduct of the colonies in the strongest colours, and urged in particular the impossibility

4

of the future exiftence of any trade to America, if this flagrant outrage on commerce, as it is pronounced, went unpunifhed. Thefe with other endeavours had the propofed effect. The refentment againft the Americans became as high and as ftrong as could be defired, within the houfe: but the ftorm was to be directed againft the *Maffachufetts*. The minifter, in debate, ftated that the oppofition to the authority of parliament had always originated in that colony; and that that colony had always been inftigated to fuch conduct, by the irregular and feditious proceedings of Bofton. It was become neceffary therefore to begin with that town. He had forgot, or would not mention, that the violent oppofition to the ftamp-act originated in Virginia.

Leave was given to bring in a bill " for the immediate 14, removal of the officers concerned in the collection of the cuftoms from Bofton, and to difcontinue the landing and difcharging, lading and fhipping of goods, wares and merchandifes, at Bofton or within the harbour' thereof." At the firft introduction of the bill it was received with general applaufe. Mr. *Bollan* however, petitioned to be heard for the Maffachufetts council, and in behalf of himfelf, and other inhabitants of Bofton. The commons refufed to admit his petition, though a few days back they had received one from him as agent for the council. The lords were actually hearing him on a petition, as a perfon duly qualified. On the third reading of the bill, another petition was prefented, in the name of feveral natives and inhabitants of North America; which infifted ftrongly on the injuftice of the act, and its tendency to alienate the affections of America; and exprefsly declared, that the attachment of America

America could not long furvive the juſtice of Great Britain. The minority members maintained, that the bill ſtood ſimply as a proſcription of one of the greateſt trading towns in the Britiſh dominions from the uſe of their port, and from all the commerce by which thouſands obtained their bread. " Have we not (ſay they) given an extent of power to his majeſty to prevent the port of Boſton from ever being reinſtated, if the king ſhould think proper? A fine is laid; the trade is prohibited until it is paid; and when the fine is paid, the town may be as far from recovering her trade as ever. The act provides, that the crown muſt have ſatisfaction, and that the laws of trade and revenue ſhall be obeyed. There is a ſting in this. The act under pretence of an indemnity to the Eaſt India Company, is meant to enforce the ſubmiſſion to taxes. America will ſee this; and the cauſe of Boſton will be made the cauſe of all the colonies. They are all as guilty as Boſton. Not one has received the tea: ſome have deſtroyed it, others ſent it back." But all oppoſition was ineffectual; for the projected meaſures of government were immutable. The bill paſſed; and was carried up to the houſe of lords, where it was warmly debated, but, as in the houſe of commons, paſſed without a diviſion.

Mar. 31.   It received the royal aſſent.

The Boſton port-bill formed only one part of the coercive plan propoſed by miniſtry. A bill was ſoon brought in for " the better regulating the government of the Maſſachuſetts-bay." The purport of it was, to alter the conſtitution of the province, to take the whole executive power out of the hands of the democratic part, and to veſt the nomination of counſellors, judges and

and magistrates of all kinds, including sheriffs, in the crown, and in some cases in the king's governor, and all to be removable at the pleasure of the crown.

In the debates it was asked of ministry, whether the colonies already regulated nearly in the manner proposed by the bill, were more submissive to the right of taxation than the Massachusetts. It was justly argued, that the disorder lay much deeper than the forms of government; that the people throughout the continent were universally dissatisfied; and that the uneasiness and resistance was no less in the royal governments than in any other. Mr. *Bollan* again made an effort in favor of his province; but the commons refused to receive his petition. The ministry having carried the preceding bill, prepared another, without which, it was said, the scheme would be entirely defective.

Lord *North* presented the third bill " for the impar- April tial administration of justice in the cases of persons 21. questioned for any acts done by them in the execution of the law, or for the suppression of riots and tumults in the *Massachusetts-bay*." This bill provided, that in case any person was indicted in that province for murder, or any other capital offence, and it should appear to the governor that the fact was committed in the exercise or aid of magistracy, in suppressing tumults and riots, and that a fair trial could not be had in the province, he should send the person so indicted, &c. to any other colony, or to Great Britain to be tried. The charge on both sides was to be paid out of the customs. The minority opposed this bill with great vehemence. They insisted that having no sort of reason for impeaching the tribunals of America, the real intention was to set up a military government, and to provide a virtual indemnity for all the murders and capital outrages which might be committed by the barbarous hands of authority. From the impoffibility of profecuting in Great Britain, they ftrenuoufly maintained that this was holding out encouragement for all kinds of lawlefs violence. Colonel *Barre*'s fpeech upon the occafion commanded the attention of the whole houfe, and clofed admirably, with " You have changed your ground. You are becoming the aggreffors, and offering the laft of human outrages to the people of America, by fubjecting them in effect, to military execution. Inftead of fending them the olive branch, you have fent the naked fword. By the olive branch, I mean a repeal of all the late laws, fruitlefs to you and oppreffive to them. Afk their aid in a conftitutional manner, and they will give it to the utmoft of their ability. They never yet refufed it, when properly required. Your journals bear the recorded acknowledgments of the zeal with which they have contributed to the general neceffities of the ftate. What madnefs is it that prompts you to attempt obtaining that by force, which you may more certainly procure by requifition. They may be flattered into any thing, but they are too much like yourfelves to be driven. Have fome indulgence for your own likenefs; refpect their fturdy Englifh virtue; retract your odious exertions of authority; and remember that the firft ftep toward making them contribute to your wants, is to reconcile them to your government."

The publications of the day quote an old member, rarely in oppofition, as having clofed his fpeech with thefe remarkable words--" I will now take my leave of the whole plan. You will commence your ruin from this day. I am sorry to say, that not only the house has fallen into this error, but the people approve of the measure. The people, I am sorry to say it, are missed. But a short time will prove the evil tendency of this bill. If ever there was a nation running headlong into ruin it is this." It is much questioned by many whether the member did not mistake in saying—the people. The same natives of America, who petitioned against May the Boston port-bill, renewed their endeavours by a pe- 2. tition against these two bills. It was pointed with an uncommon energy and spirit; and strongly indicated the effects that these bills would produce in the place where they were intended to operate. It was admitted to lie on the table, and had no other notice taken of it.

Both bills were opposed in the house of lords, and the minority entered on each a very strong protest. On both however in each house, the number of the minority continued all along very low and inadequate. Mr. *Bollan* applied for a hearing in the house of lords upon the last bill, but was refused. He has stood up in defence of the rights and liberties of the Massachusetts when no other of the numerous advocates of the colonies, out of parliament, have appeared to check the torrent of the most grievous proceedings against them, in like manner, by their learning and fortitude.

Upon the first of the two bills, the protesting lords *Richmond, Portland, Abingdon, King, Effingham, Ponsonby, Rockingham, Abergavenny, Leinster, Craven,* and *Fitzwilliam,* dissented among other reasons, " because the definitive legal offence, by which a forfeiture of the charter is incurred, has not been clearly stated and fully proved;

A a 2   neither

neither has notice of this adverse proceeding been given to the parties affected; neither have they been heard in their own defence—because all the judges are to be nominated, not by the crown, but by the governor; and all, except the judges of the superior court, are to be removable at his pleasure, and expressly without the consent of that very council, which is to be nominated by the king; the sheriff is made changeable by the governor and council, as often and for such purposes as they shall think expedient, whereby the governor and council are intrusted with powers, with which the British constitution has not trusted his majesty and privy council, and have the means of returning such a jury in each particular cause, as may best suit with the gratification of their passions and interests, so that the lives and properties of the subject are put into their hands without control." The protesting lords took occasion to mention concerning the Boston port-act, " that, unexampled on the records of parliament, it had been entered on the journals of the house as voted, *nemine dissentiente*, and had been stated in the debate of the day, to have been sent to the colonies, as passed without a division in either house, and therefore as conveying the uncontroverted universal sense of the nation: and that an unfair advantage had been taken, on the final question for passing the penal bill, of the absence of those lords, who had debated it for several hours, and strongly dissented from it on the second reading, the period on which it is most usual to debate the principle of a bill."

On the second bill, the protesting lords *Richmond*, *Fitzwilliam*, *Ponsonby*, *Rockingham*, *Portland*, *Craven*, *Leinster*, and *Manchester*, dissented among other reasons, " because the bill amounts to a declaration, that the

house

houfe knows no means of retaining the colonies in due
obedience, but by an army rendered independent of the
ordinary courfe of law in the place where they are employed; becaufe the bill feems to be one of the many
experiments toward an introduction of effential innovations into the government of the empire." They faid
" The authority given by this bill to compel the tranf-
portation from America to Great Britain, of any number of witneffes at the pleafure of the parties profecuting
and profecuted, without any regard to their age, fex,
health, circumftances, bufinefs or duties, feems to us fo
extravagant in its principle, and fo impracticable in its
execution, as to confirm us further in our opinion of the
fpirit which animates the whole fyftem of the prefent
American regulations."

His majefty gave his affent to both bills.   May
                                                                  20.
The feffion was drawing near to the ufual time of recefs, and the greater number of the members were retired into the country. In this fituation a bill was
brought into the houfe of lords, " For making more
effectual provifion for the government of the province
of *Quebec* in North America." It paffed through that
houfe with little if any obfervation. When it came
down to the houfe of commons, it met with a very
different reception. The principal objects of the bill
were, to afcertain the limits of the province, which were
extended far beyond what were fettled as fuch by the
king's proclamation of 1763—to form a legiflative council for all the affairs of the province, except taxation,
which council was to be appointed by the crown, and
the office to be held during pleafure, and his majefty's
Canadian Roman Catholic fubjects were to be entitled

to a place in it—to eſtabliſh the French laws and a trial
without jury in civil caſes, and the Engliſh laws, with
trial by jury in criminal—and to ſecure to the Roman
Catholic clergy, except the regulars, the legal enjoyment
of their eſtates, and of their tythes from all who were
of their own religion. The minority inſiſted, that the
Proteſtant religion by this eſtabliſhment enjoyed at beſt
no more than a toleration. " The popiſh clergy," they
ſaid, " have a legal parliamentary right to maintenance,
the proteſtant clergy are left to the king's diſcretion
Why are not both put at leaſt on an equal footing, and
a legal ſupport provided for both?" The minority
was uncommonly ſmall; neverthelefs, the bill produced
much greater uneaſineſs and diſcontent out of doors
than any of thoſe for puniſhing the old colonies. The
preſent policy of it is, among other things, to gain,
through the influence of the prieſts, the aſſiſtance of the
laity in ſubjugating the other provinces.

June   It received the royal aſſent, when his majeſty went to
22.   the houſe at the cloſe of the ſeſſion; the buſineſs of which
being ended, the miniſtry entertained the moſt ſanguine
expectations, that the ſubmiſſion throughout America
would be immediate, and that complete obedience and
tranquillity would be ſecured. The ſpeech from the
throne expreſſed ſimilar ſentiments. The triumphs and
mutual congratulations of all who have ſupported the
miniſterial plan, within doors and without, are unuſually
great. Theſe may be owing, not a little, to the aſ-
ſurances that governor *Hutchinſon* has repeatedly given
to many, that if the parliament would but act with reſolution, and adopt ſpirited meaſures, a ſpeedy ſubmiſſion would take place without any call for fighting.

By

By the Quebec act, the total revenue of the province
is configned, in the firft inftance, to a warrant from the
lord of the treafury, for the purpofe of penfioning judges
during pleafure, and the fupport of a civil lift. totally
unlimited. The firft lord of the treafury, without control of parliament, is therefore in actual poffeffion of
the revenues of one American province, under the authority of an act of parliament, with no other obligation expreffed, than in general to defray the expences of
the adminiftration of juftice, and to fupport civil government. The refidue, as in the tea-act, is to be referved for the difpofal of parliament. The government
of Quebec is, in truth, a legal parliamentary defpotifm
committed into the hands of the crown and its minifter;
for the crown of Great Britain is conftituted as abfolute
in the province, under an act of parliament, as any defpot that ever exifted in the world. Hence is inferred
what minifters would do through all America, did they
poffefs the power *.

Your prefent governor, general *Gage*, has been appointed as the moft proper perfon to fee to the execution of the laws, which have been paffed refpecting both
the colony and its capital : when he has fettled matters,
and eftablifhed order and due fubmiffion to the power
of parliament, Mr. Hutchinfon is to return and refume
the chair. The laft fince his arrival, has been gracioufly received : his influence with miniftry will continue,
till events convince them that they have been greatly
miftaken in relying upon his judgment on American
fubjects. A commiffion during pleafure has paffed the
great feal, granting to general Gage full power and au-

* Mr. Hartley.

A a 4   thority,

thority, where he fhall fee caufe, to pardon and remit all treafons, murders, felonies, crimes and mifdemeanors whatfoever, and all fines or penalties whatfoever incurred in the *Maffachufetts*.

————

LETTER IX.

Roxbury, Sept. 28, 1774.

THE appointment of general *Gage* to the government was not thought of by Mr. *Hutchinfon*. He expected to have been intrufted with the execution of the minifterial plan; and was rather difconcerted when he found it to be otherwife. Before he left the colony, he was prefented with a few addreffes; one by a number of gentlemen, conceived in very refpectful terms, but againft which many others entered a proteft. Had he applied himfelf vigoroufly and fteadily, to the healing of the breach between the colonies and the parent ftate, inftead of calling upon miniftry to force fubmiffion, he would have been a bleffing, and had the love of all; but now it will be well, if he does not prove a curfe to both countries, and make himfelf odious to the lateft pofterity.

May
13.   When general Gage landed on the long wharf, it was thought from appearances, that he had apprehenfions of being ill-treated by the inhabitants: but though they were highly incenfed at the port-bill, which they had
                                        juft

juſt received, they behaved toward him with the greateſt decency. He was complimented by the council, the gentlemen in the commiſſion of the peace, and others, and afterward ſumptuouſly entertained.

The next day there was a numerous town-meeting to conſider the port-bill; when they reſolved, " That it is the opinion of this town, that if the other colonies come into a joint reſolution, to ſtop all importation from and exportation to Great Britain, and every part of the Weſt Indies, till the act be repealed, the ſame will prove the ſalvation of North America and her liberties; and that the impolicy, injuſtice, inhumanity, and cruelty of the act, exceed all our powers of expreſſion: We therefore leave it to the juſt cenſure of others, and appeal to God and the world." Copies of the act arrived in different parts; were multiplied with incredible expedition; and circulated through the colonies, by which the whole country was inflamed. In ſome places they were printed upon mourning paper with a black border, and cried about the ſtreets under the title of *a barbarous, cruel, bloody and inhuman murder*: in others, great bodies of the people were called together by advertiſement, and the obnoxious law burned with great ſolemnity, ſimilar to what was done in the time of the ſtamp-act.

When the Boſton port-bill arrived at New York, captains Sears and M'Dougall wrote to the committee at Boſton, aſſuring them of the ſupport of the New Yorkers. The letter was publiſhed without their names. The Yorkers would have fixed a cenſure upon them, but could get no proof of their being the writers. Captains Sears and M'Dougall called the people together by a publication. They collected, and after a violent opposition

opposition from the tories, who had brought their whole strength upon the occasion, a vote was obtained for appointing a committee on account of the port-bill, which was to confist of fifty-one. The tories fearing the worst, had provided a lift; but all lifts were taken off the table at Mr. Sears's motion, when nominations took place, and the number of whigs and tories was nearly equal. Mr. Sears got another added, which made the committee fifty-two. The whigs in it infifted, that there muft be a congrefs. The violence of captain Sears's temper, and his influence over the populace, induced the tories to fall in with the propofal of one, rather than be expofed to the dangers of a mob; but they expected that they fhould prevent it. A letter was fent to the Bofton committee, with a recommendation to them to appoint time and place. They approved of a congrefs, but declined making the appointments. The York committee confidered the anfwer; and it was carried, to write to them afrefh upon the fubject. The tories were caught, for having agreed to the motion for a congrefs, they could not hinder it, by all their contrivances. You muft admit of my ufing for brevity fake, the terms *whig* and *tory* for the *pro*'s and *con*'s on the fubject of full redrefs to American grievances. When better can be met with, they fhall be adopted: but they are univerfally applied in this manner by the liberty party.

The Bofton committee of correfpondence were fenfible, that the utmoft delicacy and precaution, in the ufe of words and expreffions, were requifite in the prefent ftate of affairs; that fo their enemies might not difappoint them of that fupport, for which they were to make a general application to all the colonifts, and whom they

they addreſſed on the head of the port-bill, and the diſtreſſes coming upon the inhabitants, with the utmoſt
reſpect: they were careful to inſert in all their letters,
" It is hoped that Boſton will be conſidered *as ſuffering
in the common cauſe.*"

While theſe letters were circulating, the period arrived for the meeting of a new general court, which aſſembled at Boſton; when the ſervices of the election- May
day were carried on as uſual; but the hearts of many 25.
felt ſad with the apprehenſion that it would be the laſt of
the kind. Their forebodings were increaſed, by the
number and characters of the elected counſellors whom
governor Gage negatived, not leſs than thirteen. He
laid nothing before the court more than the common
buſineſs of the province; but gave them notice of their
removal to Salem on the firſt of June in purſuance of
the act. Learning that the houſe of aſſembly, to evade
removing were haſtening through the neceſſary buſineſs,
with the greateſt expedition, he adjourned the general
court to the ſeventh of June, then to meet at *Salem.*
Before that day, the inhabitants of ſeveral towns and
cities, in different parts of the continent, concurred in
expreſſing the greateſt diſapprobation of the meaſures
purſued againſt Boſton, an abhorrence of the new act,
and a condemnation of the principles on which it was
founded, with a reſolution to oppoſe its effects in every
manner, and to ſupport their diſtreſſed brethren, who
were to be the immediate victims. At *Philadelphia* a
ſubſcription was ſet on foot for the ſupport of ſuch poor
inhabitants of Boſton as ſhould be deprived of the means
of ſubſiſtence by the operation of the act. The *Virginia* houſe of burgeſſes appointed the firſt of June to
be

be set apart as a day of fasting and humiliation, devoutly to implore the divine interpofition, for averting the heavy calamity which threatened deftruction to their civil rights, and the evils of a civil war; and for giving one heart and one mind to the people, firmly to op-pofe every injury to the American rights.   This occa-fioned their diffolution, but before they feparated, eighty-nine of the members entered into an affociation, in which they declared, " That an attack made on one of our fifter colonies, to compel fubmiffion to arbitrary taxes, is an attack made on all Britifh America, and threatens ruin to the rights of all, unlefs the united wif-dom of the whole be applied."   They recommended to the committee of correfpondence, to communicate with the feveral committees of the other provinces, on the expediency of appointing deputies, from the diffe-rent colonies, to meet annually in general congrefs, to deliberate on thofe meafures, which the united interefts of America might from time to time require.

June 1.   Bufinefs was finifhed at the cuftom-houfe in Bofton at twelve o'clock at noon, and the harbour fhut up againft all veffels bound thither; and after the fourteenth none were to be allowed to depart.   The day was devoutly kept at Williamfburgh in Virginia, as a day of fafting and humiliation.   There was a folemn paufe in the bu-finefs of Philadelphia.   If we except the Quakers, near nine-tenths of the citizens fhut up their houfes; and the bells were rung muffled all the day.   It was obferved in other places as a day of mourning.

The Maffachufetts general court met at Salem ac-cording to adjournment, and a committee was appoint-ed to confider and report the ftate of the province.   Mr.
Samuel

Samuel Adams obferved, that fome of the committee were for mild meafures, which he judged no ways fuited to the prefent emergency. He conferred with Mr. *War-ren* of Plymouth upon the neceffity of giving into fpirited meafures, and then faid, " Do you keep the committee in play, and I will go and make a *caucus* * againft the evening; and do you meet me." Mr. S. Adams fecured a meeting of about five principal members of the houfe, at the time fpecified; and repeated his endeavours againft the next night; and fo as to the third, when they were more than thirty : the friends of adminiftration knew nothing of the matter. The popular leaders took the fenfe of the members in a private way, and found that they fhould be able to carry their fcheme by a fufficient majority. They had their whole plan completed, prepared their refolves, and then determined

* The word *caucus*, and its derivative caucufing, are often ufed in Bofton. The laft anfwers much to what we ftile parliamenteering or electioneering. All my repeated applications to different gentlemen have not furnifhed me with a fatisfactory account of the origin of *caucus*. It feems to mean, a number of perfons, whether more or lefs, met together to confult upon adopting and profecuting fome fcheme of policy, for carrying a favorite point. The word is not of novel invention. More than fifty years ago, Mr. Samuel Adams's father, and twenty others, one or two from the north end of the town, where all the fhip bufinefs is carried on, ufed to meet, make a caucus, and lay their plan for introducing certain perfons into places of truft and power. When they had fettled it, they feparated, and ufed each their particular influence within his own circle. He and his friends would furnifh themfelves with ballots, including the names of the parties fixed upon, which they diftributed on the days of election. By acting in concert, together with a careful and extenfive diftribution of ballots, they generally carried the elections to their own mind. In like manner it was, that Mr. Samuel Adams firft became a reprefentative for Bofton.

upon

17. upon bringing the bufinefs forward. But before they went upon it, the door-keeper was ordered to let no one whatfoever in, and no one was to go out: however when the bufinefs opened, a minifterial member pleaded a call of nature, which is always regarded, and was allowed to go out. He then ran to give information of what was doing, and a meffenger was difpatched to general *Gage*, who lived at fome diftance. The fecretary was fent off to diffolve the general court; found the door faftened; knocked for entrance, but was anfwered, that the houfe was upon very important bufinefs, which when they had finifhed, they would let him in. As he could obtain no entrance, he read the proclamation upon the fteps leading to the reprefentatives' chamber, in the hearing of feveral members and others on the outfide with him, and immediately after in the council, thus diffolving the general court. The houfe, while fitting with their doors fhut, appointed *Thomas Cufhing*, *Samuel Adams*, *Robert Treat Pain*, *James Bowdoin*, and *John Adams*, efqrs. as their committee to meet other committees, that might be convened the firft of September at *Philadelphia*, voted them five hundred pounds lawful (feventy-five pounds fterling each) and chofe a treafurer. They recommended alfo to the feveral towns and diftricts, the raifing the faid fum, by equitable proportions, according to the laft provincial tax—a recommendation which had all the force of a law. It was a triumph to many of the fons of liberty, to think that the houfe had out-generalled the governor.

Sometime before the diffolution of the general court, near upon three hundred citizens of *Philadelphia* met and appointed a committee to write to Bofton. Their

letter

letter was temperate and firm. They acknowledged the difficulty of offering the inhabitants advice upon the sad occasion that existed; wished first to have the sense of the province in general; and observed that all lenient applications for obtaining redress should be tried, before recourse was had to extremities. They remarked that it might perhaps be right to take the sense of a general congress, before the desperate measure of putting an entire stop to commerce was adopted; and that it might be right at any rate, to reserve that measure as the last resource when all other means had failed. They mentioned, that if the making of restitution to the East India company for their teas would put an end to the unhappy controversy, and leave the people of Boston upon their ancient footing of constitutional liberty, it could not admit of a moment's doubt what part they should take; but they added, it was not the value of the tea, it was the indefeasible right of giving and granting their own money, a right from which they could never recede, that was now the matter of consideration.

The importance and necessity of a general congress was soon felt by every colony, so that the measure taken by the Massachusetts was gradually adopted by the others.

Maryland, whose zeal in the cause of liberty was ardent, had a meeting of the committees appointed by the several counties, at the city of Annapolis, who June elected five deputies for that province, " to attend a 25. general congress, at such time and place as may be agreed on; to effect one general plan of conduct, operating on the commercial connection of the colonies with the

mother

mother country, for the relief of Boston and preservation of American liberty."

This meeting commenced three days before the election of deputies; and considering the distance of Salem from Annapolis, cannot be ascribed to the transaction of the Massachusetts assembly on the seventeenth; beside, it appears from the words *at such time and place as may be agreed on*, that the committees did not know, that the Massachusetts assembly had mentioned the convening of a general congress on the first of September at Philadelphia.

When the opinion of the Boston town-meeting, respecting a joint resolution of the colonies to stop all importation and exportation till the port-bill was repealed, arrived in South Carolina; it was presented to a number of the principal gentlemen in Charlestown. The mode proposed was thought to be of too much consequence to be adopted without the universal consent of the people. It was therefore determined to request a meeting of the inhabitants. That this might be as general as possible, circular letters were sent by express to every parish and district within the colony.

July 6.
A great number from almost every part of South Carolina met at Charlestown. The proceedings of parliament against Boston and the Massachusetts-bay were distinctly related to this convention of the people; on which, without one dissenting voice, they came into various resolutions. Among others they resolved, " That five gentlemen be appointed deputies on the behalf of this colony, to meet the deputies of the several colonies in North America in general congress, to consider the act lately passed, and bills depending in parliament, with regard

regard to the port of Boston and province of Massachusetts, also the grievances under which America labors,
with full power and authority, in behalf of us and our
constituents, to concert, and effectually to prosecute,
such legal measures (by which we for ourselves and them
most solemnly engage to abide) as in the opinion of the
said deputies, and of the deputies so to be assembled,
shall be most likely to obtain a repeal of the said acts,
and a redress of these grievances."—" That, while the
oppressive acts relative to Boston are enforced, we will
cheerfully, from time to time, contribute toward the relief of such persons there, whose unfortunate circumstances may be thought to stand in need of most assistance :"—" That a committee of ninety-nine persons be
now appointed, to act as a general committee, to correspond with the committees of the other colonies, and
to do all matters and things necessary to carry the resolutions into execution ; and that any twenty-one of them
met together, may proceed on business—their power to
continue till the next general meeting."

The appointment of the abovementioned deputies
was recognised, ratified and confirmed by the house of
assembly, at their next session, on the second of August.

The Connecticut house of representatives, in expectation of the event during their recess, empowered a
committee of nine, in case a congress of commissioners
from the several colonies should be convened to meet
and choose delegates to serve for that colony, and to correspond with other committees. Mr. *Silas Deane* was
of the committee, and being ambitious of going to congress, schemed their meeting at New London, (instead
of Hartford) where through the influence of a most

13. worthy father-in-law, his own policy, and his *own* vote, he obtained a majority of *one*, and became one of the four Connecticut delegates, though not viewed by those who know him most, as a person of the greatest integrity, or the truest patriotism.

At *Philadelphia*, a petition signed by near nine hundred freeholders was presented to Mr. Penn, the governor, entreating him to call a general assembly as soon as possible. This request being refused, the province proceeded to the election of deputies, who soon after met at *Philadelphia*. The resolutions passed at this meeting, carry the marks of cool and temperate deliberation, as well as affection to the mother country, more than those of many others; and are at the same time equally firm in the determination of supporting the colonial rights.

In them the deputies set out with the strongest professions of duty and allegiance, and express their abhorrence of every idea of an unconstitutional independence on the parent state, and the most ardent wishes for a restoration of the former harmony. They reprobate in the strongest terms the act and bills relative to the *Massachusetts-bay*, and declare that they consider their brethren at Boston, as suffering in the common cause. They insist upon the absolute necessity of a congress to consult together and form a general plan of conduct for all the colonies. They acknowledge, that a suspension of the commerce of that large trading province with Great Britain, will greatly distress multitudes of their industrious inhabitants, but pronounce themselves ready to offer that sacrifice, and much greater, for the preservation of their liberties; however, they express their desire, that congress will first try the gentle mode of stating

their

their grievances, and making a firm and decent claim of redrefs. They conclude with declaring, that that province will break off all commercial intercourfe whatfoever, with any town, city or colony, and individuals in them, who fhall refufe, or negleft to adopt and carry into execution, fuch general plan as fhall be agreed upon in the congrefs.

They did not undertake to appoint the delegates, but left it to the Pennfylvania affembly, who foon after fixed upon feven gentlemen. 22.

At a meeting of delegates, from the different counties in *Virginia*, at *Williamfburgh*, befide the warmeft profeffions of allegiance and loyalty, and feveral refolutions in common with the other colonies, they paffed others, which, confidering the circumftances of the colony, with its immediate dependence on the mother country for the difpofal of its only ftaple commodity, muft be confidered as very deferving of attention, becaufe ftrongly indicating the true fpirit of that people. They refolved not to purchafe any more flaves from Africa, the Weft Indies, or any other place; that their non-importation agreement fhould take place on the firft of the following November, and that if the American grievances were not redreffed by the tenth of Auguft 1775, they would export after that time, no tobacco, nor any other goods whatever to Great Britain. They recommended the cultivation of fuch articles of hufbandry, inftead of tobacco, as might form a proper bafis for manufactures of all forts; and particularly, the improvement of the breed of fheep, the multiplying of them, and the killing as few as poffible. They chofe as delegates to ge- Aug.

B b 2   neral 5.

neral congrefs, *Peyton Randolph, Richard Henry Lee, George Wafhington, Patrick Henry, Richard Bland, Benjamin Harrifon,* and *Edmund Pendleton,* efqrs.

At Newport in Rhode Ifland, an animating paper was circulated, with the motto JOIN or DIE. The ftate of Bofton was reprefented as a fiege, and as a direct hoftile invafion of all the colonies. " The generals of defpotifm (it fays) are now drawing the lines of circumvallation around our bulwarks of liberty, and nothing but unity, refolution and perfeverance, can fave ourfelves and pofterity from what is worfe than death—Slavery." The general affembly of the colony chofe two deputies to reprefent the colony in a general congrefs ; who were legally authorized for that fervice, under the hand and feal of the governor.

10.

All the other colonies, from New Hampfhire to South Carolina inclufively, adopted the meafure of electing reprefentatives to meet in general congrefs.

To judge aright of the prefent alarming ftate of affairs, you muft obferve, that it does not arife from the difcontent of a turbulent or oppreffed nobility or gentry, fo that by bringing over a few of the leaders, the reft will follow of courfe, or perfift only to their ruin : nor does it depend upon the refolution or perfeverance of a body of merchants and dealers, fo that every man, habitually ftudious of his immediate intereft, will tremble at the thought of thofe confequences which may effentially affect it : nor will a few lucrative jobs or contracts fplit the colonifts into numberlefs factions. On the contrary, the great force of the oppofition confifts in the landholders throughout America. The Britifh lands in this continent, are, in general, and more efpecially

cially in the New England colonies, the Jerfies, and in part of New York and Pennfylvania, portioned out in fuch freeholds as afford that mediocrity of condition to the poffeffors, which is fufficient to raife ftrong bodies and vigorous minds; but feldom that fuperabundance which proves fo fatal to both, in old and refined countries. The American freeholders, from many circumftances, are more enthufiaftic lovers of liberty, than ever were the Englifh yeomanry. The body of them are too bold to be defpifed without danger, and now that they are united too numerous to be bribed. Human nature being the fame in every quarter of the globe, had moderation inftead of compulfion been employed, feveral who are at prefent zealous leaders, might have been fecured, and miniftry (in colonies of fuch different manners interefts and principles, and on thefe accounts ftrongly inclined to variance with each other) might have carried many points which they will now find it difficult or impoffible to do, fince they have united them, by evidencing a defign of fubjugating each to a mode of government, to which all without exception are averfe in the higheft degree.

The Bofton committee of correfpondence received the moft encouraging anfwers to their letters; and were affured that the town of Bofton was confidered *as fuffering in the common caufe.* They had more than the ftrongeft expreffions to confole them, they had the fubftantial evidence of facts. Miniftry promifed themfelves mighty advantages from making *Salem* the feat of government, with the privilege of an open port, while the neighbouring one, in itfelf of much greater confequence, was fhut. But the merchants and freeholders of the town

difcodiscovered a most noble spirit, which will prove a sore disappointment to them. If it was expected, that incurable envy, jealousy and animosity, would be excited between the two towns, and that the refractory capital being abandoned and left alone to ruminate upon her forlorn situation, would soon be reclaimed and brought to a full sense of her duty ; the very reverse will mortify.

June 18. The day after the dissolution of the general court, the merchants and freeholders of *Salem* presented an address to the governor, and in it expressed the. most generous sentiments. They said, " We are most deeply afflicted with a sense of our public calamities ; but the miseries that are now rapidly hastening on our brethren in the capital of this province, greatly excite our commiseration, and we hope your excellency will use your endeavours to prevent a further accumulation of evils, on that already sorely distressed people."—" By shutting up the port of Boston, some imagine that the course of trade might be turned hither and to our benefit ; but nature in the formation of our harbour, forbids our becoming rivals in commerce with that convenient mart. And were it otherwise, we must be dead to every idea of justice, and lost to all feelings of humanity, could we indulge one thought to seize on wealth, and raise our fortunes on the ruin of our suffering neighbours." The governor was treated with the highest respect, and mention was made of their hoping much, from his general character, as well as from his wisdom and mildness in another command. They expressed the strongest attachment to the mother country, the deepest concern for the present unhappy troubles, and the most fervent wishes for a speedy and happy reconciliation, to obtain

which

which they were willing to facrifice every thing compatible with the fafety and dignity of Britifh fubjeets.

Marblehead, a fea-port, about three miles from Salem, and equally far with the laft from Bofton, but a town of no great trade, being engaged chiefly in the cod-fifhery, teftified its regard and compaffion for the capital, by letting the fuffering merchants have the free ufe of its wharfs and ftores. Its inhabitants offered alfo to attend the lading and unlading of their goods, and to tranfaeet for them all the bufinefs to be done at their port, without putting them to the fmalleft expence.

The pity and refentment of the country at large, were excited by obfervations publifhed on the Bofton port-bill. Thofe of Mr. *Jofiah Quincy*, jun. were moft generally read and admired. He obferved—" The Bofton port-bill condemns a whole town unheard, nay, uncited to anfwer; involves thoufands in ruin and mifery, without fuggeftion of any crime by them committed; and is fo conftituted, that enormous pains and penalties muft enfue, notwithftanding the moft perfeet obedience to its injunetions. The deftruetion of the tea which took place without any illegal procedure of the town, is the only alleged grounÞ of configning thoufands of its inhabitants to ruin, mifery and defpair. Thofe charged with the moft aggravated crimes; are not punifhable, till arraigned before difinterefted judges; heard in their own defence, and found guilty of the charge. But here a whole people are accufed; profecuted by they know not whom; tried they know not when; proved guilty they know not how; and fentenced to fuffer inevitable ruin. Their hard fate cannot be averted by the moft fervile fubmiffion, the moft implicit obedience to

Bb 4 this

this statute. Their first intimation of it was on the tenth of May, and it took place the first of June, thence to continue in full force, till it shall sufficiently appear to his majesty, that full satisfaction hath been made by or in behalf of the inhabitants of Boston, to the East India company, for the damage sustained by the destruction of their tea; and until it shall be certified to his majesty, by the governor or lieutenant governor of the province, that reasonable satisfaction has been made to the officers of the revenue and others, for the riots and insurrection mentioned in it. So short a space is given for staying the torrent of threatened evils, that the subject though exerting his utmost energy, must be overwhelmed, and driven to madness by terms of deliverance which deny relief till his ruin is inevitable."

Others said, " Had punishment been only threatened, had it been in our own option, whether we would submit or suffer, the reason for complaint would have been less. But without previous warning in the proposal of any terms that might have prevented the coming of evil upon us, it is inflicted with ineffable vengeance; so that should we servilely submit to all required, we must notwithstanding suffer almost total ruin. The conditions upon which alone our sufferings are to be removed, far from being fixed with precision, are so loose and indeterminate, that a governor may perpetuate them during his political existence, the king in council not being enabled to open the port without his certificate. The wharfs and landing places in Boston, which are the property of numerous individuals, are as to the use of them wherein only their value consists, wrested out of their hands, and put into the king's, to be disposed of at his
plea-

pleafure. Two wharfs indeed are to be opened again,
when his majefty fhall think proper ; but the refidue
are for ever interdicted the exercife of commerce."

The rough drafts of the bills " for the better regulating of the government of the *Maffachufetts-bay* ;" and
" for the impartial adminiftration of juftice in it," as
well as of that " for quartering the troops in America,"
upon their arrival at Bofton, were inftantly circulated
through the continent, and filled up whatever was before wanting, of violence and indignation in moft of
the colonies. Even thofe who were moderate or feemed wavering, now became refolute and refentful. Nothing was to be heard of, but meetings and refolutions.
Liberal contributions for the relief of the diftreffed Boftonians were every where recommended, and foon practifed. Numberlefs letters were written from diftricts,
towns and provinces, to the people of Bofton, in which,
befides every expreffion of fympathy and tendernefs,
they were commended for their paft conduct, and ftrongly
exhorted to a perfeverance in that virtue, which had
brought on their fufferings. It was in vain, that the
friends of government attended a town meeting, and
attempted to pafs refolutions for the payment of the tea,
and for diffolving the committee of correfpondence ;
they found themfelves loft in a prodigious majority,
and had no other refource than drawing up a proteft
againft the proceedings of that body. The Bofton committee of correfpondence apprehended themfelves fo fixed
in the good opinion of the public, that they ventured
to frame and publifh an agreement, entitled, *A folemn
league and covenant.*

General

General *Gage* was so alarmed at the idea of *a solemn league and covenant*, that he issued a strong proclamation against it, stiling it an unlawful, hostile, and traiterous combination. He charged all magistrates to apprehend and secure for trial, such as should have any share in aiding or abetting the foregoing or any similar covenant. The charge was needless; for the engagement was so unguardedly expressed, and so extremely insnaring, that it was severely censured by many of the best and warmest sons of liberty, in and about Boston, who refused to give it support; so that, however it might be venerated out of the colony, it sunk into obscurity at home; and changed its form into one that was less exceptionable, and yet equally well calculated to stop the trade with Great Britain, and that accorded with those entered into about the same time, in various parts of the continent, without any previous concert with each other, any more than with Boston. The coincidence of sentiments and measures, given into by individuals, and assemblies larger and smaller, in the several and most distant colonies, without any previous contrivance, has been so remarkable, that persons, the furthest removed from superstition, have inclined to ascribe it to a special providence of God. They have been seemingly actuated by one and the same spirit, nearly at the same instant. When letters have been dispatched from Boston to fellow-patriots afar, asking or giving advice; letters from these have been upon the road, giving or asking the very advice which was wanted—the like in other matters. Not that there is a uniformity in all points through the continent. The people may be divided into two great classes. One is for rushing headlong into the

greatest

greateſt extremities, without waiting till other meaſures
are tried, or receiving the general ſenſe of the colonies;
and though eager for holding a congreſs, would leave it
nothing to do, but to proſecute the violences which they
have began. The other is averſe to violent meaſures,
till all other means are ineffectually tried. They wiſh
further applications to be made to Britain, and the grievances they complain of, with the rights which they claim,
to be clearly ſtated and properly preſented. This, they
ſay, can be effectually done only by a general congreſs.
There is a third party, who are friends to the Britiſh
adminiſtration, or rather who do not totally diſapprove
of its meaſures; but their voice is ſo low, that except
in a few particular places, it can ſcarcely be diſtinguiſhed. The friends to colonial rights have a great advantage over them, not only from the goodneſs of their
cauſe, but their poſſeſſing moſt of the preſſes on the
continent. Theſe are chiefly in the hands of the whigs,
and news-papers publiſhing eſſays and other compoſi-
tions, againſt the prevailing opinions of the people, have
not a univerſal ſpread, and cannot prove ſo profitable
to the proprietors, as thoſe on the other ſide of the queſtion. The command, which the ſons of liberty have of
the preſs, gives them the ſuperiority in point of influence, over their antagoniſts in the periodical publications of the day.

As the Boſton port-bill prohibits all water-carriage,
beſide ſhutting up the port, the merchants are under
the neceſſity of adopting the expenſive mode of bringing
their goods from Salem or Marblehead, all the way
round, through Cambridge and Roxbury, to Boſton.
Had they been allowed to bring them to Charleſtown by
land,

land, and thence to crofs them over by water, they would
have faved a fourth of the way. But it is pleafing to
obferve what trade is going forward, notwithftanding
the embarraffments with which it is clogged. Bofton is
exhibiting a fcene of patience, fortitude and perfeverance,
which will make them renowned in hiftory. Though
liberal contributions have been made, are raifing, and
will be raifed, for the fuccour of fufferers; yet it may
be eafily conceived, that in a town containing feveral
thoufand inhabitants, who have fubfifted chiefly by commerce, and the various kinds of bufinefs fubfervient to
it, and where the maintenance of many families depends
merely upon locality, the cutting off of that grand fource
of their employment and fubfiftence, muft occafion great
diftreffes notwithftanding every relief. Even the rich
are not exempt from the general calamity, as a very
confiderable part of their property confifts in wharfs,
warehoufes, ftores, and thofe numerous erections, which
are deftined to the purpofes of commerce, but are now
no longer profitable.

The people at large have been for fometime preparing to defend their rights with the point of the fword.
They fee, that they are either to be terrified, or driven
into fubmiffion, by an armed force; and are for providing againft both. The countrymen, in returning
from Bofton, are daily bringing out guns, knapfacks,
&c. Every one appears defirous of being well accou-
tred. They have arms in general, the militia law requiring it of all within a certain age. Note—They are
fond of fhooting, are accuftomed to it from early life,
and are fpecial markfmen. They are perfecting themfelves in their exercife. Handling the mufket and training,

ing, are the fashionable amusements of the male inhabitants, while the females encourage them to proceed.
The sound of drums and fifes is constantly saluting your
ears.   Husbands and wives, parents and children, brothers and sisters, lovers, the young and the old, seem
possessed of, or rather to be possessed by a martial spirit,
and are fired with an enthusiastic zeal for liberty.   In
most places, but particularly in *Berkshire* and *Worcester*
counties, where the influence of government was supposed
to prevail most, nothing is to be seen or heard of, except the purchasing of arms and ammunition, the cast-
ing of balls, and the making of all those preparations,
which testify the most immediate danger, and determined resistance.

The high military tone of the country people, is to
be placed chiefly to the account of the two bills " for
regulating the government of the Massachusetts,"
and " the impartial administration of justice in it."
These bills have proposed so thorough a change in the
civil and religious liberties of towns and individuals,
that they view themselves as intentionally deprived of
every privilege, and reduced to the necessity of fighting
for all they hold dear to them.   It is of the utmost consequence that juries should not be packed.   The accus-
tomed mode of electing them is excellent, but liable
to abuse, and there " may have been instances wherein
persons who have no regard to religion and to divine revelation, have been really picked up to serve a turn *."
But this will not justify that most execrable alteration
of leaving it in the power of the governor and council,
through the aid of the sheriff, to obtain such a jury in

* The Rev. Mr. Whitney's Discourse.

each

each caufe, as may beft fuit their paffions and interefts, whereby the lives and properties of the fubject are put into their hands without control *.

It is alfo to be enacted, by the regulating bill, that after the firft of Auguft 1774, there fhall be no town-meetings, without the leave of the governor or lieute-nant governor in writing, expreffing the fpecial bufinefs of fuch meetings, firft obtained, except the annual meet-ings in March for the choice of felectmen, conftables and other officers; and in May for the election of re-prefentatives, and meetings to fill up the offices afore-faid on death or removal; and that no other matter fhall be treated of at fuch meetings, except the election of aforefaid officers or reprefentatives, nor at any other meeting except the bufinefs expreffed in the leave given. A more obnoxious alteration could fcarce have been invented.

Every town is an incorporated republic. The felect-men by their own authority, or upon the application of a certain number of townfmen, iffue a warrant for the calling of a town-meeting. The warrant mentions the bufinefs to be engaged in, and no other can be legally executed. The inhabitants are warned to attend; and they that are prefent, though not a quarter or tenth of the whole, have a right to proceed. They choofe a pre-fident by the name of Moderator, who regulates the proceedings of the meeting. Each individual has an equal liberty of delivering his opinion, and is not liable to be filenced or browbeaten by a richer or greater townf-man than himfelf. Every freeman or freeholder, as the

* The lords proteft againft the act for the better regulating of the government.

5   bufinefs

bufinefs regards either the freeholders in particular or
the freemen at large, gives his vote or not, and for or
againft as he pleafes; and each vote weighs equally,
whether that of the higheft or loweft inhabitant. At
thefe town-meetings the people are ufed to debate and
conclude upon inftructions to their reprefentatives refpecting matters before, or likely to come before the general court—freely to exprefs their fentiments regarding
public tranfactions—to agree upon the choice of a minifter, and the falary they fhall give him ; upon building or repairing the meeting houfe, and upon a variety
of other interefting matters, which concern the exercife
of their civil or facred privileges. All the New England
towns are upon the fame plan in general, though different in certain particulars. In the colony of Rhode
Ifland, they have no minifter paid by the town as a town,
nor is it allowed by the government; the falary is not
a town charge, but is made up out of the voluntary contributions of the denomination to which he is joined.

From the free exercife of all the above cited rights,
the Maffachufetts inhabitants are to be fufpended by the
aforefaid enacting claufe. When they wifh, or have occafion to hold meetings for any of the above purpofes,
they will be obliged to apply to the governor, who may
put a negative upon every application, and who will
have it in his power to prevent their fettling a minifter,
when the pulpit is become vacant, till he can be well
affured that the perfon on whom the choice will fall,
either does or will incline to fupport governmental meafures.

The bill for the impartial adminiftration of juftice,
the people confider as threatening them with military
execu-

execution, if they comply not with that for the better regulating of the government. The Englifh blood which they have derived from their forefathers, without corrupting it by foreign mixtures, for they have been too national to encourage, like fome colonies, the fettlement of foreigners among them—that blood boils in their veins at thefe two bills, and fires them to a military oppofition. The inhabitants of Connecticut mean not to be idle fpectators of the fate of their fifter colony, which can only be a prelude to their own, and are therefore giving into equal exertions for ftemming the approaching torrent.

Soon after general *Gage*'s arrival, two regiments of foot, with a fmall detachment of the artillery and fome cannon, were landed at Bofton, and encamped on the common. Thefe troops were by degrees re-inforced by the arrival of feveral regiments from Ireland, New York, Halifax, and at length from Quebec. The arrival and ftation of thefe troops, was far from being agreeable to the inhabitants; nor was the jealoufy in any degree lefs, in the minds of their neighbours of the furrounding counties. The diffatisfaction was increafed by placing a guard upon Bofton neck, the narrow ifthmus which joins the peninfula to the continent; for which meafure the frequent defertion of the foldiers was the affigned reafon. Individuals have encouraged fuch defertion; and the Bofton committee have not failed to contribute to the temptation, by making the fituation of the foldiery, as difagreeable as they could, and by counteracting all endeavours to render it comfortable. They act fyftematically for the prevention of all fupplies for the Britifh troops. Through their connection with the neighbouring

ing committees, the farmers and others are prevented selling them their straw, timber, flit-work, boards, in short every article excepting provisions necessary for their subsistence. The straw which is purchased for their service is daily burnt. Vessels with brick, intended for the army, are sunk; and carts with wood are overturned. Thus, by some contrivance or other, purchases are either prevented, or when made, the king's property is destroyed in every manner in which it can be effected. While these things are doing, a trifling circumstance gives the inhabitants of Boston a full earnest of the support they may expect from the country in case of extremity, and an opportunity of knowing the general temper of the people. A report spreads, that a regiment posted on the neck, has cut off all communication with the country, in order to starve the town into a compliance with any measures which may be proposed to it. Upon this vague report, a large body of the inhabitants of Worcester county assemble, and dispatch two messengers express to Boston, to discover the truth of the information. These envoys acquaint the townsmen, that if the report had been true, there were several thousand armed men ready to have marched to their assistance. They tell them further, that they are commissioned to acquaint them, that even though they should be disposed to a surrender of their liberties, the people of the country will not think themselves at all included in their act; that by the late act and the bills pending in the British parliament, when the last intelligence was received, their charter was utterly vacated; and that the compact between Britain and the colonies being thus dissolved, they are at full liberty to combine together, in what manner and form they think beft, for mutual fecurity.

Aug. 4.   The governor, by a proclamation for the encouragement of piety and virtue, the prevention and punifhment of vice, profanenefs and immorality, has exafperated the minds of the people, owing to the infertion of *hypocrify* among the immoralities. They have been fcoffed at and reproached by enemies, and thofe of loofer manners, for a pharifaical attention to outward forms and the appearances of religion; and therefore view this infertion as an intended infult. With the new acts, the governor received a lift of 36 new counfellors, who agreeable to the new regulations, have been appointed by the crown, contrary to the method prefcribed by the charter. About twenty-four of the gentlemen have accepted, fo that there is a fufficient number to attempt carrying on the bufinefs of government. But the courts of judicature at Bofton are fufpended, for the grand jurors refufe to take the oaths, and to act under new judges and laws. The petit jurors decline ferving, on account of *Peter Oliver* efq; ftanding impeached by a late honorable houfe of commons of the province, and of the judges of the fuperior court being made to depend upon the crown. Not only fo, but the great and petty juries through the colony, unanimoufly refufe to act in any manner under the new regulations; and the clerks of the court have found it neceffary to acknowledge their contrition in the public papers, for iffuing the warrants by which the juries were fummoned, and not only to declare that they will not act fo again, but to apologize for what they have done. At Great Barrington

2

Barrington and fome other places, the people affembled
in large bodies; and filled the court-houfe and avenues
in fuch a manner, that neither judge nor officer could
obtain entrance; and upon the fheriff's commanding
them to make way for the court, they anfwered, " We
know no court, nor any other eftablifhment, independent of the ancient laws and ufages of our country, and
to none other will we fubmit, or give way upon any
account."

At Salem the merchants, freeholders, and other inhabitants, were by hand-bills fummoned to meet on
Wednefday the twenty-fourth, to confider on meafures
for oppofing the execution of divers late acts of parliament. The day preceding the intended meeting, the 23.
governor, who refides within a few miles of the place, publifhed a proclamation prohibiting all perfons from attending. The proclamation being difregarded, a company
of foldiers were ordered into town to difperfe the meeting; but before they got to it, the bufinefs was finifhed,
and the inhabitants withdrawn. Three of the gentlemen were apprehended, but gave bonds to appear in
court, and fo were difcharged.

The proceedings of the people and their manifeft
difpofitions have alarmed the general, who has thought
it neceffary for the fafety of the troops, as well as to fecure the important poft of Bofton, to fortify the entrance
at the neck, which affords the only communication, except by water, between the town and the continent.
His own perfonal fafety, while at his country refidence
in Danvers, would have been endangered, had not the
prudence of Samuel Holten efq; M. D. a genuine, de-

termined,

termined, but confiderate fon of liberty, cooled and moderated the temper of his neighbours.

William Brattle efq; frequently an elected counfellor under the charter, having given a hint to the governor to fecure the provincial ammunition, he fent two com-

Sept. 1.

panies of foldiers acrofs the river long before day break, who poffeffed themfelves of the powder in the arfenal at Charleftown. The news circulated apace, and in the morning the inhabitants of the neighbouring towns, to the amount of feveral thoufands, affembled at Cambridge, moftly in arms. They proceeded to the lieutenant governor Oliver's houfe, and to the houfes of feveral of the new counfellors, and of others who they thought had fhown themfelves unfriendly to the province. Some of the counfellors were obliged to refign, and to declare they would no more act under, what are pronounced the arbitrary laws lately enacted. It was with difficulty that the multitude was reftrained from marching directly to Bofton, there to demand a delivery of the powder, and in cafe of refufal to attack the troops. This collection of people, and the confufion neceffarily attending their tranfactions, gave rife to a rumor, that the fleet and troops were firing upon the town of Bofton, which flew with amazing rapidity through New England; and in lefs than 24 hours after, there were between 30 and 40,000 men in arms, fome of whom marched from 20 to 30 miles toward Bofton before they were undeceived. This report and the feizure of the powder, roufed the inhabitants in the other colonies beyond New England, fo that they immediately began learning the military exercife. The tranfaction at Cambridge produced fuch

other

other rifings in the colony as obliged more of the new council to refign or to flee to Boston; whither, by the clofe of the month, the commiffioners, the cuftom-houfe officers, and all who have made themfelves particularly obnoxious, by taking an active and decided part againft the country, repaired for protection. Thus. is the feat of government at Salem abandoned, and the apparatus of a cuftom-houfe removed to a place, which an act of parliament has profcribed from all trade.

About this time the governor's company of cadets, confifting of Bofton gentlemen, difbanded themfelves, and returned him the ftandard he prefented to them upon his arrival. This flight was owing to his taking away the commiffion from Mr. Hancock, who was colonel of the corps. But Mr. *John Murray*, a colonel of the militia, having accepted a feat in the new council, twenty-four officers of his regiment refigned their commiffions in one day. Such is the prevailing fpirit, that all perfons accepting offices under the new laws, or preparing to act in conformity to them, are declared enemies to their country, and threatened accordingly.

The feizing of the powder, and the withholding from the legal proprietors what is lodged in the magazine of Bofton, and the defign carrying into execution, of repairing and manning the fortification at the entrance of the town, have occafioned the holding an affembly of delegates from the feveral towns and diftricts in the county of Suffolk, of which Bofton is the county town. After a moft fpirited preamble, they refolved among other things, " That no obedience is due from this province to either or any part of the late acts, but that they be rejected as the attempts of a wicked ad-

C c 3   miniftration

miniſtration to enſlave America :—That ſo long as the juſtices are appointed or hold their places, by any other tenure than that which the charter and the laws of the province direct, they muſt be conſidered as unconſtitutional officers, and as ſuch no regard ought to be paid to them by the people of this country :—That if the juſtices ſhall ſit and act during their preſent diſqualified ſtate, this county will bear harmleſs all ſheriffs, jurors and other officers, who ſhall refuſe to carry into execution the orders of ſaid courts :—That it be recommended to the collectors of taxes and all other officers, who have public monies in their hands, to retain the ſame and not to make any payment thereof to the provincial county treaſurer, until the civil government of the province is placed upon a conſtitutional foundation, or it ſhall be otherwiſe ordered by the propoſed provincial congreſs :—That the perſons, who have accepted ſeats at the council board, by virtue of a mandamus from the king, have acted in a direct violation of the duty they owe to their country ; this county do recommend it to all, who have ſo highly offended, and have not already reſigned, to make public reſignation on or before the 20th of this inſtant September ; all, refuſing ſo to do, ſhall after ſaid day, be conſidered by this county as obſtinate and incorrigible enemies to this country :— That the fortifications begun and now carrying on upon Boſton neck, gives us reaſon to apprehend ſome hoſtile intention againſt that town :—That the late act eſtabliſhing the Roman Catholic religion in Quebec, is dangerous in an extreme degree to the Proteſtant religion, and to the civil rights and liberties of all America :—That whereas our enemies have flattered themſelves, that they ſhall make

make an eafy prey of this numerous brave people, from
an apprehenfion that they are unacquainted with military
difcipline; we therefore, for the honor and fecurity of
this county and province advife, that fuch perfons be
elected in each town as officers in the militia, as fhall
be judged of fufficient capacity, and who have evidenced
themfelves the inflexible friends to the rights of the
people, and that the inhabitants do ufe their utmoft dili-
gence to acquaint themfelves with the art of war, and
do for that purpofe appear under arms at leaft once every
week:—That during the prefent hoftile appearances on
the part of Britain, we are determined to act merely
upon the defenfive fo long as fuch conduct may be vindicated by reafon and the principles of felf-prefervation,
but no longer:—That as we underftand it has been in
contemplation to apprehend fundry perfons of this
county, we do recommend, fhould fuch meafure be put
in practice, to feize and keep every fervant of the prefent government throughout the province, until the perfons fo apprehended be reftored uninjured:—That we
recommend to all perfons, not to engage in any routes,
riots, or licentious attacks upon the properties of any
perfon whatfoever, as being fubverfive of all order and
government; but by a fteady, manly, uniform, and per-
fevering oppofition, to convince our enemies, that in a
conteft fo important, in a caufe fo folemn, our conduct
fhall be fuch as to merit the approbation of the wife,
and the admiration of the brave and free of every age
and of every country." They then drew up an addrefs
to the governor, and voted that Dr. *Jofeph Warren* (a
phyfician, an amiable gentleman, who wifhes for a reconciliation between the colonies and the parent ftate,

C c 4   upon

upon a redrefs of grievances, and aims not at independency) with others, be a committee to wait on his excellency, to inform him how the county is alarmed, and to remonftrate againft the fortifications making on the neck, and the repeated infults offered by the foldiery, to perfons paffing and repaffing into Bofton, and to confer with him on thofe fubjects. The governor was waited upon to know if he would receive the committee with the addrefs; but defiring a private copy of it, that when he received them, he might be ready with a prepared anfwer, he was furnifhed with it, and afterward fixed on Monday the 12th for receiving the committee. The doings of the county delegates, and a copy of the addrefs to the governor have been fent off by exprefs to the general congrefs now met at Philadelphia. On the Monday, when the committee had delivered the addrefs of the county, he anfwered to it, " I have no intention to prevent the free egrefs and regrefs of any perfon to and from the town of Bofton. I fhall fuffer none under my command to injure the perfon or property of any of his majefty's fubjects; but it is my duty to preferve the peace, and to prevent furprife; and no ufe will be made of the cannon, unlefs the hoftile proceedings of the people fhall render it neceffary." The patriots are waiting earneftly for the opinion of congrefs on the Suffolk refolves, in hopes that they will be approved of; and if fo, they will go on with greater refolution and courage; for they will confider fuch approbation as a declaration, that the colony will be fupported by congrefs, in cafe hoftilities are neceffary for the prefervation of its liberties, and is alfo juftifiable in arming and training the militia.

Mr.

Mr. *Quincy* is upon the point of failing for Britain, at the requeft of feveral co-patriots. Be fo obliging as to pay a proper attention to him: you will be pleafed at finding him fo intelligent a gentleman, and may rely upon his information. Shall keep the letter open, that if the fenfe of congrefs is received time enough, it may be forwarded.

P. S. The fons of liberty are in high fpirits. The Suffolk refolves were before congrefs on Saturday morning, the 17th, and were confidered; after which it was *refolved unanimoufly*, " That this affembly deeply feels the fuffering of their countrymen in the *Maffachufetts-bay*, under the operation of the late unjuft, cruel, and oppreffive acts of the *Britifh* parliament:—That they moft thoroughly approve the wifdom and fortitude with which oppofition to thefe wicked minifterial meafures has hitherto been conducted, and they earneftly recommend to their brethren, a perfeverance in the fame firm and temperate conduct as 'expreffed in the refolutions determined upon, at a meeting of the delegates for the county of *Suffolk*, on Tuefday the 6th inftant, (that was the day of their firft meeting, but they did not finifh till the 9th) trufting that the effect of the united efforts of *North America* in their behalf, will carry fuch conviction to the *Britifh* nation, of the unwife, unjuft, and ruinous policy of the prefent adminiftration, as quickly to introduce better men and wifer meafures:—" *Refolved unanimoufly*, That contributions from all the colonies for fupplying the neceffities, and alleviating the diftreffes of our brethren at *Bofton*, ought to be continued, in fuch manner, and fo long as their occafions may require." Mr. Quincy fails to-day.

L E T-

LETTER X.

Roxbury, Feb. 3, 1775.

THE measures pursued by the British ministry, for subjecting America to parliamentary authority in all cases whatever, have united the twelve colonies, from New Hampshire to South Carolina inclusively, into a compact body. Many on the side of government flattered themselves, that the event would never exist. They had no small ground for it, considering that several of the colonies clash in their particular interests; have been frequently quarrelling about boundaries and other matters; differ greatly in manners, customs, religion and constitutions; and have local prejudices, jealousies and aversions. But they have been pressed by a common danger, threatening the most valuable rights of each individual province, so that they have all elected delegates to meet in a general congress to consult in what way to obtain a redress of grievances, and ward off the impending ruin. The ministerial influence in New York has not prevailed as was expected, to keep that colony from joining the others. Great dependence was had upon their monied men; but the cause of liberty was too popular, and the numbers that espoused it too many and too independent, either to be bribed or overawed.

Sept. 5. The delegates being arrived at Philadelphia, from all the colonies except North Carolina, they met in general
congress,

congrefs, and proceeded to the choice of a prefident, when *Peyton Randolph* efq; was unanimoufly elected, and Mr. *Charles Thomfon* was unanimoufly chofen fecretary. They refolved, that " in determining queftions, each colony fhall have one vote." Before they engaged in any fpecial bufinefs, the North Carolina delegates joined them. The number of the whole when together, is fifty-two, befide the prefident. The firft important fervice wherein they engaged, you have had an account of in the preceding poftfcript. In their fubfequent refolutions they declared, " That if the late acts of parliament Oct. fhall be attempted to be carried into execution by force, 8. in fuch cafe all *America* ought to fupport the inhabitants of the *Maffachufetts-bay* in their oppofition :—That if it be found abfolutely neceffary to remove the people of Bofton into the country, all America ought to contribute toward recompenfing them for the injury they may thereby fuftain :—And that every perfon, who fhall accept, or act under any commiffion or authority derived from the act of parliament, changing the form of government and violating the charter, ought to be held in deteftation." They have written a letter to general *Gage*, 10. in which they exprefs the deepeft concern at his proceeding in a manner that bore fo hoftile an appearance, and which even the oppreffive acts of parliament did not warrant. They reprefent the tendency this conduct muft have to irritate and force the people, hitherto welldifpofed to peaceable meafures, into hoftilities, which may prevent the endeavours of congrefs to reftore a good underftanding with the parent ftate, and may involve us in the horrors of a civil war. They exprefs their hope, that the general, to quiet the minds of the people, will

difcontinue

discontinue the fortifications in and about Boston, prevent any further invasions of private property, restrain the irregularities of the soldiers, and give orders that the communication between the town and country may be open, unmolested and free.

The general in his answer said, " No troops have given less cause for complaint, and greater care was never taken to prevent it; and such care and attention was never more necessary from the insults and provocations daily given to both officers and soldiers. The communication between the town and country has been always free and unmolested, and is so still." This assertion may appear perfectly just to a military gentleman; but may be otherwise thought of by one in a civil department, who means that the entrance into a town should have neither guards nor sentinels, either to stop or challenge passengers, whether by night or by day. The general intimated, that the hostile preparations throughout the country, and the menaces of blood and slaughter made it his duty to fortify the neck. He concluded with—" I ardently wish, that the common enemies to both countries may see, to their disappointment, that these disputes between the mother country and the colonies, have terminated like the quarrels of lovers, and increased the affection which they ought to bear to each other."

The congress have also made a declaration of rights (contained within a number of resolves) to which, they say, the *English* colonies of North America are entitled by the immutable laws of nature, the principles of the English constitution, and their several charters or compacts. In the first of these are life, liberty and property,

ty, a right to the difpofal of any of which, without their confent, they have never ceded to any fovereign power whatever. They mention, that their anceftors, at the time of their emigration, were entitled to all the rights, liberties and immunities of free and natural born fubjects, within the realm of England; and that by fuch emigration they by no means forfeited, furrendered or loft any of thofe rights; but that they were, and their defcendants now are, entitled to the enjoyment of all fuch of them, as their local and other circumftances enabled them to exercife. They then ftate, that the foundation of Englifh liberty, and of all free government, is a right in the people to participate in their legiflative council; and proceed to fhow, that as the colonifts are not, and from various caufes, cannot be reprefented in the Britifh parliament, they are entitled to a free and exclufive power of legiflation in their feveral provincial legiflatures, where their right of reprefentation can alone be preferved, in all cafes of taxation and internal policy, fubject only to the negative of their fovereign, in fuch manner as had heretofore been ufed.

To qualify the extent of this paragraph, which may feem to leave no means of parliamentary interference, for holding the colonies to the mother country, they declare, that, from the neceffity of the cafe, and a regard to the mutual interefts of both countries, they cheerfully confent to the operation of fuch acts of the Britifh parliament as are, *bona fide*, reftrained to the regulation of their external commerce, for the purpofe of fecuring the commercial advantages of the whole empire to the mother country, excluding every idea of taxation, either inter-

internal or external, for raifing a revenue on the fubjects in America wthout their confent.

They refolved, " That the refpective colonies are entitled to the common law of England, and more efpecially to the great and eftimable privilege of being tried
by their peers of the vicinage; to the benefit of fuch of
the Englifh ftatutes as exifted in the time of their colonization, and which they have found to be applicable to
their feveral and other local circumftances; and to all
the immunities and privileges granted and confirmed
to them by royal charters, or fecured by their feveral
codes of provincial laws :—That, they have a right to
affemble peaceably, confider of their grievances, and
petition the king; and that all profecutions, prohibitory
proclamations, and commitments for the fame, are illegal :—That the keeping a ftanding army in thefe colonies, in times of peace, without the confent of the legiflature of that colony in which fuch army is kept, is
againft law :—That it is rendered effential to good government, by the Englifh conftitution, that the confti-
tuent branches of the legiflature be independent of each
other; that therefore the exercife of legiflative power,
by a council appointed, during pleafure, by the crown,
is unconftitutional and deftructive to the freedom of
American legiflation."

They proceeded to claim, in behalf of themfelves
and conftituents, and to infift on the foregoing articles
as their indifputable rights and liberties, which cannot
be legally taken from them, altered or abridged by any
power whatever, without their own confent by their reprefentatives in their feveral provincial legiflatures. They
then refolved concerning eleven acts of parliament, or

parts

parts of acts, passed in the present reign, that " they are infringements and violations of the foregoing rights, and that the repeal of them is essentially necessary, in order to restore harmony between Great Britain and the American colonies." Among these is the Quebec bill, which is termed " an act for establishing the Roman catholic religion in the province of Quebec, abolishing the equitable system of English laws, and erecting a ty- ranny there, to the great danger (from so total a dissi- milarity of religion, law and government) of the neigh- bouring British colonies, by the assistance of whose blood and treasure the said country was conquered from France."

After specifying their rights and enumerating their grievances, they mention, that in hopes of being re- stored to. that state, in which both countries formerly found happiness and prosperity, they have for the pre- sent, only resolved to pursue the following peaceable measures, viz. to enter into a non-importation, non-con- sumption, and non-exportation agreement; and to prepare an address to the people of Great Britain, a memo- rial to the inhabitants of British America, and a loyal address to his majesty.

By the association they have bound themselves, and intentionally their constituents, to a strict observance of fourteen articles. They have agreed by the second, That after the first of December next, they will wholly discontinue the slave trade, and will neither hire their vessels, nor sell their commodities to those who are con- cerned in it :—By the third, That from that day, they will not purchase or use any tea imported on account of the East India company, or any on which a duty hath

hath been or fhall be paid; and from and after the firft of March next, they will not purchafe or ufe any Eaft India tea whatever, nor any of thofe goods, they have agreed not to import, which they fhall have caufe to fufpect were imported after the firft of December, except fuch as come under the directions afterward mentioned:—By the fourth, That the non-exportation agreement fhall be fufpended to the tenth of September 1775, after which, if the acts or parts of acts objected to are not repealed, they will not directly or indirectly export any commodity whatfoever to Great Britain, Ireland or the Weft Indies, except rice to Europe:—By the fifth, That they will never more have any commercial intercourfe with any Britifh merchants, who may fhip goods in violation of and with a view of breaking the affociation:—By the eighth, That they will encourage frugality, œconomy and induftry, promote agriculture arts and manufactures, difcourage every fpecies of extravagance and diffipation, and will wear no other mourning than a piece of crape or ribbon:—By the fourteenth and laft, That they will have no trade, dealings or intercourfe whatfoever, with any North American colony or province, that fhall not accede to, or that fhall hereafter violate the affociation; but will hold them as inimical to their country. This affociation, which is to continue in force, till the above acts, or parts of acts, wherein they relate to the colonies, are repealed, has been figned 24. by all the members of congrefs.

In their addrefs to the people of Great Britain, the congrefs pay the higheft praife to the noble and generous virtues of their and our common anceftors; but in a way which rather reproaches you with a fhameful degeneracy.

neracy. They tell you not to be furprifed, that they, who are defcended from the fame common anceftors, fhould refufe to furrender their liberties and the conftitution you fo juftly boaft of, to men, who found their claims on no principles of reafon, and who profecute them with a defign, that by having *our* lives and property in their power, they may with the greater facility enflave *you*. They complain of being oppreffed, abufed and mifreprefented, fo that it is become a duty to themfelves and their pofterity, and to the general welfare of the Britifh empire, to addrefs you on this very important fubject. They call upon you yourfelves, to witnefs to their loyalty and attachment to the common intereft of the whole empire; to their efforts in the laft war; and to your own acknowledgment of their zeal, and your even reimburfing them large fums of money, which you confeffed they had advanced beyond their proportion, and far beyond their abilities. They proceed to ftate and examine the meafures and the feveral acts of parliament, which they confider as hoftile to America; and reprefent the probable confequences to your country fhould miniftry be able to carry the point of taxation, and reduce the colonies to a ftate of perfect flavery. They ingenioufly endeavour to render theirs a caufe common to both countries, by fhowing, that fuch fuccefs might in the end, be as fatal to the liberties of Britain as to thofe of America. "Take care (fay they) that you do not fall into the pit preparing for us." After denying the feveral charges of being feditious, impatient of government, and defirous of independency, which they affert to be calumnies; they declare, that if neither the voice of juftice, the dictates of the law, the prin-

ciples

ciples of the conftitution, nor the fuggeftions of humanity, can reftrain your hands from fhedding of human blood in fuch an impious caufe; they muft tell you, " That they never will fubmit to be hewers of wood, or drawers of water for any miniftry or nation in the world." They afterward make a propofal, which, if duly attended to, may afford a favorable bafis for negotiation— " Place us in the fame fituation that we were in at the clofe of the laft war, and our former harmony will be reftored." The fame truth was tranfmitted to fome of the miniftry by the late reverend Mr. *Whitefield* before his death in 1770 at Newbury-port, in nearly the following words, " Would you have peace and harmony reftored through the colonies, you muft attend to the military phrafe, *right about as you were.*" The like fentiment was confirmed by a fubfequent letter, from another quarter, after a defigned conference upon the fubject with *Thomas Cufhing* and *Samuel Adams* efqrs. of Bofton, and *Thomas Lynch* efq; of South Carolina. The congrefs conclude their addrefs, by expreffing the utmoft regret at their being compelled by the over-ruling principles of felf-prefervation, to adopt meafures detrimental to numbers of their fellow fubjects in Great Britain and Ireland, in the fufpenfion of their importations from both thefe kingdoms. They finally reft their hope of a reftoration of that harmony, friendfhip and fraternal affection between all the inhabitants of his majefty's kingdoms and territories, fo ardently wifhed for by every true and honeft American, upon the magnanimity and juftice of the Britifh nation, in furnifhing a parliament of fuch wifdom, independence and public fpirit, as may fave the violated rights of the whole empire, from the

devices

devices of wicked ministers and evil counsellors, whether in or out of office.

Congress, in their memorial to the inhabitants of British America, inform the colonies, that they have diligently, deliberately and calmly inquired into all the measures, which have excited the present disturbances; and that upon the whole they find themselves reduced to the disagreeable alternative of being silent, or betraying the innocent, or of speaking out and censuring those they wish to revere. They prefer the course dictated by honesty, and a regard for the welfare of their country. After stating and examining the several laws which have been passed, and the measures which have been pursued with respect to America, since the conclusion of the late war to the present period, they inquire into the motives for the particular hostility against the town of Boston and province of Massachusetts-bay; though the behaviour of the people in other colonies, has been in equal opposition to the power assumed by parliament; notwithstanding which no step had been taken against any of them by government. This they represent as an artful systematic line of conduct, concealing several designs, adding, "It is expected that the province of the Massachusetts-bay will be irritated into some violent action, that may displease the rest of the continent, or that may induce the people of Great Britain to approve the meditated vengeance of an imprudent and exasperated ministry. If the unexampled pacific temper of that province shall disappoint this part of the plan, it is hoped the other colonies will be so far intimidated as to desert their brethren, suffering in a common cause, and that thus disunited all may be subdued." They proceed to

state

ſtate the importance of the truſt, which has been repoſed in them, and the manner in which they have diſcharged it; and deeply deplore the neceſſity which preſſed them to an immediate interruption of commerce, and apologize with ſaying, " We are driven by the hands of violence into unexperienced and unexpected public convulſions, and are contending for freedom ſo often contended for by our anceſtors. " The people of England," ſay they, " will ſoon have an opportunity of declaring their ſentiments concerning our cauſe. In their piety, generoſity and good ſenſe, we repoſe high confidence, and cannot upon a review of paſt events be perſuaded, that *they*, the defenders of true religion, and the aſſerters of the rights of mankind, will take part againſt their affectionate proteſtant brethren in the colonies, in favor of our open and their own ſecret enemies, whoſe intrigues for ſeveral years paſt have been wholly exerciſed in ſapping the foundations of civil and religious liberty." Toward the cloſe they have theſe words, " We think ourſelves bound in duty to obſerve to you, that the ſchemes agitated againſt theſe colonies have been ſo conducted, as to render it prudent that you ſhould extend your views to the moſt unhappy events, and be in all reſpects prepared for every contingency."

The addreſs of congreſs to his majeſty is clothed in the habit of an humble petition, wherein they beg leave to lay their grievances before the throne. After an enumeration of them, they implore his clemency for protection againſt them; and impute all their diſtreſſes, dangers and fears, to the deſtructive ſyſtem of colony adminiſtration adopted ſince the concluſion of the laſt war. They expreſs their apprehenſion, that as his ma-

jeſty

jefty enjoys the fignal diftinction of reigning over freemen, the language of freemen cannot be difpleafing;
adding, "Your royal indignation, we hope, will rather
fall on thofe defigning and dangerous men, who daringly interpofing themfelves between your royal perfon
and your faithful fubjects, and for feveral years paft inceffantly employed to diffolve the bonds of fociety, by
abufing your majefty's authority, mifreprefenting your
American fubjects, and profecuting the moft defperate
and irritating projects of oppreffion, have at length compelled us, by the force of accumulated injuries, too fevere to be any longer tolerable, to difturb your majefty's repofe by our complaints." They beg leave to
affure his majefty, that in regard to defraying the charge
of the adminiftration of juftice and the fupport of civil
government, fuch provifion has been and will be made,
as has been and fhall be judged, by the legiflatures of
the feveral colonies, juft and fuitable to their refpective
circumftances; and that for the defence, protection and
fecurity of the colonies, their militias, if properly regulated as they earneftly defire may be immediately
done, would be fully fufficient, at leaft in times of peace;
and in cafe of war his faithful colonifts will be ready and
willing, as they ever have been when conftitutionally required, to demonftrate their loyalty, by exerting their
moft ftrenuous efforts in granting fupplies and raifing
forces. They fay, "We afk but for peace, liberty and
fafety. We wifh not a diminution of the prerogative,
nor do we folicit the grant of any new right in our favor. Your royal authority over us, and our connection with Great Britain, we fhall always carefully and
zealoufly endeavour to fupport and maintain."—"We

D d 3

prefent

present this petition only to obtain redrefs of grievances and relief from fears and jealoufies, occafioned by the fyftem of ftatutes and regulations adopted fince the clofe of the late war, by the abolition of which fyftem, the harmony between Great Britain and thefe colonies, will be immediately reftored. In the magnanimity and juftice of your majefty and parliament we confide for a redrefs of our other grievances, trufting, that when the caufes of our apprehenfions are removed, our future conduct will prove us not unworthy of the regard, we have been accuftomed in our happier days to enjoy. For, appealing to that Being who fearches thoroughly the hearts of his creatures, we folemnly profefs, that our councils have been influenced by no other motive, than a dread of impending deftruction." They implore his majefty in the moft folemn manner, as the loving father of his whole people, connected by the fame bands of law, loyalty, faith and blood, not to fuffer the tranfcendent relation formed by thefe ties to be further violated, in uncertain expectation of effects, that if attained, never can compenfate for the calamities through which they muft be gained. They moft earneftly befeech him, that his royal authority and interpofition may be ufed for their relief; and that a gracious anfwer may be given to their petition. The clofe is a prayer, that his majefty may enjoy every felicity through a long and glorious reign, and that his defcendants may inherit his profperity and dominions till time fhall be no more.

The congrefs, a week after refolving upon the affociation, an addrefs to the people of Great Britain, a memorial to the inhabitants of the colonies, and an addrefs to his majefty, further refolved, " That an addrefs be

9   prepared

prepared to the people of Quebec, and letters to the colonies of St. John's, Nova Scotia, Georgia, Eaft and Weft Florida, who have not deputies to reprefent them in this congrefs."

Their addrefs to the French inhabitants in Canada, difcovers the moft dexterous management, and the moft able method of application to the temper and paffions of the parties, whom they endeavour to gain. They ftate the right they had, upon becoming Englifh fubjects, to the ineftimable benefits of the Englifh conftitution; and that this right was further confirmed by the royal proclamation in 1763, plighting the public faith for their full enjoyment of thofe advantages. They impute to fucceeding minifters an audacious and cruel abufe of the royal authority, in withholding from them the fruition of the irrevocable rights, to which they were thus juftly entitled. They undertake to explain to them, fome of the moft important branches of that form of government from which they are debarred; and in fo doing, quote paffages from their countryman Montefquieu, whom they artfully adopt as a judge and an irrefragable authority upon this occafion. They then proceed to fpecify and explain, under feveral diftinct heads, the principal rights to which the people are entitled by the Englifh conftitution; and thefe rights they truly fay, defend the poor from the rich, the weak from the powerful, the induftrious from the rapacious, the peaceable from the violent, the tenants from the lords, and all from their fuperiors.

They attempt pointing out numberlefs deformities in the Quebec-bill, and placing them in thofe points of view which fhould render it odious to mankind. They

renew

renew their applications to the paffions and partiality of the Canadians; and at length introduce Montefquieu as addreffing them thus: " Seize the opportunity prefented to you by providence itfelf. You are a fmall people compared with thofe who with open arms invite you into a fellowfhip. A moment's reflection fhould convince you, which will be moft for your intereft and happinefs, to have all the reft of North America your unalterable friends, or your invetcrate enemies. Your province is the only link wanting to complete the bright and ftrong chain of union. Nature has joined your country to theirs, Do you join your political interefts. The value and extent of the advantages tendered to you are immenfe. Heaven grant you may not difcover them to be bleffings after they have bid you an eternal adieu." They endeavour to obviate the jealoufies and prejudices which might arife from the difference of their religious principles, by inftancing the cafe of the Swifs Cantons, whofe union is compofed of Roman Catholic and Proteftant ftates, living in the utmoft concord and peace with one ancther, and thereby enabled to defy and defeat every tyrant that has invaded them. The congrefs, upon this article, appear to have winked out of fight their complaint about eftablifhing the Roman Catholic religion in Quebec, and to expect that it would be unknown to the Canadians, or give them no umbrage. They declare, that they do not afk them to commence hoftilities againft the government of their common fovereign, but only invite them to confult their own glory and welfare, and to unite with them in one focial compact. They conclude by informing them, that the congrefs had, with univerfal pleafure, and an

unanimous

unanimous vote, refolved, That they fhould confider the violation of their rights, by the act for altering the government of their province, as a violation of their own; and That they fhould be invited to accede to their confederation.

Before this addrefs was perfected and figned, congrefs Oct. refolved " That the feizing, or attempting to feize any 21. perfon in America, in order to tranfport fuch perfon beyond the fea, for trial of offences committed in America, being againft law, will juftify and ought to meet with refiftance and reprifal." They have alfo agreed, that another congrefs fhall be held on the 10th day of May next, unlefs the redrefs of grievances be obtained before that time.

The general congrefs, having finifhed their delibera- 26. tions, diffolved themfelves. The impartial world will go near to acknowledge, that the petitions and addreffes from the congrefs have been executed with uncommon energy, fkill and ability; and that abftractedly confidered, in refpect to vigor of mind, ftrength of fentiment, and patriotic language, they would not difgrace any affembly whatfoever. The ftudied attention that congrefs have paid to the Maffachufetts-bay and its diftreffed capital, will both confole and invigorate the inhabitants. Many however of the congreffional acts were neither carried unanimoufly, nor without much debate. Mr. Galloway of Pennfylvania, and Mr. Duane of New York, inclined to the fide of miniftry. The former became a member at the earneft folicitation of the affembly, and refufed compliance till they had given him inftructions agreeable to his own mind, as the rule of his conduct. Thefe inftructions they fuffered him to draw

draw up: they were briefly to state the rights and the grievances of America, and to propose a plan of amicable accommodation of the differences between Great Britain and the colonies, and of a perpetual union. September the twenty-eighth a plan was proposed by him, which was debated a whole day, when the question was carried six colonies to five, that it should be resumed and further considered: but it at length fell through. The ten resolutions which the congress came to in their declaration, expressing their indubitable rights and liberties, met with very considerable opposition. Mr. Duane and others who drew with him, perplexed the proposals made by the high sons of liberty, so that. the congress did not come to a single resolution for more than a fortnight, neither in stating their rights nor their grievances. When six days before that declaration, on October the eighth, the resolution was passed, " that the congress approve the opposition of the inhabitants of the Massachusetts-bay to the execution of the late acts of parliament; and if the same shall be attempted, &c. (p. 395.)" Galloway and Duane not only opposed, but wanted to have their protests entered; which being refused, on their return from congress they gave each other a certificate, declaring their opposition to that question, as they thought it a treasonable one *. In some stage of their proceedings, the danger of a rupture with Britain was urged as a plea for certain concessions. Upon this Mr. *S. Adams* rose up, and among other things said in substance, " I should advise persisting in our struggle for liberty, though it was revealed from heaven that 999.

* Parliamentary Debates relative to general Howe. Mr. Galloway's answers.

were

were to perifh, and only one of a thoufand to furvive
and retain his liberty.   One fuch freeman muft poffefs
more virtue, and enjoy more happinefs than a thoufand
flaves; and let him propagate his like, and tranfmit to
them what he hath fo nobly preferved."   It was a flight
of patriotifm, ferving to fhow the temper of the fpeaker:
but the fentiment is fo hyperbolical, as to throw it far
beyond the reach of practice.   Mr. S. Adams having
feen an happy iffue to the important deliberations of the
general congrefs, after his return repaired to the Maffachufetts provincial congrefs to aid in their deliberations.

General Gage, by the advice of his new council,
iffued writs for the holding of a general affembly at
Salem on the 5th of October.   The events which afterward took place made him think it expedient to counteract the writs, by a proclamation for fufpending the
meeting of the members returned.   But the legality of
the proclamation was called into queftion; and the new
members, to the number of 90, met according to the
precepts, on the day and at the place appointed.   Hav- Oct.
ing waited that day, without the prefence of the gover- 5.
nor, or any fubftitute for him, to adminifter the oaths
and open the feffion; on the next they appointed a committee to confider the proclamation; and on the third,
refolved themfelves into a provincial congrefs, to be
joined by fuch others as have been or fhall be chofen, to
take into confideration the dangerous and alarming fituation of public affairs.   The following day they met
in provincial congrefs and adjourned to Concord, about
20 miles from Charleftown, and when there chofe Mr. 11.
Hancock prefident.   They proceeded to appoint a committee to wait upon the governor with a remonftrance,
in

in which they apologize for their meeting, from the diftreffed ftate of the colony; exprefs the grievous apprehenfions of the people; affert that the rigor of the Bofton port-bill is exceeded by the manner in which it is carried into execution; and complain of the late laws and the hoftile preparations on Bofton-neck. They conclude with adjuring him, to defift immediately from the conftruction of the fortrefs at the entrance into Bofton, and to reftore that pafs to its natural ftate. The governor was involved in fome difficulty as to giving them an anfwer, for he could not acknowledge the legality of their affembly. Neceffity however prevailed. He expreffed great indignation at the idea's being formed, that the lives, liberties, or property of any people, except avowed enemies, could be in danger from Englifh troops; and obferved, that notwithftanding the enmity fhown to the troops, by withholding from them almoft every thing neceffary for their prefervation, they had not yet difcovered the refentment which might juftly have been expected to arife from fuch hoftile treatment. He reminded them, that while they complained of alterations made in their charter by acts of parliament, they were themfelves by their prefent affembling, fubverting that charter, and now acting in direct violation of their own conftitution: he therefore warned them of the rocks they were upon, and to defift from fuch illegal and unconftitutional proceedings. But they were not in the leaft diverted from profecuting their meafures. They adjourned to and met at Cambridge.

Oct.
17.

21.   A committee was appointed to draw up a plan for the immediate defence of the province. It was concluded to raife and inlift a number of *minute-men*, now

for

for the firſt time ſo called, from their being to turn out
with their arms at a minute's warning. Upon the ae-
bate for raiſing money to purchaſe military articles, a
thouſand pound (lawful, a fourth leſs than ſterling) was
moved for and ſeconded; then two thouſand. The
country members in common had no conception of the
expences attending warlike operations; and were dread-
fully afraid of voting away their own and their conſti-
tuent's money, however neceſſary the expenditure of it.
They are generally perſons of good underſtanding in
matters within their own ſphere, but are not competent
judges of thoſe that lie without it: and being accuſtomed
only to ſmall ſums, ſtartle at the mention of thoſe,
which to them have the comparative appearance of
enormouſly large: and yet it is needful to humor their
want of ſcientific knowledge, to prevent diſguſt and obtain their ſupport. Of this the more intelligent members of the aſſembly were ſenſible. Therefore the debate was cloſed by appointing a committee to give in
an eſtimate of the articles wanted, together with their
coſt; this being done, the committee of ſafety were
empowered to aſſemble the militia, when they ſhall judge
the ſame neceſſary for the defence of the inhabitants of
the province; and the committee of ſupplies to purchaſe ammunition, ordnance, ſtores, &c. not exceeding
the value of 20,837 l. lawful, or 15,627 l. 15 s. ſterling
—a glorious ſum with which to oppoſe the power and
riches of Great Britain! The committee of ſafety, and
the committee of ſupplies, conſiſt of different perſons,
and are intended for different purpoſes. The firſt, beſide being empowered to aſſemble the militia, are inveſted with other authority for the ſafety of the province,
and

and are to recommend to the committee of supplies the purchasing of such articles as may be deemed necessary. The last are to assist the committee of safety, not only by purchasing supplies, but by affording them help for executing the measures, which may be thought by them requisite for the public benefit. Both are to sit and continue to do business, when there is a recess of the provincial congress, as also when none existeth. It is

Oct. 25.

resolved, That all matters shall be kept private, but in such a numerous assembly it is next to impossible to effect it. Were all equally true to the same cause, each will not have the like power of retaining a secret.

27.   The honorable *Jedediah Pribble*, the honorable *Artemas Ward*, and colonel *Pomeroy*, all of whom have seen some service in the last war, were elected general officers to have the chief command of the minute-men and militia, in case they should be called out to action.

29.   The provincial congress adjourned to November 23.

As winter approached, the governor ordered temporary barracks to be erected for the troops. But such was the dislike to their being provided for in any manner, that the select men and committees obliged the workmen of the town to quit their employment, for fear of subjecting themselves to the resentments of their countrymen. The governor had as little success in endeavouring to procure carpenters from New York; so that it has been with the greatest difficulty that he has gotten those temporary lodgments erected. He has endeavoured also to procure some winter covering from that city; but the merchants have refused complying with any part of the order, and returned for answer, " They never will supply any article for the benefit of

men,

men, who are sent as enemies to their country." The general had thoughts at one time of erecting a fort upon Beacon hill. The Boston committee obtained the plan of it, waited upon him, and informed him, that they heard he had such a design, and that if he proceeded to execute it he would get himself into difficulties. He would not own that he had any such intention, but attempted rather to make them believe the contrary; on which they produced the plan, and told him it was the same that was presented to him the night before.

On the other hand, the Massachusetts committee of safety were not inattentive to their duty. They recommended to the committee of supplies the procuring of pork, flour, rice and peas, and the depositing of the same partly at Worcester and partly at Concord. They further advised the procuring of all the arms and ammunition that could be got from the neighbouring provinces; and of spades, pickaxes, bill-hooks, iron shovels and pots, mess bowls, cannon, ball, &c. &c.

Nov. 2, 8, 14, 20.

Every thing now served to increase the mutual apprehension and animosity between the government and the people. Those of Boston professed to be under no small terror, from an apprehension of danger to their property, liberties and lives. The soldiers on the other hand, considered themselves in the midst of enemies. Each side made profession of the best intentions in the world for its own part, and showed the greatest suspicion of the other. In this state of doubt and profession, matters were made still worse by a measure, which seems not of sufficient importance in its consequences to justify its having been hazarded at so critical a season. This was the landing of a detachment of sailors by night from

the

the ſhips of war in the harbour, who ſpiked up all the cannon upon one of the batteries belonging to the town.

In the mean time, through the diſpoſition and promptitude of the people, the reſolutions and recommendations of the provincial congreſs, had all the weight and efficacy of laws. At length the governor was induced to iſſue a proclamation, in which they were charged with proceedings, generally underſtood as nearly tantamount to treaſon and rebellion. The inhabitants were accordingly prohibited in the king's name, from complying, in any degree, with the requiſitions, recommendations, directions, or reſolves of that unlawful aſſembly.

Nov. 10.

23.

When the provincial congreſs met again, having Mr. Samuel Adams preſent with them, they puſhed their preparations for hoſtile oppoſition. Theſe exertions ſuited not the feelings of many in congreſs. Through timidity they began to ſicken at heart, and upon the plea of ſickneſs begged leave to return home, and were indulged. Mr. S. Adams penetrated the cauſe of their complaint; and, in order to ſtop the epidemical diſtemper, expreſſed his great willingneſs, that when members were not well, they ſhould be allowed to return, but propoſed that they ſhould be enjoined, upon getting back, to inform the towns that they were no longer repreſented, that ſo others might be ſent to ſupply their abſence. The propoſal ſoon cured the malady; for the diſordered choſe to remain in congreſs rather than incur the diſpleaſure of their conſtituents, and be ſupplanted by new ſucceſſors.

The provincial congreſs reſolved upon getting in readineſs twelve thouſand men to act upon any emergency; and directed that a quarter of the militia ſhould be inliſted lifted as minute-men, who were allowed the liberty of choosing their own officers, and were to receive pay. They sent persons to New Hampshire, Rhode Island and Connecticut, to acquaint them with what was doing, and to request that they would prepare their respective quotas to make up an army of twenty thousand men when wanted. Upon this a number of gentlemen were sent from these colonies to consult and settle with a committee of about twenty, chosen by the congress for the purpose. There was a difficulty about fixing what should be the precise period for opposing general Gage's troops; at length it was determined, that they should be opposed whenever they marched out with their baggage, ammunition and artillery; for this would carry in it an apparent intention of acting hostilely in support of British measures.

A committee was appointed to correspond with the inhabitants of Canada; and it was resolved, that the following letter be addressed to the several ministers of the gospel within this province— Dec. 6.

" REV. SIR,

WE cannot but acknowledge the goodness of heaven, in constantly supplying us with preachers of the gospel, whose concern has been the temporal and spiritual happiness of this people. In a day like this, when all the friends of civil and religious liberty are exerting themselves to deliver this country from its present calamities, we cannot but place great hopes in an order of men, who have ever distinguished themselves in their country's cause, and do therefore recommend to the ministers of the gospel, in the several towns and other places in this colony, that they assist us in avoiding that dreadful slavery with which we are now threatened."

The ministers of New England being mostly congregational, are from that circumstance, in a professional way more attached and habituated to the principles of liberty than if they had spiritual superiors to lord it over them, and were in hopes of possessing in their turn, through the gift of government, the seat of power. They oppose arbitrary rule in civil concerns from the love of freedom, as well as from a desire of guarding against its introduction into religious matters. The patriots for years back have availed themselves greatly of their assistance. Two sermons have been preached annually for a length of time, the one on the general election day, the last Wednesday in May, when the new general court have been used to meet according to charter, and elect the counsellors for the ensuing year: the other some little while after, on the artillery election day, when the officers are re-elected, or new officers are chosen. On these occasions political subjects are deemed very proper; but it is expected that they be treated in a decent, serious and instructive manner. The general election preacher has been chosen alternately, by the council and the house of assembly. The sermon is stiled *the election sermon*, and is printed. Every representative has a copy for himself, and generally one or more for the minister or ministers of his town. As the patriots have prevailed, the preachers of each sermon have been the zealous friends of liberty; and the passages most adapted to promote and spread the love of it, have been selected and circulated far and wide by means of newspapers, and read with

avidity

avidity and a degree of veneration, on account of the preacher and his election to the service of the day. Commendations both public and private, have not been wanting to help on the design. Thus by their labors in the pulpit, and by furnishing the prints with occasional essays, the ministers have forwarded and strengthened, and that not a little, the opposition to the exercise of that parliamentary claim of right to bind the colonies in all cases whatever.

The clergy of this colony are as virtuous, sensible and learned a set of men, as will probably be found in any part of the globe of equal size, and equally populous. The first settlers were early attentive to the providing of suitable persons to fill their pulpits with dignity. They saw the importance of it, and in 1636 the general court gave some hundred pounds toward a public school at Newton; but Mr. John Harvard, a worthy minister of Charlestown, dying in 1638, and bequeathing between seven and eight hundred pounds to the same use, the school took the name of Harvard college by an order of court, and the town upon the occasion changed its name for that of Cambridge. This college has been encouraged ever since, and is the first upon the continent. It is the *alma mater* to whom the youth of this colony, in particular, are sent, whether designed for the pulpit, the bar, or other callings. Here they receive the rudiments of those qualifications by which they are enabled to serve their country in a civil or sacred department. The salaries of the ministers are moderate, but in general sufficient for their support by the aid of good œconomy. They cannot approve of often bringing politics into the pulpit, yet they apprehend it

E e 2

to be right upon fpecial occafions. Who but muft admit, that " it is certainly the duty of the clergy to accommodate their difcourfes to the times; to preach againft fuch fins as are moft prevalent, and to recommend fuch virtues as are moft wanted. For example; if exorbitant ambition and venality are predominant, ought they not to warn their hearers againft thefe vices ? If public fpirit is much wanted, fhould they not inculcate this great virtue ? If the rights and duties of magiftrates and fubjects are difputed, fhould they not explain them, fhow their nature, ends, limitations and reftrictions?" You may have frequently remarked, that though the partizans of arbitrary power will freely cenfure that preacher, who fpeaks boldly for the liberties of the people, they will admire as an excellent divine, the parfon whofe difcourfe is wholly in the oppofite ftrain, and teaches, that magiftrates have a divine right for doing wrong, and are to be implicitly obeyed by men profeffing chriftianity, as if the religion of the bleffed Jefus bound them tamely to part with their natural and focial rights, and flavifhly to bow their neck to any tyrant; as if Paul was faulty in ftanding up for his Roman privileges, that he might efcape a fcourging, or falling a facrifice to the malice of his countrymen, when he appealed unto Cæfar.

The provincial congrefs chofe colonel Thomas and colonel Heath additional generals, and foon after diffolved themfelves, that they might be at home in time to keep thankfgiving with their families. It has been long a cuftom in the colony to have a faft day in the fpring, and a thankfgiving late in the fall of the year, or in the beginning of winter, when the heads of families.

lies.

lies collect their children around them; and beside attending the religious exercises of the day, feaft upon a plentiful though not a fplendid table, and are innocently merry. The obfervation of this day they call " *a keeping thankfgiving*." The appointment of both days belongs in an orderly way to the governor; but in thefe extraordinary times the provincial congrefs appointed the public thankfgiving, on which among other enumerated bleffings, a particular acknowledgment was to be made to the Almighty for the union which fo remarkably prevails in all the colonies.

The affembly of Pennfylvania met toward the clofe of the year, and were the firft legal body of reprefentatives, that ratified unanimoufly all the acts of the general congrefs, and appointed delegates to reprefent them in the new congrefs to be held the enfuing May. It is thought, that they were in a great meafure dragged into it, from the fear of a provincial convention.

No fooner did they receive at Rhode Ifland, the account of the royal proclamation, prohibiting the exportation of military ftores from Britain, but the people feized upon and removed from the batteries about the harbour, above forty cannon of different fizes. The affembly alfo paffed refolutions for procuring arms and military ftores, by every mean, and from every quarter in which they could be obtained, as well as for training and arming the inhabitants.

When copies of thefe refolutions and of the proclamation arrived at Portfmouth in New Hampfhire, the people of the province were fpirited up to make their firft hoftile movement. Though governor Wentworth's influence could not prevent their appointing deputies,

E e 3   - holding

holding a convention at Exeter, and choosing delegates for the continental congress; yet he had the address to moderate their tempers, and to keep them from acts of violence. But the example of their neighbours, and the alarming situation of affairs, at length roused them

14. to uncommon exertions. More than four hundred men collected and beset his majesty's castle at Portsmouth. Captain Cochran who commanded, ordered three four-pounders to be fired on them, and then the small arms; before.he could be ready to fire again, the fort was stormed on all quarters, and the affailants immediately secured both him and his men, and kept them prisoners about an hour and a half, during which time they broke open the powder-house, took all the powder away, except one barrel, and having put it in boats and sent it off, released him from his confinement.

The hardy inhabitants of Marblehead, used to all the toils and dangers of a seafaring life, being out of employ, have attended to military exercise for hours, three days in a week, and will soon conftitute a fine regiment of soldiers. The gentlemen of the place have encouraged them by their own example, and made it profitable to them. Something similar has been practised at Salem, and other towns. The militia of the colony will, therefore, acquire some knowledge of arms, before they are called to engage in actual service, should that unhappily be the issue of present measures.

The Virginia militia officers, under the command of lord Dunmore, convened at Fort Gower on November the fifth, have shown what may be expected from them; for though they resolved to bear the most faithful allegiance to his majesty, they declared that the love of liberty

berty and attachment to the real interefts and juft rights
of America, outweighed every other confideration, and
that they would exert every power within them for the
defence of American liberty, when regularly called forth
by the unanimous voice of their countrymen.

Barnftable in New England, and Ridgefield in Connecticut, have diftinguifhed themfelves in adopting different meafures from the other towns in their refpective
colonies. But the New York reprefentatives have given
the greateft difguft. After the affembly's taking into
confideration the regulations agreed upon at the grand
congrefs refpecting commerce, they rejected the fame.
This however was thought to be compenfated for, by 1775.
the late refolution of the Pennfylvania convention, Jan.
wherein they have declared, " That, if the petition of 23.
the continental congrefs fhould be difregarded, and the
Britifh adminiftration fhould determine by force to effect a fubmiffion to the late arbitrary acts of the Britifh
parliament; in fuch a fituation, we hold it our indifpenfable duty to refift fuch force, and at every hazard to
defend the rights and liberties of America." The convention likewife recommended in particular the making
of falt, gunpowder, falt-petre and fteel. Among the
many fons of liberty of which they were compofed, Mr.
Charles Thomfon was eminent for his inflexible fpirit;
but Mr. Thomas Mifflin was as the very foul of the capital and province. Such are his natural and acquired
accomplifhments, his unwearied exertions, his zeal, his
addrefs, his fprightlinefs, that he enlightens and invi-
gorates every thing around him.

The inhabitants of Maryland were no lefs zealous on
the prefent critical occafion, than thofe of the moft ac-

E e 4   tive

tive provinces. They were all in motion, forming county meetings, entering into affociations, choofing committees, and recommending meafures for carrying the refolutions of the continental congrefs into effectual execution. The convention has appointed a fum of money for the purchafe of arms and ammunition. Every perfon, who refufes to contribute to the purchafe, is deemed an enemy to his country. Many of the principal gentlemen are ambitious of appearing in arms to defend its liberties. They have taken the power of the militia out of the hands of the governor, and eftablifhed it by their own authority, for the defence of the Maffachufetts as well as of themfelves; and thus have fhown, to all the world, their approbation of New England meafures. The lower counties of the Delaware have acted in like manner.

27   The New Hampfhire affembly, in anfwer to a letter from Maryland, has gone further than ever before, in faying, " You may depend upon the ready concurrence of this houfe with the meafures thought neceffary to be purfued by the other colonies in the great caufe of liberty."

But the province did not truft to the complexion of the affembly. A convention of deputies was appointed by the feveral towns, and held at Exeter, when the proceedings of the continental congrefs were unanimoufly approved; and members chofen to reprefent them at the enfuing one, two days before the affembly gave their anfwer.

Moft of the New Yorkers accommodate themfelves to the meafures appointed by the general congrefs.

The

The general committee in Charleftown South Carolina, upon receiving an account of thefe meafures, immediately convened a provincial congrefs, and procured a
return of reprefentatives from every parifh and diftrict
in the colony, by which mean the body confifted of more
than two hundred, while the conftitutional affembly
amounts to no more than forty-nine. The increafe of
the reprefentatives naturally ferved the caufe of the country, by engaging a greater number of leaders in fupport
of it. This firft provincial congrefs met on the eleventh
of January, they have unanimoufly approved the proceedings of the general congrefs, and refolved to carry
them into execution. Committees of infpection and
obfervation have alfo been appointed, whofe bufinefs it
is to fee that the public refolutions are univerfally obeyed, that fo they may not be broken, through the felfifhnefs of individuals. This is the prevailing mode of
guarding againft fuch felfifhnefs in every colony.

From the former fuccefs of non-importation agreements, and a belief that the trade of America is indif-
penfably neceffary to Britain, it is generally hoped and
expected in the fouthern ftates, that the obnoxious acts
will be repealed. They have no idea of an appeal to
the fword, notwithftanding all the military parade that
exifts. A bloodlefs felf-denying oppofition is the whole
of their real intention, and all the facrifice that they imagine will be required. Similar fentiments prevail among
great numbers in the Maffachufetts; who while they are
preparing for war, expect that prefent appearances will
never terminate in it; for that Great Britain will not
fight with her beft cuftomers, but will relax and accommodate,

modate, when they find the Americans refolutely determined to ufe their arms rather than fubmit.

Perfons, who difcover great anxiety about the continuance of trade, are confidered as felfifh, preferring private intereft to the good of the country; and under this thought, the intemperate zeal of the populace in fome places, tranfports them beyond the limits of moderation, to apply fingular punifhments to individuals who counteract the general fenfe of the community.

There is however to appearance, an amazing agreement through the continent; and it may be imagined, that the inhabitants of the twelve colonies have but one heart, and but one underftanding. Affemblies, conventions, congreffes, towns, cities, private clubs and circles, are feemingly animated by one great, wife, active and noble fpirit—one mafterly foul, enlivening one vigorous body. All their acts tend to the fame point, the fupporting of the meafures of the continental congrefs. But be affured, there are great numbers in every colony, who difapprove of thefe meafures—a few comparatively, from principle and a perfuafion that the fame are wrong, and that they ought to fubmit to the mother country—fome through attachment to the late governmental authority exercifed among them—many from felf-intereft—but the bulk for fear of the mifchievous confequences likely to follow. The profeffing friends of liberty have acted in a fpirited manner, while the others have lain ftill. Such as have difcovered a difpofition to oppofe popular meafures have not been fupported, and therefore have declined making further efforts, and abfented themfelves from town and other meetings. The popular cry being againft them, they have

have fought perfonal peace and fafety in remaining quiet. But could the truth be afcertained, it would probably be difcovered, that in moft of the town and other meetings, even in New England, far more than half the parties having a right to attend, from various caufes were abfent; and that there were a great many among the abfentees, who were fuch, becaufe they knew that matters would be carried at fuch meetings contrary to their own fentiments. Not only fo but it may be reafonably fuppofed, and time may prove that feveral in affemblies, conventions and congreffes, voted againft their own opinion, to fecure themfelves from refentment and to promote their prefent intereft.

An inclination has appeared in feveral of the governmental gentlemen now in Bofton, to attempt opening the court at Worcefter, and to fupport it by the aid of two regiments. It has been the fubject of converfation. When the propofal of marching them came to be confidered in council, it was laid afide. The governor was well pleafed with the determination; he certainly does not wifh to bring on a rupture.

Now let me conclude with giving you a picture of the Maffachufetts colony, which you will be inclined to pronounce an uncommon and aftonifhing curiofity. Some hundred thoufand people are in a ftate of nature, and yet as ftill and peaceable, at prefent, as ever they were when government was in full vigor. We have neither legiflators, nor magiftrates, nor executive officers. We have no officers, but m litary ones; of thefe we have a multitude chofen by the people, and exercifing them with more authority and fpirit, than ever any did who had commiffions from a governor. The inhabitants

are

are determined never to submit to the act destroying
their charter, and are every where devoting themselves
to arms. To force upon them a form of government
to which they are absolutely averse, may not be within
the omnipotence of a British parliament. The attempt
has produced a suspension of all legal authority, and yet
individuals enjoy the same security as before, even when
they differ from the public sentiment, have they the
prudence to moderate their tempers and observe a neu-
trality. By accommodating themselves so far to the
times, they are safe at home and abroad.

The fortitude with which the town of Boston supports
its present distresses, and the determination it discovers
to endure as much as human nature can, rather than
betray the American cause and endanger the liberties
of posterity, will secure it the encomiums of future generations. Not a town or city in all the colonies would
have been likely to have exhibited so glorious a spec-
tacle, had it been called out to a similar trial; and all
the friends of American liberty through the continent
may congratulate themselves, that the storm of ministerial vengeance has fallen first upon the capital of the
Massachusetts, as in consequence of it they have enjoyed
the opportunity of providing against the worst that may
be attempted, in order to reduce them to subjection.

LETTER XI.

London, March 3, 1775.

A Strange fupinenefs prevailed, for fome time after my laft was clofed, among the great body of the Englifh nation; and the colony contefts were little regarded. Numbers flattered themfelves, that as things had formerly fo often appeared at the verge of a rupture, without actually arriving at it, fome means would be found for accommodating the prefent difpute. The opinion alfo was circulated, that a countenance of refolution perfifted in, would certainly put an end to the conteft, which (it was faid) had been nourifhed wholly by former conceffions; people in general were therefore inclined to truft the trial of perfeverance and refolution, to a miniftry who valued themfelves upon thefe qualities. The times have been highly favorable to any purpofe, which only required the concurrence of the parliament and the acquiefcence of the public. Adminiftration has taken advantage of thefe circumftances, 1774. and the late parliament has been diffolved, a twelve Sept. month before the expected time. This may be meant 30. as a preparatory ftep to the moft coercive meafures with America; but in a new houfe of commons miniftry will be left at large, to choofe or alter their line of conduct as incidents may vary, and if neceffary, can throw all the odium of the late laws upon the former parliament.

His majefty in his fpeech informed the new one, that Nov. a moft daring fpirit of difobedience to the law ftill un- 30.

happily

happily prevailed in the Maſſachuſetts, and had broken forth in freſh violences of a criminal nature ; that theſe proceedings had been encouraged in other colonies, and unwarrantable attempts been made to obſtruct the commerce of the kingdom, by unlawful combinations ; that ſuch meaſures had been taken, and ſuch orders given, as were judged moſt proper for carrying the laws into execution ; and that they might depend upon a firm reſolution to withſtand every attempt to weaken the ſupreme authority of the legiſlature over all the dominions of the crown, his majeſty being aſſured of receiving their ſupport while acting upon theſe principles.

The propoſed addreſs in the houſe of commons, produced a conſiderable debate ; and the miniſter was reminded of the mighty effects he had predicted from the late acts againſt America :—They were to humble that whole continent in the duſt, without further trouble, and the puniſhment of Boſton was to ſtrike an univerſal panic on all the colonies; that refractory town would be totally abandoned, and inſtead of obtaining relief, a dread of the ſame fate would even prevent the appearances of pity. But the addreſs was carried without any amendment, by a majority of more than three to one.

That from the houſe of lords was couched in ſtrong terms, and was warmly debated. It was rendered memorable by a proteſt, thought to be the firſt upon an addreſs, and which was very pointed ; it concluded with the following remarkable declaration : " But whatever may be the miſchievous deſigns, or the inconſiderate temerity, which leads others to this deſperate courſe, we wiſh to be known as perſons, who have diſapproved of meaſures ſo injurious in their paſt effects and their future

future tendency, and who are not in hafte, without inquiry or information, to commit ourfelves in declarations which may precipitate our country into all the calamities of a civil war.*" The addrefs was carried by a majority of 63 to 13.

Notwithftanding the hoftile tone of the fpeech, and the great majority that fupported the addreffes, there appeared an irrefolution on the fide of miniftry; and previous to the Chriftmas recefs, they feemed evidently to fhrink from all conteft upon American fubjects. The national eftimates were entirely formed upon a peace eftablifhment; and the minifter of the naval department publicly afferted in the houfe of lords, that he knew it would be fully fufficient for reducing the colonies to obedience. He fpoke with the greateft contempt both of the power and courage of the Americans; and held that they were not difciplined, nor capable of difcipline, and that formed of fuch materials, and fo indifpofed to action, the numbers, of which fuch boafts had been made, would only add to the facility of their defeat.

The eftablifhment will indeed, be fully fufficient, if the miniftry mean to employ the navy only, and to recall the military. Ships may effect that with little hazard and expence, which if once attempted by foldiers, may plunge the nation into enormous difburfements, and yet not be accomplifhed. A few fhips of the line ftationed fingly near the capital ports of the colonies, and a number of frigates employed as cruifers to ftop the Americans from fending any veffels to fea; and this meafure continued, would at length weary out

* Lords who figned the proteft—Richmond, Portland, Rockingham, Stamford, Stanhope, Torrington, Ponfonby, Wycombe, Camden.

the inhabitants of the towns and cities upon the fea-coaft of the continent, and induce one or other of them to fubmit; and if but one link of the chain gave way, the whole would foon come to the ground; and were the fea-ports once brought to adjuft the prefent difpute with adminiftration, the towns in the back country might be gradually inclined to the fame, whatever may be their prefent apprehenfions. The proper application of the navy to the American conteft would alfo exclude all foreign interference.

The congreffional proceedings were received before the Chriftmas recefs, and miniftry were difpofed to re-tract their violent meafures, and to redrefs American grievances. To this end, application was made, under the aufpices of the minifter, to the body of the American merchants, defiring them to frame petitions for the re-drefs of American grievances, and the reftoration of American rights, and promifing compliance with them, as it was moft agreeable to the miniftry to repeal the obnoxious acts, feemingly in confequence of petitions at home. While this was in agitation, letters were re-ceived from New York, affuring that the affembly would reject the proceedings of the general congrefs, and that there would be a feparation of that colony from the reft. Frefh hopes were conceived from the profpect of a divifion, upon which miniftry reverted to meafures more adapted to their own inclination *.

But during the recefs, perfons began to confider the confequences which might follow the congreffional pro-ceedings, and a general alarm was fpread. This pro-duced feveral meetings of the North American mer-

* See the Remembrancer, Part II. p. 227, the note.

5　　　　　　　　　　　　　　　　　chants

chants in London and Briftol; and petitions to parliament were prepared and agreed upon in both places. But the times were fo altered from what they were formerly, that no mercantile oppofition could prove efficacious by endangering the continuance of the miniftry.

On the firft day of the meeting after the recefs, the nobleman at the head of the American affairs, laid the papers belonging to his department, before the lords, on which Lord Chatham rofe, and expreffed his utmoft diffent and difapprobation of the whole fyftem of American meafures.

Being in poffeffion at prefent of your friend Mr. Quincy's journal, wherein he gives a particular account of his lordfhip's fpeech, of the copies of feveral letters fent by himfelf to America, and of other matters, permit me to tranfcribe from the fame, and give you the thoughts and expreffions of Mr. Quincy, with the dates.

Viewed Plymouth docks. My ideas of the riches and 1774. powers of this great nation are increafed to a degree I Nov. fhould not have believed, if it had been predicted to 11. me. I am not in any meafure reconciled to the Britifh plan of taxing America, but I fhould with cheerfulnefs accede to a contribution from the colonies, (they being the fole judges of the time and quantity of their grants) toward the charges of the Britifh government.

This morning J. Williams efq; informed me, that 18. governor Hutchinfon had repeatedly affured the miniftry, that a union of the colonies was utterly impracticable; that the people were greatly divided among themfelves in every colony; and that there could be no doubt but that all America would fubmit; that they muft, and

VOL. I. F f would

.would foon. Several of the nobility and miniftry affured Dr. Franklin of the fame facts.

19.　　　Lord N—— repeatedly faid to me, " We muft try what we can do to fupport the authority we have claimed over America; if we are defective in power, we muft fit down contented and make the beft terms we can; and nobody then can blame us after we have done our utmoft; but till we have tried what we can do, we can never be juftified in receding; and we ought to, and fhall be very careful not to judge a thing impoffible, becaufe it may be difficult; nay, we ought to try what we can effect before we can determine upon its impracticability."

24.　　　To ————. " The following language hath been reiterated to me in various companies"— " We are afraid of nothing but your divifion, and your want of perfeverance. Unite and perfevere; you muft prevail—you muft triumph."

" From parliament expect no favor, but what proceeds from fear. Depend not upon commercial plans for your fafety. Dr. Franklin is an American in heart and foul. His ideas are not contracted within the narrow limits of exemption from taxes, but are extended upon the broad fcale of total emancipation. He is explicit and bold upon the fubject."

26.　　　Governor P—— affured me, that all the meafures againft America were planned and pufhed on by Bernard and Hutchinfon. They were inceffant in their applications to adminiftration, and gave the moft pofitive affurances of fuccefs.

Dec. 6.　　　Mr. commiffioner M—— waited on me. In the courfe of converfation he faid, " You can have no idea of of the taxes of this kingdom, and the diftrefs of our poor. They are extreme poor and wretched indeed— every thing here is taxed to the utmoft. The colonies muft relieve us: they muft eafe us of our taxes, &c.' He alfo affirmed to me, that governors Bernard and Hutchinfon were principally attended to in the late meafures againft the colonies. But he added, that government had found many things had turned out different from Hutchinfon's reprefentations, and had not been at all conformable to what he foretold.

To ———. " My whole time is employed in endeavouring to ferve my country. I find every body eager to hear, moft people willing to be fet right, and almoft all grofsly ignorant of the American world. It is agreed on all hands, that your courage—your courage, I repeat it—will be brought to the teft. Should it prove anfwerable to your oftentations, and worthy your anceftors, your friends will amazingly increafe, your hearty friends will be in raptures. Prepare, prepare I fay, for the worft."

" Many of your friends here in both houfes will not take a decifive part, till they fee how you act in America. For fhould they take a determined part now in favor of that country, and in a fhort time America give back, their hopes of rife into power and office (which are the hopes of all Britifh ftatefmen) would be for ever at an end. Therefore till the colonifts difcover that union and fpirit, which all parties here agree, muft force fuccefs, you are not to expect any great exertions in your favor. But when once there is a conviction, that the Americans are in earneft, that they are refolved to endure all hazards with a fpirit worthy the prize, then

F f 2 (and

(and not till then) will you have many firm, active, per-
fevering and powerful friends.   For, ftrange as it may
feem, there is a great doubt here, among many, whether you are really in earneft, in the full force and extent of thofe words."

12.   Lord ——— appeared a very warm friend to the
Americans, and faid, " If they continue united, they
muft have all they afk."   He particularly mentioned,
that Lord M——, laft feffions, affured the houfe of
lords, that the plan they had laid would go down in
America *fine clade*; and alfo, that he had the beft intelligence what might be carried through there.   His lordfhip had no doubt that fuch affurance was grounded on
Hutchinfon's information.

14.   To E——.   " Your countrymen muft feal their caufe
with their blood.   They muft preferve a confiftency of
character.   THEY MUST NOT DELAY.   They muft—or
be trodden down into the vileft vaffalage—the fcorn—
the fpurn of their enemies—a by-word of infamy among
all men."

16.   To E——.   " Permit me to congratulate my countrymen on the integrity and wifdom, with which the congrefs have conducted.   Their policy, fpirit and union,
have confounded their foes, and infpired their friends.
All parties agree in giving them a tribute of honor and
applaufe.   My Lord N—— endeavoured to explain
away his expreffion, " I will have America at my feet."
Beware of the arts of negotiation."

      " By the way, there is no doubt but the miniftry fent
large fums to New York in order to bribe your continental delegates.   It was openly avowed and vindicated;
and great boaft was made of minifterial fuccefs in this
                                                    way,

way, with the delegates from New York. It was faid, that they had effected a dif-union which would be fatal to the caufe of America. You can't well imagine the chagrin with which the miniftry received the refult of that glorious body. They are viewed as the *northern conftellation* of glorious worthies, illuminating and warming the new world."

To Jofeph Reed efq; (of Philadelphia)   17.

" Sure I am that the miniftry have no where fuch fanguine hopes of a defection as from that quarter (New York.) Their influence is no where fo forcibly extended; it is certain they will be aftonifhingly difappointed if they do not find a fenfibility to their touch. Lord C—— faid in the houfe of lords, the other day, " Were I an American, I would refift to the laft drop of my blood." Your parliamentary friends fay, fnatch the opportunity for peace and reconciliation. Your fanguine and warm partizans fay, " You are united and infpired now, circumftances that may never happen again. Seize the happy and glorious opportunity for eftablifhing the freedom and focial felicity of all America. There is a tide in the affairs of men."

While (at Bath) viewing the moft magnificently elegant new rooms, in company with colonel Barre, he faid, pointing to the pictures taken from ruins found at Herculaneum, " I hope you have not the books containing the draughts of thofe ruins with you." I replied; " There was one fet I believed in the public library at our college." " Keep them there, (faid he) and they may be of fome fervice as a matter of curiofity for the fpeculative, but let them get abroad and you are ruined.

1775.
Jan.
2.

They will infuse a taste for buildings and sculpture; and when a people get a taste for the fine arts, they are ruined. 'Tis taste that ruins whole kingdoms. 'Tis taste that depopulates whole nations. I could not help weeping, when I surveyed the ruins at Rome. All the remains of the Roman grandeur are of works which were finished, when Rome and the spirit of Romans were no more, unless I except the ruins of the Emilian baths. Mr. Quincy, let your countrymen beware of taste in their buildings, equipage, and dress, as a deadly poison."

Colonel Barre also added in the course of conversation, " About 14 or 15 years ago, I was through a considerable part of your country; for in the expedition against Canada, my business called me to pass by land through Pennsylvania, New Jersey, York and Albany; and when I returned again to this country, I was often speaking of America, and could not help speaking well of its climate, soil and inhabitants; for you must know, Sir, America was always a favorite with me. But will you believe it, Sir, yet I assure you it is true, more than two-thirds of this island at that time, thought the Americans were all negroes." I replied, " I did not in the least doubt it, for if I was to judge by the late acts of parliament, I should suppose that a majority of the people of Great Britain still thought so, for I found that their representatives still treated them as such." He smiled and the discourse dropped. The colonel was among those who voted for the Boston port-bill.

20.   Attended the debates of the house of lords. Good fortune gave me one of the best places for taking a few minutes.

Lord

Lord Chatham rose like Marcellus. " Viros super-
eminet omnes." He seemed to feel himself superior to
those around him. His language, voice and gesture,
were more pathetic than I ever saw or heard before at
the bar or senate. He seemed like an old Roman
senator, rising with the dignity of age, yet speaking with
the fire of youth.

The illustrious sage stretched forth his hand with the
decent solemnity of a Paul, and rising with his subject,
he smote his breast with the energy and grace of a De-
mosthenes. He opened with some general observations,
on the importance and magnitude of the American
quarrel (as he called it.) He enlarged upon the dangerous and ruinous events, that were coming upon the
nation, in consequence of the present dispute, and the
measures already begun and now carrying on by his
majesty's ministers. He arraigned their conduct with
great severity and freedom. He then proceeded:

" My lords, these papers from America, now laid
for the first time before your lordships, have been, to
my knowledge, 5 or 6 weeks in the pocket of the minister. And notwithstanding the fate of this kingdom
hangs upon the event of this great controversy, we are
but this moment called to a consideration of this important subject. My lords, I do not want to look into
one of those papers; I know their contents well enough
already. I know that there is not a member in this
house but is acquainted with their purport also. There
ought therefore to be no delay in entering upon this
matter; we ought to proceed to it immediately. We
ought to seize the first moment to open the door of
reconciliation. The Americans will never be in a temper

or

or ftate to be reconciled (they ought not to be) till the troops are withdrawn. The troops are a perpetual irritation to thefe people: they are a bar to all confidence, and all cordial reconcilement. I therefore, my lords, move—That an humble addrefs be prefented to his majefty, moft humbly to advife and befeech his majefty, that, in order to open the way towards an happy fettlement of the dangerous troubles in America, by beginning to allay ferments, and foften animofities there; and above all, for preventing, in the mean time, any fudden and fatal cataftrophe at Bofton, now fuffering under the daily irritation of an army, before their eyes, pofted in their town, it may gracioufly pleafe his majefty, that immediate orders may be difpatched to general Gage, for removing his majefty's forces from the town of Bofton, as foon as the rigor of the feafon, and other circumftances indifpenfable to the fafety and accommodation of the faid troops, may render the fame practicable."

" The way, my lords, muft be immediately opened for reconciliation. It will foon be too late. I know not who advifed the prefent meafures. I know not who advifes to a perfeverance and enforcement of them; but this I will fay, that whoever advifes them ought to anfwer for it, at his utmoft peril. I know that no one will avow, that he advifed, or that he was the author of thefe meafures: every one fhrinks from the charge. But fomebody has advifed his majefty to thefe meafures, and if his majefty continues to hear fuch evil counfellors, his majefty will be undone. His majefty indeed may wear his crown; but the American jewel out of it, it will not be worth the wearing."

" What

" What more shall I say? I must not say, that the king is betrayed; but this I will say, the NATION is ruined. What foundation have we for our claims over America? What is our right to persist in such cruel and vindictive measures against that loyal and respectable people? They say you have no right to tax them without their consent. They say truly. Representation and taxation must go together: they are inseparable. Yet there is hardly a man in our streets, though so poor as scarce to be able to get his daily bread, but thinks he is the legislator of America. *Our* American subjects is a common phrase in the mouth of the lowest orders of our citizens; but property, my lords, is the sole and entire dominion of the owner: it excludes all the world besides the owner. None can intermeddle with it. It is a unity; a mathematical point. It is an atom; untangible by any but the proprietor. Touch it—and the owner loses his whole property. The touch contaminates the whole mass; the whole property vanishes.—The touch of another annihilates it—For whatever is a man's own is absolutely and exclusively his own."

" In the last parliament all was anger—all was rage. Administration did not consider what was practicable, but what was revenge. *Sine clade victoria* was the language of the ministry last sessions, but every body knew, an ideot might know, that such would not be the issue. But the ruin of the nation was a matter of no concern, if administration might be revenged. Americans were abused, misrepresented, and traduced in the most atrocious manner, in order to give a colour, and urge on to the most precipitate, unjust, cruel, and vindictive measures that ever disgraced a nation."

Gnossius

Gnossius hæc Rhadamanthus habet *durissima* regna,
   *Castigat*que, AUDITque dolos.

" My lords, the very infernal spirits, they *chastise*, *castigatque:* sed *auditque*, my lords. The very spirits of the infernal regions HEAR *before* they *punish*. But how have this respectable people behaved under all their grievances? With unexampled patience, with unparalleled wisdom. They chose delegates by their free suffrages: no *bribery*, no *corruption*, no INFLUENCE here, my lords. Their representatives meet with the sentiments and temper, and speak the sense of the continent. For genuine sagacity, for singular moderation, for solid wisdom, manly spirit, sublime sentiments and simplicity of language, for every thing respectable and honorable, the congress of Philadelphia shine unrivalled. This wise people speak out. They do not hold the language of slaves: they tell you what they mean. They do not ask you to repeal your laws as a favor: they claim it as a right: they demand it. They tell you, they will not submit to them: and I tell you the acts must be repealed; they will be repealed; you cannot enforce them. The ministry are checker-mated. They have a move to make on the board; and yet not a move but they are ruined.

" Repeal, therefore, my lords, I say. But bare repeal will not satisfy this enlightened and spirited people. What! repeal a bit of paper: repeal a piece of parchment! That alone won't do, my lords. You must go through. You must declare you have no right to tax; then they may trust you; then they will have confidence in you. I have heard a noble lord speak, who seemed to lay some blame upon general Gage. I think that
honorable

honorable gentleman has behaved with great prudence
and becoming caution. He has entrenched himfelf and
ftrengthened his fortifications. I don't know what he
could do more. His fituation puts me in mind of a
fimilar tranfaction in the civil wars of France, when the
great Condè on one fide, and Marfhall Turenne on the
other, with large armies lay many weeks very near each
other. Turenne, confcious of the terrible confequences
of a victory to himfelf and country, though the armies
were feveral days in fight of each other, never came to
a battle. On his return to the court of France, the
queen afked him, " Why, Marfhall, I think you lay
feveral days in fight of your enemy, and you might have
been up with him at any time; pray why did you not
take him ?" The general very fhrewdly replied,
" Should I have taken him, pleafe your majefty, I was
afraid all Paris would have taken me." My lords, there
are three millions of whigs. Three millions of whigs,
my lords, with arms in their hands, are a very formidable
body. 'Twas the whigs, my lords, that fet his majefty's
royal anceftors upon the throne of England. I hope,
my lords, there are yet double the number of whigs in
England that there are in America. I hope the whigs
of both countries will join and make a common caufe.
Ireland is with the Americans to a man. The whigs of
that country will, and thofe of this country ought, to
think the American caufe their own. They are allied
to each other in fentiment and intereft, united in one
great principle of defence and refiftance : they ought
therefore, and will run to embrace and fupport their
brethren. The caufe of fhip-money was the caufe of
all the whigs of England. *You fhall not take my money*
without

without my consent, is the doctrine and language of whigs. It is the doctrine and voice of whigs in America, and whigs here. It is the doctrine in support of which I do not know how many names I could——I may call in this house : among the living I cannot say how many I could, to join with me and maintain these doctrines with their blood ; but among the dead I could raise an host innumerable. And, my lords, at this day, there are very many found substantial honest whigs, who ought and who will consider the American controversy as a great common cause."

" My lords, consistent with the preceding doctrines, and with what I have ever and shall continue to maintain, I say, I shall oppose America whenever I see her aiming at throwing off the navigation act, and other regulatory acts of trade, made *bona fide* for that purpose, and wisely framed and calculated for reciprocation of interest, and the general extended welfare and security of the whole empire. It is suggested such is their design. I see no evidence of it. But to come at a certain knowledge of their sentiments and designs on this head, it would be proper first to do them justice. Treat them as subjects, before you treat them as aliens, rebels and traitors."

" My lords, deeply impressed with the importance of taking some healing measures at this most alarming distracted state of our affairs, though bowed down with a cruel disease, I have crawled to this house, to give you my best experience and counsel ; and my advice is to beseech his majesty, &c. &c. This is the best I can think of. It will convince America, that you mean to try her cause in the spirit and by the laws of freedom

and

and fair inquiry, and not by codes of blood. How can she now truft you, with the bayonet at her breaft? She has all the reafon in the world now to believe you mean her death or bondage."

" Thus entered on the threfhold of this bufinefs, I will knock at your gates for juftice without ceafing, unlefs inveterate infirmities ftay my hand. My lords, I pledge myfelf never to leave this bufinefs : I will purfue it to the end in every fhape. I will never fail of my attendance on it, at every ftep and period of this great matter, unlefs nailed down to my bed by the feverity of difeafe. My lords, there is no time to be loft ; every moment is big with dangers. Nay, while I am now fpeaking, the decifive blow may be ftruck, and millions involved in the confequence. The very firft drop of blood will make a wound, that will not eafily be fkinned over. Years, perhaps ages may not heal it. It will be *irritabile vulnus*, a wound of that rancorous malignant, corroding, feftering nature, that in all probability it will mortify the whole body. Let us then, my lords, fet to this bufinefs in earneft, not take it up by bits and fcraps as formerly, juft as exigencies preffed, without any regard to the general relations, connections and dependencies. I would not by any thing I have faid, my lords, be thought to encourage America to proceed beyond the right line. I reprobate all acts of violence by her mobility, but when her inherent conftitutional rights are invaded, thofe rights that fhe has an equitable claim to the full enjoyment of, by the fundamental laws of the Englifh conftitution, and ingrafted thereon by the unalterable laws of nature, then I own myfelf an *American*, and feeling myfelf fuch, fhall, to

6   the

the verge of my life, vindicate thofe rights againft all men, who ftrive to trample upon or oppofe them."

From the effects of this fpeech on the great audience without the bar, and from my own emotions and feelings, the miracles of ancient eloquence—*the blaze of genius and the burft of thought*—with which Grecian and Roman orators have been faid to work wonders in the fenate and the field, no longer appeared fabulous.

Lord Camden fpoke next on the fide of America and in fupport of the motion. He equalled lord Chatham in every thing, but that fire and pathos which are the *forte* of his lordfhip. In learning, perfpicuity and pure eloquence, probably no one ever furpaffed Lord Camden.

His lordfhip opened briefly upon the nature of property, the right of taxation, and its infeparability from reprefentation. " My lords (he faid) I will not enter into the large field of collateral reafoning applicable to the abftrufe diftinctions touching the omnipotence of parliament. The declaratory law fealed my mouth. But this I will fay, not only as a ftatefman, politician and philofopher, but as a COMMON LAWYER, my lords, you have no right to tax America. I have fearched the matter. I repeat it, my lords, you have no right to tax America. The natural rights of man and the immutable laws of nature are all with that people. Much ftrefs is laid on the fupreme legiflative authority of Great Britain, and fo far as the doctrine is directed to its proper object I accede to it. But it is equally true, according to all approved writers on government, that no man, agreeable to the principles of natural or civil liberty, can be divefted of any part of his property without his confent. Every thing has been ftaked on this fingle pofition, that acts of parlia-

ment

ment muft be obeyed : but this general, unconditional, unlimited affertion, I am far from thinking applicable to every poffible cafe, that may arife in the turn of times. For my part, I imagine, that a power, refulting from a truft, arbitrarily exercifed, may be lawfully refifted ; whether the power is lodged in a collective body, or fingle perfon, in the few or the many. However modified makes no difference. Whenever the truft is wrefted to the injury of the people, whenever oppreffion begins, all is unlawful and unjuft, and refiftance of courfe becomes lawful and right. But fome lords tell us ferioufly, that adminiftration muft reduce the Americans to obedience and fubmiffion, that is, you muft make them abfolute and infamous flaves, and *then*—what? We will, fay they, give them full liberty. Ah ! is this the nature of man ? No, my lords, I would not truft myfelf, *American* as I am, in this fituation. I do not think I fhould, in that cafe, be myfelf for giving of them liberty. No, if they fubmitted to fuch unjuft, fuch cruel, fuch degrading flavery, I fhould think they were made for flaves ; that fervility was fuited to their nature and genius. I fhould think they would beft ferve this country as their flaves ; that their fervility would be for the benefit of Great Britain ; and I fhould be for keeping fuch *Cappadocians* in a ftate of fervitude, fuch as was fuited to their conftitution, and might redound much to our advantage."

" My lords, fome noble lords talk very much of refiftance to acts of parliament. King, lords and commons are fine founding names. But, my lords, acts of parliament have been refifted in all ages. King, lords and commons may become tyrants as well as others.

Tyranny

Tyranny in one or more is the fame. It is as lawful to refift the tyranny of many as of one. Somebody once afked the great Mr. *Selden*, in what law book, in what records or archives of the ftate you might find the law for refifting tyranny. " I don't know, (faid Mr. Selden) whether it is worth your while to look deeply into the books upon this matter; but I'll tell you what is moft certain, that it has always been the cuftom of England— and the cuftom of England is the law of the land."

" There is a gentleman, whom I need not name, his works are well received and well known, who avoids ftating any rule, when refiftance is lawful; and he lays down the revolution as the only precedent. He fays, that the various circumftances, events and incidents, that may juftify cannot be defined; but the people at large will judge of their welfare and happinefs, and act accordingly. The fame writer fays, that whenever a cafe exactly fimilar in all its parts and circumftances to the revolution, when a cafe fhall run upon *all fours* with that, then the law feems to be fettled, that refiftance is lawful. I do not pretend to quote his words. I think his meaning is very much as I have ftated it. But undoubtedly in cafes, in many refpects diffimilar, but in equal degree tyrannical and oppreffive, refiftance may be lawful, and the people in all ages, countries and climes have at times known thefe things; and they have and will for ever act accordingly."

Lord Shelburne in the courfe of his argument faid, "My lords, we know, we all know, that juftice and injuftice, right and wrong are not at all confidered in the courfe of our parliamentary proceedings. We all know that nothing is debated in parliament for information or conviction,

viction, but for mere form. Every thing is confidered in the cabinet and brought into parliament, not for confideration, but for the fanction of the legiflature, and the fcreening the counfellors of the king. The meafures of parliament are the meafures of the minifter; and the meafures of this minifter are very often thofe of his commiffioner." The Marquis of Rockingham alfo fupported the motion.

Lords Littleton, Suffolk, Gower, Townfend, Rochford and Weymouth fpoke in oppofition. I omit relating what their lordfhips faid, left I fhould be fufpected by any who may fee this journal, of an unfair report of their fpeeches. But a very remarkable faying of Lord G—— I cannot omit. His lordfhip faid, " I am for enforcing thefe meafures (and with great fneer and contempt) let the Americans fit talking about their natural and divine rights, their rights as men and citizens, their rights from God and nature."

The houfe, at about ten, divided after the preceding debates, on the queftion contents 18. non-contents 77, including proxies.

Thus far from Mr. Quincy's papers.

The language of the lords in adminiftration was high and decifive. And it was declared, that the mother country fhould never relax till America confeffed her fupremacy, and it was acknowledged to be the minifterial refolution, to enforce obedience by arms.

The principal trading and manufacturing towns in the kingdom, having waited to regulate their conduct as to American affairs, by that of the merchants of London and Briftol, followed the example of thefe two great commercial bodies, and prepared petitions upon that subject to be prefented to parliament.

Jan. 23. The petition from the merchants of London was of courfe the firft delivered, and it was moved to be referred to the committee, appointed to take into confideration the American papers; but it was moved by way of amendment, on the minifterial fide, that it fhould be referred to a feparate committee to meet on the 27th, the day fucceeding that appointed for the confideration of American papers. This was objected to as a fhameful pitiful evafion; but upon the queftion's being put, the amendment was carried, 197 againft 81, who fupported the original motion.

A fimilar fate attended the petitions from Briftol, Glafgow, Norwich, Liverpool, Manchefter, Birmingham, Wolverhampton, Dudley, and fome other places; all of which, in turn, were configned to what the oppofition termed the committee of oblivion.

26. On the day appointed for the confideration of American affairs, a fecond and very ftrong petition was prefented from the merchants of London. On which it was moved, that the order for referring the merchants petition to a feparate committee fhould be difcharged, and that it fhould be referred to a committee of the whole houfe, appointed to confider the American affairs. The indignity and mockery offered to fo great a body as the merchants of London by the late refolution, which with an infidious affectation of civility, received the petition with one hand, and threw it out of the window with the other, was painted in ftrong colours. All the debates, on the fubject of the petitions, were attended with an unufual degree of afperity, and even acrimony on the

side

fide of oppofition. The conduct alfo of the late parliament was fcrutinized without mercy, and its memory treated with more than want of refpect. A gentleman, remarkable for a farcaftic poignancy in his obfervations, in fketching a fhort hiftory of that parliament, faid, that they began their political life with a violation of the facred right of election in the cafe of Middlefex; that they had died in the act of popery, when they eftablifhed the Roman catholic religion in Canada; and that they had left a rebellion in America, as a legacy. The queftion was rejected upon a divifion by a very great majority.

Though it was then late, a petition was offered from Mr. Bollan, Dr. Franklin, and Mr. Lee, ftating that they were authorized by the American continental congrefs, to prefent a petition from the congrefs to the king, which petition his majefty had referred to that houfe, and that they were enabled to throw great light upon the fubject: they prayed to be heard at the bar, in fupport of the faid petition. A violent debate enfued. The miniftry alleged, that the congrefs was no legal body, and none could be heard in reference to its proceedings, without giving that illegal body fome degree of countenance. It was anfwered, that the congrefs, however illegal as to other purpofes, was fufficiently legal for prefenting a petition. It was figned by the names of all the perfons who compofed it, and might be received as from individuals. It was faid, That it was their bufinefs rather to find every plaufible reafon for receiving petitions, than to invent pretences for rejecting them: that the rejection of petitions was one principal, if not the moft powerful caufe of the prefent troubles:

and that this mode of conftantly rejecting their petitions, and refufing to hear their agents, would infallibly end in univerfal rebellion, and not unnaturally, as thofe feem to give up the rights of government, who refufe to hear the complaints of the fubject. The miniftry infulted the petition as containing nothing but pretended griev-ances, while they refufed to hear and difcufs it. It was rejected by 218 to 68. This rejection muft have bee. forefeen by all who knew, that on the fourth of the month, Lord Dartmouth, by the king's orders, had written a circular letter to the governors of his majef-ty's colonies, requiring them to ufe their utmoft endea-vours to prevent the holding of any more congreffes; and that the American grievances were, in that letter, termed *pretended*. This letter was written a few days after the petition had met with an apparent gracious re-ception, and had been promifed a due confideration; but probably not before favorable advices had been re-ceived refpecting the New York affembly.

It was evident, that both houfes of parliament were ready to adopt any meafures which adminiftration fhould propofe; and it was confidently believed and afferted, that when the merchants and manufacturers were de-prived of all hopes of preventing the operation of force, it would then become their intereft to give all poffible effect to it. They would thus become by degrees, a principal fupport of that caufe, which they now fo ea-gerly oppofed.

The opinion of the efficacy of a forcible mode of pro-ceeding in America, and the hopes of compelling a great body at home to concurrence, have made the minifters more and more refolved to go through, and complete the plan with which they have begun. It may however be much doubted, whether they fufpect that the American conteft will end in blood. Some of them in all probability have fuch a firm reliance upon Mr. Hutchinfon's judgment, as to flatter themfelves that the colonifts will give way to thofe appearances of coercion, which they have adopted and mean further to adopt; and fo have engaged in the prefent hazardous politics, in hopes of enjoying a bloodlefs conqueft, and therein a complete triumph over all oppofition.

Lord Chatham perfevered in the profecution of his Feb. conciliatory fcheme with America, and accordingly 1. brought into the houfe of lords the outlines of a bill, which he hoped would anfwer that falutary purpofe, under the title of " A provifional act for fettling the troubles in America, and for afferting the fupreme legiflative authority, and fuperintending power of Great Britain over the colonies."

This bill caufed a variety of difcuffion within and without doors. The miniftry obferved, that it was a propofition of reconciliation by conceffion, which was caufe fufficient to induce them to reject it; their plan being, at prefent, to fhow a firm refolution not to give way in any inftance, while the oppofition in America continued. It was unufual in parliament to reject, on the firft propofition, any bill for an object allowed to be neceffary; and promifing, however faintly or rudely, any plan for obtaining the end propofed. But the proceeding on this occafion was different. They condemned without referve the bill in the whole, and in all its parts; and it was moved, and ftrongly fupported by all the lords on the fide of adminiftration, that the bill be

rejected

rejected in the firft inftance. The noble framer defended himfelf and his bill from the numerous attacks which were made on both, with great fpirit and vigor. The indignity offered him, feemed to renew all the fire of youth; and he retorted the farcafms, which were levelled at him from different quarters, with a moft pointed feverity. The nature of the fubjects debated, and the ftate of temper on both fides, produced much warmth, fevere altercation, and even perfonal animadverfion. The bill was rejected by a majority of 61 to 32, not being allowed to lie upon the table. The rejection of it may be of no differvice to the colonifts. It contained in it, a propofal to require of congrefs the making of a free grant to the king, of a certain perpetual revenue, fubject to the difpofition of the Britifh parliament; and congrefs was to adjuft the proportions of the feveral charges to be borne by each province, toward the general contributory fupply. Had it paffed into an act, the colonifts might not have united in the propofal, but dangerous divifions have followed, fo that you may have no occafion to regret its fate, efpecially as that will ftrengthen your union, and increafe your friends.

A petition was prefented to the commons, from the planters of the fugar colonies refiding in Great Britain, and the merchants of London trading to thofe colonies, fetting forth the diftrefs to which the Weft India iflands will be reduced, unlefs the former harmony between this kingdom and the American colonies is reftored. Like all the former upon the fubject, it was referred to the eftablifhed petition committee. The day it was prefented, the minifter opened his defigns in refpect to America. Having prepared the way by a fpeech, he
moved

moved for an addreſs to the king, and for a conference
with the lords, that it might be the joint addreſs of both
houſes. The addreſs returns thanks for the communication of the American papers; and declares, that they
find from them, that a *rebellion* actually exiſts within the
province of the Maſſachuſetts-bay; that the parties concerned in it have been countenanced and encouraged by
unlawful combinations and engagements entered into,
in ſeveral of the other colonies; that they never can
relinquiſh any part of the ſovereign authority over all
the dominions, which by law is veſted in his majeſty
and the two houſes of parliament; that they ever have
been, and always ſhall be, ready to pay attention and
regard to any real grievances of any of his majeſty's ſubjects, which ſhall in a dutiful and conſtitutional manner
be laid before them; but at the ſame time they beſeech
his majeſty to take the moſt effectual meaſures to enforce due obedience to the authority of the ſupreme legiſlature; and in the moſt ſolemn manner aſſure him,
that at the hazard of their lives and properties, they will
ſtand by him againſt all rebellious attempts, in the maintenance of the juſt rights of his majeſty and the two
houſes of parliament.

Lord North then gave a ſketch of the meaſures he
intended to purſue, which were to ſend a greater force
to America, and to bring in a temporary act to put a
ſtop to all the foreign trade of the different colonies of
New England, particularly their fiſhery on the banks
of Newfoundland, till they returned to their duty.

The addreſs was ſo loaded with conſequences, the
extent of which could not be defined, that it called up
all the powers of oppoſition; and even ſome few of the

G g 4

moſt

moſt moderate in the houſe ſeemed to feel a kind of
horror, at entering upon a meaſure ſo dangerous in the
tendency, and inexplicable in the event.

A gentleman, of the firſt eminence in the law, followed the miniſter through the whole detail of his
ſpeech, and anſwered the different poſitions. He inſiſted, that having examined with legal preciſion the de-
finitions of treaſon, the Americans were not in rebellion,
and ſaid, " Whatever the diſorders may be, they are
created by the conduct of thoſe, whoſe views are to
eſtabliſh deſpotiſm, and which are manifeſtly directed to
reduce America to the moſt abject ſtate of ſervility, as
a prelude to the realizing the ſame wicked ſyſtem in the
mother country." He concluded by maintaining, that
an oppoſition to arbitrary meaſures is warranted by the
conſtitution, and eſtabliſhed by precedent.

The other gentlemen of the minority entered but little
into the juridical part of the debate ; but maintained,
that it would be imprudent for parliament at this time
to *declare* the diſturbances rebellious. They ſaid, " It
is well known no act of violence has been committed in
the Maſſachuſetts-bay, which has not been equalled by
ſomething ſimilar in every other province, and ſome-
times even exceeded by acts of a more heinous nature ;
that therefore the only effect of this violent, but partial
declaration of rebellion, will be to delude ourſelves into
preparations of hoſtility, as if againſt one province only,
when in truth we have to contend with twelve."

On the other ſide, the crown lawyers and miniſterial
debaters maintained, that ſuch Americans as come within
certain deſcriptions, and have been guilty of certain acts,
and ſtill perſevere in the ſupport and commiſſion of ſuch

acts,

acts, are in a ftate of actual rebellion; that the punifhment of a few of the worft fort of traitors, fuch as
Hancock and his crew, may be fufficient to teach the
reft their duty in future; and that the boafted union of
the colonies will diffolve the moment parliament fhows
itfelf refolved on vigorous and fevere meafures. Some
gentlemen of rank in the army, treated all idea of refiftance by the Americans with the utmoft contempt.
They faid, " They are neither foldiers, nor ever can
be made fo, being naturally of a pufillanimous difpofition,
and utterly incapable of any fort of order or difcipline;
and by their lazinefs, uncleanlinefs, and radical defect of
conftitution, they are difabled from going through the
fervice of a campaign, but will melt away with ficknefs, before they can face an enemy; fo that a flight
force will be more than fufficient for their complete reduction." Many ludicrous ftories to that purport were
told, greatly to the entertainment of the houfe. A motion however was made for an amendment, which upon
a divifion was rejected by a large majority, 304 againft
105. The queftion being then put for the addrefs, was
carried by nearly the fame majority.

But the minority had not done with the bufinefs.
Upon receiving the report from the committee a few Feb.
days after, a noble lord made a motion to recommit the 5.
addrefs; and fupported it with many arguments. He
ftated our domeftic fituation, and inferred the impropriety and danger of a declaration from that houfe of
the exiftence of a rebellion in any part of our dominions;
and fhowed the defperate meafures into which it might
precipitate the Americans, and the advantage that might
be taken of fuch an occafion by our powerful and watch-
ful

ful neighbours, whofe ancient enmity and jealoufy were
much increafed by the glory we had acquired, and the
difgrace and lofs they had fuffered in the laft war. He
faid, " My head and my heart join in deprecating the
horrors of a civil war, which will be rendered ftill more
dreadful, by its involving in it certain confequences, a
foreign one with the combined forces of great and powerful nations."

This motion introduced the longeft and moft interefting debate that had taken place in the new parliament.
It was acknowledged on all hands, that the prefent crifis
was the moft perilous and intricate, in which the nation
had been involved fince the revolution. It was contended by thofe who oppofed the motion, that the Americans were not to be won by kindnefs or retained by
benefits; and that the tendernefs, which had been conftantly practifed by government, had produced the prefent fatal confequences. The danger from foreign powers fupporting the Americans, was faid to be imaginary:
and it was ftill contended by feveral, that an appearance of vigorous meafures, with fome reinforcement of
the troops at Bofton, would prove fufficient to quell the
difturbances in America, without the drawing of blood.

On the other fide, the addrefs was ftigmatized as
cruel, fanguinary, and unjuft. It was urged, " The
Americans have given the ftrongeft and moft unequi-
vocal demonftrations of their filial piety toward the
mother country. They have fought and bled by our
fide. In the prefent ftate of diftraction, they require no
more for the reftoration of harmony, than to be placed
in the fame fituation they were in at the clofe of the laft
war. They have been nurfed up, for a long feries of
years,

years, in ideas of certain rights, of which, the electing of their own representatives, and the disposal of their own money for the public service only through them, are among the principal. If this is an error, the crown and parliament are equally faulty with the Americans, having in their whole conduct constantly nourished the delusion. At the time of the repeal of the stamp-act, two of the first names of this kingdom, for ability as well as legal knowledge, beside many others, utterly denied the right of taxation. Is it then to be wondered at, that the Americans, with such authorities on their side, are tenacious of a right so invaluable in its nature, which has at all times been considered as the distinction between freemen and slaves, which has been confirmed by so long a prescription, and upon which, to this instant, the wisest and honestest men, even in the mother country, are divided in opinion? Philip the Second, and his seventeen provinces, are the counterpart of what we are acting. In comparing the probability of events, can any man say, Great Britain has such a prospect of victory in the event as Spain might then have expected? If we imagine, that the powers of Europe will sit still during this contest, we must suppose a system of policy now to prevail, or rather an extension of folly, all over Europe, which never before was known in any period of its existence."

Much ill temper appeared in every part of the house in the course of these debates. The ministry were charged with acting uniformly and systematically upon tory and arbitrary principles, which had thrown the whole empire into a state of confusion and distraction. "In a word," it was said, "the short and simple question

tion before the houſe, is, whether we ſhall loſe the colonies, or give up our miniſtry."

The miniſtry, on the other hand, talked much about
faction at home, and republican principles; and the
Americans being ſpirited up to their rebellion by incen-
diary writers and ſpeakers in England. After a debate,
which continued till half an hour after two in the morning, the motion for the recommitment of the addreſs
was rejected by nearly the former majority.

When it was moved in the houſe of lords, to fill up
the blank, left open in the addreſs, by the inſertion of
the words, " The lords ſpiritual and temporal, &c." to
render the inſtrument the joint act of both houſes, a
debate enſued. The queſtions of treaſon, rebellion, and
conſtructive treaſons, were deeply entered into by two
great law lords, who differed totally in their legal and
political ſentiments, and carried on a long argument
between them, with great warmth and ability; in which
a large ſtock of profeſſional and general learning was
diſplayed on each ſide. It is to be lamented, that with
all the boaſted excellency of our conſtitution, a queſtion
of ſo vaſt magnitude as to include in its conſequences,
the lives, fortunes, and honors of all the ſubjects of this
empire, ſtill remains involved in ſuch obſcurity, as not
only to admit of a difference of opinion, but that even
the great oracles of the law are bewildered in its dark-
neſs. This extraordinary debate was attended with ſome
ſingular circumſtances. Lord Mansfield, to the great
ſurpriſe of moſt of his auditors, condemned, in very explicit and unreſerved terms, the meaſure of laying on
the duties in 1767, which he declared to be the moſt
abſurd and pernicious that could be adviſed, and the
                                                    cauſe

cause of all the present impending evils. The duke of
Grafton, Lord Shelburne, and Lord Camden, who
were at that time cabinet counsellors, and held the first
offices in the state, declared separately in their places,
that they had no share in that measure, nor had ever
given it any approbation. The manner in which a measure of ministry was carried against the opinion of ministers was not explained. A disclosure relative to a
matter, which had already convulsed the whole empire,
and was still more to be dreaded in its future consequences, excited general amazement, mixt with indignation and regret in individuals. The fatal and over-
ruling secret influence, which had so long guided and
marred all public affairs, was deplored and animad-
verted upon in different parts of the house.

When the question came to be put, whether to agree
with the commons in the address, by inserting the
words necessary to fill up the blank, it was carried by a
prodigious majority. But the lords Richmond, Craven,
Archer, Abergavenny, Rockingham, Wycombe, Cour-
tenay, Torrington, Ponsonby, Cholmondeley, Abingdon,
Portland, Camden, Effingham, Stanhope, Scarborough,
Fitzwilliam, and Tankerville, protested against " an
address amounting to *a declaration of war*, which is
founded on no proper parliamentary information, which
follows the rejection of every mode of conciliation,
which holds out no substantial offer of redress of
grievances, and which promises support to those ministers, who have inflamed America, and grossly mis-
conducted the affairs of Great Britain."

The address was delivered, and an answer given, Feb.
wherein his majesty assured both houses, that they might 9.
depend

depend upon his taking the moſt ſpeedy and effectual meaſures for enforcing due obedience to the laws, and the authority of the ſupreme legiſlature.

On that or the preceding day, the petition and memorial from the aſſembly of *Jamaica* to his majeſty, was laid before the commons. It was drawn up in very ſtrong terms. The petitioners entered into a full, free, and argumentative diſcuſſion of the late claims of the mother country, and of the rights of the colonies: the former of which they combated, and the latter defended with great force. They equally deplored and beheld with amazement, a plan almoſt carried into execution for reducing the colonies into the moſt abject ſtate of ſlavery; and they ſupplicated the throne, and demanded and claimed from the ſovereign, as the guarantee of their juſt rights, that no laws ſhould be forced upon them, injurious to their rights as coloniſts or Engliſhmen; and that, as the common parent of his people, his majeſty would become a mediator between his European and American ſubjects.

10.   The next day the miniſter moved for leave to bring in a bill to reſtrain the trade and commerce of the New England provinces, to Great Britain, Ireland, and the Britiſh Weſt India iſlands, and to prohibit them from carrying on any fiſhery on the banks of Newfoundland, and other places therein to be mentioned, under certain conditions, and for a limited time. In anſwer to the objections made to it while the ſubject of debate, the charges of injuſtice and cruelty were denied, and the contrary maintained; it was declared to be neceſſary; and it was obſerved, that though the innocent were involved with the guilty, and friends with foes, the ne-

ceſſity

cellity might be lamented, but could not be helped. The motion for a bill was carried by a majority of three to one.

In the progrefs of the bill, the London merchants and traders, interefted in the American commerce, petitioned againft it, and were allowed to be heard. In confequence of this a long train of witneffes were examined, and it appeared, That in 1764, the four New England colonies employed in their feveral fifheries, no lefs than 45,880 ton of fhipping, and 6002 men, and that the produce of their fifheries in the foreign markets for that year, amounted to 322,220l. 16s. fterling:— That the fifheries were greatly increafed; that all the materials ufed in them, except falt, and the timber of which their veffels were built, were taken from this country, and that the nett proceeds of the fifh were remitted here; and that there was near a million of money owing from New England to the city of London only. They ftated to the houfe, that the calamities confequent upon the bill muft fall in a particular degree upon the innocent. The cafe of the inhabitants of Nantucket would be particularly hard. They amounted to fome thoufands, nine-tenths of them Quakers, inhabiting a barren land: but by an aftonifhing induftry they kept 140 veffels in conftant employ, eight in the importation of provifions for the ifland, and the reft in the whale fifhery.

While the bill was pending, Lord North amazed all parties, and feemed for a time nearly to diffolve his own, by a *conciliatory motion* in regard to America. It propofed, " That when the governor, council, and affembly, or general court of his majefty's provinces or colonies,

colonies, shall propose to make provision, according to
their respective conditions, circumstances, and situations,
for contributing their proportion to the common defence
(such proportion to be raised under the authorities of
the general court, or general assembly, of such province
or colony, and disposable by parliament) and shall engage to make provision also, for the support of the civil
government, and the administration of justice in such
province or colony, it will be proper, if such proposal
should be approved by his majesty in parliament, and
for so long as such provision shall be made accordingly,
to forbear, in respect of such province or colony, to levy
any duties, tax, or assessment; or to impose any further
duty, tax, or assessment, except only such duties as it
may be expedient to impose for the regulation of the
commerce, the nett produce of the duties last mentioned to be carried to the account of such province,
colony, or plantation, respectively." The numerous
high prerogative party, who had ever opposed any re-
laxation in favor of the colonies, heard the proposition
with horror, and considered themselves as abandoned or
betrayed. They pronounced it a shameful prevarica-
tion, and a mean departure from principle; and finally
concluded with declaring, that they would make no
concessions to rebels with arms in their hands; and that
they would enter into no measure for a settlement with
the Americans, in which an express and definitive acknowledgment from them of the supremacy of parliament was not a preliminary article. A gentleman of
the long robe, and who has lately distinguished himself
for his zeal in promoting all the measures for reducing
the colonies (Mr. W——) had the address in a few
minutes

minutes to hush the commotion, by convincing the mal-
contents, that the *appearance* of conceffion, lenity, and
tendernefs, which had fo much alarmed them, were of
fuch a nature, that they could not interfere with the moft
rigid meafures which they wifhed to enforce. The gentlemen in oppofition faid, " The motion is infidious,
bafe and treacherous, in the higheft degree." The minifter acknowledged it to be a cheat, and defigned for
the purpofe of dif-uniting the Americans; but it will
tend only to confolidate that common mafs of union
into which they have been thrown by the Bofton port
act. The queftion was carried by a majority of three
to one.

A petition from the merchants, traders, and principal Feb.
inhabitants of Poole, in Dorfetfhire, was prefented, in 27.
avowed oppofition to that from London, and in fupport
of the principles of the fifhery-bill. This petition fet
forth, that the reftraints upon the colonies would not by
any means be injurious to commerce; and that the foreign
markets might be amply fupplied, by extending the
Newfoundland fifhery from England. They concluded
by foliciting, no lefs for their own immediate advantage
than for the univerfal benefit of their country, fuch encouragement as parliament fhould think proper.

A petition was alfo delivered from the Quakers in
behalf of their brethren and others, the inhabitants of
Nantucket, in which they ftated their innocence and
induftry, the utility of their labors to themfelves and the
community, the hazards attending their occupation, and
the uncertainty of their gains; and fhowed, that if the
bill paffed into a law, they muft fhortly be expofed to all
the miferies of a famine.

VOL. I.   H h   In

In every stage of the bill, the debate rekindled; and, in the course of it, the minority observed, " When it was thought wisdom to overthrow established privileges, and to combat national prejudices, by starting the new claim of taxation, the Americans went no further than to deny our right of internal taxation. Having gained the point of urging them to question one right, we soon convinced them, both by argument and practice, that an external tax might be made to answer all the purposes, and to produce all the mischiefs of internal taxation. They then denied our right of taxing for supply. Parliament then proceeded to deprive them of their charter, and to change the course of justice and trials. Then they were pushed to deny the power of internal legislation. But still they had hitherto never formally rejected the power of parliament to bind their trade. We are now to convince them, however, that if but a single branch of legislative power is left to this country, we can distort that branch in such a manner, that it shall include all the purposes of unlimited tyranny." It appeared upon evidence at the bar of the house, that by the operation of the bill, many thousands of innocent inhabitants would be reduced to the sad alternative, either of perishing through want at home, or of removing to some other less rigorous government for protection and support; so that a famine among the New Englanders was predicted as the consequence of the bill.

Some gentlemen on the other side of the question, acknowledged the harshness of the measure; but lamented its being indispensably necessary. A much greater number contended, that the bill was in an high degree merciful,

merciful, and that the New England colonies did not want refources to prevent a famine. A few went fo far as to regret, that the bill did not convey punifhments adequate to the crimes of the Americans, and to dread, that the famine which had been ftrongly prognofticated, and pathetically lamented, would not take place.

Mr. Quincy fails to-morrow for the *Maffachufetts*. He is very far from being well; and has been attended upon repeatedly by Dr. Fothergill. The doctor thinks the Briftol air and water would give him perfect health; and it is greatly againft his own opinion and inclination that he takes the voyage. But he rifks his life for the good of his own colony in particular, and of America in general. His moft intimate friends infift upon his going directly to Bofton. They fay no letter can go with fafety; and that he can deliver more information and advice *viva voce*, than can or ought to be written. They urge that by going now, if he arrives fafe, he muft be of great advantage to the American caufe.

He is to tell the people of your colony, by no means to take any ftep of great confequence (unlefs on a fudden emergency) without the advice of the continental congrefs; and is to repair to that honorable body, when met at Philadelphia.

You will hear from him, how egregioufly the Americans have been infulted by feveral in both houfes of parliament, in being pronounced daftardly cowards and poltroons, *to be looked into fubmiffion* at the approach of a regiment; and that if this is your true character, there will be no great exploit in the brave general *Grant*'s marching fuccefsfully, with only five regiments, from one end of the continent to the other, of which he has

H h 2   declared

declared himſelf capable. It is ſaid, that an American durſt not look at a red coat. The ſenator holds this language in the ſenate; and the general at the head of an army. It paſſes for a maxim, and it is thought ſcepticiſm to doubt it. Every ſubaltern upon half pay looks upon himſelf as qualified for ſubduing America. If a man ſays otherwiſe, the finger is pointed at him as to an enemy of his country. Mr. Quincy will be likely alſo to give you the name of the member, who in a late ſpeech adulterated the Engliſh tongue, that he might gratify his inveteracy, by puniſhing you with *ſtarvation*.

By a future opportunity you will receive an account of the progreſs of the reſtraining and fiſhery bill through the houſe of lords; of the further proceedings of parliament and miniſtry; and of the national complexion.

LETTER XII.

Roxbury, April 26, 1775.

WHILE the Maſſachuſetts had no provincial congreſs, the active friends of government had an opportunity to try their ſtrength in a few places, and to attempt reſiſting the general current, by refuſing a compliance with the reſolutions of the colony congreſs; but the diſſentients were overwhelmed by numbers, and their attempts proved abortive.

The

The royal proclamation prohibiting the exportation of military ftores from Britain, his majefty's fpeech, and the addreffes of the new parliament, in the opinion of many, cut off all hopes of reconciliation, more efpecially in New England.

The new Maffachufetts congrefs met at Cambridge, Feb. and Mr. Hancock was unanimoufly chofen prefident. [1] They adjourned to Concord in about a fortnight, that the diftance might afford them greater perfonal fecurity, and render them lefs liable to interruption by any meafures of the governor. That the colony might be fomewhat prepared for the foreft trial, they urged in the ftrongeft terms, the militia in general, and the minute men in particular, to fpare neither time, pains nor expence, at fo critical a juncture, for perfecting themfelves forthwith in the military difcipline. They paffed refolutions for the providing and making of fire arms and bayonets, and renewed the prohibition of their predeceffors, againft fupplying the troops at Bofton, with any of thofe neceffaries peculiarly requifite for the military fervice. The committee of fafety had directed in the beginning of January, that all the cannon, mortars, cannon balls and fhells, fhould be depofited at Worcefter and Concord in the fame proportion as was done by the provifion; and while the congrefs was fitting, voted, " that the committee of fupplies do purchafe all the powder they can, and alfo all kinds of warlike ftores, [13.] fufficient for an army of fifteen thoufand men to take [21.] the field."

The propriety of the precautions taken to guard againft a furprife was manifeft from the following event.

General

26.   General Gage receiving intelligence that cannon and carriages were deposited in the neighbourhood of Salem, sent a corps of troops from the castle, under lieutenant colonel Leslie, on board a transport, to seize and bring them away. They landed at Marblehead, proceeded to Salem, found nothing there, and passed on to the draw-bridge leading to Danvers, where a number of people assembled, and those of the opposite side took up the bridge to prevent their crossing. The officer ordered it to be let down ; the people peremptorily refused, saying, " It is a private road, and you have no authority to demand a passage this way." On this refusal he determined to make use of the boats which were at hand ; his intention was perceived, and the owners jumped into their own boats, and with their axes scuttled them, to make them useless for the present ; during the transaction there was some scuffle between them and the soldiers. Things were apparently tending to an extremity. The reverend Mr. Bernard, a congregational clergyman of Salem, and other gentlemen, urged the letting down of the draw-bridge ; but it was not done, till much time had been spent in altercation, during which period the articles, that colonel Leslie was after, were conveyed away. When the opportunity of crossing offered, he marched about thirty rods, to the spot where the artificers had been employed in making carriages, &c. but finding nothing, and it being now late in the evening, returned and went on board the transport without meeting with any molestation. This expedition took place on the Lord's day, which might contribute to its ending happily without mischief. On any other day, when the people were not attending pub-

lic

lic worfhip, but difperfed about and following their fe-
cular bufinefs, the landing of the troops would have been
difcovered, and fome quarrel might have enfued while
they were making it good, or afterward upon their
march, The governor probably pitched upon the Lord's
day, in hope that it would prevent every painful cataftrophe; but the expedition fpread an alarm.

The Maffachufetts congrefs were difpleafed with the
proceedings of the New York general affembly; who
renounced all concern with the late continental congrefs,
declined choofing delegates for the propofed new one,
and in their own fingle capacity, fent a petition to the
king, a memorial to the lords, and a remonftrance to
the houfe of commons. In the remonftrance they reprefented the grievances, under which they labored, by
the innovations that had been made in the conftitutional
mode of government, fince the clofe of the laft war.
They renounced the moft diftant defire of independence,
acknowledged the fupreme government of the Britifh
parliament over the whole empire, and their authority
to regulate the trade of the colonies: remonftrated in
the behalf of their brethren in the Maffachufetts, for
whofe diftreffes they could not help feeling; but at the
fame time expreffed their difapprobation of the violent
meafures purfued in fome of the colonies. They claimed a reftoration of thofe rights which they enjoyed before the clofe of the war; but without entertaining an
idea of diminifhing the power of the mother country,
or leffening the dignity of parliament. Should the miniftry embrace the opening thus given by the general
affembly of New York, they may poffibly feparate this
central province from the others, and break the com-
H h 4 munication

munication between the northern and the southern. But the apprehension of such an event is abated by the intelligence, which the Massachusetts congress have received from the city of New York. The whig citizens, whose hearts were set upon having delegates for the new continental congress, upon the assembly's declining to appoint them, contrived to collect their fellow citizens together in order to obtain their opinion. When assembled in a body, there was a confused cry of "Congress or no congress?" After much altercation, the tories had a recourse to compulsive reasoning, and began dealing about their blows. The whigs were in the worst situation, not being provided with similar arguments, till two of their party repaired to an adjoining cooper's yard, from whence they drew forth to the assistance of their friends a number of hoop-sticks, which they reduced to a proper length, and forwarded to the combatants. The whigs, being thus supplied, soon carried the day by club law, and beat their opponents off the ground. The tories, being worsted, and not a little terrified, left the fury of captain (whom they term in a way of reproach king) Sears should lead him to head a mob, and do them some capital injury, promoted a provincial convention, which otherwise would not have existed. The battle royal at New York will prove the turning point as to that colony.

The Massachusetts congress continued their session, and recommended the sixteenth of March to be observed as the annual day for fasting and prayer, which was kept accordingly, by the inhabitants of Boston, no less than of the country. But they did not presume to rely upon religious exercises in the neglect of those civil means which

(margin note: Mar. 5.)

(margin note: 16.)

which prudence prescribed. The people, both within
and without, used every device for conveying safely from
Boston into the country, all kinds of military articles,
which might be wanted in case of a rupture. Cannon,
balls, and such like heavy stores, were put into carts
and carried out over the neck, under the appearance of
loads of dung. Half barrels of gunpowder were put
into butchers peds, or the hampers of the market people, and brought out under some slight negligent and
unsuspected cover, as they returned home in the evening. Cartridges were packed up in candle-boxes, and
sent off under that deception; but some were at length
discovered. The soldiers on the neck did not make
many prizes, however one day they seized 13,425 mus- 18.
ket cartridges, with 3000lb. weight of ball, which,
though private property, the general was warranted in
refusing to restore, on the application of the owner.

That general Gage might not succeed in seizing any
military stores in the country, should he send out troops
upon that errand, the committee of safety had voted
four days before, " that members from this committee,
belonging to Charlestown, Cambridge and Roxbury,
be desired to procure at least two men, for a watch every
night to be placed in each of these towns, and that said
members be in readiness to send couriers forward to the
towns where the magazines are placed, when sallies are
made from the army at night."

The selectmen of the town of Billerica presented a 23.
most spirited remonstrance to general Gage, on account
of an inhabitant of that town's being tarred and fea-
thered, and much abused on the 8th of the month, by
a party of his majesty's 47th regiment, under the command

mand of lieutenant colonel Nefbit. The firmnefs, refolution and freedom, with which the people both of
town and country have conducted, when their bufinefs
called them to an intercourfe with the governor, have
often embarraffed and convinced him, that they were
not wholly deftitute of fterling courage. There might
be fome ground for punifhing the perfon, whofe cafe
produced the remonftrance; but the punifhment fhould
have been under the direction of a civil and not a military officer, and of another kind; for, though it may
be deemed a retaliation upon the country, it has tended
greatly to irritate.

The Maffachufetts congrefs were folicitous to keep
their proceedings from coming to the knowledge of general Gage; but from feveral circumftances which occurred, they entertained a ftrong fufpicion, that they
had fome one among them, who betrayed their counfels. A gentleman, who is not a ftranger to many confiderable defects in the moral and political character of
Dr. Church, is apprehenfive that he is the perfon; but
is exceedingly cautious of mentioning his fufpicion, confidering the high reputation in which the doctor is among
the fons of liberty.

30.   General Gage marched out about eleven hundred
men into the country; who, doing much damage by
throwing down the ftone fences, occafioned a committee's waiting upon the Maffachufetts congrefs on the
Saturday, when upon the point of adjourning; which
kept them fitting till they received on the Monday following, accounts by a veffel from Falmouth, of what
parliament had done and was doing, in relation to their
colony.

It

It was a providental circumftance that they had fo early intelligence, and obtained it before general Gage had received his difpatches : they were careful to improve it. The intelligence fpread faft, and induced more of the inhabitants of Bofton to remove out of town. A number had been for fome time withdrawing themfelves. The town was liable to be converted inftantly, at the difcretion of the governor, into a fecure prifon ; and the people of it might be held as hoftages for the conduct of the province at large, or be kidnapped and fent to England, to ftand trial for fuppofed offences. Continuance in it was hazardous to many, who had diftinguifhed themfelves by taking an active part againft the meafures of government. But the dauntlefs courage of fome fuch inclined them to remain, though there was no knowing what private orders might be fent to general Gage ; who was not inattentive to the fervice in which he was employed, while he evidenced a prevailing defire after a peaceable accommodation. He fent private orders to the commanding officer at New York, to purchafe up all the duck, blankets, pickaxes, pots and other articles proper for camp fervice. Application was made by the officer to the Philadelphia merchants, who penetrated the defign, and no lefs nobly than unanimoufly refufed a compliance. Three of the New York merchants had for fome time been buying up, felling and fending the feveral articles to Bofton ; but at length a ftop was put to their proceedings by the influence of captain Sears, who, upon his return from Philadelphia, argued that they might want thofe things themfelves, and made a confiderable ftir upon the occafion.

cafion. But a great number were purchafed at Portfmouth, before the difcovery of the general's intention.

The news of the parliamentary proceedings encouraged the foldiery to infult the people more than ever·
their conduct feemingly intimated, that they meant to
provoke the other to begin the quarrel; while thefe bore
all with patience, as they were determined not to be the
aggreffors. Nothing was wanting, but a fpark to fet
the whole continent in a flame. The important moment, big with inconceivable confequences, was evidently approaching, when, through accident or defign,
it would be applied to thofe combuftibles, which had
been long collecting.

The grenadier and light infantry companies were taken
off duty, upon the plea of learning a new exercife, which
made the Boftonians jealous, that there was fome fcheme
on foot. A daughter of liberty, unequally yoked in
point of politics, fent word, by a trufty hand, to Mr.
Samuel Adams, refiding in company with Mr. Hancock
at Lexington, about thirteen miles from Charleftown,
that the troops were coming out in a few days. Upon
this their friends at Bofton were advifed to move out
their plate, &c. and the committee of fafety voted,
" that all the ammunition be depofited in nine different
towns; and that other articles be lodged, fome in one
place, fome in another, fo as to the 15 medicinal chefts,
2000 iron pots, 2000 bowls, 15000 canteens, and 1100
tents; and that the fix companies of matroffes be ftationed in different towns."

Mr. Adams inferred from the number to be employed, that thefe were the objects, and not himfelf and
Mr. Hancock, who might be more eafily feized in a
pri-

private way by a few armed individuals, than by a large body of troops that muft march, for miles together, under the eye of the public.

The provincial ftores had been hitherto depofited at Worcefter and Concord. To the laft of thefe places, but half the diftance of the other from Bofton, the general turned his attention; and, being continually peftered by the repeated folicitations of the American tories, with whom he was furrounded, and who perfuaded him there was no danger of refiftance, their whig countrymen being too cowardly, he determined, without the advice of the council, when and in what way to attempt the feizure of the many ftores fuppofed to be in the place.

A number of officers dined together at Cambridge, April and toward night fcattered themfelves upon the road 18. leading to Concord; and took their ftation fo as to be ready to intercept any expreffes going from Bofton to alarm and raife the country, with intelligence of the troops being upon their march. When the corps was nearly ready to proceed upon the expedition, Dr. Warren, by a mere accident, had notice of it juft in time to fend meffengers over the neck and acrofs the ferry, on to Lexington, before the orders for preventing every perfon's quitting the town were executed. The officers intercepted feveral, but fome being well mounted, efcaped their vigilance; and the alarm, being once given, fpread apace, by the ringing of bells, and the firing of fignal guns and vollies. By eleven at night, eight hundred grenadiers and light infantry, the flower of the army, embarked at the common, proceeded and landed at Phipps's farm, from whence they marched for Concord,

cord, under the command of lieutenant colonel Smith, aided by major Pitcairn, who led the advanced corps.

19.   About two in the morning, the Lexington company of militia, to the amount of one hundred and thirty, repaired to the green, close in with the meeting house. The air being chilly, and the intelligence respecting the regulars somewhat uncertain, the men, after the roll-call, were dismissed, with orders to appear again at beat of drum. Some went home, others to the adjoining public house. Word being brought between four and five, that the troops were not far off, they that were at hand collected, to the number of about seventy, by the time the regulars made their appearance. They were mostly in a confused state, and a few only were drawn up. There were present at the time about forty spectators without arms. The militia were too few to think of beginning an attack. But major Pitcairn rode round the meeting (as the meeting-house is generally called) and approaching them called out, " *Disperse you rebels, throw down your arms and disperse.*" An instant compliance not taking place, which he might construe into contempt, he rode a little further, fired his pistol, flourished his sword, and ordered the soldiers to fire, with which they complied, huzzaing upon the occasion. This produced an immediate dispersion; but the firing was continued. Individuals finding they were fired upon though dispersing, had spirit enough to stop and return the fire. Three or four were killed upon the green; the rest, making the whole number of the slain eight, were shot on the other side of the walls and fences, over which they had fled in order to escape. During this interesting period, Messrs. S. Adams and Hancock, whose re-

sidence

fidence was near at hand, quitted and removed to a further diſtance. While walking along, Mr. Adams exclaimed, " O! *what a glorious morning is this!*" in the belief that it would eventually liberate the colony from all ſubjection to Great Britain. His companion did not penetrate his meaning, and thought the alluſion was only to the aſpect of the ſky. Leſt it ſhould be ſaid and believed, that the meeting was crowded with militia, before and during the fire, let me mention that there were only a man and a boy in it. The detachment marched on to Concord. The people of the town, having received the alarm, drew up in order for defence ; but obſerving that the regulars were too numerous, retired over the north bridge and waited for reinforcements from the neighbouring towns. A party of light infantry followed, and poſſeſſed themſelves of the bridge, while the main body entered the town, and proceeded to execute their commiſſion. They diſabled two twenty-four pounders, and deſtroyed their carriages and ſeven wheels for the ſame, with their limbers, beſide ſixteen wheels for braſs three pounders, and two carriages with limber and wheels for two four pounders. They threw 500lb. of ball into the river, wells, and other places ; and broke in pieces about ſixty barrels of flour, half of which was ſaved. Theſe were all the ſtores that they could diſcover and deſtroy, on the account of which a civil war has commenced between the colonies and the parent ſtate. The inhabitants of Britain may ſee reaſon, for many ages, to curſe the memory of the man or men, who has or have been at the foundation of this fatal cataſtrophe, ſhould they ever be known. The militia being reinforced, Mr. John Butterick, of Concord, major of a

4   minute

minute regiment, and who commanded, ordered the men not to give the firſt fire, that ſo the provincials might not be the aggreſſors, for he was ignorant of what had paſſed at Lexington. Upon his advancing with them, the light infantry retired to the Concord ſide of the river, and began pulling up the bridge; and on his approaching nearer, immediately fired and killed captain Iſaac Davis of Acton, (who with his company of minute men made the front) and one of the privates. The fire was returned, a ſkirmiſh enſued, and the troops were forced to retreat, having ſeveral men killed and wounded, and lieutenant Gould (who would have been killed, had not a miniſter preſent prevented) with ſome others taken. One of their wounded, who was left behind, attempting to get up, was aſſaulted by a young fellow going after the purſuers to join them, who, not being under the feelings of humanity, barbarouſly broke his ſkull with a ſmall hatchet and let out his brains, but neither ſcalped him nor cut off his ears. This event may give riſe to ſome malevolent pen to write, that many of the killed and wounded at Lexington, were not only ſcalped, but had their eyes forced out of the ſockets by the fanatics of New England: not one was ſo treated either there or at Concord. You have the real fact. The poor object languiſhed for an hour or two before he expired.

The party was joined by the main body; and the whole detachment retreated with the utmoſt expedition; for all the country was now up in arms, and attacked the troops on every quarter. In their march of ſix miles back to Lexington, they were exceedingly annoyed, not only by thoſe who preſſed upon their rear;

but

but by others, who fired upon them from behind the stone walls and other coverts, which supplied the place of lines and redoubts to the provincials. At Lexington they were joined by a detachment under Lord Percy.

The news of what had happened at Lexington in their way to Concord, flew to Boston and the neighbourhood. But the slaughter of the militia men was carefully concealed from general Gage, who was not made acquainted with it till late in the afternoon. He had however, early intelligence of the rising of the country; and therefore detached, about eight in the morning, Lord Percy with 16 companies of foot, and a number of marines, 900 men in the whole, and two pieces of cannon, to support colonel Smith. The brigade marched out, playing, by way of contempt, *Yankee Doodle*, a song composed in derision of the New Englanders, scornfully called *Yankees*. A smart boy observing it as the troops passed through Roxbury, made himself extremely merry with the circumstance, jumping and laughing, so as to attract the notice of his lordship, who, it is said, asked him at what he was laughing so heartily; and was answered, " To think how you will dance by and by to *Chevy Chase*." It is added, that the repartee stuck by his lordship the whole day.

You may wish to know the origin of the term *Yankee*. Take the best account of it which your friend can procure. It was a cant, favorite word with farmer Jonathan Hastings of Cambridge, about 1713. Two aged ministers, who were at the college in that town, have told me, they remembered it to have been then in use among the students, but had no recollection of it before that period. The inventor used it to express excellency. A Yankee good horſe, or Yankee cider and the like, were an excellent good horſe and excellent cider. The ſtudents uſed to hire horſes of him; their intercourſe with him, and his uſe of the term upon all occaſions, led them to adopt it, and they gave him the name of Yankee Jon. He was a worthy honeſt man, but no conjurer. This could not eſcape the notice of the collegiates. Yankee probably became a by-word among them to expreſs a weak, ſimple, awkward perſon; was carried from the college with them when they left it, and was in that way circulated and eſtabliſhed through the country (as was the caſe in reſpect to *Hobſon's choice**, by the ſtudents at Cambridge in Old England) till from its currency in New England, it was at length taken up and unjuſtly applied to the New Englanders in common, as a term of reproach.

The junction of the brigade under Lord Percy, with the detachment under colonel Smith, gave the laſt a breathing time, eſpecially as they now had cannon, which awed the provincials from preſſing upon the rear in a direct line. But the whole force ventured not to halt long; for far and wide the minute-men and militia were collecting, in order to cut off their retreat to Boſton. They ſoon renewed their march; conſtant ſkirmiſhing ſucceeded, and a continued fire, though often irregular and ſcattering on their ſide, as well as on the part of the provincials. The cloſe firing from behind the walls, by good markſmen, for ſuch were almoſt all the provincials, put the troops into no ſmall confuſion, and made it ſo dangerous for the officers, that they were more attentive to their ſafety than in common. Major Pitcairn

* See The Spectator, N° 509.

quitted

quitted his horfe, which was taken with the piftols in the holfters. The foldiers loaded and fired over the ftone walls, when there was not a fingle man behind them. They were incommoded by the wind's blowing the fmoke ftrongly back upon them all the time they were retreating; during which they burnt fome houfes, attempted others, and plundered many of every thing valuable, deftroying what they could not carry off. They killed feveral innocent unarmed perfons; and murdered two old men at Menotomy. Before they reached this place, a few Americans, headed by the Rev. Mr. Payfon of Chelfea, who till now had been extremely moderate, attacked a party of twelve foldiers carrying ftores to the retreating troops, killed one, wounded feveral, made the whole prifoners, and gained poffeffion of their arms and ftores, without any lofs whatever to themfelves. The regulars, when near Cambridge, were upon the point of taking a wrong road, which would have led them into the moft imminent danger, but were prevented by the direction of a young gentleman refiding at the college; by which mean they made good their retreat a little after fun fet over Charleftown neck to Bunker's-hill, but fpent and worn down by the exceffive fatigues they had undergone, having marched that day between thirty and forty miles. Here they remained fecure till the next day, when they croffed at Charleftown ferry and returned to Bofton.

Lieutenant-colonel Smith was much difpleafed with the foldiers' firing at Lexington; probably general Gage had given orders that they fhould not fire unlefs they were firft fired upon. Major Pitcairn undoubtedly directed them to fire from the miftaken apprehenfion he

had

had entertained of American refolution, for he has the character of a good tempered officer. There were never more than about four hundred provincials together, attacking at one and the fame time; and often fcarce that number. But as fome tired and gave out, others came up. They had very little appearance of difcipline. Privates and officers fired away as they had opportunity of doing execution, without waiting for the word of command: and ufed their knowledge of the country, to gain the opportunity, by croffing fields and fences, of acting as flanking parties againft the regulars while thefe proceeded along the road. Colonel Pickering of Salem had the command of a fine well exercifed provincial regiment: had he pufhed on with his men, fo as to have headed the Britifh before they had gained Charleftown neck, (and he was near enough) they muft have clubbed their firelocks, for they were quite wearied out with the fervices of the day, and had but a round or two of ammunition remaining. No fatisfactory reafon has been affigned for the want of greater alertnefs in colonel Pickering's regiment. The Britifh officers are aftonifhed, chagrined, and mortified beyond meafure at what has happened. It's death to all their glorying, that their beft troops have been obliged in this manner to flee before a number of *Yankees*, " when all the officers in general did every thing that men could do, and when the foldiers behaved with their ufual intrepidity *." They are fore at heart upon the occafion. They have had 1 lieutenant killed, 2 lieutenant colonels wounded, Smith is one, 2 captains and

* See general Gage's account of the behaviour of the troops in the London Gazette.

9 lieu-

9 lieutenants wounded, 1 lieutenant miffing, 2 enfigns wounded, 1 fergeant killed, 7 wounded, 2 miffing, 1 drummer killed, 1 wounded, 62 rank and file killed, and 157 wounded ; in all 65 killed, 180 wounded, and 28 made prifoners ; total 273.

Of the provincials 50 have been killed, 34 wounded, and 4 are miffing ; in all 88. The following officers and gentlemen are of the number, viz. juftice Ifaac Gardner of Brookline, capt. Ifaac Davis of Acton, capt. Jonathan Wilfon of Bedford, lieut. John Bacon and fergeant Elifha Mills of Needham, and Deacon Jofiah Haynes of Sudbury killed ; capt. Eleazer Kingfbury of Needham, capt. Samuel Williams of Cambridge, captains Charles Miles, Nathaniel Barret and George Minot of Concord, capt. Oliver Barns and Deacon Aaron Chamberlain of Chelmsford wounded. The perfons who have fallen are regretted with the deepeft concern, and are honored not only as patriots, but as martyrs, who have died bravely in the caufe of their country.

Captains John Ford and Oliver Barron, and Deacon Davis, all of Chelmsford, diftinguifhed themfelves in the courfe of the day. It can be fully proved that capt. Ford killed five regulars. James Howard, a private in the Acton company, and a regular coming out of a houfe, caught fight of each other, and difcharged their pieces at the fame inftant ; both fhots taking effect, the laft dropt down dead, and the firft expired a few hours after. A big boy joined in the chafe of the retreating troops, and was very expert in firing at them, at length a ball from the enemy grazed his head, and produced

I i 3   a flefh

a flesh wound: he soon recovered the shock, bound up his head with a handkerchief, and renewed his pursuit.

Two British officers who have been taken, and the privates, who are wounded and prisoners, are treated with humanity by the provincials; and general Gage may, if he pleases, safely send his surgeons to dress and attend them.

If the contest is to become general between the colonies and the mother country, it may be deemed a happiness for them that it has commenced in the Massachusetts, where all the inhabitants are so connected with each other by descent, blood, uniformity of manners, similarity of religious and civil sentiments, mediocrity of circumstances, and a general equality, that the killing of a single individual interesteth the whole province in the event, and makes them consider it as a common cause.

The inhabitants are now every where in arms; and collecting in such numbers about Boston, that they will not only invest the town effectually, but excite disagreeable apprehensions in general Gage. No one is suffered to go in or out at present. The provincials have for their commander in chief, a native of the Massachusetts, general Ward; the honorable Jedediah Prebble having, more than a month ago, declined on account of his bad health. General Ward might have pleaded the like excuse; but he wishes to serve his country to the utmost of his abilities, and is ready to risk his life in the cause of American liberty. He is to be trusted, being a gentleman of great integrity. His commission as commander in chief of the Bay troops was delivered to him

on

on the 20th, by the provincial congrefs. Three days 20.
after, they chofe general John Thomas lieutenant
general.

The day general Ward received his commiffion, the
committee of fafety fent letters to New Hampfhire and
Connecticut, with an account of the enemy's proceedings the day before, and praying all the affiftance in
their power. The next day they agreed upon inlifting
8000 men out of the Maffachufetts forces: but the provincial congrefs being adjourned from Concord to Watertown, refolved the fucceeding day, " that an army of
30,000 men be immediately raifed and eftablifhed; that
13,600 be by this province; and that a letter and dele-
gate be fent to the feveral colonies of Hampfhire, Connecticut and Rhode Ifland." Head quarters are at
Cambridge; and the ftudents quit the college that the
provincials may be accommodated. General Thomas
commands at Roxbury. He is a cool, courageous, dif-
cerning, and active officer, well qualified for guarding
the important poft he occupies, and preventing the
enemy's making a fally over the neck into the country,
fhould they be inclined to attempt it: but for the prefent they are more afraid of being attacked.

General Gage, to fecure the people within from taking
up arms againft the king's troops, in cafe of an affault,
has agreed with the committee of the town, after a long 22.
conference; that, upon the inhabitants in general lodg-
ing their arms in Faneuil-hall, or any other convenient
place, under the care of the felectmen, all fuch inhabitants as are inclined may depart from the town with
their families and effects; that thofe who remain may
depend upon his protection; and that the arms afore-

laid, at a fuitable time, fhall be returned to the owners.
The town agreed to this propofal, and their vote upon
it was read by the committee, upon their return to his
excellency, who accepted it; and further agreed, that
the inhabitants may remove from town by land and
water with their effects, within the limits fpecified by
the port-act.   He alfo informed the committee, that he
would defire the admiral to lend his boats to facilitate
the removal of the effects of the inhabitants; and that
he would allow carriages to pafs and repafs for that purpofe.   He faid likewife, that he would take care that
the poor, who may remain in town, fhall not fuffer for
want of provifions after their own ftock is expended; and
defired that a letter might be written to Dr. Warren,
chairman of the committee of congrefs, that thofe perfons in the country, who may incline to remove into
Bofton with their effects, may have liberty fo to do
without moleftation.   An account of thefe proceedings
was fent to Dr. Warren; who was further informed by
the town-committee, " Permiffion will be given for
25.   30 waggons to enter the town at once, to carry away the
effects of the inhabitants; fo foon as thofe have returned
to the end of the caufeway leading to Roxbury, then
others will be permitted to come in.   None will be
permitted to enter till after fun rife, nor remain after
fun fet.   If any veffel or boat now in the harbour be
employed to remove the inhabitants effects, fecurity
muft be given that it be returned.   It is expected, that
leave be obtained for fome perfons to go to the different
parifhes, to give notice to fuch perfons who incline to
come with their effects into Bofton, that they may come
without moleftation; and it is defired, that the waggons
and

and veffels employed to come to carry away the goods
of the inhabitants of Bofton, may bring the effects of
thofe who are defirous to leave the country, they paying
half the charge."

Doctor Warren has this day written to general Gage. 26.

" S I R,

THE unhappy fituation into which this colony is
thrown, gives the greateft uneafinefs to every man, who
regards the welfare of the empire, or feels for the diftreffes
of his fellow men; but even now much may be done to
alleviate thofe misfortunes which cannot be entirely re-
medied; and I think it of the utmoft importance to us,
that our conduct be fuch, as that the contending parties
may entirely rely upon the honor and integrity of each
other, for the punctual performance of any agreement
that fhall be made between them. Your excellency, I
believe, knows very well the part I have taken in public
affairs. I ever fcorned difguife. I think I have done
my duty; fome may think otherwife: but be affured,
Sir, as far as my influence goes, every thing, which can
reafonably be required of us to do, fhall be done; and
every thing promifed fhall be religioufly performed. I
fhould now be very glad to know from you, Sir, how
many days you defire may be allowed for fuch as defire
to remove to Bofton with their effects, and what time
you will allow the people in Bofton for their removal.
When I have received the information, I will repair to
congrefs, and haften as far as I am able the iffuing a
proclamation. I beg leave to fuggeft, that the condition of admitting only thirty waggons at a time into the
town, appears to me very inconvenient, and will pre
vent

vent the good effects of a proclamation intended to be issued for encouraging all waggoners to assist in removing the effects from Boston with all possible speed. If your excellency will be pleased to take the matter into consideration, and favor me as soon as may be with an answer, it will lay me under a great obligation, as it so nearly concerns the welfare of my friends in Boston. I have many things which I wish to say to your excellency, and most sincerely wish I had broken through the formalities which I thought due to your rank, and freely had told you all I knew or thought of public affairs, and I must ever confess, whatever may be the event, that you generously gave me such opening as I now think I ought to have embraced; but the true cause of my not doing it, was the knowledge I had of the vileness and treachery of many persons around you, who I suppose had gained your entire confidence.

I am, &c. &c."

The committee of safety have sent letters to Rhode Island and Connecticut, importuning immediate assistance; and that as large a number of troops as can be spared, may be immediately marched forward, well stocked with provisions and ammunition, and accompanied with as large a train of artillery as can be granted. They express their determination, at all events, to act their parts with firmness and intrepidity, knowing that slavery is far worse than death.

The committee appointed to examine into the damages done on the 19th at Cambridge, Lexington and Concord, have reported that by fire, robbery and destruction, the same are as follows: at Cambridge 901 l.

16 s.

16s. 5d. ¼; at Lexington 1320l. 16s. 0d ¼; and at Concord 206l. 2s. 5d. ¼, in all 2428l. 14s. 11d. ¼ sterling. The parties exhibited their accounts on oath, and the greatest care was taken, that the state of the damages might be just.

My friend Quincy has sacrificed his life for the sake of his country. The ship in which he sailed, arrived at Cape Anne within these two days: but he lived not to get on shore, or to hear and triumph at the account of the success of the Lexington engagement. His remains will be honorably interred by his relations. Let him be numbered with the patriotic heroes, who fall in the cause of liberty; and his memory be dear to posterity. Let his only surviving child, a son of about three years, live to possess his noble virtues, and to transmit his name down to future generations. You have my warmest acknowledgments for your last manuscript. See that you embrace every safe opportunity of continuing your correspondence; you will find me in that line of conduct.

The supreme power now extant in the Massachusetts has given their first naval commission to captain *John Derby* of Salem, who is intrusted by the provincial congress with dispatches for Dr. Franklin, containing an account of the Lexington fight, and an address to the inhabitants of Great Britain. He sails without delay. In the address the congress profess to place much dependence on the honor, wisdom and valor of Britons, from which they hope for their interference in preventing the prosecution of present measures. They make great professions of loyalty: but declare, that they will not tamely submit to the persecution and tyranny of a

4   cruel

cruel miniftry; and that they are determined to die or
be free.   They appeal to Heaven for the juftice of their
caufe. Should not an accommodation take place, Heaven
muft grant them its fpecial protection, or they will be
crufhed before the power of Britain, notwithftanding all
that the other colonies can do for them: unlefs the
officers, who are employed againft them, are not fupplied with an adequate force, or are wretchedly defective
in courage, inclination, activity, prudence, or other military abilities: or unlefs fome foreign power, for its
own intereft and to injure the parent ftate, takes them
by the hand.   Their military ftores are fcarce worth
mentioning.   They reckon upon fixteen field pieces.
It is well if fix of them are calculated for much actual
fervice.   There are four brafs ones, of a fmall fize, that
may anfwer a good purpofe.   They have a few large
iron cannon, two or three mortars and howitzers, cannon
ball, and fhells; but they have only eighty-two half
barrels of powder belonging to the public ftore; moft
towns have a fmall quantity, that however will be foon
exhaufted.   Confidering what ought to be the cafe, to
warrant a reafonable expectation of fuccefs, in a military
conteft with a nation that abounds in all the apparatus
of war, they may be pronounced deftitute of every article but men; and, though thefe are not wanting in
natural courage, it will take a confiderable time to make
them thorough good foldiers.   They have neither money
nor magazines.

LETTER XIII.

London, June 12, 1775.

THE reftraining and fifhery bill did not pafs through the houfe of lords with lefs oppofition than what it had met with in the houfe of commons. Upon the motion for committing it after the fecond reading, the marquis of *Rockingham* oppofed it with great ability; and in the courfe of his fpeech fhowed, that in 1704 the whole amount of the exports to the New England colonies was only about 70,000 l. annually; that in 1754 it had arifen to 180,000 l. in the fucceeding ten years to 400,000 l. and in the laft ten years had nearly doubled that fum.

The bill was carried by a majority of more than three to one; but was productive of a proteft, figned by fixteen lords. It is particularly diftinguifhed, by the fevere cenfure paffed upon a lord high in office, who in the late debates, moft unadvifedly threw out a charge of general cowardice againft the Americans.

The fifhery bill had fcarcely cleared the houfe of commons, when Lord North brought in another, " To Mar. reftrain the trade and commerce of the colonies of New 9. Jerfey, Pennfylvania, Maryland, Virginia, and South Carolina, to Great Britain, Ireland, and the Britifh iflands in the Weft Indies, under certain conditions and limitations." While this bill was in agitation, a long feries

of

of evidence, in behalf of the West India merchants
and planters, was laid before the house. It appeared,
that upon a very moderate computation, the capital
in the West India islands, consisting of lands, buildings, negroes, and stock of all kinds, did not amount
to less than sixty millions sterling; that their exports of late years to Britain, ran to about 190,000
hogsheads and puncheons of sugar and rum annually;
amounting in weight to 95,000 tons, and in value about
4,000,000l. exclusive of a great number of smaller articles, and of their very great export to North America;
that their growth was so rapid, and improvement so
great, that within a few years, their export of sugar to
this kingdom was increased 40,000 hogsheads annually,
amounting to about 800,000l. in value. The probability was apparent, that more than half of the capital of
60,000,000l. was either the immediate property of persons resident in this country, or owing to them; and
also that the revenue gained above 700,000l. a year upon
the direct West India trade, exclusive of its eventual
and circuitous products, and of the African trade.

20. Mr. Burke made a number of conciliatory proposi-
tions with respect to the colonies, contained in a set of
resolutions, which he accompanied and elucidated by a
celebrated speech. He traced that unconquerable spirit
of freedom, that violent passion for liberty, by which
the colonists are distinguished from all other people of
the world, from the sources of their descent, education,
manners, religious principles, forms of government, and
distance from the head of the empire. He made it appear, that the whole exports to North America, the
West Indies and Africa, in 1704, (from England it
must

muſt be, for the union of the two kingdoms had not then taken place) amounted only in value to 569,930l. but the comparative value of money at that period was much greater than at preſent. In 1772, the exports from Great Britain to the ſame places, amounted at a medium, to no leſs than 6,024,171 l. He alſo ſhowed, that the *whole export* trade of England, including that to the colonies, amounted in 1704, only to 6,509,000l. Thus the trade to the colonies alone was, in 1772, within leſs than half a million of being equal to what was carried on by England with the whole world, at the beginning of the preſent century. However aſtoniſhing this general increaſe of the whole colonies may appear, the growth of the province of Pennſylvania is ſtill more extraordinary. In 1704, the whole exports to that colony amounted to no more than 11,459l. and in 1772, they were riſen to 507,909l. being nearly fifty times the original demand, and almoſt equal to the whole colony export at the firſt period. This aſtoniſhing growth of the colonies, within little more than half a century, and the prodigious ſhare they contribute to our greatneſs, makes them a matter of the firſt importance to ourſelves, and muſt excite the admiration of future ages.

The previous queſtion was moved on the firſt propoſition, and carried by 270. to 78 ; and thus ended the buſineſs.

But the ill ſucceſs which has attended all conciliatory propoſitions hitherto, excepting thoſe which have originated from government, did not deter Mr. Hartley 27. from making a ſimilar attempt. The motion however was rejected without a diviſion.

During

During the progress of the second restraining bill, an additional clause was moved for by the minister, whereby the counties of Newcastle, Kent and Suffex on the Delaware, were included in the prohibitions of that bill, and carried without a division.

While these matters were transacting, several petitions were received from manufacturing towns in Britain and Ireland against the coercive acts. Some counter-petitions were also received, calling for an enforcement of the laws of Britain, as the only means of preserving a trade with the colonies. Much altercation arose on the truth of facts alleged on both sides, as well as on the manner of obtaining the signatures, and the quality of those who signed. The minority insisted, that the most who signed the war-petitions, as they called them, were persons who had little or no interest in the American trade, but of that description of warm and active partymen commonly called tories. And they entered into several examinations to prove the truth of the former part of their assertion. This produced many long and hot debates. Other petitions were presented to the crown, and equally disregarded: one from the British settlers in Canada against the Quebec bill; one from the quakers, in which besides endeavouring to diffuse the influence of that spirit of peace, which is the predominant principle in their religious system, they declared themselves persuaded, that there are not in his majesty's extensive dominions, subjects more loyal, and more zealously attached to his royal person, his family and government, than in the provinces of America, among all religious denominations. His majesty however, went in person to the house, and gave the royal

                                                                    affent

affent to the reftraining and fifhery bill in the ufual form. In this feafon of public difcontent, when the minds of all were agitated on one fide or other, the city of London, not difcouraged by the fate of all its applications for a number of years paft, once more approached the April throne, with an addrefs, remonftrance and petition, 10. upon a fubject, and in a manner, as little calculated to obtain a favorable reception as any of the preceding. In this remonftrance they recapitulated the whole catalogue of American grievances; declared their abhorrence of the meafures which had been purfued, and were then purfuing; and juftified the refiftance to which the Americans had been driven, upon the great principles of the conftitution; " actuated by which," they faid, " at the glorious period of the revolution, our anceftors transferred the imperial crown of thefe realms to the illuftrious houfe of Brunfwick." They befeeched his majefty immediately and for ever to difmifs from his councils, thofe minifters and advifers, who had been at the bottom of the preceding meafures. His majefty delivered the following anfwer, " It is, with the utmoft aftonifhment, that I find any of my fubjects capable of encouraging the rebellious difpofition, which unhappily exifts in my colonies in North America. Having entire confidence in the wifdom of my parliament, the great council of the nation, I will fteadily purfue thofe meafures which they have recommended for the fupport of the conftitutional rights of Great Britain, and the protection of the commercial rights of my kingdom."

The earl of Effingham has uniformly oppofed the whole fyftem of meafures purfued againft the Americans; and finding that the regiment in which he ferved

was at length deftined for America, and thinking it inconfiftent with his character, and beneath his dignity, to
enforce meafures with his fword, which he had fo utterly
condemned in his legiflative capacity, he wrote a letter
of refignation to the fecretary of war. In it he deeply
regretted his being neceffitated to quit the military profeffion; but faid, " I cannot, without reproach from
my own confcience, confent to bear arms againft my
fellow fubjects in America, in what, to my difcernment,
is not a clear caufe." Pity that it is not a point of honor
with all military officers, to confider the merits of the
caufe wherein their fwords are to be employed, and
when they are not fatisfied in their own judgments, to
practife as the noble earl has done. Such a point of
honor might hinder many a war.

The Britifh ambaffador at the Hague applied to the
ftates to forbid their fubjects fupplying the Americans
with arms, ammunition, gunpowder, &c. and they by
proclamation prohibited the exportation of all fuch articles, in Dutch or foreign fhips, from any of their dominions, without licence, on penalty of forfeiting about
90l. fterling. Judge, whether the profits of the voyage
will not be fo great as to make it worth the merchants
while to run the rifk of that fum. Let the American
veffels repair to Holland, and the Dutch will furnifh
them with gunpowder in large glafs bottles of feveral
gallons dimenfion, under the notion of fpirits or liquor
of one kind or other *. France was alfo applied to,
and could have crufhed all affiftance, by exprefs prohibition; but only told her fubjects, that if they afforded
any, it was at their own rifk, tantamount to—if you

* This was practifed.

will

will venture you may. Spain roundly refused giving the leaft hinderance to her fubjects.

His majefty went to the houfe of peers, and gave the 13. royal affent to the bill for reftraining the trade of New Jerfey, Pennfylvania, &c. Thus the probability of the colonies dividing from each other is leffened, and their union becomes more eftablifhed. Some future proceedings in the provinces of New York and North Carolina, will be likely to confolidate the whole continent.

The American fifheries being now abolifhed, meafures were neceffary to fupply their place, and to guard againft the confequences of the foreign markets, either changing the courfe of confumption, or falling into the hands of ftrangers. It was alfo expedient to pay a greater attention to the interefts of Ireland, than what had been practifed for many years. The minifter therefore moved for a committee of the whole houfe to con- 27. fider of the encouragement proper to be given to the fifheries of Britain and Ireland. The committee in its progrefs granted feveral bounties to the fhips of Britain and Ireland, for their encouragement in profecuting the Newfoundland fifhery; and two refolutions were introduced and paffed in favor of the latter kingdom. Complaints however were made, that claufes were infidioufly ftolen into the act to prevent its operating in any confiderable extent. The committee agreed alfo to the granting of bounties for encouraging the whale fifhery, and to take off the duties payable upon the importation of oil, blubber, and bone from Newfoundland, &c. and on the importation of feal fkins.

Miniftry have not confined themfelves to the making of laws; they have alfo fent out againft the Americans,

general

generals Howe, Clinton and Burgoyne, in the Cer-
28.   berus. The tranſports with troops to re-enforce governor
Gage, ſailed a week after from Corke.

May   Toward the cloſe of the ſeſſion, Mr. Burke acquainted
15.   the houſe, with his having received a paper of great importance from the general aſſembly of New York. He
obſerved, that it was a complaint, in the form of a re-
monſtrance, of ſeveral acts of parliament, ſome of which
they affirmed, had eſtabliſhed principles, and others
had made regulations, ſubverſive of the rights of Engliſh ſubjects. He afterward moved, that it might be
brought up. The miniſter immediately moved an
amendment, which proved an indirect but effectual negative upon Mr. Burke's motion. The amendment was
carried by a majority of 186 to 67; the queſtion being
then put upon the amended motion, it was rejected
without a diviſion. The New York memorial to the lords
was brought in by the duke of Mancheſter, who moved
for its being read. After ſome altercation the queſtion
was called for, and upon a diviſion the motion was rejected by a majority of 45 againſt 25. The petition to
the king was received, but the prayer of the petitioners
was not granted. Such is the fate of the applications
made by the general aſſembly of New York, for a redreſs of their ſuppoſed grievances. It muſt tend to
widen the breach between Britain and the colonies.

17.   Lord Camden preſented a petition to the houſe of
lords from the Britiſh inhabitants of the province of
Quebec, in which they ſtated their grievances, and im-
plored their lordſhips favorable interpoſition, that the
Quebec-act might be repealed or amended, and that
they might enjoy their conſtitutional rights, privileges,

4   and

and franchifes. His lordfhip, after expatiating on the
evils of the act, propofed a bill, which was read, for
the repeal of the late act. This meafure was ftrongly
oppofed by adminiftration, and a motion was made by
lord Dartmouth, that the bill be rejected, which was
carried by a majority of fixty out of eighty-eight, there
being only twenty-eight lords who fupported the bill.
Much cenfure having been expreffed or implied, both
within doors and without, relative to the whole conduct
of the bifhops in the Canada tranfaction, the reverend
father of that bench, ftood up during the debate to
juftify the Quebec-act, fo far as it related to religious
matters, which he did upon the principles of toleration,
the faith of the capitulation, and the terms of the definitive treaty of peace; but many were far from being
convinced, that thefe principles required fuch a full and
perfect eftablifhment of the popifh religion, as is granted by the act itfelf.

Sir George Saville prefented to the houfe of commons, 18.
another petition from the fame inhabitants of Quebec,
in which among other things, they reprefented with too
much truth, that the petition to his majefty, in the
name of all the French inhabitants of that province,
and upon which the late law had been avowedly founded, was not fairly obtained, and had neither received
the concurrence of the people in general, nor even been
communicated to them, but had been carried about in
a fecret manner, and figned by a few of the nobleffe,
advocates, and others, who were in their confidence.
They affirmed that the inhabitants in general were as
much alarmed as themfelves, at the introduction of the
Canadian laws. They concluded by praying, that the

said

said act might be repealed or amended. Sir George examined and laid open the weak or obnoxious parts of the act, and threw new light even upon those which had already undergone the highest degree of colouring, and then concluded his speech with moving for a repeal of the late act for the better government of the province of Quebec. . Confiderable debates enfued, in the course of which the minister avowed his intention, if it should become necessary, of arming the Canadians against the other colonies. But he declared his firm persuasion, that the troubles in America, would be speedily and happily settled without bloodshed. Notwithstanding this declaration it was whispered, that he was uneafy, and from what general Gage wrote last, dreaded the news by the April packet. For some, who professed to have the best information, afferted that orders were fent to apprehend Messrs. Cushing, Samuel Adams, Hancock and others, and to transport them to Great Britain; and that the receipt of these orders had been acknowledged; but that second orders had been dif-patched to hang them at Bofton. Sir George Saville's motion was rejected by a majority of more than two to one, the numbers being 174 to 86.

26.   The speaker, when he prefented the money bills for the royal affent, gave an affurance in his speech to his majefty, that if the Americans perfifted in their refolu-tions, and the fword muft be drawn, the commons would do every thing in their power to maintain and support the fupremacy of this legiflature.

The king gave his royal affent to the feveral bills, both public and private, which remained to be paffed
into

into acts; and clofed the feffion by a fpeech from the throne, in which he expreffed the moft perfect fatisfaction in the conduct of the parliament, during the courfe of their feffion; and his perfuafion, that the moft falutary effects muft, in the end, refult from meafures formed and conducted on fuch principles, as thofe on which they had acted. A favorable reprefentation was made of the pacific difpofition of other powers, and the ufual affurance given of endeavouring to fecure the public tranquillity.

Captain Derby arrived with his difpatches for Dr. 28. Franklin, got to London in the evening, and delivered them to Dr. Lee, as the other agent had left the country. The circulated accounts of the action were vague; it was plain however, that the troops had been worfted; and that government feared it, though they difclaimed all knowledge of what had happened.

The Sukey, captain Brown, though fhe failed four days before captain Derby's veffel, did not arrive till June the ninth of June with general Gage's difpatches. The 9. Gazette has given us the governmental account of the Lexington engagement. From the praifes beftowed upon officers and men for their activity and bravery, it is evident, that the Americans made the bufinefs of the day a hard, difficult and dangerous fervice to them. The nation in general is not fo fhocked with this tranfaction, as the importance of it requires. It was a fatal miftake to fend foldiers inftead of fhipping; and no lefs fo to order them to Bofton, inftead of planting them in New York (where government has a ftrong intereft) and fecuring a fortified line of communication from
thence

thence to Canada, with which to divide the southern from the New England colonies.

Six more regiments of foot have received orders to hold themselves in readiness to embark for America. They are encouraged by an expectation, into which they are drawn by the informations given them, of possessing farms and other confiscated property.

THE END OF THE FIRST VOLUME.

ERRATA.

Page 67, line 12, *read*, proprietary, the burgesses and those freemen. P. 120, *dele* the side date 1753. P. 121, l. 12, add on the side 1753. L. 25, *for* sat, *read* set. P. 135, l. 24, *read* was to be made. P. 140, l. 16 and 17, *read* Barnstable in Barnstable county. P. 144, l. 8, *read* engaged. P. 183, l. 28, *read* beset. P. 197, l. 12, *insert*—at the end. P. 318, l. 2, *read* with that amazing.

The reader is desired to correct the above noted errors, and candidly to excuse what other typographical ones have escaped observation.